AMERICAN SCHOOLS OF ORIENTAL RESEARCH
PUBLICATIONS OF THE JERUSALEM SCHOOL

Archaeology: Volume III

PALESTINIAN CERAMIC CHRONOLOGY
200 B.C. – A.D. 70

by

PAUL W. LAPP

Director, American School of Oriental Research

Jerusalem, Jordan

WIPF & STOCK · Eugene, Oregon

Wipf and Stock Publishers
199 W 8th Ave, Suite 3
Eugene, OR 97401

Palestinian Ceramic Chronology
200 B.C. - A.D. 70
By Lapp, Paul W.
Softcover ISBN-13: 978-1-6667-5105-5
Hardcover ISBN-13: 978-1-6667-5106-2
eBook ISBN-13: 978-1-6667-5107-9
Publication date 6/16/2022
Previously published by American Schools of Oriental Research, 1961

This edition is a scanned facsimile of the original edition published in 1961.

TO

G. ERNEST WRIGHT

PREFACE

This study was originally a dissertation submitted in March, 1960, to the Doctoral Committee of the Divinity School of Harvard University "in partial fulfillment of the requirements for the degree of Doctor of Theology in the subject of Biblical Studies." It has been slightly revised to incorporate suggestions of the Thesis Committee and more recent literature.

Evidence for refining and correcting the conclusions here reached has continued to appear while printing proceeded, notably from Khirbet Mird and Murabba'ât, and a wealth of new stratified material should soon be available from excavations at Jerusalem and 'Arâq el-Emîr, not to mention the imminent publication of stratified Nabataean deposits from Petra and 'Abdeh. Some additions and corrections that would ordinarily have been possible during the course of printing have been precluded by the fact that the entire book has been set by hand, and the first pages were printed nearly a year before the last.

The method of printing has also made precise *infra* references difficult, but this has been overcome in part by reference to chapter and the footnote number nearest the pertinent material. Fonts with adequate diacritical marks are unavailable here, and perhaps their use should have been abandoned entirely. Only the circumflex was available in the fonts selected, and it was used for nearly all long vowels in names diacritically marked. It may also be noted that there was a shortage of l's, and the turn of the era is indicated by a zero. (In any case, the tradition of avoiding the zero seems to be based on the faulty assumption that zero with reference to time denotes a continuum, not a point.)

The work suffers from typical dissertation sins of omission and commission. Certain aspects of the subject have not received adequate treatment. No systematic discussion of the chronological and typological developments of the various wares has been attempted, to say nothing of petrographical analysis. A statistical concern is almost wholly lacking in regard to the relative frequencies of forms from a horizontal or vertical perspective and in the description of typological change. These omissions are explained in part by the limitations of available evidence and practical considerations, but, at bottom, they are the result of the author's skepticism about the chronological value of previous ceramic studies oriented to these emphases.

In the Chapter VI Corpus conclusions are committed to specific dates. This is done with some hesitation because a false impression of precision might be given to the casual reader. Yet, advances in precision can best be made when specific hypotheses articulating available evidence are set down and subsequently refined. The reader is warned that these precise conclusions are based on the limited stratigraphic evidence now available. There is no intention of confining provenience of a given form to the chronological limits indicated by stratified data, unless this is specifically stated.

This study is part of a project to systematize Palestinian ceramic chronology in the Persian, Hellenistic, Roman, and Byzantine periods. It is a joint project of the writer and his wife, and the appearance of this volume is as much the result of her efforts as his. It is a pleasure to thank Professor O. R. Sellers for permission to publish material from the 1957 Beth-zur campaign, Mrs. Herbert Huffmon for inking the plates, Mr. G. R. H. Wright for designing the cover, Miss Beatrice Habesch and the staff of Commercial Press for their patient coöperation in printing the volume, and the American Schools of Oriental Research and the chairman of its Publications Committee, Professor W. F. Albright, for accepting this book for the Publications of the Jerusalem School Archaeology Series. The constructive suggestions of the Thesis Committee, Professors George M. A. Hanfmann, Frank M. Cross, Jr., and G. Ernest Wright, have been deeply appreciated. Besides giving permission to publish the valuable Shechem evidence, Professor Wright has been the guiding spirit in this project; his encouragement and friendship have made even the drudgery of pots a pleasure. To him this volume is dedicated.

Jerusalem, Jordan   P. W. L.
September 24, 1961

CONTENTS

	PREFACE	v
	LIST OF ABBREVIATIONS	viii
I.	INTRODUCTION	1
II.	AN ANALYSIS OF THE STRATIFIED DEPOSITS	8
III.	AN ANALYSIS OF OTHER CHRONOLOGICALLY SIGNIFICANT POTTERY GROUPS	23
IV.	AN ANALYSIS OF THE CHRONOLOGICAL SIGNIFICANCE OF IMPORTED WARES	56
V.	AN ANALYSIS OF OTHER PALESTINIAN CERAMIC MATERIAL	99
VI.	A CORPUS OF PALESTINIAN POTTERY, 200 B.C. – A.D. 70	137
	APPENDIX A. – ECONOMIC AND CULTURAL IMPLICATIONS	221
	APPENDIX B. – HISTORICAL IMPLICATIONS	230

LIST OF ABBREVIATIONS

AASOR	*Annual of the American Schools of Oriental Research*
Agora IV	Howland, Richard Hubbard. *Greek Lamps and their Survivals.* (The Athenian Agora, Vol. IV.) Princeton: American School of Classical Studies at Athens, 1958.
Agora V	Robinson, Henry S. *Pottery of the Roman Period: Chronology.* (The Athenian Agora, Vol. V.) Princeton: American School of Classical Studies at Athens, 1959.
AJA	*American Journal of Archaeology*
'Alâyiq	Pritchard, James B. "The Excavation at Herodian Jericho, 1951," *AASOR*, XXXII-XXXIII (1952–54). New Haven: American Schools of Oriental Research, 1958.
Antioch I	Elderkin, George W. (ed.). *Antioch on-the-Orontes I: The Excavations of 1932.* Princeton: Princeton University Press, 1934.
Antioch II	Stillwell, Richard (ed.). *Antioch on-the-Orontes II: The Excavations, 1933–1936.* Princeton: Princeton University Press, 1938.
Antioch III	Stillwell, Richard (ed.). *Antioch on-the-Orontes III: The Excavations, 1937–1939.* Princeton: Princeton University Press, 1941.
Antioch IV	Waagé, Frederick O. (ed.). *Antioch on-the-Orontes IV*, Part I: *Ceramics and Islamic Coins.* Princeton: Princeton University Press, 1948.
Antiq.	Josephus. *Antiquities.*
BA	*Biblical Archaeologist*
BASOR	*Bulletin of the American Schools of Oriental Research*
Bel. Jud.	Josephus. *Bellum Judaicum.*
Bethany	Saller, Sylvester J. *Excavations at Bethany (1949–1953).* Jerusalem: Franciscan Press, 1957.
Beth-shan I	Rowe, Alan. *The Topography and History of Beth-shan.* Vol. I. Philadelphia: University Press, 1930.
Beth-shan II, II	Fitzgerald, Gerald M. *The Four Canaanite Temples of Beth-shan;* Vol. II, Part II: *The Pottery.* Philadelphia: University Press, 1930.
Beth-shan III	Fitzgerald, Gerald M. *Beth-shan Excavations 1921–1923;* Vol. III: *The Arab and Byzantine Levels.* Philadelphia: University Press, 1931.
BIES	*Bulletin of the Israel Exploration Society*
Broneer	Broneer, Oscar. *Terracotta Lamps.* (Corinth, Vol. IV, Part II.) Cambridge: Harvard University Press, 1930.
Caves	De Vaux, R. "Exploration de la région de Qumrân," *RB*, LX (1953), pp. 540–61.
CBZ	Sellers, Ovid Rogers. *The Citadel of Beth-zur.* Philadelphia: Westminster Press, 1933.

Corinth I	Broneer, Oscar. *The South Stoa and its Roman Successors.* (*Corinth*, Vol. I, Part IV.) Princeton: American School of Classical Studies at Athens, 1954.
CPP	Duncan, J. Garrow. *Corpus of Palestinian Pottery.* London: British School of Archaeology in Egypt, 1930.
Cyprus I-III	Gjerstad, Einar, et al. *The Swedish Cyprus Expedition: Finds and Results of the Excavations in Cyprus, 1927–1931*; Vols. I-III (3 vols. of text and 3 vols. of plates). Stockholm: Swedish Cyprus Expedition, 1934–1937.
Cyprus IV	Vessberg, Olof, and Westholm, Alfred. *The Swedish Cyprus Expedition*; Vol. IV, Part III: *The Hellenistic and Roman Periods in Cyprus.* Stockholm: Swedish Cyprus Expedition, 1956.
DJD I	Barthélemy, D., Milik, J. T., et al. *Qumrân Cave I.* (*Discoveries in the Judaean Desert*, Vol. I.) Oxford: Clarendon Press, 1955.
Feshkha	De Vaux, R. "Fouilles de Feshkha: Rapport préliminaire," *RB*, LXVI (1959), pp. 225–55.
Gezer I-III	Macalister, R. A. Stewart. *The Excavation of Gezer: 1902–1905 and 1907–1909.* 3 vols. London: John Murray, 1912.
Hazor I	Yadin, Yigael, et al. *Hazor I: An Account of the First Season of Excavations, 1955.* Jerusalem: Magnes Press, 1958.
HE I-II	Reisner, George Andrew, Fisher, Clarence Stanley, and Lyon, David Gordon. *Harvard Excavations at Samaria, 1908–1910.* Vol. I: *Text.* Vol. II: *Plans and Plates.* Cambridge: Harvard University Press, 1924.
IEJ	*Israel Exploration Journal*
Iliffe I	Iliffe, J. H. "Sigillata Wares in the Near East: A List of Potters' Stamps," *QDAP*, VI (1936), pp. 4–53.
Iliffe II	Iliffe, J. H. "Sigillata Wares in the Near East: II, More Potters' Stamps," *QDAP*, IX (1939), pp. 31–76.
Kahane I-III	Kahane, P. "Pottery Types from the Jewish Ossuary-Tombs around Jerusalem," *IEJ*, II (1952), pp. 125–39 (*Kahane I*), 176–82 (*Kahane II*); III (1953), pp. 48–54 (*Kahane III*).
Lachish III	Tufnell, Olga. *Lachish III: The Iron Age* (a vol. of text and a vol. of plates). London: Oxford University Press, 1953.
PAM	Palestine Archaeological Museum, Jerusalem, Jordan
PEFA	*Palestine Exploration Fund Annual*
PEF QS	*Palestine Exploration Fund, Quarterly Statement*
PEQ	*Palestine Exploration Quarterly*
QDAP	*Quarterly of the Department of Antiquities in Palestine*
Rapport I	De Vaux, R. "Fouille au Khirbet Qumrân: Rapport préliminaire," *RB*, LX (1953), pp. 83–106.

Rapport II	De Vaux, R. "Fouilles au Khirbet Qumrân: Rapport préliminaire sur la deuxième campagne," *RB*, LXI (1954), pp. 206–36.
Rapport III	De Vaux, R. "Fouilles de Khirbet Qumrân: Rapport préliminaire sur les 3ᵉ, 4ᵉ et 5ᵉ campagnes," *RB*, LXIII (1956), pp. 533–77.
RB	*Revue Biblique*
SS I	Crowfoot, J. W., Kenyon, Kathleen M., and Sukenik, E. L. *The Buildings at Samaria*. (*Samaria-Sebaste*, Vol. I.) London: Palestine Exploration Fund, 1942.
SS III	Crowfoot, J. W., Crowfoot, G. M., and Kenyon, Kathleen M. *The Objects from Samaria*. (*Samaria-Sebaste*, Vol. III.) London: Palestine Exploration Fund, 1957.
Tarsus I	Goldman, Hetty (ed.). *Excavations at Gözlü Kule, Tarsus.* Vol. I: *The Hellenistic and Roman Periods* (a vol. of text and a vol. of plates). Princeton: Princeton University Press, 1950.
TBM I	Albright, William F. "The Excavation of Tell Beit Mirsim. Vol. I: The Pottery of the First Three Campaigns," *AASOR*, XII (1930–31). New Haven: American Schools of Oriental Research, 1932.
TBM III	Albright, William F. "The Excavation of Tell Beit Mirsim. Vol. III: The Iron Age," *AASOR*, XXI–XXII (1941–43). New Haven: American Schools of Oriental Research, 1943.
TCHP	Thompson, H. A. "Two Centuries of Hellenistic Pottery" (The American Excavations in the Athenian Agora, Fifth Report), *Hesperia*, III (1934), pp. 311–480.
TN I	McCown, Chester Charlton. *Tell en-Nasbeh I: Archaeological and Historical Results.* Berkeley and New Haven: The Palestine Institute of Pacific School of Religion and the American Schools of Oriental Research, 1947.
TN II	Wampler, Joseph Carson. *Tell en-Nasbeh II: The Pottery*. Berkeley and New Haven: The Palestine Institute of Pacific School of Religion and the American Schools of Oriental Research, 1947.

CHAPTER I

INTRODUCTION

An "archaeological expedition" without chronological concern can well be designated a treasure hunt. An archaeologist who cannot date his discoveries with accuracy makes no significant contribution to historical understanding. A great mass of archaeological material would be of little historical significance except for one thing, the chronological significance of pottery—the most universal and abundant material available to the archaeologist from late Neolithic to modern times.

The discovery of the chronological importance of pottery came close on the heels of the first excavation of a stratified mound. Less than a decade after Schliemann's initial excavation at Hissarlik came the first publication which considered the chronological significance of decorated pottery by Furtwängler and Loeschcke.[1] A decade later, in 1890, Sir Flinders Petrie undertook the first Palestinian excavation at Tell el-Hesî where he became convinced of the indispensable chronological value of undecorated pottery—or kitchen pottery, as it is sometimes called. At once he was able to give fairly accurate absolute dates to certain strata which contained Syro-Palestinian pottery identical with that previously found in datable Egyptian tombs.[2] Except for some initial skepticism[3] and certain instances where pottery studies have been ignored or only superficially mastered,[4] pottery study has been a fundamental part of every Palestinian excavation.

This does not mean that misdatings of several centuries were confined from the start to excavators who ignored pottery. It can easily be understood that gaps in occupation between successive strata of occupation could not be identified from the

---

1. Adolf Furtwängler und Georg Loeschcke, *Mykenische Thongefässe* (Berlin, 1879). Cf. by the same authors, *Mykenische Vasen* (Berlin, 1886).
2. W. F. Albright, *From the Stone Age to Christianity* (Garden City, 1957), pp. 50-51.
3. C. R. Conder, "Chronology of Pottery," *PEF QS*, 1891, p. 69. Wilhelm Nowack, *Lehrbuch der hebräischen Archäologie*, I (Leipzig, 1894), p. 265.
4. A striking example is Teleilât el-Ghassûl where the date of Father Mallon was some 1500 years too late. Alex Mallon, Robert Koeppel, and René Neuville, *Teleilât Ghassûl*, I (Rome, 1934), pp. 87ff. Cf. W. F. Albright, "Presidential Address: Palestine in the Earliest Historical Period," *Journal of the Palestine Oriental Society*, XV (1935), pp. 203-205; W. F. Albright, *Archaeology of Palestine* (London, 1960), pp. 36, 45. For a more detailed description of the Ghassûl controversy cf. G. Ernest Wright, *The Pottery of Palestine from the Earliest Times to the End of the Early Bronze Age* (New Haven, 1937), Chap. II.

The German excavation at Shechem was notorious in this respect since pottery was ignored from the beginning of Sellin's work in 1913 up to 1934 when H. Steckeweh finally began utilizing ceramic evidence. Cf. Albright, *The Archaeology of Palestine*, pp. 45-46; G. Ernest Wright, "The First Campaign at Tell Balâtah," *BASOR*, 144 (Dec., 1956), p. 10.

start.⁵ Clearly stratified evidence from several contemporary sites (which in early stages was correlated with absolutely dated Egyptian remains) had to be available before accurate typological development could be traced.⁶ A clear description of that development has been the contribution of W. F. Albright and members of his school, notably G. Ernest Wright.⁷ Thanks to their efforts Palestinian pottery can be dated with accuracy from its initial appearance in Palestine before 5000 B.C. down to the end of the Divided Monarchy, 587 B.C.⁸

In striking contrast to this situation is the state of Palestinian ceramic chronology from exilic down to modern times. Here the archaeologist generally has been limited to the designations "Persian," "Hellenistic," "Roman," "Byzantine," "Arabic," and "modern," with occasional designations of "early" or "late."⁹ G. L. Harding pertinently comments,

> It is a strange anomaly that pottery of the Middle and Late Bronze Ages, can in Palestine at any rate, be dated by its contexts to within 25 or 50 years, with reasonable accuracy whereas as soon as the historically far better-known Roman period is reached, a couple of centuries seems to be the closest limit one can hope for.¹⁰

This is still true despite the abundance of imported pottery, more complete and reliable

---

5. The early excavation at Gezer, for example, failed to recognize such a gap. Albright, *The Archaeology of Palestine*, p. 111; *TBM I*, pp. 76-77; *TBM III*, p. 143.

6. Albright points to the fact that "at an early stage of archaeological research in any given country" the inductive work of the stratigrapher takes precedence while in later stages of research "the trained typologist eventually acquires an advantage over the mechanical stratigrapher, except in dealing with undisturbed deposits." Albright, *From the Stone Age to Christianity*, pp. 53-54. It may be observed that research in the Hellenistic and Early Roman periods in Palestine is still in the earlier stage as is reflected in the methodology of this study.

7. Wright has analyzed the earliest pottery of Palestine in his dissertation, *The Pottery of Palestine from the Earliest Times to the End of the Early Bronze Age*. The latest revision of his views is to be found in his chapter in the forthcoming Albright *Festschrift*. The publication of the well-stratified pottery from Tell Beit Mirsim in the *Annual* of the American Schools of Oriental Research by Albright has provided a framework for Palestinian ceramic chronology in the Middle and Late Bronze Ages and in the Iron Ages I and II. Subsequent evidence has not required any major alterations of this framework although certain refinements have been achieved, most notably through the stratigraphical evidence from Hazor and Samaria for Iron II. *V. Hazor I*, pp. 22-23; *SS III*, pp. 94-134, 198-209; Y. Aharoni and Ruth Amiran, "A New Scheme for the Sub-Division of the Iron Age in Palestine," *IEJ*, VIII (1958), pp. 171-84; G. Ernest Wright, "Israelite Samaria and Iron Age Chronology," *BASOR*, 155 (Oct., 1959), pp. 13-29.

8. Accuracy varies from the dark Early Chalcolithic period (4300-3600 B.C.) where the outlines of ceramic development are only beginning to appear, to the eighteenth to sixteenth centuries B.C. where characteristic pottery can be roughly dated within a century from purely ceramic evidence.

9. Recent examples of the broad use of the terms are "Stratum IV" at Ramat Rahel which is designated "Persian-Hellenistic-Early Roman" and the publication of a sounding at Pella where two illustrated vessels are labeled "Hellenistic-Roman," although neither of these vessels should be dated prior to the Roman annexation of Palestine and the former may even be post-Roman. Y. Aharoni, "Excavations at Ramath Rahel, 1954," *IEJ*, VI (1956), pp. 105, 137-39 and Figs. 7 and 8. R. W. Funk and H. N. Richardson, "The 1958 Sounding at Pella," *BA*, XXI (1958), p. 81, Fig. 1 and p. 87, Fig. 4. Cf. Chap. V, esp. n. 137.

10. G. Lankester Harding, "A Nabataean Tomb at 'Amman," *QDAP*, XII (1942), p. 60.

historical records, and numismatic evidence beginning in the fifth century B.C.[11]

Several factors have contributed to this situation. Some of the earlier archaeologists who unearthed post-exilic pottery either were unaware of the possibilities of a precise ceramic chronology or had not developed archaeological technique to the point where stratigraphic excavating could produce relevant evidence.[12] Ever since archaeological techniques have been refined to such an extent that they make possible a precise ceramic chronology, significant post-exilic remains have been discovered only occasionally. For example, the highest levels of Tell en-Nasbeh, Megiddo, and Lachish contain remains from the Persian period, but, as surface strata, they present problems of erosion and contamination.[13] Other factors, such as the chance choice of sites and excavation areas on sites, the sparseness of population in the Persian period,[14] the supposed lack of Biblical connections in the post-exilic period, the predilection of many archaeologists for the earliest possible remains, the comparatively slow change of certain pottery forms,[15] and the increased number of other chronologically significant artifacts,[16] should be mentioned though their relative significance is difficult to assess.

The situation for the period from about 200 B.C. to A.D. 70 has changed considerably in the last few years as a result of excavations at Beth-zur, Qumrân, 'Alâyiq, Bethany, Samaria, and Shechem.[17] At Beth-zur, Qumrân, and 'Alâyiq clearly defined strata from the Late Hellenistic and Early Roman periods have been recognized.

---

11. The earliest coin yet found in Palestine is reported from Shechem. Cf. Wright, *BASOR*, 144, pp. 19-20.

12. The early excavations at Gezer and Samaria are cases in point.

13. R. S. Lamon and G. M. Shipton, *Megiddo I* (Chicago, 1939), pp. 88ff.; *Lachish III*, pp. 71ff.; and *TN I*, pp. 175ff. Cf. G. Ernest Wright's MS for the Albright *Festschrift*, p. 26.

14. Albright, *The Archaeology of Palestine*, p. 142 vs. R. H. Pfeiffer, *History of New Testament Times* (New York, 1949), p. 7.

15. The globular cooking pot provides a good example of slow development (Cf. Chap. II).

16. It may be noted that even dated coins are frequently of less chronological significance than pottery since the "heirloom" factor is much more likely in the case of coins. This is especially true of silver and gold coins. Illustrative is the hoard of bronze coins from Samaria dated 94-74 B.C. which contained one silver coin dated to 131 B.C. *HE I*, p. 253. Note the divergent views of Oscar Broneer and H. S. Robinson on the chronological value of coins. In 1930 Broneer, in his classic treatment of Corinthian lamps, stated that "coins are, of course, the most accurate means of dating..." *Broneer*, p. 4. Writing in 1959, Robinson states that coin evidence has "proved chiefly of negative value in confirming the chronology" of Roman pottery from the Agora. *Agora V*. p. 1, n. 4. Robinson's view is confirmed by the archaeological experience of the last three decades.

17. R. W. Funk, "The 1957 Campaign at Beth-zur," *BASOR*, 150 (Apr., 1958), pp. 8-20. *Rapport I*, pp. 83-106; *Caves*, pp. 540-61; *Rapport II*, pp. 206-36; *Rapport III*, pp. 533-77. J. L. Kelso and D. C. Baramki, "Excavations at New Testament Jericho and Khirbet en-Nitla," *AASOR*, XXIX-XXX (1949-1951); '*Alâyiq*. S. Saller, "Excavations in the Ancient Town of Bethany," *Liber Annuus*, II (1951-52), pp. 119-62; *Bethany*. *SS III* (although the Joint Expedition took place over twenty years ago the final report has just appeared). Wright, *BASOR*, 144, pp. 9-20; G. Ernest Wright, "The Second Campaign at Tell Balâtah (Shechem)," *BASOR*, 148 (Dec., 1957), pp. 11-28.

These strata can be dated absolutely by correlation of numismatic and literary evidence.[18] A correlation of this stratified evidence with pottery groups from sealed loci at Bethany, Samaria, Shechem, and Jerusalem[19] can produce a closely dated series of pottery types from Late Hellenistic and Early Roman times.[20]

Such an expectation justifies the following attempt at a detailed and comprehensive examination of all available evidence bearing on the development of Palestinian

---

18. Paul and Nancy Lapp, "A Comparative Study of a Hellenistic Pottery Group from Beth-zur," *BASOR*, 151 (Oct., 1958), pp. 17-18. '*Alâyiq. Rapport I*, pp. 83-106; *Rapport II*, pp. 206-36; *Rapport III*, pp. 533-77.

19. R. W. Hamilton, "Street Levels in the Tyropoeon Valley," *QDAP*, I (1931), pp. 105-110; J. W. Crowfoot and G. M. Fitzgerald, "Excavations in the Tyropoeon Valley, Jerusalem, 1927," *PEFA*, 1927. C. N. Johns, "The Citadel, Jerusalem," *QDAP*, XIV (1950), pp. 121-90. R. W. Hamilton, "Excavations against the North Wall of Jerusalem, 1937-8," *QDAP*, X (1940), pp. 1-53.

20. This terminology requires some comment. In theory the pre-exilic typological classifications of Bronze and Iron Ages were continued through 330 or 300 B.C. with the terms (Early) Iron III or Late Iron, but in practice the historical designation Persian has been most commonly used. Cf. *TN I*, p. 2. The term Early Iron III should be avoided since it has been used for both the last phase of Iron I and the phase following Iron II. Cf., e.g., J. Naveh, "Khirbat al-Muqanna'—Ekron," *IEJ*, VIII (1958), p. 95, and contrast Aharoni and Amiran, *IEJ*, VIII, p. 171, n. 1. The term Babylonian has been used for the period from 587-539 B.C. Albright, *The Archaeology of Palestine*, p. 142. That there may be a trend toward designating even pre-exilic periods by historically oriented terminology is suggested by Aharoni and Amiran, *IEJ*, VIII, p. 172. The major periods after 330 B.C. have been called Hellenistic and Roman. The Hellenistic Period ends in Palestine with the Roman conquest in 63 B.C. The date 50 B.C. is often used for convenience and corresponds to the date given to the Hellenistic-Roman break in excavations in the vicinity of Palestine. Cf., e.g., *Cyprus IV*, pp. 72ff. The Hellenistic Period may be divided into three periods designated historically as Ptolemaic (323-198 B.C.), Seleucid (198-150/130 B.C.), and Hasmonean (165-63 B.C.). It is frequently divided into Early and Late Hellenistic, the terminology being left unspecified, but the latter generally indicating the Hasmonean Period. The Roman Period (63/50 B.C.—A.D. 350) is also divided into Early and Late Roman, the break coming about A.D. 150. Cf. especially Kelso and Baramki, *AASOR*, XXIX-XXX, p. 22. Both the Early and Late Hellenistic and the Early and Late Roman divisions correspond approximately to those of the Swedish Cyprus Expedition (cf. ref. *supra*) and are similar to those suggested by P. Kahane (*Kahane I*, p. 127). Cf. also *TN I*, p. 2, where the period 100 B.C.—A.D. 100 is called Hellenistic-Roman. The terminological usage in this study corresponds to the following scheme:

587-539 B.C.	Babylonian	
539-330 B.C.	Persian	
330 - 63 B.C.	Hellenistic	
330-198 B.C.	Ptolemaic—Early Hellenistic	
198-165 B.C.	Seleucid	Late Hellenistic
165-100 B.C.	Early Hasmonean	
100 - 63 B.C.	Late Hasmonean	
63 B.C.—A.D. 350	Roman	
63 - 37 B.C.	Pre-Herodian	
37 - 4 B.C.	Herodian	Early Roman
4 B.C.—A.D. 70	Post-Herodian	

It is recognized that at times "Herodian" has been used for the period 50 B.C.—A.D. 70 (cf. Kelso and Baramki, *AASOR*, XXIX-XXX, p. 22); however, this leads to confusion because it does not correlate with the use of the terms "Augustan" and "Tiberian." The division between Early and Late Hasmonean is convenient because several important Hellenistic sites are abandoned about 100 B.C. Actually, in this study a period is usually referred to by one of its normative stratum (e.g., "Qumrân II horizon").

pottery in these periods. The purpose of the study is *a clear presentation of Palestinian ceramic development between about 200 B.C. and A.D. 70.*

Methodology

This study is so organized that each of Chapters II to V presents an analysis of a different category of evidence with respect to its contributions to the stated purpose of the study. The final chapter summarizes the results of Chapters II to V in the form of a corpus (hereafter called "the Corpus") which, it is hoped, achieves the purpose of a "clear presentation of Palestinian ceramic development between about 200 B.C. and A.D. 70." The economic, cultural, and historical implications of the study are discussed briefly in appendices, but their full explication would involve another study of even broader proportions than the one attempted here. Below is a brief explanation of the analyses undertaken and their relationships.

1. Analysis of stratified deposits. — The study begins with a detailed examination of the stratigraphical evidence of the period which has come to light in recent excavations at Beth-zur, Qumrân, and 'Alâyiq. After determining absolute dates for the strata at these sites through literary and non-ceramic archaeological evidence, the pottery types from these strata are discussed with a view to establishing chronologically significant variations between similar types in the successive strata. This is the basic analysis which provides the framework of the Corpus presented in the final chapter. Evidence subsequently discussed could not produce such a framework and cannot be adequately understood without reference to it. A really reliable presentation of ceramic development for any period is possible only if a series of independently dated strata is available. The multiplication of parallels from groups of pottery dated by expert opinion, which has been the common *modus operandi* with pottery of this period, is really a multiplication of imprecise guesses that lead either to confusion, or, what is worse, to a false assumption of archaeological precision.

2. Analysis of other significant pottery groups. — These groups are of two types. One type is a homogeneous group from a pit, cistern, room, or tomb which has no related stratification of significance. Homogeneity is established by the close affinity of the ceramic forms with those of one or more of the stratified groups. Precise *termini* may be determined by attention to the chronologically significant forms, that is, those forms with the latest *termini post quem* and the earliest *termini ante quem*. The deposit under the steps of Bethany Cistern 61 and Beth-zur Locus 279 are examples of this type.

The other type of group comes from an imported fill. Such groups are very common in this period as most excavated debris consists of imported fills. A single imported fill is of little significance except when its material can be dated by relation to a stratified Corpus. If a series of these fills occurs and the latest pottery of each can be isolated, a significant contribution to the understanding of ceramic development is possible. Again, absolute dating is possible only with reference to stratified evidence.

Even coins or imported pottery are of little assistance in establishing precise dates since they may represent only the earliest or latest horizon of the fill, and perhaps neither. Coins may be used as supporting evidence if the latest are dated from the same period that stratified parallels indicate for the latest pottery. The chronological use of imported pottery is even more difficult because the dating of such pottery at sites outside Palestine needs careful scrutiny, and neither lines of trade nor business practices involved in the distribution of foreign pottery in Palestine are clearly understood. Samaria and Shechem provide groups of this latter type.

A judicious treatment of evidence from these two types of ceramic groups adds significant support to the validity of the stratigraphical analysis and provides supplementary material for the Corpus. These groups are analyzed in Chapter III.

3. Analysis of imported pottery. — A rather small portion of the pottery from the strata and groups discussed in Chapters II and III is imported or imitation thereof. Chronological conclusions regarding imported wares or their imitations are of the same nature as those for other kinds of pottery, but further investigation is necessary to determine chronological relations with similar pottery discovered outside Palestine. Basic to an understanding of these relations is careful evaluation of the methods used in dating non-Palestinian material. If the basis of such dating is sound, chronological relations can be established, and in some cases the Corpus may gain in scope or precision from such comparison. If the basis is unsound or completely lacking, Palestinian evidence may help clarify ceramic chronology in other territories.

One might think that the extent of non-Palestinian evidence would make an analysis within the limited scope of this study impossible. Yet, when material without chronologically significant context is eliminated, only a small fraction remains for consideration. The few sites with material considered chronologically normative in the literature are discussed in detail. The chronological significance of the groups from loci or strata is analyzed, and the dates assigned them are evaluated in the light of Palestinian and other non-Palestinian evidence. Other groups which have little relevance for Palestine or are too small to merit separate treatment are referred to in the course of the discussion. Through such procedure some light is shed on forms or wares that occur in Palestine for which Corpus evidence is lacking or ambiguous. Where Corpus evidence is relatively clear, however, it can gain little from non-Palestinian material, which is only in rare instances of comparable chronological significance.

Actually, the establishment of chronological relations is difficult.[21] The place of origin of various wares, the spread of imitations, the extent of decentralized manufacture, the policies and procedure of trade,[22] and native corpora are either unknown or known

---

21. P. Kahane's study of pottery from Jerusalem ossuary tombs *(Kahane I-III)* illustrates the difficulties.

22. Significant chronological considerations in this area are suggested in Virginia Grace's study of Rhodian wine jar handles, "Stamped Amphora Handles found in 1931-1932," *Hesperia*, III (1934), pp. 216-17. The time when the jar stamp could be legally (?) used, the time when the jars were part of the potter's stock awaiting sale, the time when they were in the hands of the wine maker, the length of the aging process, the time spent in port awaiting shipment, the time spent in transit, and the time while in the stock

in very rudimentary fashion.[23] These uncertainties, coupled with the general absence of a precise chronological framework for analyzing the non-Palestinian pottery, increase the difficulty of reaching significant conclusions about chronological and other relationships. Only when corpora comparable to the one developed here are available for a number of geographical areas in the Mediterranean world will major progress in establishing relationships be possible.

4. Analysis of other Palestinian groups. — Published Palestinian pottery not considered in Chapters II and III because of its lack of chronological significance is considered in Chapter V. An attempt is made to date groups for which homogeneity is indicated by Corpus parallels. The ability of the Corpus to indicate homogeneity, especially in some of the larger groups, tends to further confirm the validity of the Corpus since a confused Corpus could hardly serve to define a large homogeneous group. These groups add little to the Corpus, but in a few cases where *termini* indicated by Corpus parallels can be correlated with historical references certain conclusions can be drawn. A few sites where pottery of the period under study is reported but not yet published are also included.

5. Summary of analyses. — Chapter VI summarizes the conclusions reached regarding typological development of Palestinian pottery between 200 B.C. and A.D. 70. The framework is provided by the evidence of Chapter II and supplemented with material from Chapter III; a few refinements from Chapter V are included. The material discussed in Chapter IV properly belongs with non-Palestinian corpora. Under each type are listed sites discussed in Chapter V in which that type occurs. This facilitates reference to this material without mixing it with the chronologically significant material of Chapters II and III. An attempt is made to present this summary in a form clear and concise enough to be of value to a Palestinian field archaeologist.

---

of the wholesaler (?) and the retailer in the country of sale are all possible factors to be considered; the unusual length of any one of these would jeopardize chronological deductions based on analysis of the original stamp. The dates assigned individual potters are themselves open to some question. Thus, even in the case of inscribed imported ware, extreme care must be exercised in drawing chronological conclusions.

23. M. Rostovtzeff observes: "As regards pottery, we know practically nothing of the ware used and made in Egypt and especially in Alexandria in the second and first centuries B.C. . . . We are similarly ignorant in respect of Italy." *The Social and Economic History of the Hellenistic World* (Oxford, 1941), II, p. 919. Regarding territories further east he states, "No comprehensive comparative study of Hellenistic pottery found in Palestine, Phoenecia, and South Syria on the one hand, and in North Syria and Mesopotamia on the other, has ever been carried out." *Ibid.*, III, p. 1445, n. 311.

CHAPTER II

AN ANALYSIS OF THE STRATIFIED DEPOSITS

Before identifying the stratified deposits to be discussed in this chapter it is necessary to consider the definition of the term stratum. G. Ernest Wright has pointed out that in the history of Palestinian archaeology the terms stratum and level have often been used synonymously. Strictly speaking, the term level is properly used for expressing a horizontal dimension of the tell or excavated site, if possible in relation to a survey bench mark.[1] In early Palestinian excavation the method of stripping off successive horizontal "levels" of the tell was considered sound archaeological technique.[2]

A broad use of the term stratum is found in some of the work of Israeli archaeologists. For example, at Ramat Rahel a single (?) layer containing the site's Persian, Hellenistic, and Early Roman debris is designated Stratum IV.[3] Miss Kenyon applies the term "stratification" to observed layers or disturbances of the soil.[4] One or more of these layers may be related to a single period of occupation.[5] The use of the term stratum here adopted corresponds to what Miss Kenyon designates a period. A stratum is an empirically observed layer or layers which can be limited to a short, distinct period of continuous occupation or erosion.

In this chapter only those strata are considered which

1. have been excavated in Palestine (excluding Transjordan beyond the Jordan Valley);
2. belong to the period 200 B.C.—A.D. 70;
3. can be dated absolutely to a period of less than a century;
4. can be dated independent of comparative ceramic material;
5. contain a significant corpus of pottery that is accessible to the writer or has been published in sufficient detail to be of use to this study.

Perhaps the third criterion is rather arbitrary, but it can be pragmatically justified on

---

1. Kathleen M. Kenyon, *Beginning in Archaeology* (London, 1956), pp. 119-20.
2. Petrie used this method from the time he inaugurated Palestinian archaeological work in 1890. Cf., *e.g.*, the publication of much of the pottery from his excavations in *CPP* where the horizontal level of the tell at which the vessels occurred is usually recorded. This method with some deference to empirically observed stratification was still in favor at the time of the Lachish excavations. The term level is properly used in the Lachish publications, but in some cases, *e.g.*, Level II (597-587 B.C.), the term stratum, as defined below, would be more precise.
3. Y. Aharoni, "Excavations at Ramath Rahel, 1954," *IEJ*, VI (1956), p. 137.
4. Kenyon, *Beginning in Archaeology*, pp. 69-71. Note, however, her confusing use of the terms "building level" and "destruction level" on p. 70.
5. *Ibid.* and cf., *e.g.*, *SS III*, pp. 94-98.

the ground that there are corpora of pottery within this limit that do provide the basis for tracing a precise typological development. Three sites offer stratified material which meets these qualifications.

Stratification

Beth-zur (Khirbet et-Tubeiqah)

There is no evidence from sherds or other artifacts that there was any occupation of the Field II area of the 1957 Beth-zur campaign between about 587 B.C. and the second century B.C. when another widespread occupation of the site is indicated.[6] Two clearly defined strata from the second century were unearthed. The first is to be dated to the time of Antiochus Epiphanes (175-163 B.C.), the second primarily to the time of John Hyrcanus (134-104 B.C.).

The literary sources studied in the light of the coin evidence from the two campaigns indicate "intensive occupation" at the time of Antiochus Epiphanes,[7] a very limited occupation between 160 and 145 B.C.,[8] and a larger community again during the reign of John Hyrcanus.[9] The location of Field II on the periphery of the tell suggests that the two strata are to be identified with the two periods of more intensive occupation.

Two coins of Antiochus Epiphanes were recovered from the lowest preserved floor of the earlier stratum. The pottery immediately underneath the floor was homogeneous with that on and above it, indicating the same horizon of occupation.[10] A precise *terminus post quem* is impossible to determine; yet, since no evidence in either campaign from this peripheral area indicates occupation before the reign of Antiochus Epiphanes, the date 175 B.C. used in this study can hardly be off more than a few years.

The *terminus ante quem* of the earlier stratum can with some confidence be placed at 165 B.C. since the first intensive occupation of the site probably ceased when Judas captured Beth-zur in that year.[11] The discovery of a bath belonging to the earlier

---

6. This discussion is based on the writer's observations as a member of the Beth-zur staff and is presented with the kind permission of the excavation's director, O. R. Sellers. For the location of Field II and other details, see Funk, *BASOR*, 150, pp. 8-20.

7. The 124 Antiochus Epiphanes coins, none of them from hoards (*CBZ*, pp. 69-70), are striking even though his coins are comparatively numerous in Palestinian excavations. The number exceeds by 44 the total recovered by both the Harvard and Joint Expeditions at Samaria. Cf. *HE I*, p. 253, and *SS III*, p. 47.

8. No coins of Demetrius I or Alexander Balas were recorded in the 1957 campaign. The paucity of coins from this period in the 1931 campaign (O. R. Sellers and W. F. Albright, "The First Campaign of Excavation at Beth-zur," *BASOR*, 43 [Oct., 1931], p. 10 and *CBZ*, p. 70) led Sellers and Albright to state that "the Syrian garrison was either entirely removed during most of this period [160-145 B.C.], or that it was reduced to the smallest possible number." Sellers and Albright, *BASOR*, 43, p. 12. However, 1 Macc. 10:12-14, *Antiq.* xiii. 2.1 and xiii. 5.6 might indicate that this is a slight overstatement of the case.

9. *CBZ*, p. 70.

10. The Beth-zur pottery drawn in the Corpus is from the floor or above it while the pottery below the floor is compared to it.

11. *Antiq.* xiii. 7.5. 1 Macc. 4:26-61; 6:5-7.

stratum fits this date well. It is hardly possible that the bath would have been built outside the fortifications of Judas[12] or Bacchides[13] in the troubled times when the population of Beth-zur was small.[14]

It can also be stated with considerable probability that the beginning of the second major occupation under Demetrius II (145-139/8 B.C.) is to be associated with the reconstruction of Simon about 142 B.C.[15] The fact that the city was not violently destroyed when Simon captured it[16] is reflected in the archaeological evidence which does not indicate violent destruction between the two strata. The *terminus ad quem* of communal life at Beth-zur is near the end of the reign of John Hyrcanus.[17] Therefore, the upper stratum and the cistern pottery related to it can be dated about 140 to 100 B.C.[18] The upper date should be placed a few years after Simon's victory since occupation at the edge of the tell would probably not begin immediately. Beth-zur, then, provides two closely defined strata of significance for this study, Beth-zur II (175-165 B.C.) and Beth-zur I (140-100 B.C.).

Khirbet Qumrân

The popularity of the Dead Sea Scrolls accounts for the common knowledge of the stratification at Khirbet Qumrân even though only the preliminary reports are available.[19] There are some remains from the eighth and seventh centuries B.C. and the time of the Second Jewish Revolt, but the site flourished only in the Late Hellenistic and Early Roman Periods. De Vaux divides this latter occupation into three periods. Period I extends from the reign of John Hyrcanus (?) to 31 B.C. Large scale building operations that took place probably during the reign of Alexander Jannaeus (103-76 B.C.) are suggested as a convenient point of division between an earlier (Ia) and a later (Ib) phase of the period.[20] Period II is dated from the reign of Archelaus (4 B.C. – A.D. 6) to A.D. 68, and Period III, which is beyond the horizon of this

---

12. *Antiq.* xii.7.7. 1 Macc. 4:61; 6:7.
13. 1 Macc. 9:52. Cf. Sellers and Albright, *BASOR*, 43, p. 11, and C. Watzinger, *Denkmäler Palästinas*, II (Leipzig, 1935), pp. 24-25. Probably without intention Josephus omits Beth-zur in *Antiq.* xiii.1.3.
14. For a discussion of the bath see P. and N. Lapp, *BASOR*, 151, p. 18, n. 10.
15. Cf. *Antiq.* xiii.5.6, 10-11 and 1 Macc. 11:65-66; 13:33, 41 with 1 Macc. 14:33. Cf. Sellers and Albright, *BASOR*, 43, p. 11; C. Watzinger, *Denkmäler Palästinas*, II, pp. 24-25; *CBZ*, p. 11.
16. *Antiq.* xiii.5.6. Cf. 1 Macc. 11:65-66.
17. This is indicated by the numismatic evidence of both campaigns. *CBZ*, pp. 11, 13, 70, 89-90. Sellers and Albright, *BASOR*, 43, pp. 10-12. P. and N. Lapp, *BASOR*, 151, p. 11, n. 3. "Near" specifically includes the possibility that the occupation may have terminated a few years after Hyrcanus' reign.
18. Cf. P. and N. Lapp, *BASOR*, 151, pp. 16-18.
19. *Rapport I-III*. "Chronique archéologique: Khirbet Qumrân," *RB*, LXI (1954), pp. 567-68, and *RB*, LXIII (1956), pp. 73-74.
20. Evidence for dating Qumrân Ia is primarily numismatic. This evidence is very difficult to interpret, however. There are one or two coins of Antiochus VII (139/8-129 B. C.) from Trench A. J. T. Milik, *Ten Years of Discovery in the Wilderness of Judaea*, trans. J. Strugnell (Naperville, Illinois, 1959), p. 51, mentions "a few silver coins of the Seleucid kings," but see the preliminary report of the second campaign, *Rapport II*, p. 230, where one silver coin of Antiochus VII is recorded with mention of another illegible coin

study, from A.D. 68 to the end of the century.[21] Actually, the two major periods of occupation, from which most of the pottery of *Rapport I-III* comes, are Qumrân Ib and II.

De Vaux concludes that there is a gap in occupation from 31 B.C. through the end of the reign of Herod.[22] He bases his argument on the fact that there were only five coins from his relatively long reign. In this view he is followed by Cross,[23] but Milik says that comparative paucity of coins is typical and contends for a small occupation until the major rebuilding of the site in the time of Archelaus.[24] Whichever view is accepted, there was quite probably a gap in pottery manufacture at this time so that

of the same type. In addition to Cross' warning about using silver coins to establish *termini ante quem* (F. M. Cross, Jr., *The Ancient Library of Qumran* [Garden City, 1958], p. 43, n. 13), it should be noted that the coin of Antiochus VII comes from Trench A, the debris of which De Vaux assigns to Ib. Although the possibility cannot be excluded that the debris removed from the buildings at the beginning of II included some Ia remains, it is most likely that De Vaux's attribution is correct. In this case the silver coins cannot be used as evidence bearing on the beginning of Ia.

None of the fifteen copper coins of John Hyrcanus (135-104 B.C.) can be assigned precisely to Ia, but they are the best evidence available for delimiting the phase archaeologically. That the Ia occupation was small is indicated by the scantiness of the remains, their limited extent, and the limited facilities for water storage (*Rapport III*, pp. 537-38). The period of occupation indicated by these remains and coins is impossible to determine precisely. De Vaux sees the period as of very short duration, possibly in the reign of Hyrcanus I, although that this period may fall entirely within the reign of Jannaeus is not excluded (*Rapport III*, p. 538). Milik, p. 51, suggests that Ia may have "lasted ten, twenty, or forty years." Cross, p. 43, considers the coin evidence decisive against "any dating of the beginnings at Qumrân more than a half dozen years before Hyrcanus" and makes it highly probable that Ib commenced "no later than the reign of Alexander Jannaeus." Suffice it to say that the archaeological evidence would not be contradicted if other evidence pointed to a more specific date between 140 and 100 B.C. for the founding of the community.

If Cross' strong case for the identification of the Wicked Priest with Simon is accepted (pp. 95-119), and if the Teacher of Righteousness personally led his flock into the desert as tends to be further confirmed by the identification of Qumrân as the land of Damascus (pp. 91, 59, n. 46), the beginning of Ia could be attributed to the last years of Simon. At least such a date fits the archaeological evidence (and the texts as well) better than Milik's identification of the Wicked Priest with Jonathan (Milik, pp. 84-85).

The paleographic evidence further confirms the dating of Ia to the last half of the second century B.C. No sectarian works were composed before the second paleographic period (Hasmonean, 150-30 B.C.). Thus, it is not necessary to think of sectarian scribal work before 150 B.C. (Cross, pp. 89-90).

The date of the beginning of phase Ib is also disputed, but the different views are separated by less than twenty years. Milik states that "it is certain ... that the site entered into its most flourishing stage" during the reign of Hyrcanus I (p. 51). He relates its expansion to Hyrcanus' persecution of the Pharisees at the end of his reign (p. 89). De Vaux contends just as unequivocally (*Rapport III*, p. 538) that Ib began under Jannaeus. The troubled times of the civil war (93-88 B.C.) during his reign would also provide a suitable historical context for the expansion.

Thus, the period indicated for the founding of the site on archaeological grounds (140-100 B.C.) is not contradicted by historical, textual, or paleographic considerations. The date Ib began cannot be fixed definitively on the basis of present evidence. The date 100 B.C. may be used for convenience since it is within a decade of being absolutely correct.

21. *Rapport III*, pp. 566-69.
22. *Rapport III*, p. 565.
23. Cross, p. 44.
24. Milik, pp. 53-54.

there is a quarter-century between the pottery of Ib and that of II. The 31 B.C. earthquake was accompanied by a major conflagration that clearly separates the pottery of I from that of II.[25]

Another disagreement between De Vaux and Milik concerns the analysis of Loci 86 and 89, the pottery storage pantry adjoining the refectory.[26] De Vaux thinks that the pottery from Locus 89 was ruined in the 31 B.C. earthquake, and this debris was walled up when the site was renovated at the beginning of II. Milik contends that the pottery in both Loci 86 and 89 was used through the end of II. He argues that an incised bowl has typical first century A.D. script, that the corner of the room behind the purported walling up was reinforced, that there was no clear wall between Loci 89 and 86, that sherds were found behind, before, and *under* the purported wall, and that the pottery of Locus 89 does not differ significantly from that of II.[27] In view of this disagreement it seems advisable to postpone consideration of Locus 89 until the next chapter. Trench A will also be considered with the loci groups because it is not stratigraphically related to Ib.

The question of the propriety of using the Qumrân strata in the basic structure of this study might be raised in view of the conservative "closed" nature of the community.[28] It might be argued that the pottery, too, should reflect conservative tendencies. This possibility has been seriously considered, but, as will be seen in the discussion in Appendix A, there are no obvious conservative tendencies in the ceramic development at Qumrân. In fact, significant evidence points to the same ceramic developments at Qumrân as at other sites.

In summary, then, since there is no significant pottery corpus available from Ia, there are two pottery corpora which satisfy the qualifications prescribed for this study, the group from Ib dated about 100-31 B.C. and the group from II dated about A.D. 0-68. On the archaeological principle that the pottery from any given stratum usually belongs to the last years of occupation it seems desirable to date the groups respectively about 50-31 B.C. and A.D. 50-68.

Tulûl Abû el-'Alâyiq (Herodian Jericho)

The building at Herodian or New Testament Jericho excavated by J. B. Pritchard in 1951 contained pottery from an occupation of less than a century that lay between Early Bronze and Arabic remains. The limits are not precisely defined by destruction layers, but can be firmly set between 30 B.C. and A.D. 50 on numismatic and histori-

---

25. Milik, p. 93, suggests that the earthquake and fire at the end of Ib need not be contemporaneous, but the evidence permits him, at most, to separate the two events only by a few years.

26. *Rapport III*, p. 562. Milik, p. 55, n. 1.

27. Milik's argument is difficult to follow. He states that there was not a clear wall and at the same time that pottery was found under what the excavators purport to be a wall. If whatever was discovered represented the remains of a wall, the finding of pottery under it could be used in favor of a walling up of the debris in Qumrân II.

28. The possibility is suggested by G. Lankester Harding, "Khirbet Qumran and Wady Muraba'at," *PEQ*, 1952-1953, p. 105.

cal grounds.[29] Since it is unlikely that Herod constructed this building at the beginning of his reign,[30] and it is usual that pottery from the latter part of an occupation predominates,[31] it seems safe to consider the pottery from this building (except that which is obviously Early Bronze or Arabic) as belonging substantially to the first half of the first century A.D.

A methodological rigidity might suggest limiting the consideration to pottery represented on Plates 38 and 39 of 'Alâyiq which came from the lowest levels of debris in the building, but the combination of numismatic and historical evidence plus the obvious homogeneity of all the Roman pottery from the building would make such procedure pedantic. It can be deduced, however, that the pottery on these two plates would probably come from the first quarter of the first century A.D. or slightly earlier.

The precise relation of this building to the *opus reticulatum* complex described by Kelso and Baramki is still unclear.[32] The nearby presence of Herodian masonry (under the *opus reticulatum* stratum) further confirms the fact that Herod carried on building operations in this area, whether he or Archelaus was responsible for the *opus reticulatum* installations.[33] The coins from the building excavated by Pritchard indicate that it was in use during the phase characterized by Herodian masonry as well as during the phase characterized by the *opus reticulatum*. The rapid disintegration of these buildings could perhaps be presumed from the absence of further literary evidence for their use after Archelaus. The five coins of Herod Agrippa I, however, can be considered strong evidence against such an hypothesis. It is not unlikely that the villa fell into disuse after his reign, and the numismatic evidence prevents a serious presumption of its use beyond A.D. 50.

Summary

Of all the excavations reported for the period, 200 B.C.—A.D. 70, only these three sites present strata which meet the qualifications described above. An attempt must now be made to trace the development of ceramic forms through these strata:

Beth-zur II	175-165 B.C.
Beth-zur I	140-100 B.C.
Qumrân Ib	50 - 31 B.C.
'Alâyiq	A.D. 0-50
Qumrân II	A.D. 50-68

---

29. *'Alâyiq*, pp. 24-28, 56-58.

30. Jericho was in the hands of Cleopatra between 34 and 30 B.C. when Augustus returned it to Herod. *Bel. Jud.* i. 18.5; i. 20.3 // *Antiq.* xv. 7.3. Herod had been in Jericho in 35 B.C. at a feast given by Alexandra, but there is no indication that he had buildings there at that time. *Bel. Jud.* i. 22.2 // *Antiq.* xv. 3.3-4. Thus, it is very unlikely that the building of Herod under consideration antedates the last quarter of the first century B.C. The fact that no coins from the building antedate his reign also argues against construction at a date early in his reign.

31. Cf. the remarks of Cross, p. 43.

32. *'Alâyiq*, p. 58. Kelso and Baramki, p. 11.

33. For the references to the theater, amphitheater, and hippodrome at Jericho which were used by Herod see Emil Schürer, *Geschichte des Jüdischen Volkes im Zeitalter Jesu Christi* (Leipzig, 1907), I, pp. 413-18; II, p. 61.

Typology

Jars

Only sherds of jars have been recovered from the Beth-zur strata. All the rims are at least somewhat everted. The sections may be divided into rounded and collared types.[34] The former group is most common in Beth-zur II, the latter in Beth-zur I. In fact, no examples of the rounded type are clearly from Beth-zur I. The handles show the typical careless lower attachment although several examples from Beth-zur I indicate a trend toward more careful attachment.[35] Most of the handles are wet-smoothed and have a more or less oval cross-section. The double ridged handle with typical careless attachment should be noted.[36] Only round bases could be definitely attributed to the jar class.[37] The first of these shows a characteristic spiral, and the others have a smudge at the inside base point which is very common.

An unusually large number of whole and reconstructed large jars have been recovered at Khirbet Qumrân in addition to those from the caves. Because these jars are not standardized, some of them are rather difficult to classify. Only two of the published examples are from Qumrân Ib. One is placed in Corpus Type 11 which is rather awkwardly characterized as "cylindrical to bag-shaped."[38] It has a rounded rim which is not found on any of the Qumrân II jars. The other is a large ring-based jar of inverted ovoid shape which has a close parallel from Qumrân Locus 89 which belongs to the Qumrân Ib horizon.[39]

Fifteen large jars from Qumrân II are segregated into six major types. Corpus Type 11 is represented by a jar with simple rim,[40] another probably of the same class but without a preserved rim,[41] and a third with a tall collar rim.[42] The last is a much taller collar than any of the rims from Beth-zur II or I. Three inverted ovoid jars, similar to one of the jars from Qumrân Ib, occurred in Qumrân II.[43] These have a plain rim and ring base. Two have the usual vertical loop handles, but one has two ledge handles. There are four large bell-shaped jars, two with clear ridges at the base of the neck.[44] Five jars have been classed as cylindrical footed jars.[45] These very in slenderness and, unlike any of the jars mentioned so far, are without handles, except for one which has four pierced ear handles. Another has a shoulder flange.[46] The more slender are characterized by sharp breaks at the base and shoulder. A rather

---

34. Rounded: Corpus 11.3. A – C, E. Collared: Corpus 11.2. A – D.
35. Corpus handle sections 11.9. A – C from Beth-zur II have the typical careless attachment. An example of the careful attachment is represented in the Corpus by the oval handle section, 11.9. E.
36. Corpus 11.9. B.   37. Corpus 11.9. K – M.
38. Corpus 11.3. H.
39. Corpus 13. A. Cf. the discussion of Locus 89 in Chapter III.
40. Corpus 11.1. B.   41. Cf. Corpus 11.1. C.
42. Corpus 11.2. G.   43. Corpus 13. B – C.
44. Corpus 12. D provides the typical example and gives references to the other examples.
45. Corpus 14.1. A – C and 14.2. A.
46. Corpus 14.2. A.

unusual "neckless" jar with an open funnel base is also published.[47] It is of inverted ovoid profile and has two handles.

In addition to the large specimens there are three smaller jars from Qumrân II.[48] No development can be traced for these since no similar jars or fragments clearly associated with them were found at 'Alâyiq or Beth-zur.

Only fragments of large jars have been recovered by Pritchard at 'Alâyiq. The Qumrân II bell-shaped jar type is represented by two sherds with a ridge at the base of the neck.[49] Similar rims with grooves at the base of the neck are also illustrated,[50] as is a simple neck with thickened rim.[51] Handles typical of the same jars are also illustrated.[52] The handle hole representing almost a complete circle is common on these jars which are only known from first century A.D. strata. Another jar rim belongs with the simple rim variety of Corpus Type 11.[53]

Chronologically significant characteristics in jar development seem to be the gradual lengthening of the collared rim throughout the period, the disappearance of the rim with rounded section in the first century B.C., and the appearance of the ridged or grooved neck near the beginning of the first century A.D.

Jugs

There appears to be only one common type of jug represented by more than isolated sherds in the stratified evidence. Whole or nearly whole specimens of this type occur in the Beth-zur I cistern[54] and Qumrân Ib and II.[55] It is represented by fragments from Beth-zur II and 'Alâyiq.

The fragments from Beth-zur II indicate that the jugs frequently had thicker ware and heavier rims than those of Beth-zur I.[56] The three base fragments representing this jug type in Beth-zur II show a similar tendency.[57] Typical features of the Beth-zur I jugs include an everted rim coming more or less to a point at the brim and separated from the neck by a definite exterior break, a piriform body with concave base, and a carelessly made handle of more or less ovoid section coming to a rather sharp point at either end, attached to the body at the brim and very roughly at the shoulder.[58] The workmanship is careless throughout with the brim at times somewhat askew.[59] With one exception,[60] the ware is comparatively thin. Corpus 21.1.B is exceptionally thin ware for Beth-zur II.

---

47. Corpus 19. A.
48. Corpus 15. A — C.
49. Corpus 12. C, E.
50. Corpus 12. F — G.
51. Corpus 12. H.
52. Corpus 11.9. H — J.
53. Corpus 11.1. A.
54. Corpus 21.1. F — H. Cf. P. and N. Lapp, *BASOR*, 151, p. 20, Fig. 2:4 — 8.
55. Corpus 21.1. Q — R.
56. Corpus 21.1. A — B.
57. Cf. Pottery Reg. Nos. 168, 524, and esp. 486 of the 1957 Beth-zur excavation. The Pottery Register is available at the American School of Oriental Research in Jerusalem, Jordan, or can be obtained from the author.
58. Corpus 21.1. F — G.
59. Cf., *e.g.*, Pottery Reg. No. 137 of the 1957 Beth-zur excavation.
60. Cf. *ibid.*, Pottery Reg. No. 144.

A jug of the same general size and shape occurs in Qumrân Ib and II.[61] The treatment of the brim and base is different, however. The rims from Ib and II have a vertical outside face and a small inside shelf which could hold a lid. The beginning of this rim might be seen in the rim from Beth-zur I with a vertical outside section without a shelf.[62] The base of a Qumrân II jug is similar to those from Beth-zur I except that it is distinctly pointed at the outside edge.[63] There also seems to be a tendency for the neck to become narrower in the Qumrân examples. Thus, there appear to be obvious developments in the formation of the rims and bases of these jugs taking place in the first half of the first century B.C.

Fragments from 'Alâyiq indicate that the jug used there had rims and bases similar to those from Qumrân Ib and II.[64] There is no evidence for rim or base treatment comparable to the Beth-zur I examples.

A jug type with narrow neck and flat base is represented by a single example from Qumrân Ib.[65] Ring bases probably indicating other jug types are included in the Corpus although evidence for such types is lacking at present.

Flasks

Flask fragments occur in Beth-zur II and I[66] and at 'Alâyiq,[67] while the only whole flask occurs in Qumrân Ib, and it is obviously misshapen.[68] No chronologically significant development can be derived from such meager evidence, but a trend toward a longer neck above the upper handle attachment should be noted.

Juglets

Besides the reconstructed globular juglet from the Beth-zur I cistern,[69] there are only a few insignificant juglet fragments from Beth-zur. The cistern juglet has a cup-shaped rim; narrow, short, and rather undefined neck; almost round body; and slightly twisted strap handle attached at the rim and shoulder, the shoulder attachment displaying especially careless workmanship. The ware is very thin and has distinct rippling.

Juglets of this type occur in Qumrân Ib and II.[70] The modifications from the Beth-zur juglet have been discussed,[71] but they cannot be asserted strongly on the basis of the limited stratified evidence now under consideration. The juglet from Beth-zur does have a shorter, less clearly defined neck and is larger than the examples from Qumrân. An examination of some of the unpublished globular juglets from Qumrân sustains this judgment, but trustworthy conclusions must await subsequent evidence.

---

61. Corpus 21.1. Q–R.   62. Corpus 21.1. H.
63. Corpus 21.1. R. Cf. the evidence from Trench A in Chapter III.
64. Corpus 21.1. R. The two fragments published in 'Alâyiq, Pl. 58:23 and 59:9, come from the same vicinity, and it is possible that they come from a single vessel.
65. Corpus 21.2. B. Cf. a similar jug from Qumrân III, (Rapport II, Fig. 6:7) and the discussion of the pottery from Qumrân Cave 1 in Chapter V.
66. Corpus 29. B–C.   67. Corpus 29. G.
68. Corpus 29. E. For the normal form of this vessel see Corpus 29. F from Qumrân Trench A.
69. Corpus 31.1. C.   70. Corpus 31.1. D_1, D_5, E.
71. P. and N. Lapp, BASOR, 151, p. 22.

Another apparent difference between the Beth-zur and the Qumrân Ib-II juglets occurs in the treatment of the rim. Beth-zur rims begin with a vertical line while those from Qumrân II are slightly inverted. One slightly elongated juglet from Qumrân II, on the other hand, does have an everted rim.[72]

The juglet and fragments from 'Alâyiq[73] tend to duplicate the features of the Qumrân juglets such as inverted rim, longer neck, and slightly twisted handle. The juglet is slightly elongated; together with the elongated juglet from Qumrân II, a first century A.D. tendency might be indicated.

Three other juglet types have appeared in the Qumrân preliminary publications. The first is a wide-mouthed, squat juglet somewhat reminiscent of the small one-handled cooking pot.[74] A similar shape occurs in the 'Alâyiq building.[75] Another type is an elongated piriform juglet with everted rim and flat base.[76] A similar juglet with slightly concave base and more piriform in shape occurs at 'Alâyiq.[77] A spherical juglet with flat base and straight neck also comes from Qumrân II.[78] A very similar base fragment may indicate its presence also at 'Alâyiq.[79] A final type is represented by a pointed base, evidently of a juglet, from 'Alâyiq.[80] Further evidence is needed for delimiting the chronological development of these forms.

Mortaria and Craters

There is no evidence of craters from Beth-zur II or I, but mortarium fragments are common.[81] They are not standardized, but may be generally characterized as shallow with thick heavy ware, wide diameter, and probably ring bases.[82] All sherds indicate that these vessels were very carelessly executed. The great variations in the individual examples make it impossible to trace any development between Beth-zur II and I.

In contrast with Beth-zur, there is no evidence of mortaria at Qumrân, but craters are well represented. Three virtually identical examples of a two-handled crater come from Qumrân II.[83] Two handleless craters from Qumrân II have different shapes.[84] One of these has a rim like those of the two-handled type. These rims are sharply everted and thickened with end slightly concave. Two smaller bowls have forms corresponding to the handleless examples.[85] These bowls are actually too small to be considered craters, but they are so classified because they appear to belong typologically with the larger vessels. Only one larger and one smaller crater are as yet published from Qumrân Ib.[86] The typological relation of these to the Qumrân II craters is unclear.

---

72. Corpus 31.1.F.　　　　　　73. Corpus 31.1.E.
74. Corpus 34.B.　　　　　　　75. Corpus 34.A.
76. Corpus 33.B.　　　　　　　77. Corpus 33.A.
78. Corpus 32.2.A.　　　　　　79. 'Alâyiq, Pl. 59:10.
80. Corpus 38.B.　　　　　　　81. Corpus 41.A—E, K.
82. Corpus 41.K. The bases from Beth-zur II are similar to that reconstructed for the Samaria vessel.
83. Corpus 45.3.A.　　　　　　84. Corpus 45.1.B—C.
85. Corpus 45.2.B is similar to Corpus 45.1.B. Corpus 45.2.C is similar to Corpus 45.1.C.
86. Corpus 45.2.A and 49.A.

From 'Alâyiq come a number of crater rims. These seem to represent both the two-handled and the handleless varieties from Qumrân II.[87]

It seems, then, that mortaria must have gone out of use between Beth-zur I and Qumrân Ib, and craters apparently began to be used in that same period. The everted rim with concave end seems to be characteristic of the first century A.D. although it is also represented in Locus 89 of the Qumrân Ib horizon.[88]

Bowls

A sherd from Beth-zur II represents the small hemispherical bowl type,[89] and several varieties of small plates come from Beth-zur II and I.[90] Not enough evidence is available to trace any development in the second century B.C.

A large variety of deep and shallow bowls, cups, and plates comes from Qumrân Ib and II. The large number of these vessels published in *Rapport I-III* can be divided into several types, a few of which display significant differences between Qumrân Ib and II. The small bowl with incurved rim is represented by eight examples from Qumrân Ib and ten from Qumrân II,[91] but the great variety of individual forms makes the tracing of a typological development impossible. Similar small bowls which are more hemispherical in shape are also represented in Qumrân Ib and II.[92] No typological development has been observed. Small deep bowls with everted rims also occur in Qumrân Ib and II.[93] Here it seems that Corpus Type 51.8.B with its slight cyma profile and carefully formed base can be distinguished from the forms of Qumrân II which appear less delicate and not so carefully executed.[94] Cups with inverted to vertical sides[95] as well as cups with everted sides[96] are common in Qumrân Ib and II, but no development is apparent. Miscellaneous single bowls and cups with unique features from Qumrân Ib and II should be mentioned for the sake of completeness.[97] A number of small, rather flat plates occur in Qumrân Ib but are not represented in Qumrân II.[98] The common "plate" in Qumrân II is apparently the bowl with vertical rim.[99] This type is not represented in Qumrân Ib although a few early prototypes occur in loci of Qumrân Ib horizon.[100] Light is shed on this striking difference between Qumrân Ib and II "plates" by the typological development of Eastern Sigillata A forms.[101]

---

87. Corpus 45.1.A, C; 45.3.A.
88. Cf. the discussion of Locus 89 in Chapter III.
89. Corpus 51.2.A.   90. Corpus 53.A—C, F—G.
91. Corpus 51.1.C—F (Ib), J—M (II).
92. Corpus 51.2.F—J (Ib), K—L (II).
93. Corpus 51.8.A—B (Ib), C—D (II).
94. Cf. forms from Qumrân Locus 89 and Trench A which support this distinction which would be extremely tenuous if based exclusively on the single Qumrân Ib vessel.
95. Corpus 52.1.A (Ib), B—D (II).
96. Corpus 52.2.B—D (Ib), E—F (II).
97. Corpus 51.6.A; 51.7.A; 52.9.A, C—D.
98. Corpus 53.H—L.   99. Corpus 54.1.A—D; 54.2.D—K.
100. Cf. the discussions of Qumrân Locus 89 and Trench A in Chapter III.
101. Cf. the discussion of the Roman Ia deposit at Samaria in Chapter III.

From 'Alâyiq come examples of the small bowl with incurved rim[102] and a small bowl of heavy ware apparently belonging to the earlier Beth-zur II-I tradition.[103]

The general picture of development indicated by the stratified evidence is somewhat as follows. Small, carelessly made bowls with incurved rim or hemispherical profile are used throughout the period 200 B.C. – A.D. 70. These vessels do not display any kind of standardization and no development is apparent. There seems to be some evidence of the "degeneration" of form in the small deep bowls or cups with everted rim between Qumrân Ib and II. No development is evident in the case of the cups with inverted to everted sides from Qumrân Ib and II which do not appear in the Beth-zur II-I horizon. The variety of small, rather flat plates of careless workmanship appear in Beth-zur II-I and Qumrân Ib but are replaced in Qumrân II by the bowls with vertical rims.

Lids, Stands, and Funnels

No lids are provided by the Beth-zur or 'Alâyiq groups, but three lids each are illustrated from Qumrân Ib and II.[104] The Qumrân Ib lid in the shape of a small bowl with everted rim and handle inside is unique.[105] The other two Qumrân Ib lids present a more rounded appearance than those from Qumrân II where the more or less vertical sides are sharply broken from the top of the lid. That this difference is not significant is shown by evidence from the Qumrân caves.[106]

One short, small, heavy stand is illustrated from Qumrân II.[107]

A large funnel (a flower pot if Kelso is correct) occurs at 'Alâyiq.[108] Two rather large funnels come from Qumrân II.[109]

Cooking Pots

The development of the globular cooking pot has been partially presented in the preliminary publication of the cistern associated with Beth-zur I.[110] No evidence for a distinction between the globular cooking pots of Beth-zur II and I can be illustrated although a slight tendency for the ware to become finer and lighter in weight can be sensed in working with the pottery. The ware may be smooth or slightly rippled.[111] The typical Beth-zur pot[112] might be characterized as having a width and height of about 16-22 centimeters. The width may slightly exceed the height and vice versa. The straight neck (vertical to slightly everted) is at least 2.5 centimeters long. There

---

102. Corpus 51.1. G–H. 103. Corpus 53. M.
104. Corpus 61. B–C, 63. A (Ib); 62 A–C (II).
105. Corpus 63. A. 106. Cf. Chapter V, n. 158.
107. Corpus 65. A.
108. Corpus 68. B. Cf. Kelso and Baramki, p. 31.
109. Corpus 68. C–D.
110. P. and N. Lapp, *BASOR*, 151, p. 22.
111. This rippling should not be confused with Byzantine ribbing. It is impossible to confuse the smooth rippled surface of Late Hellenistic and Early Roman pottery with the sharp rough surface of Byzantine ribbed ware. Difficulty arises when the rippling is exaggerated in drawings so that it appears to be ribbed.
112. Cf. Corpus 71.1. A–E.

is a definite break in the line where the shoulder extends downward and outward at about a 45° angle. The greatest diameter is reached about mid-body and below this the lower third of a circle is formed. The thin strap handles are carelessly attached at the rim and shoulder. The body never protrudes as much as three centimeters beyond the handle. Some of the rims are simple, usually rounded at the top. Others appear to have been shaved so that they have a sharp inside or outside angle.[113]

The Qumrân Ib cooking pots[114] are similar to those from Beth-zur, but they display certain developments. One of the vessels resembles the Beth-zur pots in size, but the others are significantly larger and all are proportionately more squat. The fact that no rims with a sharp inside angle occur in Qumrân Ib, Qumrân II, or at 'Alâyiq may also be significant.

The Qumrân II pots[115] continue the more squat form of Qumrân Ib, but they tend to have a shorter and less sharply differentiated neck. That the development was not unilateral, however, can be seen in a small pot which continues the Beth-zur form.[116]

The evidence from 'Alâyiq tends to conform to this development since both Qumrân Ib and II features are represented.[117]

The shallow cooking pot or casserole appears in three distinct variations in Qumrân II. The first has a rim extending outward horizontally and provides a slightly concave shelf for a lid.[118] It is also represented in Beth-zur II.[119] In the second the rim and shoulder form somewhat of a semi-circle which is completed by the handle.[120] Sherds representing this variant also come from 'Alâyiq.[121] The third variant has a relatively simple rim which continues the line of the shoulder.[122] No lines of development for the casseroles are apparent.

Lamps

Lamps are poorly represented in the stratified evidence. Only one lamp fragment came from Beth-zur II. It has a rounded body, rather long straight neck, and rounded nozzle.[123]

From Qumrân Ib came a decorated lamp with bowed spout[124] and loop-handled lamps with round bodies tapering into long necks.[125] From Qumrân II three simple bow-spouted Herodian lamps are published.[126]

---

113. Corpus 71.1.C represents the simple rim. Corpus 71.1.A and B represent the outside "shaving" and D and E the inside "shaving." Corpus 71.1.F also displays inside "shaving" and has an inside ridge at the base of the neck. Its unusually short neck and orange ware distinguish it from the usual Beth-zur pots. However, it cannot be confused with the Qumrân II pots.

114. Corpus 71.1.K_2.
115. Corpus 71.1.N_2. Cf. P. and N. Lapp, *BASOR*, 151, p. 21.
116. Corpus 71.1.K_2.
117. Corpus 71.1.K_2 (Ib) and 71.1.N_1, P, Q. The latter do not have parallels from Qumrân II listed in the Corpus, but they do display the less differentiated, shorter neck.
118. Corpus 72.1.K.
119. Corpus 72.1.F.
120. Corpus 72.2.B.
121. Corpus 72.2.A.
122. Corpus 72.3.A.
123. Corpus 83.1.A.
124. Corpus 82.2.A.
125. Corpus 84.A–D.
126. Corpus 82.1.B–D.

The 'Alâyiq stratum presents five bowed spouts, two decorated with circles.[127] There is also a fragment of a molded lamp of the rounded type with slight nozzle barely protruding and a small oil hole.[128]

The absence of the Herodian bow-spouted lamp from the Beth-zur strata and its presence in Qumrân Ib, Qumrân II, and 'Alâyiq should be noted, as should the absence of the Qumrân Ib loop-handled lamps from Qumrân II.

Unguentaria

Sherds of the heavy ware fusiform unguentarium[129] occur in Beth-zur II,[130] and a base of the thin ware variety comes from 'Alâyiq.[131] The piriform bottle is represented by numerous examples from 'Alâyiq[132] and a fragment from Qumrân II.[133] Two other smaller bottles attributed to the piriform unguentarium group also came from Qumrân II.[134] Note should be taken of the thick, heavy ware of the Beth-zur II fusiform unguentarium fragments as compared with the light thin ware of the 'Alâyiq example. The single fusiform unguentarium compared with the large number of piriform unguentaria from 'Alâyiq also proves of significance in the light of subsequent evidence.[135]

Hellenistic Decorated Ware[136]

Fragments of Hellenistic Decorated Ware were common at Beth-zur but did not occur at Qumrân or 'Alâyiq. The forms represented are a jug,[137] bowls with incurved rims,[138] a bowl with outcurved rim,[139] bowls with pinched handles,[140] and fish plates.[141] A number of ring bases from such small bowls are also included in the Corpus for the sake of completeness.[142] No development between Beth-zur II and I is apparent.

Eastern Sigillata A[143]

Four fragments of Eastern Sigillata A came from 'Alâyiq.[144] Their significance will be interpreted in terms of evidence discussed in Chapter III.

---

127. Corpus 82.1. A—B.   128. Corpus 85. A.

129. The possible intimation of an original use as a lachrymatory makes the designation "tear bottle" unsatisfactory. Cf. *TCHP*, p. 473.

130. Corpus 91.1. B—D.   131. Corpus 91.2. C.

132. Corpus 92. A—E. Cf. *'Alâyiq*, Pl. 19:1.

133. Corpus 92. D.   134. Corpus 92. F—G.

135. A glance at Corpus 91.2 will show that the single fusiform unguentarium from 'Alâyiq is the only one from an A.D. context.

136. This designation is used for those forms that have a common tradition throughout the Eastern Mediterranean and which are decorated with various shades of black, brown, or red glaze, paint, slip, or wash during the Hellenistic Period. The vessels of this ware from the second and early first centuries B.C. display such universally careless workmanship that it is impossible to treat them as an imported ware even if the forms are not considered exclusively local imitations. In Palestine, as will become clear in Chapter III, the repertory of forms is limited to a variety of small bowls and plates with occasional fragments of jugs and bottles. Some of the forms frequently occur in ordinary local "kitchen" ware.

137. Corpus 139. A.   138. Corpus 151. D—E.

139. Corpus 151.3. A.   140. Corpus 151.4. A—B.

141. Corpus 153.1. K—N.   142. Corpus 151.9. A—C.

143. For the definition of this term cf. *SS III*, pp. 283–84.

144. Corpus 253.1. L—M.

West Slope Technique[145]

A single fragment displaying the West Slope Technique is recorded from Beth-zur II.[146] It must be considered with non-Palestinian evidence discussed in Chapter IV.

Rhodian Amphora

A critical evaluation of Miss Grace's intensive study of Rhodian amphora stamps and handles is beyond the scope of this study. Two Rhodian stamped handles did occur in Beth-zur II. These are dated by Miss Grace 200-190 B.C.[147] and 180-150 B.C.[148]

---

145. The term West Slope Technique is used because the designation "West Slope Ware" could imply Athenian provenience, whereas by the second century B.C. the manufacture of this kind of ware had been at least partly mastered elsewhere. This ware is distinguished from Hellenistic Decorated Ware both by the forms which it utilized and its painted and incised decorative motifs. For a detailed discussion of pottery displaying West Slope Technique v. Chapter IV.

146. Corpus 353.1.A.

147. Beth-zur Obj. Reg. No. 28; cf. Grace, *Hesperia*, III, p. 227, No. 47.

148. Beth-zur Obj. Reg. No. 97; cf. *Tarsus I*, p. 142, No. 42.

CHAPTER III

AN ANALYSIS OF OTHER CHRONOLOGICALLY SIGNIFICANT POTTERY GROUPS

The previous chapter has presented the limited stratified evidence of ceramic typological development in Palestine between 200 B.C. and A.D. 70. The purpose of this chapter is to analyze other ceramic groups which confirm and supplement that evidence. The first group analyzed is the pottery group from under the steps of Locus 61 at Bethany. It can be dated by the stratified typology to approximately the second quarter of the first century B.C. This tends to confirm the accuracy of the typology and the stratigraphical analysis from which it was derived; if the stratigraphy were inaccurately observed or incorrectly dated, or if the typology misrepresented the evidence, it is highly unlikely that the stratified typology could closely date any large pottery group. Once the pottery group has been closely dated, those new or transitional forms that occur in it can be used to supplement the typological Corpus. The capacity of the Corpus to date a large pottery group closely, of course, only confirms its relative accuracy unless evidence for absolute dating is found with the deposit. Yet, the absolute chronology can hardly be questioned in light of the literary and archaeological data used in establishing the absolute dates in the Corpus strata.

At Samaria a series of deposits predate successively 150, 107, 55, and 25 B.C. Unfortunately, their *termini a quo* go back to the beginning of the Hellenistic period or earlier. These deposits also provide evidence to confirm the validity of the stratified Corpus and to supplement it. The fact that none of the material in these deposits must postdate its *terminus ante quem* according to Corpus parallels attests the validity of the Corpus. Miss Kenyon's discussion is especially concerned with new pottery forms which appear for the first time in one of the three later deposits. Thus, a new form in the pre-25 B.C. deposit should have a *terminus a quo* of 55 B.C. if the pre-55 B.C. deposit is of significant extent and the form itself is not rare. Especially since a number of sigillata forms can be dated in this manner, the Corpus can be significantly supplemented.

The fact that the stratified Corpus (correlated with other evidence) provides a satisfactory solution to a difficult stratigraphical problem in Field II at Shechem also confirms its validity. The forms from Beth-zur II and the fill of the Hellenistic Fort Wall at Samaria correlate closely with forms from the Black Earth Level at Shechem while the underlying debris from Room 1 of the Hellenistic House can be dated by the stratified Corpus to the second half of the second century B.C. Similar confirmation comes from Locus 279 of the 1957 excavation at Beth-zur, Locus 89 and Trench A at Qumrân, and several smaller groups from Jerusalem.

Bethany Cistern 61

The pottery from this locus comes from debris beneath the steps leading into the cistern.[1] Many of the types represented have close parallels with the stratified material discussed in Chapter II. No imported wares were discovered, and there were no coins or other datable objects in the debris. The context is not of chronological significance. The pottery must be dated by relationships with the stratified evidence.

There are no vessels or sherds that must date before 100 B.C. In fact, development beyond Beth-zur I forms is evident in a number of instances, indicating a *terminus post quem* sometime after 100 B.C. Two of the three collar rims from Cistern 61 have slightly longer collars than examples from Beth-zur I.[2] Rims with ridges at the base of the neck that are known from 'Alâyiq and Qumrân II are represented in the Bethany deposit.[3] No such forms occur in Beth-zur II or I, and their absence from Qumrân Ib is not significant since so few large jars from Ib have been published. Two small flattish plates are of lighter ware than the Beth-zur examples[4] and have a close parallel in Qumrân Ib.[5] The Bethany jugs are definitely post-second century B.C. because of their squared rims with inside groove and their sharp bases.[6] Juglets with more clearly defined necks than the juglet from the Beth-zur cistern are published.[7] Two bowed lamp spouts, which first occurred in Qumrân Ib, are also reported.[8]

On the other hand, no form must be placed in the Christian era, and several forms definitely predate a first century A.D. horizon. These include jar rims with collars which are definitely shorter than those of the first century A.D.[9] and the flat plates which do not appear after Qumrân Ib.[10] Both these forms were common in this locus.[11] Further, it seems likely that a jug (*sic!*) and three cooking pots should be dated before Qumrân Ib.[12] Arguments from silence are tenuous even when dealing with rather large groups such as this one, but it can be noted that there is no evidence

---

1. For a diagram of the locus see Saller, *Liber Annuus*, II, p. 128, Fig. 8.
2. Corpus 11.2.E. The third is classed with Corpus 11.2.B from Beth-zur II, but it is also similar to Corpus 11.2.C which is found in Beth-zur II and I. The large jar with simple rim from Cistern 61 should also be mentioned (Corpus 11.1.C). This jar cannot be certainly attributed to the Cistern 61 group under study because it was not found in debris definitely under the steps. Cf. *Bethany*, Fig. 31 and p. 198. It should also be noted that this vessel was reconstructed, and there was no join between the handle and the neck. *Bethany*, p. 198. Yet the form of the body is similar to Corpus 11.2.F from Trench A of the Qumrân Ib horizon (cf. *infra*) and a similar rim occurs on a jar from Samaria Roman Ia (Corpus 11.1.A) dated near the turn of the era. It seems probable, therefore, that the jar belongs to the same horizon as the rest of the group.
3. Corpus 12.A? and B and cf. C – F.
4. Corpus 53.A – G.   5. Corpus 53.H.
6. Corpus 21.1.M.
7. Corpus 31.1.D$_1$. Contrast 31.1.C from Beth-zur I.
8. Corpus 82.1.B and cf. 82.2.A.
9. Corpus 11.2.B, E, and contrast G.
10. Corpus 53.H.   11. *Bethany*, pp. 200, 204.
12. Corpus 21.1.F – G; 71.1.K; and cf. *Bethany*, Pl. 118:5 – 7.

of mortaria which do not occur after Beth-zur I nor is there any evidence of Eastern Sigillata A which is uncommon before 50 B.C. (cf. *infra*).[13]

Accordingly, evidence points to the second quarter of the first century B.C. as a period when all the forms from this locus could occur. It might be argued that the group should be dated between the earliest and latest possible dates that can be assigned to any of the extant forms. This would give a range of dates from somewhere in the third century B.C.[14] through at least the first century A.D.[15] Such procedure is objectionable because it fails to distinguish forms which show chronologically significant development from those which are relatively stable. In the absence of evidence to the contrary in a rather large pottery group, it seems quite defensible to place the entire group within the chronological limits prescribed by its most chronologically significant forms.[16]

Having established this date for the group, one can add the new forms which occur in it to the Corpus. These forms include three jug rims,[17] two juglet forms,[18] a small vase,[19] and two lamp types.[20] The provenience of these types in the second quarter of the first century B.C. is established, but their precise chronological limits and developments cannot yet be determined.

Samaria Deposits

A number of loci at Samaria have precisely fixed *termini ante quem*. The filling contemporary with the Hellenistic Fort Wall (henceforth HFW) is prior to the middle of the second century B.C., and the "Post Hellenistic Fort Wall" deposit (henceforth PHFW) is probably to be dated before 107 B.C.[21] Vault Cisterns 1 and 2 were filled with debris and sealed by building operations related to the construction of the Temple of Augustus, 30-20 B.C.[22] This is attested by the coins from the debris, four of which probably are to be dated between 100 and 40 B.C.[23] The Street

---

13. Three painted sherds occurred in the locus, but they are not adequately described for detailed consideration. *Bethany*, p. 296, Nos. 2119, 2120, and 2538.

14. The jar rim, Corpus 11.2.B, is known from third century B.C. contexts at Shechem, but proof must await detailed analysis of this period.

15. Cf., *e.g.*, Corpus 21.1.M with 21.1.R.

16. One form that might seem to suggest a date after 50 B.C. is the bow-spouted ("Herodian") lamp (Corpus 82.1.B). Actually, the earliest context for these lamps in Palestine aside from Bethany is a Tyropoeon Valley deposit dated 37–4 B.C. While there is no incontrovertible evidence to prevent placing the *terminus ante quem* of the deposit later than 50 B.C., there is no positive evidence for doing so even in the case of the bow-spouted lamp. The nearest parallels to the bow-spouted lamp from Corinth and Athens certainly predate 50 B.C. Cf. *Broneer*, Pl. IV:163 and pp. 50-51, and *Agora IV*, Pl. 45:516 and p. 124.

17. Corpus 21.1.N–P and 21.2.A (?). 18. Corpus 31.2.A and 32.1.A.

19. Corpus 38.A. 20. Corpus 81.1.A and 81.2.A.

21. *SS III*, pp. 218–20, 233.

22. *Antiq.* xv. 8.5. *Bel. Jud.* i. 21.2. Cf. *HE I*, p. 49; *SS I*, p. 123. Note incomplete note 1. Henceforth, the mean date for the building of the Augustan Temple, 25 B C., will frequently be used.

23. *HE I*, p. 52.

Cistern in Strip 3, as well as debris under the street which seals the cistern, is to be dated prior to the constructions of Gabinius about 57-55 B.C.[24] Deposits under the Gabinian floors of the Lower Terrace (L.T.)[25] and of the houses to the north of the retaining wall of the forecourt of the Augustan Temple[26] are also to be dated prior to 55 B.C. The *termini a quo* of these deposits unfortunately go back to Seleucid, Ptolemaic, and, in the case of the HFW, Israelite times.[27] They are therefore substantially of little independent chronological significance. However, the isolation of pottery types occurring in these deposits which do not occur in deposits with earlier *termini ante quem* proves of the highest significance. After a discussion of certain weaknesses in the stratigraphical delimitation of these groups, they will be analyzed individually in detail.

Miss Kenyon argues that sigillata ware can be given a conclusive *terminus post quem* of 150 B.C. because it was not found in the "enormous" mass of pottery associated with the building of the Hellenistic (Reisner's Greek) Fort Wall about 150 B.C.[28] Deposits with *termini ante quem* of 107 B.C., when Hyrcanus destroyed the town, are scanty, but there is no sigillata ware in them.[29] Two types of Eastern Sigillata A occur under the floors of the Gabinian rooms north of the Augustan Temple, and the same types occurred in sub-Gabinian deposits of the Harvard Expedition according to Fisher.[30]

On the basis of evidence from the Harvard Expedition Reisner had argued that sigillata was introduced in the second century B.C. or even earlier.[31] Miss Kenyon opposes this contention with typological, stratigraphical, and historical arguments.[32] The pre-Gabinian sigillata is very similar to that from between the Gabinian floors and the construction of the Temple of Augustus. It is

> intrinsically improbable that the vessels should be dated late second century B.C., for they are extremely close in ware and form to the groups datable 30-20 B.C. It is most unlikely that the industry should remain static for seventy-five years or more, especially in view of the marked development between c. 30 B.C. and the beginning of the first century A.D.[33]

Stratigraphically all that can be said of the sigillata Reisner dates to the second century B.C. is that it has a *terminus ante quem* of 57-55 B.C.[34] Yet, since the remains dated between 150-107 B.C. (which do not contain sigillata) are scant,[35] the stratified

---

24. *HE I*, p. 304. *SS III*, p. 285.   25. *HE I*, p. 304.
26. *SS III*, p. 285. Cf. *SS I*, pp. 121–22. The map designation, *SS III*, p. 285, should read 501 – 525 N, 591 (not 541) – 613 E. Cf. *SS I*, p. 121.
27. *SS III*, pp. 218, 220. *HE I*, pp 52, 74, 304, *et passim*.
28. *SS III*, pp. 218–19, 284. Cf. *infra*.
29. *SS III*, p. 284. Note that henceforth the term "sigillata" will be used to refer explicitly to to Eastern Sigillata A.
30. *SS III*, p. 285.
31. *HE I*, p. 304. Cf. *SS III*, p. 306, where a similar view is still held by Mrs. Crowfoot.
32. *SS III*, p. 285.   33. *Ibid*.
34. *Ibid*.   35. *SS III*, p. 284.

evidence is not conclusive. The conclusion of Reisner that Hyrcanus' razing of Samaria was so complete that there was a gap in occupation until Gabinius' reconstruction seems less likely than Miss Kenyon's view that continued occupation was not precluded by the extent of the destruction.[36]

Miss Kenyon concludes from the Samaria evidence that sigillata had come into "fairly common use" in Palestine by about 60 B.C., "but that a date much earlier than this cannot be proved."[37] She apparently specifies 60 B.C. because of the close typological relation between the two pre-Gabinian and the immediately subsequent forms; but that these forms are subsequent is disputed below. A more cogent argument for this date, discussed in Appendix A, is the possible shift in trade policies beginning with the Roman accession. Yet, 60 B.C. seems to be an absolutely minimal date, and in this study the date of the pre-Gabinian types will be given as the second quarter of the first century B.C., a date perhaps more adequately reflecting the imprecision of the limited evidence. It should be emphasized that this date is accepted only as a working hypothesis, because there is no evidence that would absolutely exclude the introduction of sigillata ware at the end of the second century B.C.

The material sealed in loci at the building of the Temple of Augustus, as discovered by the 1931 Expedition, was found on Gabinian floors and included nearly whole plates of very fine ware, according to Miss Kenyon.[38] However, the evidence cited for locating these vessels on the floor is not of the category of empirical stratigraphy, but is based on a rather tenuous assumption that vessels nearly intact would not be found in the make-up of the floor, whereas, if there had been smaller sherds, they *might have been* part of the make-up. Her assumption that the building operations were so "brusquely" carried out that there was no time to remove such vessels from the houses would be more acceptable if the Romans had bulldozers and if the plates had been entirely intact. Such considerations cannot exclude the possibility that these vessels were in use before the operations of Gabinius. Miss Kenyon herself admits this on grounds of their potential value as treasures.

These observations must be related to Miss Kenyon's typological argument for bringing the pre-Gabinian sigillata down to about 60 B.C. If the material attributed to the Gabinian floors can actually be considered with the pre-Gabinian material, the forms of the two groups are contemporary and no typological development need be expected; then the date of the introduction of Eastern Sigillata A at Samaria is more difficult to fix precisely.

Miss Kenyon observes that Vault Cistern 2 has a *terminus ante quem* identical with the material from the Gabinian floors, and that its contents "represent debris from

---

36. The Josephus passage, the exegesis of which is disputed, is *Antiq.* xiii. 10.3. Here it is stated that Hyrcanus destroyed every indication that Samaria had existed as a city. This is obviously an exaggeration, but there is disagreement regarding the extent of the exaggeration. Cf. *HE I*, pp. 57–58, and *SS III*, p. 306, with p. 285. *V.* also Appendix B *infra*.

37. *SS III*, p. 285. 38. *Ibid.*

the pre-Herodian houses."[39] It must be added that the debris shifted about in the Herodian operations is in no locus exclusively "pre-Herodian" (55-25 B.C.). This is explicitly true of Vault Cistern 2 which contained coins from the third to first centuries B.C.[40]

In summary, Miss Kenyon's contention that a date for the introduction of sigillata into Palestine about 60 B.C. cannot be disproved. It does appear that the evidence favoring this minimal date may be a bit overdrawn. What the 1931 Expedition has shown is that sigillata was not introduced by 150 B.C., and probably not by 107 B.C. Two types in sigillata occur in debris predating the Gabinius building operations and several other types occur in loci prior to the construction of the Augustan Temple. The attribution of the pre-Gabinian material to the second quarter of the first century B.C. and the pre-Herodian material to the second and third quarters of that century seems to be as minimal a chronology as is defensible.

A final locus at Samaria is dated by parallels to a stamped Arretine plate to the turn of the era.[41] Unlike the other groups no stratigraphy fixes the precise date assigned to this group, but observation indicates that the local pottery associated with it should also form a fairly homogeneous group. Accordingly, if the local pottery can be dated by comparison with the Corpus to the same period as that of the imported ware, a confirmation of the typology here developed and of the dating of the imported ware will result. The latter is true especially in view of the fact that identical stamped sigillata vessels in Europe and Palestine cannot, uncritically, be assumed to have had an identical chronological history.[42]

1. Filling for the Hellenistic Fort Wall.—None of the HFW pottery has close affinities to the pottery from 'Alâyiq or Qumrân. Many of the sherds closely resemble Beth-zur types, and where a distinction between Beth-zur II and I is possible, the relationship with II is closest. A number of earlier forms occur. Some of these can be designated as pre-second century B.C. with reasonable confidence because they have affinities with unpublished third century B.C. material from Shechem. Forms with no parallels in the stratified Corpus may be earlier, but they are perhaps second century forms not yet represented in the Corpus. Most of these forms are included in the Corpus, and the year 200 B.C. is always placed in parenthesis to indicate that an earlier *terminus post quem* must be considered. In addition, the possibility of a pre-200 B.C. date is specifically indicated for some of the forms. A detailed discussion of the HFW pottery (*SS III*, Figures 37-42) follows.

---

39. *SS III*, p. 285.   40. *HE I*, p. 52.
41. *SS III*, p. 286.
42. Cf. Miss Kenyon's remarks on the spotty geographic spread of Megarian bowls where the chronological differences in provenience are attributed to differences in local demand and development of trade. *SS III*, p. 218. The same point is argued by Waagé (*Antioch IV*, p. 5) where a striking illustration is cited.

In general, the HFW fish plates[43] are very similar to the Beth-zur fish plate fragments in ware and decoration. Only the "drooping rim" variety occurs in Beth-zur II and I, and it is represented by six examples in the HFW deposit.[44] There is no evidence of central depression among the Beth-zur sherds.[45] An adequate discussion of these plates, however, is only possible in the light of the Tarsus evidence presented in Chapter IV. This evidence suggests that, with two exceptions, the Samaria fish plates belong to the horizon of the top level of the Middle Hellenistic Unit and the Late Hellenistic Unit (late third and second centuries B.C.).[46] The dating of these plates to the first half of the second century B.C. is determined by the evidence which assigns the HFW a pre-150 B.C. date, and it is confirmed by the fish plates in the PHFW and Beth-zur I which have features that distinguish them from the HFW examples.[47]

One of the HFW bowls with outcurved rim has a close parallel probably from Beth-zur II.[48] The example illustrated from Samaria has red slip, but the Beth-zur example has poor black glaze as do the majority of bowls of this class.[49] Miss Kenyon suggests that the other two HFW bowls with outcurved rim are slightly later examples of the type because their profiles are more angular than the example with a Beth-zur parallel.[50] This is doubtful because both the rounded and angular types occur also in the PHFW.[51]

HFW bowls with incurved rims have both ring and disc bases.[52] Parallel rim fragments occur in Beth-zur II, one example with rather poor mottled red to dark red

---

43. Corpus 153.1.A—J. (References to the original publication are cited in the Corpus. If the material is not included in the Corpus, the original publication is cited directly.) Miss Kenyon uses the term, "fish plates," broadly to include plates without a central depression. This is certainly defensible in view of the fact that nearly identical forms occur with (Corpus 153.1.B) and without (Corpus 153.1.H) the depression. For evidence that this depression is not a chronologically significant feature v. Chap. IV under Tarsus.

44. Cf. Corpus 153.1.K—N with 153.1.B and H. "Drooping rim" is Miss Jones' term, cf. *Tarsus I*, Fig. 178:26, A.

45. Cf. Corpus 151.9.A—C and n. 43 *supra*.

46. The exceptions are Corpus 153.1.A (cf. *infra*, Chap. IV, n. 50 and Corpus 153.1.F (cf. *Tarsus I*, Fig. 178:D and E from third century B.C. contexts). The latter might be questioned in the light of two examples from the Black Earth deposit at Shechem. Cf. *infra*. The top level of the Middle Hellenistic Unit is dated late third to early second century B.C., but according to the principle adopted in this study the pottery probably belongs to the latter part of the period, i.e., early second century B.C.

47. Cf. the discussion of the PHFW, *infra*.

48. Corpus 151.3.A. In Beth-zur Field II, Area I, from which this sherd came, there were very few sherds from Beth-zur I, which merged with the cultivation level in this area. Evidence of the Beth-zur I stratum in one corner of Area I was observed too late to separate its sherds from those of Beth-zur II, to which all subcultivation material was attributed.

49. *SS III*, p. 223.

50. Corpus 151.3.B—C. Cf. *SS III*, p. 223.

51. Corpus 151.3.D—F.

52. Corpus 151.1. Corpus 151.1.D is probably to be dated much earlier than the second century B.C. Cf. the parallel cited, *SS III*, p. 224.

glaze and another with poor worn black to red glaze.⁵³ Examples of the same form in plain "kitchen" ware from Beth-zur II may also be noted.⁵⁴ Some of the ring bases of Hellenistic Decorated Ware may belong to this type, and undecorated disc bases from Beth-zur II, probably from this form of bowl, may be noted.⁵⁵

The Samaria evidence indicates that both ring and disc bases were extant in the first half of the second century B.C. The scanty evidence from Beth-zur does not indicate a development in this form between Beth-zur II and I, but if the disc type does represent a breaking down of the form, this breakdown is in process in the second quarter of the second century B.C. since both types are clearly represented in Beth-zur II and in the HFW fill at Samaria.

The only form of Figure 39 represented at Beth-zur is a bowl with pinched handle. A rim of this type was found in Beth-zur II; another comes from Beth-zur II-I.⁵⁶ This bowl therefore occurs in the second century B.C., and in light of the dating of the HFW group, in the first half of that century. Some of the other forms represented in Figure 39 are discussed in Chapter IV in connection with parallel material.

The mortaria that are common in Beth-zur II and I are also represented in the HFW deposit.⁵⁷ There is such a wide variety of forms that it is doubtful whether a development in the second century B.C. can ever be traced. It is interesting to note that Miss Kenyon reconstructs a base (which she says is uncertain) for one of the mortaria which has close parallels in Beth-zur II.⁵⁸ The other forms of Figure 40 have no parallels in the Corpus so far developed.⁵⁹

The HFW cooking pots are divided into two groups, the globular type with more or less vertical neck and the type with neck shaped to receive a lid, the latter group being most common. At Beth-zur the former type is by far the more numerous. The sherds of the globular type are compared to Beth-zur I parallels in the Corpus.⁶⁰ Some of these parallels are not close, but the variety displayed by the Beth-zur I cistern pots indicates that the type was not highly standardized. It should be recalled that no difference in *form* could be observed between Beth-zur II and Beth-zur I pots, so the Beth-zur I parallels do not indicate a post-150 B.C. date. The shaved outside rim may be noted in four of the HFW examples.⁶¹ The short neck tapering into the shoulder in one of these makes it a closer parallel of a first century A.D. pot. Perhaps it is intrusive.⁶²

---

53. Corpus 151.1.E, Beth-zur Pottery Reg. Nos. 1140 and 1183 respectively.
54. Corpus 51.2.A.   55. Corpus 151.9.A—C. and cf. 53.B.
56. Corpus 151.4.A—B. Evidence from the 1931 Campaign (cf. *CBZ*, Pl. XI:10 and Fig. 39) clearly relates the HFW sherd and those from Beth-zur to the same type of bowl.
57. Corpus 41.A—E (Beth-zur) and F—G, J—K (Samaria HFW).
58. Corpus 41.K.
59. *SS III*, Fig. 40:6 and 7 are not included in the Corpus; they would demand a special classification since their decoration is not that of Hellenistic Decorated Ware.
60. Corpus 71.1.A—C.   61. Corpus 71.1.B.
62. Fig. 41:3 listed under Corpus 71.1.B is similar to Corpus 71.1.N_2.

Two rims shaped to receive a lid were recovered from Beth-zur II, none from Beth-zur I.[63] The Samaria HFW fragments[64] obviously belong to the same kinds of pots as those from Beth-zur, but there is a large variety of forms, and no close parallels can be cited. Actually, the closest Corpus parallel to several of the HFW sherds is a shallow pot from Qumrân II.[65] If the evidence of the single Qumrân vessel is accepted, it seems that this type continued in use until the first century A.D. without apparent change or, perhaps, was reintroduced in that century. As can be noted in the Corpus, evidence of its use in Palestine in the first century B.C. is weak. The lid type pots are divided in the Corpus between deep and shallow vessels although this division is not completely satisfactory.[66] No Corpus evidence sheds further light on the lid or the pan of Figure 41.[67]

The holemouth jar, Figure 42:1, is omitted from the Corpus because there is no evidence of holemouth jars in the second century B.C. A rim of a large storage jar, Figure 42:2, is also omitted because of its lack of relation to any other published Palestinian pottery. The flask may be earlier than the Beth-zur examples because of its shorter neck and untwisted handles.[68] The juglet has a rim parallel from Beth-zur II-I.[69] It is a similar but less delicate juglet than the Beth-zur I cistern example.[70] Jug rims, Figure 42:5 and 7, have a Beth-zur II-I parallel,[71] and the thickness of ware and roundness of rim indicate a date before the horizon of the Beth-zur I cistern jugs.[72] The jug rim, Figure 42:6, is shaped like the end of an inverted crescent, a type which is common in pre-second century contexts at Shechem (compare *infra*). Jar rims, Figure 42:8, 11, and 12, are similar to jar rims from Beth-zur II;[73] the necks of the HFW examples are more clearly defined, however. Jar rims, Figure 42:9, 10, and 14, are probably earlier since they have parallels from third century B.C. pottery groups from Shechem and are therefore not included in the Corpus. Figure 42:13 is perhaps also a form that occurs before 200 B.C.[74]

2. *Post-Hellenistic Fort Wall Deposit.* — This deposit postdates the building of the Fort Wall about 150 B.C. and has a probable terminal date of 107 B.C.[75] The deposit is small, and the types are represented in Figure 43.

The first is a fish plate which is characteristic of the PHFW deposit.[76] The rounded sharply turned-down rim does not occur in the HFW deposit.[77] A rim of

---

63. Corpus 72.1. B, F.   64. Corpus 72.1. A, D—E and 71.2. A.
65. Corpus 72.1. K.
66. *SS III*, Fig. 41:15 is put with the shallow type (Corpus 72.1. A) because of its profile, but its 13 cm. diameter makes this attribution dubious.
67. Lid: Corpus 61. A. Pan: 78. B.
68. Corpus 29. A.   69. Corpus 31.1. A.
70. Corpus 31.1. C.   71. Corpus 21.1. C and cf. D.
72. Corpus 21.1. F—G.
73. Corpus 11.3.C, E. No. 5 is properly drawn with a proposed handle. It is not a jar as stated in the text, *SS III*, p. 232. Note the rippling of No. 7 and cf. p. 34 and n. 102.
74. Corpus 11.3. D.   75. *SS III*, p. 220.
76. Corpus 153.1. N.   77. *SS III*, pp. 220, 222—23.

the same type occurs in Beth-zur I, but this type is absent from Beth-zur II.[78] Figure 43:2 is a similar form noted for a creamy buff ware absent in the HFW pottery. A striking confirmation of this observation comes from Beth-zur where most of the glazed ware was described as deep reddish buff, reddish buff, or buff. There are no sherds definitely belonging to Beth-zur II that are described as buff; the two sherds with buff ware can be attributed to Beth-zur I. The buff description is undoubtedly to be identified with Miss Kenyon's creamy buff. This evidence is especially striking since the Beth-zur pottery registrar was unaware of the chronological significance of this difference in ware. Miss Kenyon notes also that the HFW glaze is characterized by merging of colors while the later group from the PHFW has sharply defined color zones (due to stacking in the kiln).[79] It must be noted, however, that some of the HFW examples do have the sharp color zone.

Figure 43:3 is a local imitation of a fish plate with a crude disc base.[80] This type is not found in the HFW deposit.[81]

As has been pointed out above, Miss Kenyon's discussion of bowls with outcurved rims is confusing. She states that Figure 43:4 is late because of its angularity and proportionate depth, but she had made the same comment about Figure 37:16 from the HFW.[82] The less angular type also occurs in the PHFW (Figure 43:6) and the HFW (Figure 37:14) deposits.[83] It is therefore impossible to show a chronological development of this type in the second century B.C. from the Samaria evidence.

A parallel to the West Slope fragment comes from Tarsus.[84] A mortarium rim from Beth-zur II provides a close parallel for Figure 43:8 with its rolled rim reminiscent of the Middle Bronze type.[85] Beth-zur provides no comparative material for Figure 43:9, which may be an example of the concave exterior profile of a fish plate.[86] No Corpus jars have handles attached to the rim or are as heavy as Figure 43:10. Figure 43:11 is a jug rim that shows the beginning of the shelf inside the rim which is characteristic of Bethany and Qumrân jug rims.[87]

Two cooking pot rims have Beth-zur I parallels,[88] and one has a parallel in the Shechem Black Earth deposit discussed *infra*.[89] Another rim of the lid type cooking pot is illustrated from the PHFW.[90] Miss Kenyon suggests in her discussion of this vessel that flatness of rim is an indication of lateness.[91] The evidence from the HFW (compare *supra*) and Shechem (compare *infra*) does not support Miss Kenyon's observation. No development of this type in the second century B.C. has yet been traced.

---

78. Corpus 153.1.N.
79. *SS III*, p. 220.
80. Corpus 53.D.
81. *SS III*, p. 225.
82. *SS III*, pp. 223, 233. Corpus 151.3.D and C respectively.
83. Corpus 151.3.F and A respectively.
84. Fig. 43:7. Cf. Chap. IV under Tarsus.
85. Corpus 41.B.
86. *V*. Chap. IV under Tarsus and the discussion of the HFW fish plates *supra*.
87. Corpus 21.1.L–M, Q–R.
88. Corpus 71.1.A, D.
89. Corpus 72.1.C.
90. Corpus 72.1.G.
91. *SS III*, p. 230.

Figure 64 illustrates the Megarian sherds present in the PHFW deposit which are absent from HFW fill. The fact that no Megarian sherds were discovered at Beth-zur can be attributed to exigencies of trade.[92] For a treatment of Megarian bowls see Chapter IV.

Summary of the HFW and PHFW deposits.—When the earlier or dubious material from the HFW is eliminated, Beth-zur II and I and Samaria HFW and PHFW present the second century B.C. Palestinian pottery horizon. The division between the earlier and later deposits at each site is suggested on non-ceramic grounds to be near 150 B.C. There was probably a gap in occupation of the Field II area of Beth-zur between about 165-140 B.C.[93] In addition to citing comparative material, Miss Kenyon notes that the evidence of the Rhodian jar stamps and the coins from the HFW support a terminal date near 150 B.C.[94] This point of division is confirmed by ceramic evidence from both sites. Especially striking is the case of the fish plates with elongated, drooping rim and creamy buff ware which are represented only in the later deposits.[95] The contrast between the jugs from the first and second half of the second century B.C. is also obvious.[96]

The problem of the *terminus a quo* for the HFW deposit cannot be solved with satisfaction. All that can be stated is that some material earlier than that from Beth-zur II which has a *terminus a quo* of 175 B.C. (or perhaps slightly earlier) is present. Some of this material has been removed because of its affinities with third century B.C. material from Shechem. Some is included in the Corpus but with clear indication of its problematical dating. There is no evidence that there is any significant difference in the *termini ante quem* for Beth-zur II and the Samaria HFW deposit. The *termini ante quem* of Beth-zur I near 100 B.C. fits well with the suggestion that the PHFW deposit was complete in 107 B.C. Except for the forms that appear to be earlier than Beth-zur II, *the HFW and the PHFW can be assigned approximately the same dates as Beth-zur II and I respectively.*

The significance of this conclusion should be noted. The fact that so many parallels between pottery groups from a northern and a southern Palestinian site can be adduced is indeed striking. This provides an entirely different picture from, for example, the obvious differences between northern and southern Palestinian pottery in Iron II. The lack of preciseness in certain parallels cited is far outweighed by the similarities in pottery forms. Further, while the Samaria HFW repertoire may be broader even after the elimination of earlier forms, this can probably be attributed more to political

---

92. Cf. *SS III*, p. 218.

93. See the discussion in Chap. II. The main argument involves attributing the two strata to the two periods of prosperous occupation cited in the historical literature, the earlier period confirmed by numismatic evidence.

94. *SS III*, pp. 218—19. The fact that the latest coin had a terminal date of 187 B.C. and only two of a of number of Rhodian handles are to be dated 180—150 B.C. could indicate a terminal date for the deposit somewhat before 150 B.C., and, for convenience, the terminal date of Beth-zur II, 165 B.C., could be suggested.

95. Corpus 153.1. N.

96. Contrast Corpus 21.1. C with 21.1. F—G, K—L.

and economic disparities between the two sites than to geographical factors. This indicates that methodologically local variation should be used in explaining ceramic developments in this period only as a last resort. This principle should be followed despite the fact that the common forms in the second century B.C. are not highly standardized.

3. Pre-Gabinian Deposit. — This deposit predates the building operations of Gabinius at Samaria which took place 57-55 B.C. It is the earliest deposit of chronological significance in Palestine that contains *terra sigillata*. Miss Kenyon discusses the sherds from this small deposit which are not published except for examples of the two sigillata forms.[97] She refers to some sherds which are similar to the HFW pottery, but she only mentions in detail those "closely connected" with the PHFW groups. The creamy buff ware and sharply defined color zones of the Hellenistic Decorated Ware, the fish plates with elongated drooping rim, and Megarian sherds are reported as characteristic of this group as they were of the PHFW deposit.

Miss Kenyon believes there is a development of the cooking pot toward a taller more vertical neck and ribbed body.[98] The Corpus evidence does suggest a slightly taller neck for a number of pots of the horizon of Qumrân Ib and later.[99] The necks of cooking pots in the latter part of the first century B.C., however, are not more vertical than second century B.C. necks.[100] It is in comparison with the common first century A.D. pots that the cooking pot necks of first century B.C. examples appear tall and more clearly defined.[101] Ribbing, or as is preferred here, rippling, certainly occurs at this time; however, since it is present throughout the period 200 B.C.—A.D. 70, it can hardly be used as a chronological indicator.[102]

The two sigillata forms represented in Figure 65 have close parallels in the deposit with *terminus ante quem* at the building of the Augustan Temple in 30-20 B.C.[103] As pointed out above these forms may well be contemporary and need not reflect development.[104] Establishing a date for the introduction of *terra sigillata* is therefore most difficult. Although the pre-Gabinian ceramic context does not exclude a date at the very beginning of the first century B.C., a minimal date of the second quarter of the first century B.C. has been adopted in this study.[105] Its absence from the Samaria PHFW and Beth-zur I deposits should also be noted although these scanty deposits are not of decisive significance. That no evidence outside Palestine urges its introduction before 75 B.C. is noted in Chapter IV.[106]

---

97. *SS III*, pp. 288—89, 291.
98. *SS III*, p. 289. Cf. pp. 228, 294 under Fig. 67:4.
99. Corpus 71.1. K_2.
100. Note the vertical or near vertical necks of Corpus 71.1. B, D—E.
101. Cf. Corpus 71.1. K_2 with 71.1. N_1—N_2.
102. Note the rippling on the HFW jug, Fig. 42:7, and cf. Chap. II, n. 111. Cf. also Chap. IV at n. 35 for an early rippled pot from Tarsus.
103. *SS III*, p. 285.   104. P. 27 *supra*.
105. Cf. pp. 26—28 *supra*.
106. N.B. Chap. IV at n. 162 ff.

4. Roman I Deposits. — Miss Kenyon's Herodian (Roman I) Period contains deposits sealed by the Herodian construction. These are the make-up of the ramp against the outer north wall of the Temple of Augustus, the filling of the Israelite casemate robber trench, the make-up of the floors beneath the Herodian house overlying the Israelite casemate, and the filling of the HFW robber trench. Sherds from these deposits are represented in Figures 66 and 67 of *SS III*. From the same period is the pottery from Vault Cistern 2 of the Harvard Expedition, the sigillata ware being illustrated in Figure 185 of *HE I*. As Miss Kenyon points out,[107] none of these deposits has a fixed *terminus a quo* since they consist of disturbed debris.

Four elegant plates of Eastern Sigillata A from the Roman I deposit represent one of the two sigillata forms extent in the pre-Gabinian deposit.[108] These are the nearly intact plates Miss Kenyon avers to have been in use at the time of the construction of the Temple of Augustus.[109] Figure 66:5 is probably an early sigillata type since it does not occur in definitely later contexts at Samaria and it was present in the 17-0 deposit at Antioch.[110] The floors of these five plates are stamped with various rosette, palmette, and rouletted circle motifs. They are noted for their technical excellence, which is not approached in later sigillata.[111] Whether these date to the third or second quarter of the first century B.C., or slightly earlier, cannot be definitely determined. In the case of such fine vessels the possibility that they might have been in use through the entire period can never be ignored.

The other sigillata type represented in the pre-Gabinian deposit also has a parallel in the Roman I deposit.[112] This hemispherical bowl type is also represented in Roman I by an example in black glaze (except for the base which is of red glaze).[113] This example is classified with the Hellenistic Decorated Ware as there is some indication that the form had affinities with the Hellenistic tradition;[114] still, it is not of a piece with the poor quality of Hellenistic Decorated Ware that stems from second century B.C. deposits. It comes from the time when the Eastern Sigillata A tradition was being established and may indicate experimentation or imperfect technique. The bowl with outcurved rim, a form common in Hellenistic Decorated Ware, is also represented in Roman I by a red-glazed example.[115] This bowl gives the appearance of being deeper than the other bowls of the class, but it may well belong before the Roman I horizon. Miss Kenyon notes that its glaze and ware belong to the "earlier" black glaze technique. She also notes that the black-glazed hemispherical bowl and the

---

107. *SS III*, p. 292.
108. Corpus 253.4. B—E and cf. A.
109. *SS III*, p. 292.
110. Cf. Chap. IV following n. 318 where the deposit is dated toward the end of the first century B.C. For earlier plates of similar form in black glaze, cf. *TCHP*, D 1 and E 22-26. V. Corpus 253.5. A.
111. *SS III*, p. 285.   112. Corpus 251.2. A.
113. Corpus 151.2. A.
114. A similar bowl occurs at Athens, *TCHP*, E 46.
115. Corpus 151.3. G.

red-glazed bowl with outcurved rim show "two stages in the transition from black to red glazed ware."[116] Such a statement could prove misleading. There is no conclusive evidence of a gradual trend toward the popularity of red decoration. Much of the Hellenistic Decorated Ware was undoubtedly black-glazed, but red-glazed vessels occur at least as early as the third century B.C. and represent a persistent tradition through the second century B.C.[117] It would seem best to speak of a transition from the use of the decadent Hellenistic Decorated Ware (which was mostly black but partly red) to the use of Eastern Sigillata A (which was predominantly red, perhaps after a brief period of experimentation).

Except for the cooking pot with a Qumrân Ib parallel,[118] none of the other material in Figure 67 is included in the Corpus. Figure 67:9 is the upper part of a jug with upswept handle and crescent rim; both of these features are unknown in second century B.C. contexts in Palestine, and Shechem evidence points to a third century B.C. date.[119] Figure 67:3 and 5-8 are omitted because there is no Corpus evidence to indicate that they, too, may not belong with earlier material in the Roman I group.[120]

Vault Cistern 2 excavated by the Harvard Expedition supplements the evidence concerning Herodian sigillata. *HE I*, Figure 185, illustrates seven forms distinctly different from those published by the 1931 Joint Expedition for this period, including examples of the plate, bowl, crater, and jug classes. Figure 185:1a—c are flat based plates with short sides extending upward at about a 45 degree angle.[121] Figure 185:4b is also a flat plate but with vertical sides and ring base.[122] The projection of the floor of the plate beyond the vertical side is a distinctive feature. Figure 185:6a is a small bowl with flat bottom, everting wall, turned-down decorated rim, and ring base.[123]

---

116. *SS III*, p. 294.

117. Cf. the top level of the Middle Hellenistic Unit at Tarsus (*v.* Chap. IV) and note the lamps from Group III, *Tarsus I*, p. 88 and Nos. 15-35. The three illustrated examples of the bowl with outcurved rim from the HFW are also in the red-glazed tradition. Corpus 151.3. A—C and cf. descriptions *SS III*, p. 223. Note also the large portion of vessels with red decoration in *HE I*, Fig. 174. Conversely, note black-glazed sigillata ware, e.g., *Tarsus I*, pp. 184—85.

118. Corpus 71.1.K_2. Miss Kenyon's remarks about the development of the cooking pot under her description of this pot, *SS III*, p. 204, Fig. 67:4, are along the same lines as those rejected in the discussion of the pre-Gabinian group. Cf. p. 34 *supra*.

119. The parallel with a PHFW jug handle cited by Miss Kenyon is extremely remote. Cf. *SS III*, Fig. 67:9 with Fig. 43:11. Note further Mrs. Crowfoot's remark about *SS III*, Fig. 58:10 on p. 269. The crescent rim appears in third century B.C. contexts at Shechem. Cf. p. 31 *supra* and the discussion of the Shechem deposits *infra*.

120. Miss Kenyon states that the jug with fluted rim does not occur earlier, but apparently this was the only fragment of this type recovered. In the case of odd, unusual vessels the principle of utilizing the new material from each of a series of deposits as chronologically significant does not apply. In this instance, the fact that a similar jug rim was found with the 1931 material from Beth-zur (cf. *CBZ*, Fig. 39, right side, second sherd down) indicates that the type probably antedates 100 B.C. Another Samaria example is published in *HE I*, Fig. 184:31a, from Lower Terrace 5. This context is of no help chronologically; it contained a coin of the second and another of the first century B.C. Cf. *HE I*, p. 261, No. 20, and p. 267, No. 4.

121. Corpus 253.3. A—B.   122. Corpus 254.2. A.

123. Corpus 253.2. A.

Figure 185:9a is the upper part of a rather deep small bowl with three ridges on the inside rim.[124] Figure 185:10a-b are bowls with slightly concave bottom, rather long everting wall, and a short trumpet foot.[125] Figure 185:11a-b are examples of a crater with everted rim and heavy ring base.[126] Figure 185:14a is a small jug with flat base, distinct nearly horizontal shoulder, long neck, rim with inside groove, and ring base.[127] The handle attaches at the outer shoulder and upper neck. The rim treatment is the same as that of the undecorated jugs of Bethany and Qumrân Ib and II.[128]

The shallow broad-floored plate with ring base represented in the pre-Gabinian and Roman I deposits is also common in the Vault Cistern 2 group.[129] These examples are smaller and not so carefully made, a fact which may suggest that they date after rather than before 57-55 B.C.[130] The carefully formed notch in the ring base where it attaches to the body is either absent or less clearly formed in the Vault Cistern 2 examples. Fragments parallel to this latter type were found at 'Alâyiq,[131] indicating that the form persisted into the first century A.D.

The hemispherical bowls are of two types, those with straight rims[132] and those with slightly everted rims.[133] The former type has close parallels in the pre-Gabinian and Roman I deposits.[134] No development between 75 and 25 B.C. is apparent for either type.

Other pottery from Vault Cistern 2 published in *HE I* includes juglets, a cup, a funnel, lamps, and fusiform unguentaria. The globular juglet is represented by a whole specimen and two rims.[135] The whole specimen is of the smaller size with more sharply defined neck characteristic of first century B.C. examples.[136] The globular type, then, belongs to the 75-25 B.C. horizon of the Vault Cistern 2 sigillata. A similar juglet which is slightly larger and has a slightly concave base may belong to the same period, but since the deposit contained earlier objects, this is not certain.[137] The bottom of a small cup with incised design[138] is not included in the Corpus since there is no comparative material for establishing its date. A small funnel which could also be earlier than the first century B.C. is included in the Corpus.[139] Three delphiniform lamps with ray motif from Vault Cistern 2 are classed with two similar lamps

---

124. Corpus 251.2b.A.   125. Corpus 252. A–B.
126. Corpus 253.3. A.   127. Corpus 228. A.
128. Corpus 21.1. M, Q–R.   129. Corpus 253.1. A–K. Cf. 253.4. A–E.
130. This typological consideration would imply that the larger Roman I as well as the pre-Gabinian plates may predate 57-55 B.C.
131. Corpus 253.1. L–M.   132. Corpus 251.2. A.
133. Corpus 251.2a. A–C.   134. Cf. Corpus 251.2. A.
135. Corpus 31.1. D_1-D_3.
136. Corpus 31.1. C* from the Beth-zur I cistern has a diameter of 11+ cm. while Corpus 31.1.D_1* from Qumrân Ib has a diameter of 8+ cm. A plausible reconstruction of *Bethany*, Fig. 61:5 (Corpus 31.1.D_1) also shows a diameter of 8+ cm. All these examples from Bethany and Qumrân Ib have the sharply defined neck.
137. Corpus 31.2. B.   138. *HE I*, Fig. 186:5c.
139. Corpus 68. A.

which belong definitely to the third quarter of the first century B.C.[140] The fragments of fusiform unguentaria of thin ware[141] also have parallels from the latter part of the first century B.C.[142]

5. *The Roman Ia bath fill.*—This deposit (*SS III*, Figures 68 and 69), it may be recalled, has no stratigraphic *termini* but is dated by a stamped Arretine Augustan plate, a cup resembling an Arretine form, and two cooking plates of Pompeian Red ware.[143] Parallels to these forms indicate a date near the turn of the first century B.C.—first century A.D.[144] The following detailed comparison of the remaining forms with those of the Corpus suggests a similar date. That the dating of Arretine and Pompeian Red ware in widely scattered sites is also valid for Palestine is thereby confirmed.

---

140. Corpus 83.2.B—D; cf. 83.2.A.

141. Note the discussion of the drawings of *HE I* under Samaria in Chapter V where it is held that the thickness of the ware is exaggerated in the drawings. Cf. n. 146 *infra*.

142. Corpus 91.2.A—B. The example from Beth-zur II is probably intrusive, and the single example from 'Alâyiq is probably from near the turn of the era when this form was being replaced by the piriform unguentarium.

143. *SS III*, pp. 228, 289—90, 295—96.

144. Cf. *SS III*, p. 296. Characteristic Arretine pottery is assigned to the last third of the first century B.C. and the first two decades A.D. Cf. Felix Oswald and T. Davies Pryce, *An Introduction to the Study of Terra Sigillata* (London, 1920), p. 4. Miss Kenyon observes that the Arretine plate, Corpus 354.2.A, is a more developed form than any that appear at the Oberaden campsite which is dated 13—9 B.C. (Miss Kenyon gives the date 12—8 B.C.) Cf. Christoph Albrecht, Kurt Regling, and August Oxé, *Bodenbefund, Münzen, Sigillaten und Inschriften*, Band II, Heft 1 of *Das Römerlager in Oberaden und das Uferkastell in Beckinghausen an der Lippe*, ed. Christoph Albrecht (Dortmund, 1938), pp. 9, 36, 59, and Pl. 41:1—13. Note the stamps of L. TETTIVS SAMIA. The Samaria plate has two closely dated parallels, one from Haltern (11 B.C.—A.D. 9 or less likely A.D. 16) and another from Agora Group G, Layer II (A.D. 0—37); cf. Chap. IV at n. 268. Siegfried Loeschcke, "Kermische Funde in Haltern," *Altertums-Kommission für Westfalen, Mittheilungen*, V (1909), p. 127 and Pl. 2a. *Agora V*, p. 26 and Pl. 62 (G 34). J. H. Iliffe in his study of sigillata stamps had classed the Samia stamp group as South Gaulish (his last stamp being identical with the Samaria example), but in his later study he tacitly omits this designation. *Iliffe I*, p. 45; *II*, p. 64. His strictures against those who fail to distinguish Gallic and Italian ware (*Iliffe I*, p. 22) are interesting in this connection. Miss Kenyon mentions an occurrence of the stamp at Inzigkofen in 15 B.C., but the parallels in form indicate that the stamp must have been used until near the turn of the era, the probable date of the Samaria example.

The cup with flaring, concave rim, Fig. 68:8, is a very common first century A.D. type. Mrs. Crowfoot found it represented in fifteen of the eighteen sites she analyzed, and concluded that it is a form "as characteristic of the first century A.D. as the plates with incurved rim and hemispherical bowls which proceeded them are of the first century B.C." *SS III*, p. 338. For comparative material cf. under Form 23, *SS III*, pp. 346ff. Mrs. Crowfoot fails to mention in her discussion of Alexandria that this form also occurs there. Rudolf Pagenstecher, *Die Gefässe in Stein und Ton, Knochenschnitzereien*, Band II, 3, of *Die Greichisch-Aegyptische Sammlung Ernst von Sieglin*, ed. Ernst von Sieglin (Leipzig, 1913), pp. 105—106, No. 58. Crucial for dating this form, which occurs contemporaneously in several wares, to near the turn of the era, are T. Knipowitsch, *Die Keramik römischer Zeit aus Olbia in der Sammlung der Eremitage*, Heft IV, I, of *Materialien zur römisch-germanischen Keramik* (Frankfurt, 1929), pp. 12, 31, Type 24, Pl. II:24, IV:6; Albrecht, Regling, and Oxé, *Oberaden*, p. 9 and Pl. 41:29—30; *Tarsus I*, Pottery Nos. 412—419 (first century A.D. deposits). Perhaps this form is inspired by a similar type in West Slope ware from Athens

The two larger, broad-floored sigillata plates which are illustrated from Roman Ia show the development of this form over the pre-Gabinian and Roman I examples.[145] That these examples are later is indicated by their less brilliant glaze, the sharper inside angle where the side joins the floor, the lack of a notch where the base joins the body, the heavier walls, and especially the heavier foot.[146] The first example has a step in the base similar to an example from Vault Cistern 2.[147] A similar plate with a horizontally everted rim is also published.[148] It also has a step underneath. Two sherds of this type are reported from the Roman I group.[149]

The deep plate with vertical side and flange at the body join is represented in Figure 68:6.[150] Another plate has a somewhat more everted rim and a less evident flange.[151] Mrs. Crowfoot's classification of this example separately from the plates with vertical rims seems unnecessary, and the term "profiled" does not distinguish it.[152] Figure 68:6 is paralleled by a single example in Vault Cistern 2.[153] This led Miss Kenyon to place the appearance of the form with the prominent flange about 25 B.C.[154] This observation agrees with the fact that local imitations of this form do not occur in Qumrân Ib but are represented in Qumrân II.[155] Figure 68:7 is the rim of a jug[156] for which a reconstruction is suggested by Mrs. Crowfoot based on unstratified parallel material.[157] Figure 68:9 is the hemispherical bowl type which occurs in the earliest sigillata deposits. This example can be dated later than the others because of its poor glaze.[158]

Group F (last quarter of the first century B.C.); cf. Chap. IV at n. 238 ff. *Agora V*, F 16, 17. A later development of the form (*ca.* A.D. 40–60) comes from Hofheim, E. Ritterling, "Das frührömische Lager bei Hofheim i. T.," *Annalen des Vereins für Nassauische Altertumskunde und Geschichtsforschung*, XXXIV (1904), p. 23 and Pl. VI:14. Note that the rim becomes more inverted and the base becomes more blunt.

Parallels to the Pompeian Red ware are cited in detail by Miss Kenyon, *SS III*, p. 298. Cf. also *Iliffe I*, pp. 23–24.

145. Corpus 253.4. F–G.

146. *SS III*, pp. 292, 294, 296. The smaller plates of this type from Vault Cistern 2 (Corpus 253.1. A–K) appear to have comparably heavier walls than the pre-Gabinian and Roman I examples, but the general exaggeration of ware thickness in the *HE I* Hellenistic drawings should be remembered in this connection. Cf. n. 141 *supra*.

147. Cf. Corpus 253.4. F with 253.1. G.

148. Corpus 253.6. A.

149. *SS III*, p. 287. There is a parallel from Tarsus (*Tarsus I*, Fig. 188:C and cf. Chap. IV at n. 117) and others from the 17–0 deposit at Antioch (Type 105:f, k, p). For the dating of the 17–0 deposit to the last quarter of the first century B.C., cf. Chap. IV following n. 318.

150. Corpus 254.2. A.   151. Corpus 254.2. B.

152. *SS III*, pp. 331–32 and Fig. 79:13–22.

153. Corpus 254.2. A.   154. *SS III*, p. 296.

155. All plates with sharply vertical sides come from Qumrân II. Cf. Corpus 54.2. D–K. An example from Trench A belongs with the later forms of that group. Cf. Chap. IV at n. 295.

156. Corpus 228. B.

157. *SS III*, Fig. 83:2. No certain chronological conclusions can be drawn about this unusual form except that it is extant by the first years of Christian era.

158. Corpus 251.2. B and cf. A.

Miss Kenyon's suggestion that the crater, Figure 69:1, may be an heirloom survival in the Roman Ia deposit[159] seems to be borne out by the discovery of a sherd of similar ware and decoration in a late third century B.C. deposit at Shechem.[160] A close parallel to the piriform bottle comes from 'Alâyiq.[161] The rims of Figure 69:3 have parallels in the lid type cooking pots, but the form of the vessel is not that of a cooking pot. Since there are no known parallels, the chronology of the form cannot be determined. It is therefore not included in the Corpus.

In general the cooking pots from Roman Ia (Figure 69:4 – 10) reflect a stage of development comparable to that at 'Alâyiq. In both groups the rather tall, sharply differentiated neck characteristic of Qumrân Ib[162] as well as the shorter, less differentiated neck of the first century A.D.[163] are present. The neck of Figure 69:9, the best representative of the later type, does not yet have as short and undifferentiated a neck as the typical Qumrân II pot.[164] The fact that most of the pots are of the Qumrân Ib type could indicate that the transition to the later type was beginning. The one-handled pot with neck join somewhat less sharp than the normal Qumrân Ib pot is apparently a usual first century B.C. variant.[165] Figure 69:6 is proportionally deeper than the rest of the Roman Ia pots, and its close parallel in Beth-zur I may suggest a date earlier than that assigned the Roman Ia deposit.[166] Figure 69:5 is a form that does not seem to belong with the other Corpus cooking pots from the period under study. Since it could belong to a pre-200 B.C. horizon, it is not included in the Corpus. Figure 69:10 is one of the two fragments of an unusual pot with tall neck with a ridge inside just below the rim to receive a lid. Since this type is rare, its occurrence in this deposit (a fill containing earlier material) does not preclude an earlier date.[167]

The jar rim, Figure 61:11, has a collar much taller than an example from Trench A (Qumrân Ib horizon) and is nearly as tall as an example from Qumrân II.[168] A date about the turn of the era is therefore likely. Figure 69:12 is a similar jar (whole) with a simple rim without exact parallels but quite probably to be dated as the preceding example.[169]

Also from this group are two Herodian bow-spouted lamps (*SS III*, p. 368) which can be dated to the turn of the first century B.C.—first century A.D. since they have parallels from Qumrân Ib and II and 'Alâyiq.[170]

From the fact that all but a few of the forms from this deposit date near the beginning of the Christian era, support is given to the dating of the Arretine and Pompeian Red ware forms to this same time. Accordingly, their dating in Palestine corresponds to their dating at other sites. The striking correlations in date between

---
159. *SS III*, p. 298.
160. Unpublished material from the East Gate area, Locus 3. Pot. Reg. No. 2129.
161. Corpus 92. A.   162. Corpus 71.1. K_2.
163. Corpus 71.1. N_1.   164. Corpus 71.1. N_2.
165. Corpus 71.1. L.
166. The body shape is that of Corpus 71.1. D and the rim that of 71.1. C.
167. Corpus 72.1. J.   168. Corpus 11.2. F–G.
169. Corpus 11.1. A.   170. Corpus 82.1. B.

the "kitchen" pottery and the imported wares are a significant confirmation of the validity and reliability of the Corpus.

Since there is no assurance that any of the vessels from Roman 2a or subsequent deposits predate A.D. 70, they are not considered in this study.

Shechem Deposits

A most perplexing problem in working out the stratification at Shechem was the relation of the debris from Room 1 of the Hellenistic House in Field II to the Black Earth debris overlying it.[171] The debris in Room 1 included forms that the Corpus clearly dates toward the end of the second century B.C. and a coin of Antiochus VIII, dated 121/120 B.C.[172] It also contained ring burnished bowl fragments identical in form, ware, and burnishing technique with the common small burnished bowls of Iron II, as well as several other Iron II sherds.[173] Only at the bottom of this debris do Hellenistic pottery forms occur which are prior to the Hellenistic forms in the Room 1 deposit and to the second century B.C. forms of the Black Earth Level above the Room 1 deposit. A coin probably of Ptolemy II[174] may date this bottom level (presumably the make-up of the floors of the Hellenistic House though these could not be observed) to the third century B.C. There was no Hellenistic Decorated Ware except at the bottom of the Room 1 debris although all the other major local forms in the Corpus in the period 140−100 B.C. are represented. It is also interesting to note that fragments of the same jar[175] and cooking pot[176] were separated by some thirty centimeters of debris; the debris also contained a large number of small bowls of very poor workmanship[177] together with other numerous Hellenistic and some Iron II sherds.

These facts indicate that the debris in Room 1 (except the lowest level) must be

---

171. The problem was further complicated by the fact that in the level from about 10 cm. above the walls of the Hellenistic House down through the first few stone courses of the house another level intervened which contained, in addition to material in common with the Black Earth Level and the Room 1 deposit, a black-glazed sherd from the end of the fifth century B.C. (Obj. Reg. No. 50; Cf. Peter E. Corbett, "Attic Pottery of the Later Fifth Century," *Hesperia*, XVIII [1949], p. 327 and Pl. 91:53), another sherd possibly from the same period (Obj. Reg. No. 106), and a rouletted base (Obj. Reg. No. 107=Pot. Reg. No. 316) and rim (Pot. Reg. No. 265 joins Obj. Reg. No. 67), probably from the same plate, with lustrous red glaze and brown spots of Miss Kenyon's Eastern Sigillata A, ware 1 (*SS III*, p. 284). This mixed material between the Black Earth and the Room 1 debris has been eliminated from the two deposits being considered, and is probably to be construed as debris from surface occupation subsequent to the filling of Room 1. In this case, the sigillata base definitely indicates that Room 1 debris was deposited before the later part of the first century B.C. since the base is closely paralleled by Corpus 253.4. B−E, E even having identical rouletting. Cf. n. 212 *infra* for a discussion of the dating of the construction, use, and abandonment of the Hellenistic House.

172. Obj. Reg. No. 321. Henceforth, numbers merely prefixed by No. refer to Pottery Registration Number.

173. Nos. 1956, 1191, 1065, 1085, 1088.

174. Obj. No. 348. The attribution is that of the American Numismatic Society supplied through the courtesy of G. Ernest Wright.

175. No. 1058=1183=1188. Corpus 11.2. B.

176. No. 1042=1181. Corpus 71.1. H.

177. Corpus 51.1. B.

considered displaced debris which did not accumulate by continuous occupation in the Room 1 area.[178] This is obviated by Iron II sherds, the 121/120 B.C. coin, the fact that parts of the same jar and cooking pot were separated by thirty centimeters of debris, and the a priori consideration that accumulation of the debris much higher than the threshhold of the house would make its habitation difficult.[179]

That the black debris overlying the Hellenistic House is also displaced debris is proved by the fact that its latest pottery is of an earlier date than that of the latest pottery in the Hellenistic House beneath it (compare the discussion below). It also contained Iron II sherds[180] and a coin probably of Ptolemy I.[181]

In dealing with a displaced deposit one must constantly be aware of the fact that one or any number of objects may be originally from a stratum other than the one that preponderates in the deposit. In the following analysis there is an attempt to exercise extreme caution in dealing with any material that cannot be confidently compared to forms in the Corpus.

Since the pottery has not yet been published, it is referred to by Pottery Registration Number in the Corpus.

1. The Black Earth Level over the Hellenistic House.[182] — This level is immediately under a dump of the German excavators and was apparently the sub-surface level before that time, the pottery being relatively homogeneous. The pottery is closely related to the HFW deposit at Samaria and Beth-zur II. No forms necessarily predate 200 B.C. except certain obviously Iron II sherds.[183] The dating is confirmed especially by the close relation of the Hellenistic Decorated Ware to that from the HFW fill at Samaria. Both have the earlier orange to red paste. A detailed analysis of the registered pottery follows.

One jar rim has a more or less rounded to oval head and a more or less definite break in line between the rim and neck. There are close parallels from Beth-zur II and the HFW deposit for this rim.[184] An examination of the Beth-zur Pottery Register indicates that there are no examples of this rim type from Beth-zur I as compared with ten registered examples definitely from Beth-zur II. A jar rim from Room 1 of the

---

178. For a similar argument based on widely separated pieces of the same vessel cf. Corbett, *Hesperia*, XVIII, p. 300. *Agora V*, p. 10.

179. G. Ernest Wright has suggested that the accumulation of debris in the house may be due to a leveling off of the mound at the end of the second century B.C. as seen in the earth moving operations at the East and Northwest Gates. The Black Earth Level may be a result of the same operations or a later process of erosion.

180. *E.g.*, Nos. 585, 780.

181. Obj. Reg. No. 147. Attribution as n. 174 *supra*.

182. This Black Earth Level continued under the German dump to the south of the Hellenistic House, but here the debris included sigillata ware (Obj. Reg. No. 602), a jug rim (No. 600) closely parallel to Corpus 21.1. H* from Beth-zur I, and Hellenistic Decorated Ware of creamy buff characteristic of the latter part of the first century B.C. (Nos. 604 and 679).

183. One sherd of Eastern Sigillata A (No. 391) is located toward the the top of the Black Earth Level and undoubtedly belongs with the surface level between the Black Earth and the German dump.

184. Corpus 11.3. E.

Hellenistic House is similar, but on the inside the rim is beginning to be squared, which indicates that it should be considered later.[185] This rounded type is characteristic of the first half of the second century B.C. and rare, if extant, later. Two jar handles are registered, but they are too fragmentary to give a clear typological representation.[186] One of these has an incised triangle near the lower body join. The handle attachment to the body is not carefully executed although it is not as carelessly joined as many Hellenistic examples from Shechem.

A date in the first half of the second century B.C. fits the jug rims well. Two are of a rounded type reminiscent of the rounded jar rims.[187] Another rim is similar but more squared.[188] All three have thicker ware than any jugs from the Beth-zur I cistern. The first two rims have parallels from the HFW and Beth-zur II-I; the last has its closest parallel from Beth-zur II.[189] Another smaller jug rim probably belongs with the two rims of the rounded type.[190]

A mortarium fragment from the Black Earth Level is of the same type which is especially common in Beth-zur II and the Samaria HFW deposit.[191] Another mortarium with a rough outside groove could be considered with them, but the chalky ware may indicate that it is to be dated before the second century B.C.[192] It is therefore not included in the Corpus. A mortarium with the typical heavy, hard ware has a rim grooved to receive a lid.[193]

In the bowl class there are a number of Iron II sherds.[194] A single bowl base, belonging to the type of very carelessly made small bowls with incurved rim that are common in the Shechem Room 1 deposit, is registered.[195] This may indicate that these

---

185. Corpus 11.3. F*. 186. Corpus 11.9. F.

187. Corpus 21.1.C (Nos. 157 and 793). The drawing of No. 157 is deceptive, showing three apparently decorative ridges which upon examination prove to be the result of the potter's carelessness.

188. Corpus 21.1.H. 189. Corpus 21.1.C and H.

190. Corpus 21.1.C (No. 156).

191. Corpus 41.D. Note that only examples of Corpus Type 41 are definitely from the last half of the second century B.C.

192. No. 149. 193. Corpus 41.H.

194. Discussion of these bowl sherds and several other Iron II sherds seems in order at this point since there has been a tendency to consider certain Iron II forms such as ring-burnished bowls and holemouth jars as continuing into the Hellenistic Period. A red burnished bowl (No. 585) with ring burnishing inside and on the rim is characteristic of the latter part of Iron II. The burnishing technique and the drab reddish buff ware with gray core further confirm an Iron II date. A carinated bowl burnished outside and on the rim (No. 591) has parallels at Samaria from the end of the eighth century B.C. Cf. *SS III*, Fig. 11:22, 23; 32:3, 4. Two rims were at first considered Hellenistic counterparts of the Iron II holemouth jar rim (Nos. 153, 582=594). Actually, they are from craters and have Iron II parallels. Their ware is definitely Iron II and not Hellenistic; the thick black to gray core and many fine to large white grits do not occur in the Hellenistic period. Cf. *Hazor I*, Pl. LXV:3 (Stratum VI) with No. 153. Cf. *Hazor I*, Pl. LIV:2 (Stratum IV), Pl. LVI:25 (Stratum V), and Pl. LXX:2 (Stratum IV) with No. 582=594. A date toward the end of the eighth century is also indicated for these Hazor crater parallels. Another crater rim, No. 580, and a bowl base, No. 586, are also of the Iron II ware just described. The late eighth century B.C. appears to be a satisfactory date for all the Iron II sherds from the Black Earth Level.

195. Corpus 51.2. B—C.

bowls began to be manufactured toward the end of the first half of the second century B.C.

One of the cooking pot rims is of the Iron II double-ridged type with typical ware containing many small white grits.[196] It is hardly to be attributed to random selection that the other three cooking pot rims from the Black Earth Level are of the type with definite inside projection to receive a lid.[197] Rather, this fact points to a situation comparable to that at Samaria at the time of the HFW deposit. Here the lid type was much more common than the globular type.[198] This is apparently true at Shechem also although it is not the case in the south at Beth-zur where the deep type dominates. No precise parallels to the Shechem examples are found at Samaria, but this is not surprising in view of the great variety of lid type rims illustrated from the HFW.[199] The closest parallels are the two examples of this type from Beth-zur II.[200] The light pink outside surface of one example indicates that it was probably never used as a cooking pot.[201] It may also be noted that two of the cooking pot rims from the Room 1 deposit have an inside projection, but it is not as pronounced as that of the Black Earth examples.[202] This shows the development of this form and may indicate its tendency to merge with the deep type that dominates the deposits in the second half of the second century B.C.

One fragment of a fusiform unguentarium from the Black Earth Level is registered.[203] A similar base comes from Beth-zur II.[204] Complete specimens of this type are common but not from chronologically significant contexts.[205]

The closest parallels to the Hellenistic Decorated Ware are found in the HFW deposit and Beth-zur II. Exceptional is a beautiful glazed jug form, undoubtedly an import, which has no parallel in the Corpus.[206] Another example comes from the Samaria summit but from an unstratified context.[207] The Shechem jug is included in the Corpus because of its predominant context, but it may well belong before 200 B.C. The small bowls with incurved rim are represented by an example with close parallels from Beth-zur II and the HFW.[208] A fish plate with incurved rim is represented by two examples. These have a close parallel from the HFW.[209] The Tarsus evidence suggests that this form may be earlier,[210] but the ware and poor glaze of these examples from Shechem are certainly typical of other Hellenistic Decorated Ware from the first half of the second century B.C.

---

196. No. 780.
197. Corpus 72.1. B, C, F.
198. *SS III*, pp. 228, 230, and cf. *supra*.
199. Cf. *SS III*, Fig. 41:8–21. Note that one of the examples finds its closest parallel in the PHFW group, Corpus 72.1. C.
200. Corpus 72.1. B, F.
201. Corpus 72.1. C.
202. Corpus 72.1. H.
203. Corpus 91.1. A.
204. Corpus 91.1. D.
205. Cf., *e.g.*, *HE I*, Fig. 178:9–11.
206. Corpus 128. B.
207. *SS III*, Fig. 58:4.
208. Corpus 151.1. E.
209. Corpus 153.1. F.
210. P. 29 and n. 46 *supra*.

2. The debris from Room 1 of the Hellenistic House. — This debris was under the Black Earth Level[211] in a room which was entered from the north by a well-constructed doorway. From the debris came a coin dated 121/120 B.C. and sherds of the latter half of the second century B.C. with which a few Iron II sherds were mixed. This displaced debris which filled the house contained no sigillata ware. A number of forms from this deposit which show apparent development in the second century B.C. could be from the first half of the century, but, since none have to be, they are all dated with that material which can be more precisely limited to the latter half of the century. In the foundation level beneath this deposit material appeared which definitely antedates 200 B.C. including Hellenistic Decorated Ware with highly metallic glaze and a coin probably of Ptolemy I.[212]

The rounded jar rims common in Beth-zur II and found also in the Samaria HFW deposit apparently develop a more squared angle inside the rim in the second half of the second century B.C. as seen in two jar rims from the Room 1 deposit.[213] This type seems to have disappeared by the time of Bethany Cistern 61. Two other rims, classed with the rounded type, have the squared inside angle, but the rim has been pressed against the neck on the outside in such a way as to obscure the rounded profile.[214] The ware of these rims is identical with that of the clearly rounded examples. Jars with both the very short, squared collars and the slightly taller, more rounded collars of the second century B.C. are represented in the Hellenistic House debris.[215] Examples of the taller collar were more common, and this seems to be the more characteristic type of the second half of the century. Two rims of dark gray ware and brown and white grits belong to the Iron II period.[216] Registered jar handles from Room 1 display the careless lower attachment.[217] However, a number of the handles from Room 1 saved for study by Professor Howard Kee are much more carefully joined and confirm the evidence for a trend toward better attachment noted in Beth-zur I.[218]

The ware of a number of jug fragments appears to be too thin to occur before 150 B.C. on vessels of this size. One of these is similar to the Beth-zur I cistern

---

211. Cf. n. 171 *supra*.

212. This evidence can be interpreted to indicate that the Hellenistic House was built sometime in the third century B.C. and was occupied through most of the second century B.C. Room 1 was filled with debris contemporary with that left at the time of abandonment. It is to be expected that the house floors may have built up slightly from debris, but most of the debris prior to the last years of occupation was probably cleared out regularly. The careful blocking up of the north doorway may have taken place at any time during the second century B.C. occupation, and no pottery from the time of the blocking would necessarily have survived.

213. Corpus 11.3. F.   214. Corpus 11.3. G.
215. Corpus 11.2. A—C (form C only Nos. 1048, 1185).
216. Nos. 1065 and 1085. A parallel to No. 1085, with gray clay and brown grits, comes from Hazor. *Hazor I*, Pl. LVII:4 (Stratum V).
217. Corpus 11.9. F (Nos. 1046, 1072, 1084, 1184, 1187).
218. Cf. p. 14 *supra*.

jug rims but has a sharp angle just inside the rim.[219] Another is similar to the single example with a rather squared rim from the Beth-zur I cistern.[220] The last is a base typical of the cistern jugs in form and thin ware.[221] A handle with part of the neck and shoulder also belongs with the Beth-zur I cistern jug type.[222] The ware of another base is as heavy as that of the heaviest cistern examples.[223] Its slightly concave line above the base before it turns outward may indicate the beginning of the development toward a pointed base.[224]

The mortarium type which is common in the second century B.C. is represented by a single registered sherd.[225] Because of the apparent lack of craters in the second century B.C., a crater rim from the Hellenistic House debris is probably of Iron II horizon.[226]

Two sherds of Iron II burnished bowls were registered from the Room 1 debris.[227] A plain heavy bowl, very similar in form to the heavy second century B.C. bowls, is definitely to be attributed to the Iron II period because of its close similarity in form and ware to a bowl from a pure Iron II pottery cache at Beth-zur.[228] Another bowl rim probably belongs with this Iron II group.[229]

A considerable number of small cups or bowls were recovered from the debris. Seventeen of the complete or nearly complete specimens were registered. Only one of these has a horizontally everted rim.[230] The others are classed with the hemispherical or incurved rim varieties.[231] All of the bowls have flat or slightly concave disc bases. A few have a pronounced central depression.[232] The color of the ware is from orange and reddish buff to buff and drab. The ware of all cups except the two with the more definitely inverted rim[233] is uniform. These latter have orange and red ware with a distinct drab layer in the center in the heavier part near the base. White grits varied from many to few and small to large, but the normal description specified few grits.

This bowl was the most common type in the Samaria HFW group "in all varieties of quality, both imported and local imitation."[234] The fact that only six of 135 examples in the HFW deposit had disc bases suggested to Miss Kenyon that the disc-based

---

219. Corpus 21.1.E.
220. Corpus 21.1.H.
221. Corpus 21.1.F–G.
222. Corpus 21.1.F–G.
223. Corpus 21.1.J.
224. Cf. Corpus 21.1.M.
225. Corpus 41.D.
226. No. 1087. This is confirmed by parallels from the Black Earth Level of more characteristic Iron II ware (Nos. 153, 582=594, 605). Cf. also *Hazor I*, Pl. LXII:16, for a similar small crater or store jar rim (Stratum V).
227. Nos. 1056, 1191. No. 1191, burnished on the inside and rim, has a close parallel from the Black Earth Level (No. 585). No. 1056 is also burnished on the outside and can be dated earlier in the Iron II period.
228. No. 1088 // Beth-zur Pot. Reg. No. 877=915=918. The ware is orange buff toward the outside with a burnt gray core. The grits are small to large in reddish brown and white.
229. No. 1182.
230. Corpus 53.E.
231. Corpus 51.1.B and 51.2.B–C. Only representative examples are listed.
232. Cf., e.g., Corpus 51.1.B.
233. Corpus 51.1.B.
234. *SS III*, p. 223.

examples "only seem to appear towards the middle of the second century B.C."[235] This agrees with the evidence from the Black Earth Level from which only one base of this type was registered.[236] The evidence from Beth-zur is ambiguous. Beth-zur II contains a number of flat bases in "kitchen" ware, no doubt belonging to cups of this type; the absence of such bases from Beth-zur I, however, does not appear significant. On the other hand, Miss Kenyon's suggestion that their development is in the direction of shallowness and more sharply incurved rims is contradicted by the evidence from Shechem, Beth-zur, and Samaria itself. The cups from the Hellenistic House with pronounced incurved rims[237] are as deep or deeper than those of hemispherical form. Two rims of Hellenistic Decorated Ware from Beth-zur II[238] are decidedly incurved, while a HFW example is hardly incurved at all although it has the later disc base.[239] The fact that this form continues, apparently without development, in Qumrân Ib, ʻAlâyiq, and Qumrân II makes it a very unsatisfactory form for chronological purposes.[240] It might be noted that no examples of this type with ring bases are known to occur after 150 B.C.

Both lid and globular type cooking pots occur in the Room 1 deposit. This same situation was true at Beth-zur I[241] and the Samaria PHFW.[242] The two examples of the lid type from the Hellenistic House show an apparent development over the three Black Earth Level rims in that the place where the inside ridge is expected is beginning to be rounded.[243] Two examples from the PHFW with pronounced ridges could cast doubt on this development, but they may belong with earlier material in that deposit.[244] Similarly, Miss Kenyon's suggestion that there is a development toward a more horizontal rim is not borne out by evidence from Shechem, Beth-zur, or Samaria itself.[245] It should also be noted that one of the examples is of much heavier ware than the other.[246]

Two rims of globular cooking pots are close parallels to a Beth-zur I pot.[247] The ware of these rims is of the lighter, thinner kind that is more characteristic of the latter part of the second century B.C. Another more everted neck of a pot with a ridge inside the rim is illustrated in the Corpus.[248] The ware of this example is thicker than that of the first two rims, and it displays distinct rippling. A very similar form

---

235. *SS III*, p. 225. The Tarsus evidence cited by Miss Kenyon at this point is not conclusive. Cf. Chap. IV following n. 64.
236. Corpus 151.2.B—C.   237. Corpus 51.1.B.
238. Cf. Corpus 151.1.E.
239. Corpus 151.1.F and cf. *SS III*, Fig. 38:7.
240. Corpus 51.1.C—M.
241. Corpus 72.1.F and 71.1.A—E.
242. Corpus 72.1.C and 71.1.A, D.
243. Cf. Corpus 72.1.H with 72.1.B, C, F.
244. Corpus 72.1.C, G. Cf. *SS III*, p. 220.
245. None of the more horizontal lid rims like Corpus 72.1.G occurred in either the Black Earth Level or Room 1 deposit or Beth-zur II—I. The HFW deposit at Samaria, on the other hand, produced the nearly horizontal lid type rim, Corpus 72.1.E.
246. Corpus 72.1.H.   247. Corpus 71.1.C.
248. Corpus 71.1.H.

with a shorter neck occurs in Beth-zur II.[249] It may be emphasized again that the variety of forms makes it impossible to distinguish a development in the second century B.C., but the thinning and lightening of the ware does appear to be a significant trend.

The body of an imported jug of very thin ware is a *bibelot*.[250] It has an unstratified parallel from Samaria.[251] Being an unusual vessel in an imported fill, its dating to the last half of the second century B.C. must remain tentative.

Also from this deposit are two rims of stone hemispherical bowls and a Rhodian handle fragment.[252] The stone rims have profiles similar to what Miss Kenyon calls a measure. She further states that similar objects have been found in Jewish tombs near Jerusalem.[253] The Rhodian handle is of the later shape which Miss Grace attributes to the last quarter of the third century B.C.[254] The Shechem handle is just as angular and has an even rounder section so that a date in the last half of the second century B.C. fits it well. These objects, therefore, also fit the dating of this deposit to the second half of the second century B.C.

The registered sherds from the lowest level of Room 1 are here singled out for attention.[255] Most of these sherds belong to the 150—100 B.C. horizon. Two short collar jar rims are close parallels to rims already mentioned from the Hellenistic House debris.[256] Another jar rim is of the rounded type with inside projection which also occurred in the house.[257] A jar handle following the careful attachment trend of some of the Room 1 examples is also represented.[258] One of the common, small, hemispherical bowls also occurred at this level.[259] However, a crescent-shaped rim that belongs to a pre—200 B.C. horizon should be noted.[260] It has parallels in the deposit in Room 2 from the same level. The same horizon is suggested by sherds of Hellenistic Decorated Ware with metallic black glaze from about the same level.[261] The glaze is better than any that can be dated to the second century B.C.

3. The debris from Room 2 of the Hellenistic House. — Nine sherds were registered from Room 2 between 140—160 centimeters below the top of Wall f. Five of these are Iron II sherds.[262] The remaining four probably belong to the third century

---

249. Corpus 71.1. G.
250. Corpus 128. C.
251. *HE I*, Fig. 183:22a.
252. Nos. 1044, 1052, and 1059 respectively.
253. *SS III*, p. 466, Fig. 118:8.
254. Grace, *Hesperia*, III, pp. 203, 214, 306. Contrast Pl. II:4 and 5.
255. From 120 cm. below the top of the east doorpost down sherds of the third century B.C. began to appear. This indicates that foundation material had been reached although no clear floor level had been preserved.
256. Corpus 11.2.C (Nos. 1195, 1196).
257. Corpus 11.3.F (No. 1197).
258. Corpus 11.9.F (No. 1192).
259. Corpus 51.2.B—C (No. 1193).
260. No. 1194.
261. Obj. Reg. Nos. 292, 293.
262. Four of these have parallels at Hazor. No. 928 // *Hazor I*, Pl. LX:4, 8 (Stratum V); No. 921 // Pl. LXXIII:30 (Stratum V; form only); No. 930 // Pl. LXX:1, 3, 4 (Stratum IV); No. 927 // Pl. LXVIII:8 (Stratum V). The fifth, No. 929, is a red bowl burnished interior and rim as *TBM I*, Pl. 61:14 (Stratum A).

B.C. Three are of drab ware,[263] and the fourth of drab ware on the outside and orange ware with a drab surface on the inside.[264] The four sherds registered from the foundation level of Room 2 are of the same ware as those just preceding, indicating a pre-200 B.C. date.[265]

A comparison of the pottery from Room 1 with that of Room 2 indicates that Room 2 was filled with debris of a different age (Iron II and early Hellenistic) than that found in Room 1.[266] Pottery of the same horizon occurs at the bottom of both rooms. A careful analysis of this pottery from the foundation level will provide a *terminus post quem* for the building of the Hellenistic House.

Beth-zur Locus 279

After the removal of Iron II and other earlier sherds, Locus 279 in Field I of the 1957 campaign at Beth-zur produced a homogeneous group of second century B.C. pottery which can be correlated with the pottery of Beth-zur II-I. A few forms supplement the second century B.C. Corpus material. A brief indication of parallels substantiating the dating of this group will be presented together with special attention to the material supplementing the Corpus. The material was studied in three groups,[267] but since no difference was noted between them, this distinction is not preserved in the following discussion.

All the registered jar sherds are common second century B.C. forms.[268] Most of the jug sherds[269] have close parallels in the Beth-zur I cistern jugs, but the heavier ware of two examples indicates that they are probably from the Beth-zur II horizon. A new juglet rim form is listed with the globular juglets, but its classification with this type is not certain.[270] Three similar bases also suggest a juglet type not yet represented in the Corpus.[271] A bowl or mortarium type with two horizontal handles can be dated

---

263. No. 931 is a jar with the short collar with everted and pointed top. No. 932 is a well-rounded jar rim of the type that disappears by *ca.* 150 B.C. No. 920 is of the heavy bowl class. Its ware has a greenish cast. The ware of the second century B.C. tends to have more of a brownish or orange cast. Cf. the description of small bowls from the Hellenistic House, p. 46 *supra*.

264. Jug rim and handle No. 933. This example may be from the first half of the second century B.C., but its heavy ware precludes a date after 150 B.C.

265. No. 925 is a jug rim with gray interior to orange exterior ware. Its semicircular rim is missing from second century B.C. contexts and seems to be common earlier. Nos. 923, 924, and 926 are of drab ware. No. 924 is another jug rim similar in shape to the preceding one. No. 926 is a jar rim similar to the jug rims but with a more pointed top. All three are related to the crescent rim from the bottom of Room 1 (No. 1194). No. 923 is a crater rim of identical ware with No. 932 from the debris in the upper level of Room 2. There are no certain crater examples from the second century B.C.

266. This conclusion is based on the few registered sherds from Room 2 which are considered characteristic.

267. Baskets 3, 7, 12, and 14 were from the northwest; baskets 17, 19, 20, and 22 from the west; and baskets 15, 21, 23, and 26 from the east of the locus.

268. Corpus 11.2. A—C; 11.9. B, D.

269. Corpus 21.1. A, D, F—G, K.

270. Corpus 31.1. B. 271. Corpus 39. B.

by its context to the second century B.C.[272] All the bowl sherds have parallels in Beth-zur II-I.[273] The cooking pot fragments also have second century B.C. parallels, but again it is impossible to see a difference between earlier or later forms in this century.[274] The absence of the lid type is to be explained by its comparative rarity at Beth-zur. The lower half of a fusiform unguentarium of very thin ware was recorded from Locus 279, but there was some confusion about its registration.[275] It may have come from a small group of first century B.C. sherds nearby. If this was the case, the evidence of the Corpus is consistent in placing the sherds of heavier, more carelessly made unguentaria in the second century B.C. contexts and the fragments of the thinner, more carefully executed examples in first century B.C. groups.[276] The Hellenistic Decorated Ware also reflects a second century date in its parallels to Beth-zur II and I.[277] A juglet handle of this ware may also be noted.[278] A Rhodian jar stamp, probably to be dated 180—150 B.C., supports the second century dating of the deposit.[279] A Rhodian jar base also fits this context.[280]

Qumrân Deposits

Locus 89.—This is the locus which De Vaux would date with Qumrân Ib and Milik with Qumrân II. A comparison of the pottery from Locus 89 with the Ib and II groups indicates that De Vaux's contention is correct. The material from the locus clearly reflects the state of development of the small bowls at the end of Qumrân Ib. The development correlates remarkably with the development of the corresponding sigillata forms. Having established this dating, certain forms can be used to supplement the Corpus. A detailed discussion of the Locus 89 pottery found in *Rapport III*, Figure 2, follows.

Figure 2:1 is a jug with a base typical of the Beth-zur I cistern jugs and a squared rim (presuming the left side of the drawing to be accurate) which also has a close parallel in one of the Beth-zur I jugs.[281] This jug has not yet developed the shelf inside the rim or the sharper base illustrated from Bethany Cistern 61 and Qumrân II.[282] The body is more elongated than the Beth-zur jug illustrated in the Corpus.[283]

Figure 2:2 is a large crater which has a slightly larger parallel from Qumrân II. 'Alâyiq offers rim sherds probably of the same type.[284] The rim of the Locus 89 example gives the appearance of being more pressed back against the body like the 'Alâyiq rims, but the limited evidence makes it impossible to substantiate a development.

---

272. Corpus 41. L.
273. Corpus 53. B—C, G.
274. Corpus 71.1. A—E.
275. Corpus 91.2. A.
276. If this development is sustained, it contradicts the assumption that a form usually appears in a high state of development and then declines or degenerates. Cf. Chap. IV, n. 150.
277. Corpus 151.1. E, 151.4. C, 151.9. A—C, 153.1. K, M, P.
278. Corpus 139. B.
279. No. 1057. Cf. Grace, *Hesperia*, III, p. 230, No. 59.
280. No. 986.
281. Corpus 21.1. H.
282. Corpus 21.1. M, R.
283. Corpus 21.1. H*.
284. Corpus 45.1. A—B.

In any case, this context indicates that the everted rim with concave end common in Qumrân II apparently makes its appearance in the first century B.C.

Figure 2:4 is a single variant of the common cups with everted rim, Figure 2:8 and 9.[285] These cups certainly belong to the Qumrân Ib horizon rather than with Qumrân II.[286] This is clear from the fact that the examples from Qumrân II have flat bases whereas the earlier examples have carefully formed ring bases. The small hemispherical bowls display a similar tendency. The 708 bowls of the type represented in Figure 2:11 and 12 with carefully formed ring bases are the standard for Qumrân Ib.[287] This type does occur with ring bases in Qumrân II, but they are not as carefully formed and the workmanship of the vessels as a whole is poorer.[288] The twelve examples of this type with flat bases from Locus 89, represented by Figure 2:3, apparently indicate the beginning of the development or degeneration reflected in the Qumrân II examples.[289]

The shallow bowls, Figure 2:5—7, have no close parallels in Qumrân Ib. Figure 2:5 is very similar to Qumrân II examples.[290] That the single example of Figure 2:5 is to be considered a step in the development toward bowls with vertical sides that characterize Qumrân II is indicated by a similar development in sigillata forms. The plate with vertical sides is represented by one example from Vault Cistern 2, which Miss Kenyon interprets as indicating that the form begins to appear about 25 B.C.[291] Thus, the form represented in Figure 2:6 and 7 is characteristic of Qumrân Ib and displays the beginning of the "turning up" of the sides of the plates.[292]

The large jar, Figure 2:10, has a parallel from Qumrân Ib, and it supplies the form of the rim which was not preserved in the Qumrân Ib example.[293]

Trench A.—The Trench A deposit, according to De Vaux's hypothesis contained debris cleared from the Qumrân building complex when the community returned after the exodus of 31 B.C.[294] Its pottery should therefore be of the Qumrân Ib horizon with the possible admixture of a few later sherds to be attributed to the renovators. This is precisely the situation reflected in a detailed examination of the published evidence, *Rapport II*, Figures 1:4 and 2.

Figure 2:4, 23, and possibly 20 would better fit a context at the beginning of the first century A.D. The plate with vertical sides, Figure 2:4, is characteristic of Qumrân II.[295] The cooking pot, Figure 2:23, has a less differentiated neck than the Qumrân Ib examples, but does not have the high-shouldered, squat shape of typical Qumrân II pots.[296] A date at the beginning of the first century A.D. would be quite

---

285. Corpus 52.9. B and 51.8. B.
286. Contrast Corpus 51.8. A—B with C—D.
287. Corpus 51.2. F—G.
288. Corpus 51.2. L.
289. Corpus 51.2. K. Cf. 51.2. H.
290. Corpus 54.1. A—B.
291. Corpus 254.2. A. Cf. *SS III*, p. 296.
292. Corpus 54.2. A—B and cf. C—K.
293. Corpus 13. A.
294. *Rapport II*, p. 214.
295. Corpus 54.2. D and cf. E—K.
296. Corpus 71.1. N_1.

satisfactory. The juglet body, Figure 2:20, is of the more elongated form that seems to be characteristic of first century A.D. globular juglets.[297]

A number of the pottery types can be dated quite definitely before the first century A.D. The plates, Figure 2:3, 5, 8, and 9 have parallels in Qumrân Ib, not Qumrân II.[298] The small hemispherical bowls, Figure 2:24 and 26, and the cup or bowl with everted rim, Figure 2:25, have carefully formed ring bases characteristic of Qumrân Ib.[299] The lamps, Figure 2:15 and 16, could hardly be dated later than the first century B.C.[300]

Other forms probably to be dated with the Qumrân Ib material are a flask,[301] the bowls with proto-vertical sides,[302] the small bowls with incurved rims,[303] the small heavy cups,[304] a stand,[305] and a one-handled cooking pot.[306]

Trench A, then, presents primarily the Qumrân Ib pottery horizon with a few forms that probably belong to the first years of the Christian era.

Jerusalem Deposits

There are no large corpora of pottery published in detail from any of the numerous excavations and soundings in and around Jerusalem. Material for such a corpus from the Citadel soundings is apparently available in the Palestine Archaeological Museum and would undoubtedly make a substantial contribution to this study.[307] Smaller, "typical" groups, which corroborate the dates assigned some of the Corpus types, have been published.

1. Citadel Sounding C. — Comparison with the Corpus indicates that a pottery group from Sounding C at the Citadel is quite homogeneous and belongs to the same pottery horizon as Qumrân Ib.[308] The provenience of the pottery is given as deposits (= layers) *e—h*, and it is attributed to the first century B.C. Most of the pottery is from *f*.

Layers *e*, *f*, and *g* can be associated with Herod's erection of Hippicus, Phasael, and Mariamne, the three towers guarding the northwest corner of the city where his palace was located. Layer *e* is considered contemporary with or subsequent to the second building phase.[309] Johns postulates that this phase was completed about 100 B.C. This is the earliest date permitted by the numismatic evidence on which he chiefly

---

297. Corpus 31.1. E and cf. F.   298. Corpus 53. H, J, L.
299. Corpus 51.2. F—J; 51.8. B.
300. Corpus 83.2. A; 84. B. Neither type has any parallels after the first century B.C.
301. Corpus 29. F.   302. Corpus 54.2. C.
303. Corpus 51.1. C—E.
304. Corpus 51.2. D—E; 52.8. A. These actually have no close Corpus parallels but should undoubtedly be dated with the dominant Qumrân Ib horizon.
305. Corpus 65. A. This example has a close Qumrân II parallel, but the evidence is insufficient to exclude a Qumrân Ib date.
306. Corpus 71.1. L.   307. Johns, *QDAP*, XIV, p. 144, n. 3.
308. The pottery is found in *ibid.*, Fig. 14, p. 145. Cf. *infra*.
309. *Ibid.*, p. 135.

relies.[310] However, the sherds from *e* and the contemporary middle tower are reported to correspond to the types of Figure 14 (mostly from *f*) which, as a group, can hardly antedate 50 B.C.[311] The *e* debris fills the deep trench of the second building phase and forms a thin, gradually sloping deposit over *d* into which the *e* trench was cut.[312] Deposit *e* consists of uniform reddish earth with a homogeneous pottery group which contrasts strikingly with the mixed pottery of *f*.[313] It seems likely that *e* is an imported fill of rather homogeneous material used to "landscape" the second building phase, which by its latest contents may date to the early part of Herod's reign or possibly the time of Antipater after he became procurator of Judea in 47 B.C.[314] The fact that the second phase is characterized by marginal draft masonry which is so typically Herodian concurs with the lower date suggested by the pottery.

It seems certain that *f* is to be associated with the third phase of construction, the building of Phasael and the filling of the gap between it and the north curtain wall.[315] Layer *f* is characterized as "highly mixed and laid in even patches as if tipped in small loads."[316] Therefore, one should be alert to the possibility that earlier material might be included, but Figure 14 indicates that Johns has been judicious in selecting the latest.

The covering of deposit *g* with dressers' chips from the building operation makes it certain that it is also associated with the third building phase. Johns suggests that *h* may well have been Herodian, and there is no reason why such a revetment should not be considered the last operation of the third phase of construction especially since a lamp from *h* is not known to survive 25 B.C.[317]

These considerations indicate that the latest pottery from *f—h* is to be dated between the beginning of Herod's reign (37 B.C.) and 29 B.C. when the three towers were completed.[318] Pottery from *e* could be slightly earlier, but together with that from *f* to *h* it belongs to the same horizon as Qumrân Ib. With this the numismatic evidence agrees. There are no post-Herodian coins from Layers *e—h*, but the reign

---

310. There are structural arguments for relating the second build of the north curtain with the construction of the adjacent middle tower. The latest coin from the north curtain belongs to John Hyrcanus and coins of Alexander Jannaeus (one in the middle of the level [*b*] that preceded the construction of the tower) provide the *terminus post quem* for the tower. Johns suggests that the building operation was begun at the end of Hyrcanus's reign and completed by Jannaeus. Cf. *ibid.*, p. 136.

311. *Ibid.*, p. 144, and cf. *infra*.   312. *Ibid.*, Fig. 5, p. 127.

313. That this apparently is meant only relatively is indicated by the fact that pre-Hellenistic types did occur in *e*. *Ibid.*, p. 136.

314. *Bel. Jud.* i.x. 3—4 mentions that Antipater repaired walls at Jerusalem overthrown by Pompey, and it is not impossible that Pompey overthrew walls outside the temple area. Contrast Johns, *QDAP*, XIV, p. 140.

315. According to Johns' interpretation *f* was deposited between the time of building the tower and the north curtain although he considers these two operations part of a single construction plan. *Ibid.*, p. 137. Since *f* lies against the lowest course of phase three (to the height of nearly a meter), it is possible to suggest that *f* was deposited during the building, after the first course was laid. In this case, *f* may have been used as a platform from which the second course was put in place after which the trench, *g*, was filled in.

316. *Ibid.*, p. 143.   317. Corpus 85.2. A.

318. Johns, *QDAP*, XIV, p. 144, and references there cited.

of John Hyrcanus II (63—40 B.C.) is represented, and there is a single Herodian coin.[319]

A detailed comparison of the forms of Figure 14 with the Corpus supports this conclusion. Only one of the fragments in Figure 14 is possibly of pre-Herodian date.[320] Most of the remainder have close parallels in Qumrân Ib or nearly contemporary deposits.[321] The tall collar of Figure 14:1 has its closest parallel from Qumrân II, but a similar tall rim comes from Samaria's Roman Ia group which dates only slightly later than the Citadel deposit.[322] The small number of published large jars from Qumrân Ib should be remembered in this connection.[323] There is no certainty that such collars did not occur as early as the Qumrân Ib horizon. There is no close parallel to the juglet base drawn with Figure 14:4c, but its angular base indicates that it belongs after the second century B.C.[324] The lid type cooking pot rims, Figure 14:2b, have many parallels in the second century B.C.,[325] but a similar pot also occurs in Qumrân II.[326] Accordingly, the Citadel sherds may fill an important Corpus gap. Figure 14:8 is of Eastern Sigillata A, Ware 2;[327] the treatment of the base is similar to that of a vessel from Vault Cistern 2, but the attribution of this incomplete specimen to the same type is uncertain.[328]

2. *Tyropoeon Valley "lower level."* — The "lower level" of a sounding in the Tyropoeon Valley belongs to a similar Herodian horizon. Typical pottery from this level is drawn on page 109 of *QDAP*, I. With this group belongs some of the pottery on Plates XI, XII, and XVII of the 1927 *PEFA*. The group includes material with parallels from the latter part of Herod's reign and the first century A.D.[329] However, the group should not be dated later than the first century B.C.; this is indicated by the flat plates, cooking pots, folded lamps, and fusiform unguentaria.[330] This evidence

---

319. *Ibid.*, p. 146.

320. The globular juglet, Fig. 14:4b, has a less sharply differentiated neck that is with some hesitancy considered a characteristic of second century B.C. juglets. Cf. p. 16 *supra*.

321. Corpus 11.2. F—G; 11.3. H; 21.1. H; 29. E; 32.1. A; 39. C; 51.1. C—E; 53. J; 71.1. K_2 (for a close parallel to the rim right of Fig. 14:2a cf. *Rapport II*, Fig. 3:22); 72.1. D; 81.2. A; 83.2. A; 91.2. B; 251.2a. A.

322. Corpus 11.2. G.

323. *Caves*, pp. 544—47. Figs. 1—2 probably contain some jars belonging to Qumrân Ib, especially those from Cave 29 which contained a lamp of the Qumrân Ib type. Cf. Chap. V at n. 156 and following.

324. Corpus 39. C. Cf. the jug base, Corpus 21.1. M.

325. Corpus 72.1.   326. Corpus 72.1. K.

327. *SS III*, p. 284.   328. Corpus 251.2a. A.

329. The closest parallels to the jar rims come from 'Alâyiq and Qumrân II, but it should be noted again that almost no large jars from Qumrân Ib are published. Corpus 12. C—D; 19. C. The cooking pot with shorter less differentiated neck is also represented. Corpus 71.1. N_1.

330. For the flat plates represented in Qumrân Ib but not 'Alâyiq or Qumrân II, cf. Corpus 53. H. A cooking pot fragment illustrates the type with the sharply differentiated neck that is more typical of Qumrân Ib. Corpus 71.1. K_2. The small folded lamps of both open and closed varieties are not known in A.D. contexts. Corpus 81.1. A. 81.2. A. The fusiform unguentaria of thin ware are disappearing at the end of the B.C. period. Corpus 91.2. B. Other material from the group can be dated without difficulty to the end of the first century B.C. Corpus 29. E; 31.1. D_4—D_5; 33. A; 82.1. A—B.

may suggest a slightly later date than that of the Citadel group, and the time of Herod's reign is assigned to this typically Herodian group.

3. North Wall Sounding B. — In his Sounding B against the North Wall at Jerusalem Hamilton recovered from the bottom stratum a pottery group (*QDAP*, X, page 30, Figure 14) which he dated to the first two centuries A.D. Stratigraphically the material was attributed to a time before the construction of the North Wall. Close parallels to the pottery from 'Alâyiq and Qumrân II legitimate the hypothesis that this group antedates A.D. 70.[331]

It might be objected that this group may date after A.D. 70 since the study provides no control beyond that date; that is, perhaps the ceramic repertory remained rather unchanged for a considerable period after A.D. 70. While not establishing conclusively the hypothesis that this group antedates A.D. 70, the following considerations tend to lend it strength. The fact that the excavators had no trouble separating this group from the next pottery group which probably does not antedate A.D. 250[332] indicates a gap in occupation during which time there was a substantial ceramic development. Further, in Sounding C a pottery group deposited shortly after A.D. 70 was discovered.[333] Though a presentation of evidence is beyond the scope of the present study, this group does contain material which shows immediate development beyond the A.D. 70 group.[334] The fact that the only two coins from the lowest stratum of Sounding B (one questionable) are dated A.D. 9/10 and 42/43 fits the above analysis.[335] The close parallels of some of the forms with ossuary pottery of the Christian era also tends to confirm this hypothesis.[336]

---

331. Corpus 11.9. H; 12. E—F; 19. C; 29. G; 31.1. E; 71.1. N$_1$; 72.2. A; 82.1. B.

332. R. W. Hamilton, "Excavations against the North Wall of Jerusalem, 1937-8," *QDAP*, X (1940), p. 11.

333. *Ibid.*, pp. 52—53. Cf. M. Avi-Yonah, "Greek and Latin Inscriptions from Jerusalem and Beisan," *QDAP*, VIII (1938), p. 55.

334. Hamilton, *QDAP*, X, p. 44, Fig. 20. Note especially Fig. 20:2, 12—14. The lamp fragment, Fig. 20:12, is apparently from a common Roman molded lamp type with round body, nozzle barely protruding, and small oil hole. The type seems to be represented by a sherd from 'Alâyiq (Pl. 49:6), but otherwise there is no evidence for its occurrence in Palestine before A.D. 70.

335. Hamilton, *QDAP*, X, p. 35.

336. Cf. Chap. V. Note especially the pottery from *kokhim* complexes in the Dominus Flevit excavations which contain ossuaries antedating A.D. 70 on paleographic grounds.

CHAPTER IV

AN ANALYSIS OF THE CHRONOLOGICAL SIGNIFICANCE OF IMPORTED WARES

A discussion of the relationship between the ceramic development in Palestine and in adjacent and more distant lands is beset with difficulties.[1] Difficulty arises out of the unsystematic selection of sites in such a vast territory, parts of which are relatively unknown from an archaeological viewpoint. Further, the publications of many of the excavations are practically inaccessible and most often provide little helpful material for a stratigraphically derived corpus. Much of the material is as yet unpublished.[2] The common kitchen pottery frequently receives little or no attention. Descriptions of the vessels, especially of their ware, glaze, and decoration, are often inadequate and are not consistent among the various publications. Even the designations of the various kinds of ware have been most confusing.

Only since the publication of Miss Kenyon's thorough analysis of much of this material from a broad perspective in *SS III* have certain of these difficulties been overcome. Miss Kenyon's method of adhering to critically evaluated stratified evidence

---

1. For the methods employed in this chapter cf. pp. 6–7 *supra*, and note that material discussed in this chapter is limited to those forms and wares which appear in Palestine in some quantity. Forms and wares that occur rarely, such as Western sigillata, are not considered. Where such examples occurred in stratified context, comparative material was cited, as *e.g.*, p. 38, n. 144.

The breadth of treatment varies, too, between Hellenistic Decorated Ware and Eastern Sigillata. Doris Taylor in her admirable study of "black-glazed" pottery from Cosa points out that "it is still too early . . . for a classification of the black-glaze pottery of the Western Mediterranean area," and, in any case, "the workshops of black-glaze pottery which were sending their wares abroad in the Western Mediterranean in the second and first centuries did not, as far as I have been able to determine, export to the Eastern Mediterranean." (Doris M. Taylor, "Cosa: Black-Glaze Pottery," *Memoirs of the American Academy in Rome*, XXV [1957], pp. 190, 192.) Accordingly, a detailed analysis of Western varieties of Hellenistic Decorated Ware would not help in clarifying the Palestinian chronology. It is instructive to note the very similar repertory of forms and wares. Cf. *op. cit.* and esp. Nino Lamboglia, "Per una classificazione preliminare della ceramica campana," *Atti del I° Congresso Internazionale di Studi Liguri* (1950), pp. 139–206. The forms are so similar that identical problems of classification occur, *e.g.*, the distinction between hemispherical and incurved-rim bowls. Cf. Taylor, p. 73. The influence of the Etruscan tradition on Eastern Sigillata forms also deserves further investigation. Cf. Taylor, pp. 192–93.

In the case of Eastern Sigillata, on the other hand, the broadest possible treatment is indicated, for example, by the fact that the dating of events at Timna' in South Arabia and Virampatnam-Arikamedu on the eastern shores of India is dependent largely upon the dating of Italian (Arretine) sigillata from Roman campsites in Germany such as Haltern, Hofheim, and Oberaden. Cf. Howard Comfort, "Imported Pottery and Glass from Timna'," *Archaeological Discoveries in South Arabia*, Richard LeBaron Bowen, Jr., Frank P. Albright, *et al* (Baltimore, 1958), esp. pp. 200–201.

2. Mrs. Crowfoot, for example, uses unpublished material from six sites in her study of the Samaria sigillata. *SS III*, p. 346.

stands in sharp contrast to the typological presentations of Mrs. Crowfoot, based on rather uncritical compilations of comparative material, in the same volume. The chronological conclusions of Miss Kenyon, although not always beyond dispute because of the scantiness of the stratified evidence, show how carefully observed stratigraphy at one site can be of much greater chronological significance than a score of tenuously dated pottery parallels without carefully delimited context.

This study can add little to the perspective established by Miss Kenyon, much less solve more satisfactorily some of the problems that are still elusive such as the precise proveniences of wares. The following detailed examination of individual sites with stratigraphically significant material for the Corpus has three major goals. The primary goal is to confirm, sharpen, and supplement the Corpus. The second is to indicate any evidence from the Corpus bearing on the dating of the deposits discussed. The third is to gain as adequate a picture as possible of the geographical spread of the forms in the Corpus, and, accordingly, bring together evidence bearing on the problems of the cultural trends and influences reflected in the Palestinian ceramic 200 B.C.—A.D 70. The order in which the sites are discussed is determined by a somewhat subjective opinion of their decreasing significance for Palestinian ceramic chronology.

Tarsus

The Tarsus expedition, although mainly seeking prehistoric material,[3] has more adequately published a larger and more significant corpus of Hellenistic and Roman pottery than most excavations oriented to these periods. The various deposits[4] are dated by the coins, lamps, and stamped amphora handles found in the deposits.[5] No attempt is made to correlate the deposits with literary references to the history of the site.[6] The deposits contain later intrusive material which is considered "unavoidable,"[7] and "no particular hypothesis is needed to explain the appearance, at any level of a site of this character, of stray finds of an earlier date."[8] In fact, in several instances the majority of the datable coins are earlier than the dates assigned the deposit.[9] These

---

3. *Tarsus I*, p. 4.

4. Some of these deposits are referred to in abbreviated form: MHU (Middle Hellenistic Unit), LHU (Late Hellenistic Unit), HRU (Hellenistic-Roman Unit).

5. *Tarsus I*, pp. 29, 84.

6. For instance, a detailed study of the literary sources might suggest the dating of the MHU between the time Tarsus was apparently overcome by the Egyptians in the Third Syrian War (246 B.C.) and the time Antiochus IV went there to quell a revolt *ca.* 171 B.C., although in the latter case a destruction is not necessarily indicated. Cf. A. F. Pauly, G. Wissowa, and W. Kroll (eds.), *Real-Encyclopädie der classischen Altertumswissenschaft*, Vol. IV A (Stuttgart, 1932), p. 2418.

7. *Tarsus I*, p. 29.   8. *Tarsus I*, p. 137.

9. The middle level of the MHU contained seven coins dated to the fourth century B.C. (*Tarsus I*, pp. 64 ff., Nos. 2, 3, 25, 31, 38, 40, 41), one coin from the late fourth-early third century B.C. (No. 45), three coins from the first half of the third century B.C. (Nos. 57, 62, 63), and four coins (Nos. 71, 72, 82, 83) from 226—187 B.C. The deposit is dated in the last half of the third century B.C. The top level of the MHU has three fourth century B.C. coins (Nos. 7, 18, 37), five coins from the first half of the third century B.C. (Nos. 47, 48, 59, 60, 61), five coins dating between 226—187 B.C. (Nos. 73, 84—87), and later coins dating 160—155 B.C., 116—95 B.C., and A.D. 217-218. This level is dated to the very end of the third century and the early years of the second century B.C. *Tarsus I*, pp. 30—31.

intrusive factors bring into question the dating of the pottery forms in a given deposit. Any individual sherd may be considered an earlier (more likely) or later intrusion. This evidence further suggests that the dates assigned to a deposit may need alteration in the direction of eliminating the *terminus a quo* and assigning the deposit a *terminus ante quem* consistent with its latest contents.[10]

The dates assigned the various units and levels at Tarsus should be construed as dating construction phases, but the pottery within the unit or level cannot be so dated because each new phase apparently began with an imported fill which contained earlier material, as is obvious from the dated coins, lamps, and stamped handles in the successive deposits. It is therefore only the new forms appearing in each fill that are chronologically significant. This fact is recognized, for example, when the excavators assign the *floruit* of Group II lamps to the earlier levels of the MHU, because new types appear in the top level.[11] But this fact is difficult to keep constantly in mind especially when there are also later intrusions. Whether the latest materials are to be regarded as crucial for dating the deposit or intrusive is a decision that must be based on careful field observation balanced by a knowledge of comparative material. In the case of the HRU Miss Kenyon has shown that, in the light of subsequent evidence,

---

10. This consideration makes crucial an examination of the method by which ceramic evidence can be used to date architectural remains. This methodology has been recently discussed by G. Ernest Wright in his criticism of *Samaria III* (*BASOR*, 155, p. 21). In the case of a given stone building the archaeologist would like to be able to date the time of construction, the period during which the floor levels were in use, and the time of abandonment or destruction.

Ceramic evidence for the date of construction is afforded by the latest sherds from the fill and foundation trenches of the building and the earliest sherds above the lowest floor that are contemporary with or later than the latest foundation sherds. If the two groups of sherds are contemporary, the construction date can be closely established, but if there is a definite gap, one is dealing with an imported fill or construction after a gap in occupation at the locus in question. In the latter case the construction date will probably be nearer the date of the earliest sherds postdating the foundation ware. If a long, uninterrupted occupation follows the initial construction, it is possible that initial construction should be dated considerably before the earliest post-foundation materials. (That most of the material from a given construction dates from the end of its occupation has been affirmed above.) Help might be gained from the sherds the workers could have left in the foundation deposit or in the sherds on the lowest floor that may never have been cleaned out, but these sources would tend to produce, at most, scanty evidence.

Dating of the succeeding floors should follow the same principle. The construction date of the floor is to be delimited by the latest sub-floor material (i.e., new forms which did not occur in the previous deposit) and the earliest material above the floors that is contemporary with or postdates the sub-floor pottery. This is true in the case of a continuous build-up of occupation debris (which is to be expected in mud-brick construction), in which case the latest material will be immediately under the new floor, but it is also true in the case of an imported fill where the latest material might be represented in that fill and/or in the material just above the previous floor.

The dating of the final occupation is indicated by the material between the latest floor and the destruction level and/or by the latest material in the destruction level. If the building is abandoned, the problem is more difficult, but the same principle applies: use the earliest sherds contemporary with or postdating the latest sub-floor material, since erosion or subsequent earth moving operations are liable to have mixed the abandoned remains with earlier and/or later material.

11. *Tarsus I*, p. 88.

the excavators' judgment erred in considering intrusive the latest material that should have been used to date the phase.[12] The sigillata and other artifacts from the HRU indicate a *terminus ante quem* similar to Vault Cistern 2 at Samaria, about 25 B.C.[13] Combined with evidence cited below, the latest material in the LHU should be dated near 100 B.C. and the sigillata sherd No. 271 considered intrusive. The datings assigned to the top level of the MHU (late third and early second centuries B.C.) and the Hellenistic House in Section A (about 150 B.C.) appear satisfactory; this sustains the judgment of the excavators that the coins from the top level of the MHU (Nos. 108, 132, and 239) are intrusive.

The deposits dated to the first century A.D. present special problems. All twelve of the coins from the Roman Fill were dated from the third to the first centuries B.C.,[14] but the pottery consistently belongs to the first half of the first century A.D. The fill under Grave 38 contained eight lamp fragments, all of which could be dated in the first half of the first century A.D.,[15] but pottery Nos. 262 and 263 belong to the first century B.C. (as could *some* of the lamps). The Circuit Wall Deposit contained a second century B.C. (No. 152) and a first century B.C. (No. 184) coin, a first century A.D. lamp (No. 174), and pottery that could generally be dated to the first half of the first century A.D. (but compare No. 81). Trench 6 and the Concrete Wall Chambers, dated to the end of the first century A.D., also contained artifacts and pottery from earlier periods.[16]

Since the individual sherds in each deposit cannot be closely dated from context alone, the following discussion is devoted to the Tarsus pottery types and their relation to the Corpus. The evidence is sifted so as to change or supplement chronological conclusions only in light of the new forms appearing in the successive deposits that can hardly be considered intrusive. Even here certain conclusions are somewhat tenuous. Continued occurrence in successive levels is considered of corroborative significance only

---

12. *SS III*, pp. 286—87. This is to be accounted for primarily on the basis of their assumption of an early date for the introduction of sigillata. Cf. *Tarsus I*, p. 14. Another injudicious interpretation of material as intrusive is the case of the "Roman Pergamene" in the HRU. Cf. *Tarsus I*, p. 173, and *SS III*, p. 287.

13. *SS III*, p. 287. The excavators note that there is no difference between the three arbitrary divisions of this material. *Tarsus I*, p. 32. This is to be expected on a priori grounds. A deposition of well over a half meter of occupation debris (*Tarsus I*, p. 15) in a stone house which probably had a low roof seems unlikely. The fact that this debris contained a number of earlier objects (cf. n. 10) and that the latest objects were found at different levels (cf. *SS III*, p. 287) indicates that the material is to be considered an imported fill like that in Room 1 of the Hellenistic House at Shechem and should be treated like that deposit.

14. Nos. 58, 135, 152, 163, 164, 180, 188, 190, 192—94, 208.

15. Nos. 65—68, 85, 129, 147, 170.

16. This was especially true of the latter. Cf. coin No. 141, amphora handle No. 57, pottery Nos. 17, 110, 114, 121, 123, 244, 245, 713, and Fig. 200:D, and lamp No. 28. Earlier material in Trench 6 included coin Nos. 150 and 187 and pottery No. 722. For the dating of other Tarsus levels and loci falling outside the limitations of this study which can be accepted at least relatively, if not absolutely, see *Tarsus I*, pp. 29—37.

when it parallels Corpus provenience. The added possibility of local differences is also a constant concern, but it is remarkable that it plays such a small role in the following comparisons.

Kitchen Ware. — Few large jars, or pithoi as they are designated by Miss Jones, are illustrated. Figure 186:205 from the middle level of the MHU (last half of the third century B.C.) is closest in form to jar rims from the deposit in Room 1 of the Hellenistic House at Shechem.[17] The Tarsus context indicates that this kind of rim was also used in the third century B.C., and unpublished evidence from Shechem corroborates this conclusion for Palestine. No parallel to Figure 191:357 occurs, and from context it may date from 300—30 B.C. Figure 201:713 is from the Concrete Wall Chambers. It has a close parallel from Beth-zur II and Shechem Room 1.[18] It has the everted, squared rim common on jars of the second century B.C. It can be dated with the second century B.C. material from the deposit, a coin, No. 141, and an amphora handle, No. 57.

Jugs 195—198 have no close parallels from the Corpus, and all can tentatively be dated prior to the second century B.C. by their contexts. Jug 710 from the Roman Fill also has no parallels and cannot be closely dated. From the Concrete Wall Chambers comes a juglet which has parallels from 'Alâyiq and Qumrân II;[19] it can accordingly be assigned a first century A.D. date.

A number of mortaria are presented as illustrating the development of these vessels from heavier to thinner ware and from exterior thickened to simple thickened, then to narrow horizontal rim.[20] Even if the limited evidence clearly indicated this development (which it does not[21]), the fact that all these contexts contain artifacts dated to the second century B.C.[22] would make it dubious. The thinner ware, heavier ware, and horizontal rim are represented in Samaria's HFW deposit.[23] If no development can be observed, it is possible to consider the examples from the later deposits intrusive and to attribute all mortaria to the second century B.C. or earlier.[24] This would agree with the Corpus which illustrates no mortaria after 100 B.C. The Tarsus evidence, however, does tend to indicate that mortaria were used there after 100 B.C., but it is not necessary to assume an identical typological history for Palestine.

---

17. Corpus 11.3. G.
18. Corpus 11.2. A.
19. No. 711 // Corpus 34. A—B.
20. *Tarsus I*, pp. 167, 178, 197.

21. The simple grooved rim, for example, occurs in the LHU (No. 192), the Hellenistic House in Section A (No. 193), the HRU (No. 351 and Fig. 190:B), and in the Concrete Wall Chambers (Fig. 200:D). To be sure, Miss Jones only argues for a *floruit* in her Hellenistic-Roman period, but the extent of the published evidence and the nature of the contexts make the proposal extremely vulnerable. Cf. also a profile with horizontal rim from the top level of the HRU (Fig. 186:C).

22. LHU: coins, Nos. 103, 104, 110, 119, 120, 126, 138, and amphora stamp, No. 44. Hellenistic House: amphora stamp, No. 83. HRU: coins, Nos. 105—107, 109, 111—113, 115, 116, 118, 127, 130, 133, 134, 137, 139, 140, 146, 147, 151, 166, and amphora stamps, Nos. 40, 42, 43, 45, 48, 49, 52, 53, 55, 56, 59, 61. Concrete Wall Chambers: coin, No. 141, and amphora stamp, No. 57.

23. Corpus 41. F—G, J—K.

24. The assumption behind this argument is that only new material in a series of contaminated deposits is significant chronologically.

Miss Jones' classification of "decorated kitchen ware" consists chiefly of craters decorated with laurel or ivy leaves about the neck.[25] Craters of this type are represented in the Samaria HFW deposit with the characteristic short, rather vertical collar above a rounded shoulder and horizontal rim.[26] The decoration is in the West Slope tradition and is termed West Slope Technique in the Corpus.[27] At Tarsus these craters first occur in the top level of the MHU.[28] Both the Samaria and Tarsus contexts suggest the early years of the second century B.C. for these craters. The two examples from the HRU could date from the same period or indicate that this type continued into the first century B.C., at least at Tarsus.[29]

Craters of the first century A.D. with outturned, thickened rim and slightly concave end occur in the Circuit Wall Deposit and the Concrete Wall Chambers, which are predominantly first century A.D. deposits.[30] Similar rims occur predominantly in first century A.D. contexts in Palestine.[31] This type could well be a development of the earlier decorated form.

A lid in the shape of an inverted, nearly flattened "V" comes from the LHU while one with vertical sides comes from the Circuit Wall Deposit.[32] Lids with a slightly convex profile are illustrated from the top level of the MHU and from Trench 6.[33] No development in form is apparent. Even the types of vessels with which the various lid shapes should be associated are not definitely established.

The few published sherds of cooking ware from specified contexts make little contribution to the Corpus and receive little refinement from it. The shallow lid type is illustrated from the LHU and HRU.[34] Neither example has a close Corpus parallel. Miss Jones' suggestion that this "casserole" type continues into the first century A.D. fits the Corpus evidence, but no examples are presented. The globular type is found in the middle and top levels of the MHU (Figure 187:222, B, C), the HRU (Figure 191:363), the Circuit Wall Deposit (Figure 201:726, 727) and the Concrete Wall Chambers (Figure 201:H). Note the rippling of the early pot, Figure 187:C.[35] A second century B.C. date fits Figure 187:B and C, and Fig. 191:363 may well date from the end of that century.[36] The sharply defined, nearly horizontal shoulder of Nos. 725 and 726 is apparently a local development as is Figure 201:H.

The presence of pan No. 722 in Trench 6 may indicate that this type, represented in the Corpus only from the HFW deposit, continues into the first century A.D. although this deposit contains earlier objects.[37] In any case, if the pan does continue to be used in Palestine in the first century A.D., it is rare in the sites studied so far.

---

25. Nos. 212—215. No. 216 is of a different, probably later shape.
26. Corpus 345.1.A. 27. Cf. Chap. II, n. 145.
28. Nos. 212, 213, Fig. 186:I. 29. Nos. 214 and 215.
30. Figs. 200:E—J; 201:B. 31. Corpus 45.1; 45.3.
32. Figs. 187:223 and 201:I respectively. For the latter type cf. Corpus 62.
33. Fig. 186:H and No. 715 respectively.
34. Fig. 187:221 (LHU) and 191:362 (HRU).
35. Cf. Chap. III, n. 102. 36. Cf. Corpus 71.1.A—B.
37. *Tarsus I*, Coins, Nos. 150, 187. Cf. Corpus 78.A—B.

Fusiform unguentaria occur primarily in the MHU, LHU, and HRU.[38] The two examples from the Concrete Wall Chambers are probably to be considered with the other early material from that deposit.[39] Two other examples are without doubt intrusive in their assigned contexts.[40] Accordingly, the evidence points to the disappearance of the form about the beginning of the Christian era, but Miss Jones' analysis of its typological development must be rejected.[41] With one exception, piriform unguentaria from specified deposits are from the first century A.D. and later contexts.[42] The evidence from 'Alâyiq indicates that this type, which may be an imitation of a glass form,[43] has become popular in the first half of the first century A.D., the four examples from the Tarsus Roman Fill being contemporary with those from 'Alâyiq.[44] The single piriform unguentarium in the HRU reflects the beginning of transition from the fusiform to the piriform unguentaria, and the 'Alâyiq evidence, with a single fusiform unguentarium, its end.[45]

None of the other kitchen ware from Tarsus is of sufficient quantity or spread to be of chronological significance. The stamped amphorae have been referred to above.

---

38. Nos. 224–247 and cf. Figs. 135 and 187.
39. Nos. 244–245.   40. Nos. 246–247.
41. The development described by Miss Jones (*Tarsus I*, pp. 171–72) is not supported by the evidence published. The LHU examples are supposed to have developed "an elegant and tapered" form and reduced capacity. This is not apparent in comparing the examples from the MHU (Nos. 225–232) with those from the LHU (No. 233–237). No. 232 is described as "perhaps slightly more bulbous" than No. 236, but No. 230 is cited as similar to No. 235. Cf. pp. 229–30. No. 232 from the top level of the MHU is cited as a close parallel of No. 236 from the LHU. This is to be expected since much material from each group is contemporary. In the HRU "another version" is supposed to appear with broad, flat shoulder. However, this difference between No. 225 from the middle level of the MHU and No. 243 from the HRU is so slight that a development can hardly be maintained, if it be assumed that No. 243 dates to the first century B.C. Note also that No. 239 from the HRU hardly fits the development toward smaller capacity and shorter cavity. The Corpus evidence, on the contrary, suggests the thinning of the ware, and consequently the increasing of capacity in the first century B.C. This is supported by a bulbous example from Haltern, a Roman outpost in Germany, occupied from 11 B.C.–A.D. 16. (There is an argument as to whether the major occupation of this site ceased already in A.D. 9. For the most recent discussion cf. Howard Comfort, "Imported Pottery and Glass from Timna'," *Archaeological Discoveries in South Arabia*, Richard LeBaron Bowen, Jr., Frank P. Albright, *et al* [Baltimore, 1958], p. 200, where the pertinent literature is sited.) S. Loeschcke, *Mittheilungen*, V, Pl. XI:30. Similar bulbous examples come from Agora Group F (*Agora V*, F 48, 49) from the last quarter of the first century B.C. Cf. *infra*.
42. Nos. 730–736. Cf. Fig. 159 and 203. The exception, No. 730, from the HRU need not be dismissed as intrusive since the HRU contained material from the third quarter of the first century B.C., a time when the piriform unguentarium may have been beginning to make its appearance. Cf., *e.g.*, an example from Agora Group F (*Agora V*, F 50) from the last quarter of the first century B.C.
43. Cf. *Cyprus IV*, p. 68.
44. Cf. the cache of piriform unguentaria illustrated in '*Alâyiq*, Pl. 19:1 with Nos 731–34.
45. Corpus 92.1.C. At Haltern (11 B.C.–A.D. 16) both fusiform and piriform unguentaria also occur together. Cf. Loeschcke, *Mittheilungen*, V, Pl. XI:30 and 31. Cf. also Agora Group F 48–49 (fusiform unguentaria) and 50 (piriform unguentarium). Unpublished evidence from Corinth cited in *TCHP*, p. 473, indicates that the piriform unguentarium was used when the city was refounded in 44 B.C. This remark is misinterpreted by P. Kahane (*Kahane I*, p. 136).

"*Glazed Ware.*"—The Corpus "fish plates" are divided into five classes by Miss Jones, who limits the term to one of these classes and calls the others saucers, although she admits the possibility of two of the saucer types being fish plate imitations.[46] The Corpus follows Miss Kenyon in using the term more broadly to include all plates of the same general form including those without the characteristic central depression.[47] The Tarsus evidence indicates that the type reached its *floruit* about 200 B.C. and gradually declined in popularity through the second century B.C., becoming rare, if extant, thereafter.[48] The evidence for tracing a development in the type is very tenuous.

The variant designated "fish plate" by Miss Jones has a sharply downturned rim with a groove at the top and a groove and ridge forming the central depression.[49] This type is not represented in the Corpus,[50] and may be a local variant. Typologically, one might expect the variants with the grooved horizontal and grooved rounded rims to be a development of Miss Jones' "fish plate" variant, but such is not supported stratigraphically, nor can any development within these classes be traced from the little evidence available.[51]

The fish plate variant that Miss Jones appropriately designates as the drooping rim type is apparently more common at Beth-zur and Samaria.[52] It is this type that probably evolves into a more elongated, turned-down rim characteristic of the last half of the second century B.C. in Palestine.[53]

The most common variant at Tarsus has a thickened, folded-in rim, usually rather horizontal, but sometimes more everted.[54] A development is suggested from convex to straight to concave exterior profile (and thus a shallower bowl), but the evidence is not conclusive. A very concave profile occurs already in the middle level of the

---

46. *Tarsus I*, p. 156.   47. *SS III*, pp. 220-22.

48. Seventeen examples (Nos. 23, 24, 26—37 and Figs. 178:A and 179:A, B) from the top level of the MHU, four (Figs. 178:B and 179:C, D, G) from the LHU, one (No. 38) from the Hellenistic House in Section A, and three (Figs. 178:C and 179:E, F) from the HRU are published. These last may be considered with the second century B.C. material from the HRU. A similar history of the form may be suggested for the Samaria plates.

49. Fig. 178:A might better be classed with the next drooping rim class.

50. *SS III*, Fig 37:1, has a sharply downturned rim but none of the other characteristics of this class. Precisely what Miss Kenyon means by "this form" that occurs in the MHU and LHU is unclear. Apparently she refers to Miss Jones' "fish plates," but these are also recorded from the HRU. She refers to a parallel from the top level of the MHU which she does not specify, but Fig. 37:1 almost certainly predates this level and has no close published parallels in it (cf. *supra*). Miss Kenyon observes that "from ware, this [Fig. 37:1] should be considerably earlier" than most of the HFW material. *SS III*, p. 222.

51. The grooved horizontal rim is not illustrated. For the grooved rounded rim cf. Fig 179:39, 40, E, F. Cf. *Tarsus I*, pp. 155-56. Even the loss of "crispness of line" is not apparent in the published examples.

52. Fig. 178:26, A. Cf. Corpus 153.1.B, L, M, P.

53. Corpus 153.1.N.

54. Fig. 179:32, D. Cf. Corpus 153.1.E-F and *v. SS III*, p. 222.

MHU.[55] The convex profile occurs on examples from the bottom and middle levels of the MHU and could indicate a third century date.[56]

The presence or absence of a central depression in these variants does not appear to be chronologically significant.[57] Third century B.C. examples are without depressions while from the MHU come examples which have them.[58] The virtual absence of central depressions at Beth-zur should be considered a local phenomenon. Further, a consistent chronological development from ring to slightly concave disc bases in the second century B.C. is not clearly discernible.[59]

The evidence regarding bowls with outcurved rims (Miss Kenyon's designation) or bowls with angular profile (Miss Jones' designation) from Tarsus only confirms the conclusion derived from the Samaria evidence; no development in the second century B.C. is apparent.[60] A sigillata[61] bowl, similar in form to an example of this type in Hellenistic Decorated Ware from Roman I at Samaria, occurs in the HRU.[62] It can therefore be considered with the first century B.C. sigillata repertory.[63]

The Tarsus evidence confirms the conclusions about bowls with incurved rims reflected in the Corpus material.[64] The fact that examples from the MHU do not have disc bases, while such bases do occur in the HRU,[65] fits the hypothesis that disc bases did not begin to appear on this bowl type until the second quarter of the second century B.C. The contention that shallowness (sagging walls) is a sign of lateness is questionable in the light of "shallow" examples from the bottom and top levels of the MHU.[66] In fact, these are the shallowest examples illustrated. The Tarsus evidence does seem to indicate a tendency to develop a more sharply incurved rim. The few

---

55. Fig. 178:F.
56. Fig. 178:D and E respectively. A third century date can accordingly be suggested for Corpus 153.1.F. Miss Kenyon's statement (*SS III*, p. 222) that the concave interior wall tends to be early appears confused. Corpus 153.1.E has the concave exterior which Miss Jones considers late.
57. Cf. *SS III*, Fig. 37:2 and 11, which are nearly identical in form except that the latter lacks the central depression.
58. Cf. Fig. 178:D, E with Fig. 179:C, G. Note also the crude imitation fish plates from the PHFW deposit, Corpus 153.1.Q. It has a pronounced central depression and certainly cannot be dated before 150 B.C.
59. The disc type is represented in the top level of the MHU (Fig. 179:A, B), the LHU (Fig. 179:C, D), and the HRU (Fig. 179:E, F).
60. Miss Kenyon comes to the conclusion that angularity is a local feature rather than an indication of lateness at Tarsus, but she considers angularity chronologically significant at Samaria. *SS III*, p. 223. Cf. Chap. III, p. 29 and n. 51, where her view is questioned. It may also be noted that a Tarsus example from the top level of the MHU is nearly as flat-floored as PHFW example, Corpus 151.3.G.
61. See *SS III*, p. 282, for arguments against use of the term "Hellenistic Pergamene." As previously noted, the term sigillata is used in this study for Miss Kenyon's Eastern Sigillata A unless otherwise specified.
62. No. 290. Cf. Corpus 151.3.G.
63. Cf. *SS III*, Fig. 77:7 and p. 326.
64. Cf. esp. pp. 29 and 44 *supra*.
65. Fig. 180:N, 72. Miss Kenyon (*SS III*, p. 225) evidently prefers to consider only Fig. 180:N a disc base, but its difference from Fig. 180:72 is infinitesimal.
66. *Tarsus I*, p. 157. Cf. Fig. 180:A, C.

third century B.C. examples are less incurved than those of the first century B.C.,[67] but evidence from Palestine indicates that this tendency is probably local since it is not apparent in the Corpus material.

It should be noted that a bowl or skyphos type with pinched-back handle, represented in second century B.C. Palestinian contexts, comes from a third century context at Tarsus.[68] An angular skyphos with a pushed-up horizontal handle is represented in the top level of the MHU and a later deposit.[69] This type has an unstratified parallel at Samaria.[70] Skyphoi with vertical ring or strap handles are also represented by a few fragments.[71] These handles may be rounded or may extend outward horizontally and turn sharply downward, being frequently spurred at the turn. A handle and sidewall of the latter type also occurs in the HFW deposit at Samaria.[72] All examples have a red to brown "glaze." The Tarsus examples occur in the bottom and top levels of the MHU and the HRU. Since the examples from the HRU may belong with earlier artifacts from that deposit, only a provenience from the third and early second centuries B.C. is assured. The limited evidence suggests a similar date for the skyphos types with horizontal handles.

Another "glazed" piece from the second century B.C. of significance for the Corpus is a jug rim with handle attachment comparable to a fragment from the Black Earth deposit at Shechem.[73] Both the top level of the MHU and the Black Earth deposit suggest a date early in the second century B.C.

The rim of West Slope ware with ivy trail from the PHFW at Samaria is very similar to an example from the middle level of the MHU.[74] A sherd of a plate with West Slope decoration from Beth-zur II is comparable to an unstratified example from Tarsus.[75] Smaller bowls of the same type occur from the bottom of the MHU to the HRU. A jug neck from Beth-zur II is possibly an imitation of a Tarsus jug of West Slope Technique from the top level of the MHU.[76] No chronological precision is indicated for the Corpus sherds or the Tarsus evidence.

An impressive series of bowls from Tarsus has been classified as Megarian,[77] "Hellenistic Pergamene," and "Roman Pergamene." The Megarian bowls are represented in the Corpus by a few sherds from Samaria.[78] Stratigraphically, the Megarian type occurs at Tarsus from the third century B.C. through the third quarter of the first

---

67. Cf. Fig. 180:51, A, B and Fig. 180:L—N, 72.
68. No. 82. Cf. Corpus 151.4.
69. Fig. 122:A and No. 82 respectively.
70. *SS III*, Fig. 57:3, 3a.
71. Nos. 83—86, Fig. 181:A—C.
72. Corpus 151.5.A.
73. No. 91. Cf. Corpus 128.B.
74. *Tarsus I*, p. 160 and Fig. 125:H. Cf. Corpus 353.2.A.
75. No. 133. Cf. Corpus 353.1.A.
76. *Tarsus I*, pp. 160—61, No. 117. Cf. Corpus 139.A.
77. While there is no proof that Megarian bowls were ever made at Megara, no attempt has been made to eliminate this term which, as Thompson notes, has "a very definite connotation in the minds of those who interest themselves in such things." *TCHP*, p. 311, n. 2.
78. Corpus 158. Cf. *SS III*, p. 274.

century B.C.[79] The "Hellenistic" and "Roman Pergamene" molded bowls are discussed together, thereby indicating agreement with Miss Kenyon's arguments against a sharp break between "Hellenistic" and "Roman Pergamene."[80] These bowls occur preponderantly in the HRU[81] and continue to appear in contexts of the first and second centuries A.D.[82]

Miss Kenyon's contention that the provenience of Megarian bowls is related to exigencies of trade[83] is further supported by the fact that not a single Megarian sherd was recovered from a considerable mass of third-second century B.C. debris at Shechem in 1957. Her stratigraphically based contention that their absence from the HFW deposit indicates their introduction at Samaria after 150 B.C. must take precedence over contrary views expressed in the same volume.[84] After their later introduction the Samaria Megarian bowls apparently had a similar history to that at Tarsus although stratified evidence is scant.[85]

Characteristics of chronological significance within the Megarian group are not as many as might be expected. The slight inversion or eversion of the rim appears to have no chronological import,[86] but the general shape of the bowl does show development. The Megarian bowls tend to be deep with nearly straight and vertical sides and rounded bottom;[87] the later bowls of genuine Eastern Sigillata A appear to take over this shape,[88] flatten the base already in the first century B.C.,[89] and evert and shorten the sides in the first century A.D.[90]

The decorative motifs are of limited help in dating. Human and animal figures are uncommon until the HRU. They are "relatively common" in that unit but the floral patterns again preponderate in the sigillata bowls.[91] More evidence is needed to establish this apparent trend toward the use of human figures in the first century B.C. In the sigillata bowls six major motifs are distinguished.[92] The first, the body covered with large leaves, occurs only in the HRU and can therefore be dated to the middle

---

79. Sherds occurred in the MHU, the LHU, the Hellenistic House in Section A, and in relatively greater frequency in the HRU. There are no certain later occurrences, the six fragments from the Concrete Wall Chambers (Nos. 171–176) belonging to the earlier material in that deposit and No. 177 from the Middle Roman Unit undoubtedly being intrusive.

80. *SS III*, pp. 282–87.

81. To be dated in light of the Samaria evidence 75–25 B.C. Cf. *SS III*, p. 287, and *supra*. During this same period the Megarian bowls are dying out.

82. *Tarsus I*, pp. 177–78.

83. *SS III*, p. 218. 84. *SS III*, pp. 218, 220, 273–74.

85. Cf. n. 78 and *infra*. Unfortunately, the Megarian bowls of genuine sigillata ware cannot be distinguished clearly by the description given. For example, the ware and motif of *SS III*, Fig. 62:8, indicate that it is probably a sigillata bowl. Cf. *SS III*, p. 280, Fig. 63:22.

86. *Tarsus I*, p. 164. 87. Fig. 183:152, 159, 160, 173, 174.

88. Fig. 189:305. 89. Fig. 189:306, 309, from the HRU.

90. Fig. 189:331, 338, 339, and 341, which unfortunately are all from post-first century A.D. or unstratified contexts. A similar profile is to be assumed for first century A.D. examples of this class from Trench 6 (Nos. 332–335) and the Roman Fill (Fig. 141:B–F).

91. *Tarsus I*, pp. 164–65, 177. 92. Cf. Nos. 305ff.

half of the first century B.C. The sixth, body covered with scattered decoration, occurs exclusively in first and second century A.D. contexts with the exception of one sherd from the HRU[93] which should be considered intrusive. If one accepts the theory that these bowls represent a trend toward the decentralized manufacture of a standardized product,[94] detailed stratified evidence from a number of sites is needed before a more detailed analysis of these motifs would be of substantial significance. The large number of molds involved also lends support to the theory of decentralized manufacture and complicates the task of a detailed analysis.[95]

The ware of the Hellenistic Megarian bowls is described as "buff to red-buff and orange-red;" similarly, that of the sigillata bowls is "buff, buff-red, orange-red or red." Both contain some mica. Generally speaking, then, the Hellenistic Megarian ware and the sigillata ware must be distinguished by differences in glaze color and quality rather than by differences in ware.[96] Some of the Hellenistic Megarian bowls have a distinctive gray ware, but bowls of this ware are consistently decorated with black glaze, which even more obviously distinguishes them from sigillata bowls.

Keeping in view revisions in the stratigraphical evidence and the rejection of a sharp break between Hellenistic and Roman sigillata, the Tarsus sigillata substantially confirms and supplements the Corpus evidence and justifies a detailed analysis of several forms. The most popular form at Tarsus, accounting for more than a third of the registered Hellenistic Pergamene[97] and more than half of the Early Roman Pergamene pieces[98] is the hemispherical bowl. At Samaria this form was represented in the pre-Gabinian, Roman I, and Roman Ia deposits, that is, from before 55 B.C. to the first years of the Christian era.[99] This simple form occurs primarily in the HRU,[100] but not all the examples from later contexts can be dismissed as intrusive,[101] especially those

---

93. Fig. 141:A.
94. *Tarsus I*, p. 163. Cf. Antioch *infra*. Three molds definitely of this period have been found at Antioch (*Antioch IV*, p. 29) and one at Samaria (*HE I*, p. 307); other bowls are considered Delian or Spartan (*SS III*, pp. 272–73). The argument of Waagé (*Antioch I*, p. 68; *IV*, p. 29) followed by Mrs. Crowfoot (*SS III*, p. 272) for the Antiochene origin of the Samarian Megarian bowls is not supported by the evidence of the molds. Neither the three molds from Antioch nor the single mold from Samaria come from a pottery shop; all are chance finds. The 3:1 ratio is not significant. What is significant is the fact that the bowls were made both at Antioch and Samaria.
95. Of some 78 sigillata bowl fragments, only two were definitely from the same mold and these were possibly from the same bowl. *Tarsus I*, p. 177, No. 239.
96. Cf. *SS III*, p. 280, Fig. 63:22.
97. Nos. 271–289.
98. Nos. 423–499. This number is unusually high because of an apparent hoard of these bowls in the Roman Fill, but seven examples are also registered from Trench 6.
99. Corpus 251.2.
100. Nos. 272–278. A variant with slightly everted rim is illustrated in Fig. 188:E // Corpus 251.2a.
101. Nos. 279–286. No. 282 with buff ware from the Middle Roman Unit is almost certainly intrusive. Nos. 279, 280, and 285 of orange-red ware from first century A.D. contexts prove that the simple first century B.C. form occurred, albeit infrequently, in the first century A.D. No. 271 from the LHU either indicates that some material in this deposit belongs to the first century B.C., or, more probably, should be considered intrusive.

with orange-red clay which is as typical of the first century A.D. as buff and pinkish buff is typical of the first century B.C.[102] Possibly to be considered with the later examples are two bowls from Trench 6 with a somewhat shallower appearance.[103] The typical hemispherical bowl of first century A.D. Tarsus is characterized by an elaborately profiled foot and rim.[104] Of the stratified examples[105] only two[106] come from post-first century A.D. contexts and are undoubtedly intrusive. The fact that this profiled type is infrequently represented at Samaria,[107] taken with subsequent evidence, supports Mrs. Crowfoot's judgment that "during the Roman period sigillata flourished at Tarsus while it dwindled away at Samaria."[108] This sigillata form is especially valuable chronologically since it is one of the few that can be limited to the first century A.D.

A striking confirmation of this dating comes from the stamps on these bowls. In contrast to the decorative stamps of the first century B.C.,[109] the stamps from the first century A.D. contain a potter's name, a greeting, or a single rosette. The greeting is by far the most common and most frequently is simple XAPIC.[110] These stamps are found in the center of the floor of the plate or bowl. This kind of stamp occurs *only* on pottery which is to be associated with first century A.D. contexts at Tarsus, and is found on most of the hemispherical bowls with elaborate profile.[111] None of these

---

102. *Tarsus I*, p. 181. The orange-red ware does occur in the HRU, however. Cf., *e.g.*, Nos. 293, 302, 303.

103. Fig. 193:A—B.

104. Cf. Fig. 194:424. *Tarsus I*, p. 181, notes that this development of elaborate profiles is contrary to the general tendency toward simplification of profile. Local Palestinian typological developments also suggest that this "general tendency" is rather dubious. The common jugs develop a much more distinctive base and rim in the first century B.C. (Corpus 21.1). The necks of the globular juglets also are more carefully delineated in the first century B.C. (Corpus 31.1). In the case of the hemispherical bowls the profiled foot and rim of the first century A.D. is probably the result of influence by western sigillata wares. Cf., *e.g.*, an elaborately profiled imitation of an Arretine form in Eastern Sigillata A from Roman Ia. Corpus 251.6.A.

105. Nos. 423—464.   106. Nos. 456—457.

107. Examples in Form 24, p. 338 and Fig. 81:19, 22—24.

108. *SS III*, p. 348.

109. The first century B.C. sigillata stamp consists of two concentric groups of two to four rouletted circles. Between these groups may be five palmettes or Isis symbols and possibly a rosette in the center. Cf. *Tarsus I*, p. 208; *SS III*, Figs. 66, 73—76 and pp. 316—20.

110. Iliffe originally considered XAPIC a potter, but has accepted the correction of Oxé in his second collection of these stamps. His two collections (*Iliffe I, II*) plus Comfort's supplement to the first ("Supplementary Sigillata Signatures in the Near East," *Journal of the American Oriental Society*, LVIII [1938], pp. 30—60) are basic to their study. These stamps, like the Rhodian and related wine amphora stamps, constitute an area of research beyond the scope of this study. Iliffe cautions against "supposing that any of the considerable number of stamps hitherto published has added, from the context in which it has been found or otherwise, any definite chronological evidence" (*Iliffe II*, p. 33). Although there is no evidence for pre-Tiberian *in planta pedis* stamps, even his evidence for their appearance beginning A.D. 10—15 is not absolutely convincing (*Iliffe I*, pp. 19—20). He considers significant the fact that only one example is found at Haltern, although in the next sentence he states that "in Germany as a whole it is rare" (*Iliffe I*, p. 20).

111. *Tarsus I*, p. 209, notes two Hellenistic and two Late Roman stamps of a similar nature which, however, are stamped on different parts of the vessel.

bowls or other vessels from sure first century A.D. contexts contain the stamps characteristic of the first century B.C.

Considered as characteristic of the early sigillata ware as the plain hemispherical bowl is the plate or shallow bowl with broad floor, incurved rim, and ring base.[112] It is represented in the first century B.C.,[113] but there are no clear examples from the first century A.D. deposits.[114] At Samaria the form occurs in pre-Gabinian, Roman I, and Roman Ia deposits as did the hemispherical bowl.[115] Two Tarsus examples have the exterior groove where the foot joins the body which is also found on early Samaria examples.[116] A number of variants may generally be considered developments that occur infrequently toward the end of the first century B.C. or in the first century A.D. These include the thickened everted rim,[117] a plain "thickened" rim,[118] a low vertical rim,[119] an everted rim,[120] and another variant with higher walls.[121]

A type with only one example from a first century B.C. context and two from a first century A.D. context is the plate with turned-down, decorated rim.[122] This type also occurs in Vault Cistern 2.[123]

The type of broad plate with interior rim molding is represented by examples from the HRU and Circuit Wall Deposit.[124] This type is also represented in the Roman I group at Samaria.[125] The bowl with outcurved rim, common in Hellenistic Decorated Ware, is represented by sigillata examples from the HRU and the Circuit Wall Deposit.[126] The latter example may indicate that this rather uncommon form was also extant in the first century A.D., but it could belong with the earlier material from that deposit.[127] The sigillata jug fragments from the HRU are rather similar to a reconstructed jug from Vault Cistern 2.[128] The long slender bottles with everted, squared rims are not represented in the Corpus and probably date to the third quarter of the first century B.C.[129]

---

112. *Tarsus I*, p. 175. Cf. Corpus 253.1; 253.4.
113. Nos. 257–261.
114. Both the stamps and ware of Nos. 262 and 263 indicate an early date, and Nos. 264 and 264a are too fragmentary to classify with certainty, 264a having unique decoration.
115. Corpus 253.4. A–G and 253.1. A–K. The examples from 'Alâyiq, 253.1. L–M could be from the early years of that deposit.
116. Nos. 258–259. Cf. Corpus 253.4. B–E.
117. Fig. 188:C. Cf. Corpus 253.6. A from Roman Ia.
118. Fig. 192:366.
119. Fig. 188:A, which cannot belong to the MHU.
120. Fig. 188:B.
121. Fig. 188:270. This example is out of place in the Middle Roman Unit.
122. Fig. 137:269, A, B.
123. Corpus 253.2. A.
124. Nos. 252 and 253 respectively.
125. Corpus 253.5. A.
126. Nos. 290 and 500 respectively.
127. Cf., *e.g.*, coins, Nos. 153, 184.
128. No. 296 and Fig. 189:A. No. 296 // Corpus 228. A. The second fragment is similar but the rim treatment is different.
129. Nos. 297–303. Since No. 297 is similar to No. 298 and Nos. 298–303 are from the HRU, this conclusion seems relatively safe.

Among the types which first appear in first century A.D. deposits at Tarsus is the large class of shallow bowls with broad floor and vertical sides,[130] the vertical sides frequently having rather elaborate profiles. Related to these are similar bowls with ring bases, concave to straight shoulders, and similar vertical to slightly concave rims.[131] Another probable first century A.D. type is the broad-floored, shallow bowl with incurved rim;[132] the type is apparently rare, and the few examples should not be considered conclusive evidence of a first century A.D. date. Another rare form is a bowl with a nearly flat base with two steps underneath and a wall everting to a horizontal rim.[133] Two similar examples have grooved rims.[134] All three examples are from Trench 6, suggesting a date late in the first century A.D. A single example of a hemispherical bowl with constriction at mid-body comes from the Roman Fill.[135] It may also belong in the first century A.D. Bowls with flat bases and everting walls come from first century A.D. deposits, but their presence in Vault Cistern 2 proscribes an exclusively first century A.D. date.[136] The later examples give a somewhat deeper appearance.

The extensive repertory of wares in first century A.D. Tarsus included, according to Miss Jones' classification, mottled sigillata, black-glazed sigillata, metallic red-glazed ware, brown-glazed ware, "Samian" or Eastern Sigillata B, Arretine ware, barbotine ware, "thorn" ware, and lead-glazed wares. Since these wares are only rarely represented in Palestine,[137] a detailed examination of them is beyond the scope of this study. Mention needs to be made of the Arretine ware which does not appear before the Roman Fill, a provenience corresponding to the dating of the popular Arretine bowl form from the Roman Ia deposit at Samaria.[138] A single lead-glazed vessel in the Berlin Antiquarium is reported as coming from Jerusalem.[139]

Lamps. — In contrast to the other pottery types, the lamps from Tarsus are of little significance for the rather meager representation in the Corpus. The observation that each site has a slightly different set of lamp types and that even the Antioch repertory "varies considerably from the Tarsus types,"[140] at least partially explains the situation. The Herodian bow-spouted type, without glaze and side knob, is apparently a local adaptation of Tarsus Group III. The greatest number of Tarsus examples come from the HRU[141] and only one example occurs in a first century A.D. context that

---

130. Nos. 372—391. An example from Vault Cistern 2, Corpus 254.2. A, indicates that this form was beginning to appear about 25 B.C. A slightly later parallel comes from Roman Ia. Corpus 254.2. A.

131. Nos. 412—419. These appear to be imitations of an Arretine Augustan form. Cf. Corpus 251.6. A, a sigillata vessel of this type, which obviously imitates an Arretine form. For references cf. Chap. III, n. 144.

132. No. 396. Nos. 420—421 are similar but their floors are not as broad.

133. Fig. 193:C.   134. Nos. 409—410.

135. No. 411.   136. Nos. 501—502. Cf. Corpus 253.3. A—B.

137. The fact that none of these wares except Arretine are represented in the extensive excavations at Samaria makes it doubtful that these wares will turn up in any quantity in future excavations in Palestine proper.

138. Corpus 354.2. A.   139. *Tarsus I*, p. 195, n. 144.

140. *Tarsus I*, p. 84.   141. Nos. 20—27.

contained much earlier material.[142] The Bethany and Qumrân Ib examples are contemporary with those from the HRU, but the form continued to be popular in the first century A.D. at 'Alâyiq and Qumrân II.[143] The handled lamps from Qumrân Ib[144] are reminiscent of Tarsus Group VI with their long spouts and loop handles. Type A with a ridge around the oil hole and Type B with the ridge extending to and around the wick hole are rudimentarily represented at Qumrân. The lack of decoration, glaze, and spade-shaped spout mark these as crude imitations of the Tarsus examples, which occurred in deposits from the end of the third century B.C. into the first century A.D.

Athenian Agora — Hellenistic Period

If any work is considered normative for the study of Hellenistic pottery of the Near East—to judge from the numerous references, all whole-heartedly accepting its chronology—it is Homer Thompson's "Two Centuries of Hellenistic Pottery."[145] One is therefore surprised to discover the limitations of the evidence upon which the ceramic chronology is based. Instead of empirical stratigraphy, the developments suggested are derived from a series of five sealed loci containing displaced debris. The same limitations as were applicable in the case of the Shechem, Samaria, and Tarsus deposits apply. Any single example may date quite differently from the more or less homogeneous group. A situation similar to the Tarsus units exists; Groups C, D, and E are dated near their sealings, but they contain coins dated considerably earlier than the pottery.[146] The actual dating of the pottery groups is largely based on subjective typological considerations. While these have their place, they do not seem appropriate in a study which is attempting to establish a ceramic chronology for a relatively obscure period.[147] Further, although the most pertinent parallels are cited, their stratigraphical contexts are not critically analyzed and, indeed, are frequently unknown.

Although Thompson's study is an admirable presentation of the Agora material, it is to be criticized on three grounds. First, his chronological argument relies too heavily on the homogeneous nature of each deposit.[148] Secondly, he frequently considers a development assured on the basis of too little evidence.[149] Thirdly, he proposes developments which are derived primarily from a priori subjective considerations.[150] In the

---

142. No. 28.   143. Cf. Corpus 82.1; 82.2.
144. Corpus 84.   145. *TCHP*.
146. *TCHP*, pp. 347, 370, 394.   147. Cf. Chap. I, n. 6.

148. In only one instance does he suggest a possible intrusion (*TCHP*, p. 455 for E 83) Other sherds should be considered intrusive according to his own typology (*e.g.*, C 16, 17, D 29, E 67 and cf. pp. 444—45, 452) although in one case he does suggest three typological stages within a given group (lamps in Group A, *TCHP*, p. 460). These instances justify suspicion of other material in these groups.

149. Cf. the discussion of the "black-glazed" dinner plates, imbricated Megarian bowls, unguentaria, etc., *infra*. The best example is the West Slope amphora where he describes seven characteristics of formal development from five published examples.

150. The arbitrary assumption that the ideal shape of the Megarian bowl in the mind of the Athenian potter is *obviously* illustrated by A 74 (*TCHP*, p. 454) cannot be accepted, and if it were, it would be no substitute for empirical observation in seeking chronologically significant factors. Related to this frame of thought is his assumption that the forms and workmanship of the period degenerate consistently along set lines (*e.g.*, toward poorer "glaze," "less artistic" shape). Cf. *TCHP*, p. 454.

light of these observations the following principle in dealing with the Agora evidence may be suggested. When parallels to Corpus types do occur in contemporary or near contemporary deposits, they may be considered confirmatory or supplementary evidence, but a larger quantity of unambiguous evidence than is presented in the Agora Groups would be necessary to force any significant alterations in the Corpus.

Evidence from the last three of Thompson's five groups is pertinent here. Group C is dated to the beginning of the second century B.C. primarily on the basis of lamp parallels in a tomb at Gabalou in Aetolia. Group C also contained four coins from the first half and two from about the third quarter of the third century B.C.[151] Group D is dated to the middle of the second century B.C. by the latest coin which cannot precede 166 B.C. and lamp parallels from Corinth predating 146 B.C.[152] Group E is dated "to the turn of the second and the first century and to the early years of the first [century B.C.]."[153] The debris contained a stele dated 122/1 B.C., and it is suggested that the debris was produced about 86 B.C. when Sulla paid a destructive visit to Athens.

The evidence is considered by type in the order of Thompson's discussion, *TCHP*, pages 429—474.

Black-glazed ware and sigillata.—Thompson points to a trend toward more and more slavish imitation of metal vessels in the third and second centuries B.C. This is observed especially in forms which are ceramically impractical and in the gradual thinning of the ware.[154] However, any attempt to use the metallic prototypes chronologically is doomed by the fact that their durability makes them dubious as chronological indicators, that evidence for the chronological relation between individual types and their copies is lacking, and that metal vessels have not been discovered in contexts of greater chronological significance than the pottery imitations themselves.

Miss Kenyon notes that (even according to her broad definition of the term) Thompson publishes no fish plates[155] and that Watzinger also noted their rarity at Athens.[156] Some plates from Athens do have similarities to the fish plate family, however. Thompson's classes of ordinary dinner plates,[157] tea plates,[158] and little saucers with furrowed rims[159] are described as developing lighter ware, greater depth, and turned-down rims. Similar developments are echoed at Tarsus, but, except for the early characteristic of convex outside line, they have been rejected in this study as not agreeing with the published evidence.[160] The evidence from Athens is not so impressive or so precisely related to the evidence from Tarsus and Palestine as to override this rejection.

---

151. *TCHP*, p. 347.   152. *TCHP*, p. 370.
153. *TCHP*, p. 394.
154. *TCHP*, Fig. 116:D and pp. 432, 434—35.
155. *TCHP*, p. 347, however, mentions that a "few fragments" of fish plates were found in Group C.
156. *SS III*, p. 220.   157. Fig. 116:A 70, C 1, E 1.
158. Fig. 116:B 5, E 19, E 21.
159. Fig. 117:A 38, A 3, E 27. Cf. *SS III*, Pl. 40:6, from the HFW.
160. Cf. pp. 63—64 *supra*.

A large plate with sharply offset rim, represented in Groups D and E, is found in the Roman I deposit at Samaria in sigillata ware.[161] It seems clear, therefore, that the sigillata form, at least, was inspired by a ceramic rather than a toreutic prototype.

Only two fragments of sigillata occur in Group E.[162] The two sherds of sigillata amid a mass of "black-glazed" ware suggest that sigillata was just beginning to appear at this time.[163] Unfortunately, the precise date is by no means clear. The attribution of the destruction debris to Sulla's visit in 86 B.C. is merely a suggestion. Even if this be accepted, some time could have intervened before the debris was thrown into the cistern, and the sigillata sherds could easily have been associated with the deposit at this later time. Accordingly, the Athens evidence does not prove the existence of Eastern Sigillata A before the second quarter of the first century B.C.

The bowls with outcurved[164] and incurved[165] rims further illustrate the difficulty of substantiating the general lines of development suggested for black-glazed plates and bowls. The thinning of the ware between Groups A and D in both classes can be noted in the examples selected for illustration, but E 33 and E 46 revert to ware as heavy as the examples from Group A (end of the fourth century). The depth of the outcurved bowl A 71 does not differ significantly from that of D 5, and the outcurved bowls have a "great variety of sizes and depths" already in the fourth century B.C.[166] The angularity of A 71 is hardly distinguishable from D 5, and examples of the more rounded A 9 shape might be expected in the latter part of the second century B.C., as at Samaria.[167] The hemispherical bowls with simple tapering rim from E should be noted because this form became one of the two earliest known sigillata forms.[168] A similar bowl with black "glaze" occurred in the Roman I deposit at Samaria. Both the Agora and Samaria bowls may be dated to the first century B.C.[169]

C 8–10 are "black-glazed" jugs. C 9 has a parallel from the top level of the MHU at Tarsus and the Black Earth deposit at Shechem although rim treatments vary.[170] Jugs with this type of handle treatment are apparently widespread in the second century B.C. C 8 and 10 are different types of jugs but have the upswept handle which is not known to occur in Palestine after the third century B.C.[171] The bowl with pushed-up horizontal handles occurs in Groups D and E. These contexts suggest

---

161. D 1 and E 22–26. Cf. Corpus 253.5. A.

162. E 151 and 152. Thompson identifies E 151 as "probably Pergamene," but Miss Kenyon identifies it as Eastern Sigillata A, Ware 1. Cf. *TCHP*, p. 435, with *SS III*, p. 286.

163. The form is also represented in the earliest (pre-Gabinian) sigillata at Samaria. Cf. *SS III*, Fig. 65:3.

164. Fig. 117:A 9, A 71, D 5, and E 33.

165. Fig. 117:A 20, D 9, E 46.

166. *TCHP*, p. 435.   167. Corpus 153. F.

168. E 46–48. Cf. Corpus 251.2. A.

169. Miss Kenyon notes that the Samaria Roman I deposit contains earlier material. *SS III*, p. 292. Cf. p. 35 *supra*. In light of this it might be suggested that both Agora and Samaria bowls could date from the early first century B.C.

170. *TCHP*, Fig. 29:C 9. *Tarsus I*, Fig. 182:91. Corpus 128. B.

171. Cf. p. 36 *supra*.

a second century B.C. date for this type.[172] A similar date is suggested by a Tarsus parallel from the top level of the MHU.[173] It is therefore likely that the unstratified example from Samaria[174] is to be dated to the second century B.C. An askos from Group B is of much better quality than an example from the HFW deposit.[175] Parallels to the Agora askos may indicate an earlier date than the 300—250 B.C. date assigned Group B,[176] and the dating of the Samaria example is not aided.

In concluding the discussion of the Agora Hellenistic "black-glazed" ware Thompson states that especially the dinner plates, saucers with furrowed rims, and little bowls with outcurved lips "extend over the entire period and careful observation will show that they underwent a consistent development."[177] Exception must be taken to this conclusion if the above observations are true. There may be *tendencies* of development that could be documented if enough evidence were published, but none of the general characteristics of development cited is carried through *consistently* in the evidence from Tarsus or Athens, except the general decline in workmanship noted in glaze, ware, and form. This decline is difficult to define or publish precisely, and a specific description of decline within the second century B.C. is too precise a demand for the evidence presented. For example, thin metallic black glaze is characteristic of both Groups C and E.

Ceramic evidence which presents only slight developmental tendencies in periods of over a century is of dubious chronological significance. It is even more dubious when the "early" and "late" characteristics may occur at the beginning and end of the period in question. The evidence available from Tarsus and Athens is of basic value if the picture of slow and somewhat ambiguous development is true of the period, but this will remain uncertain until evidence of more precise chronological significance is available.

West Slope Ware.—It seems appropriate to discuss in detail evidence of this ware from the site where it was first distinguished and named by Carl Watzinger[178] and where Thompson's evidence offers opportunity for "studying the development of the ware over a considerable period of time on a single site."[179] To demonstrate that the ware occurs in Palestine in more than isolated cases, it suffices to point to *SS III*, Figure 44. Thompson arbitrarily fixes the beginning of West Slope Ware proper when

---

172. D 17—18. E 52—53. Cf. Fig. 118:D 17.

173. *Tarsus I*, Fig. 122:A. Another example from the Tarsus Circuit Wall Deposit is obviously intrusive (Fig. 122:81).

174. *SS III*, Fig. 57:3, 3a.

175. Cf. Fig. 21:B 31 with Corpus 128. A.

176. *TCHP*, pp. 340—41.   177. *TCHP*, p. 438.

178. Carl Watzinger, "Vasenfunde aus Athen," *Mitteilungen des kaiserlich deutschen archäologischen Instituts, Athenische Abteilung*, XXVI (1901), esp. pp. 67—68, 87—88. Thompson (*TCHP*, p. 311, n. 2) notes that it could as well be called North Slope Ware, but any change from the traditional designation would only be confusing. Its priority at Athens is generally accepted although it was manufactured elsewhere. *TCHP*, p. 446. *SS III*, p. 236.

179. *TCHP*, p. 438.

thinned clay and white paint were first used to decorate large vessels, at the end of the fourth century B.C. These decorative techniques had been used earlier on small vessels, and, together with incision, which became common later,[180] constitute the means of decorating West Slope Ware.[181]

Decorative motifs only rarely include men or animals.[182] Common motifs are a necklace with painted pendants, sometimes giving the impression of suspension between the upper handle attachments; a wavy band of water; designs inspired by ivy and the grape vine; and geometric motifs, especially the checkerboard, concentric rectangles, and cross-hatching. Geometric stars, rosettes, and pairs of dashes set at right angles also occur with the geometric motifs. Decoration is usually limited to the neck and upper shoulder in closed shapes. Features of decoration that are described as chonologically significant include the development of a rough zigzag line from the thin precise line used earlier to attach necklace pendants, development in the treatment of the surface of the waves with thinned clay to treatment by incision, development of increased stylization in the treatment of ivy and vine motifs, and the introduction of cross-hatching in Group E.[183] None of these developments are traced in detail through the five groups, but the later characteristics are generally attributed to the second century Groups C—E.

The most common large vessel decorated with West Slope techniques was an amphora, usually with twisted handles; its origin is unknown.[184] Five examples, two from B, two from D, and one from E, are published in *TCHP*. On the basis of these five examples Thompson isolates the following chronologically significant features: (1) the later metallic "glaze" and masks applied at the bottom handle attachment,[185] (2) the development from "well proportioned" body to examples in which the neck is too short or too long,[186] (3) a tendency of the rim to flare unduly and become squared and slightly concave on the outside in the later period,[187] (4) the tendency of later handles to disturb the general lines of the vase,[188] and (5) the degeneration of the base to a ring of insignificant height.[189]

It might be expected on a priori grounds that such a list of developments overestimates the limited evidence upon which it is based, even if the developments are not

---

180. "Later," according to Thompson's usual usage, refers to characteristics observed in Groups C—E, Groups A—B being considered earlier.

181. *TCHP*, pp. 438—39.

182. In addition to the examples cited in *TCHP*, p. 440, n. 1, the dolphin occurs on fragments of West Slope Ware from Samaria (*SS III*, Fig. 44:5) and Tarsus (*Tarsus I*, Fig. 125:117, 126:125). *Tarsus I*, Fig. 125:117 also has a satyr head.

183. *TCHP*, pp. 440—41.

184. *TCHP*, p. 444. Cf. *SS III*, p. 236 and Fig. 44.

185. D 25 and 26, E 59.   186. Contrast B 3, 35 with D 26, E 59.

187. D 26, E 59.

188. D 25. The tendency of the Rhodian handles toward a sharper bend near the end of the third century is paralleled by the limited Agora evidence. Cf. Grace, *Hesperia*, III, pp. 203, 214, 306, and Pl. II:4 and 5. This is at least a safer criterion than a rather subjective opinion as to what is "disturbing to the general lines of the vase" (*TCHP*, p. 444).

189. This feature is not clear in illustrations.

sharply drawn. Support for this expectation comes from three fragments of a West Slope amphora found in an unstratified context at Samaria.[190] There is no reason to question Mrs. Crowfoot's judgment that these fragments are Attic imports,[191] but her conclusion that the fragments date to the first half of the third century B.C. raises a question regarding one of Thompson's criteria which she does not discuss. The Samaria amphora apparently had an early non-metallic glaze and a late mask. At least one must question the mask as a late feature, and this might be true of other characteristics. A similar vessel from the top level of the MHU at Tarsus[192] with a band handle and reeded body is considered an Attic import. In addition to masks at upper and lower handle attachments, it has a sharply flaring rim (late) and dolphin and satyr figures (chiefly early). Its predominant context indicates a dating about 200 B.C. which does not conflict with the Athens evidence.

The other popular West Slope form is the kantharos, frequently with reeded body in addition to the other common decorative techniques.[193] Only two fragments are recorded in second century B.C. contexts,[194] and these may be intrusive. The unstratified examples from Samaria also may well predate 200 B.C.[195] The fragmentary Tarsus evidence indicates that there the skyphos[196] was the more popular form for West Slope decoration, and that this form continued in use at least through the second century B.C.[197]

Also belonging to the repertory of forms receiving West Slope decoration are saucers and shallow bowls[198] and, infrequently, jug and juglet types.[199] The limited and fragmentary nature of the evidence, however, gives no chronological help that is not related to the general development or degeneration of the techniques already described. The most that can be concluded from the evidence discussed is that examples of West Slope technique from imprecise contexts in Palestine can be dated to the second or early first century B.C. if they display primarily those characteristics described by Thompson as "late."

Lagynoi. — The lagynos first appeared in Group C. One specimen is partly preserved from this group, three from D, and four from E.[200] This indicates they were used in the second century B.C. This form seems to be continued in the first century B.C. by an example from the HRU at Tarsus and a sigillata jug from Vault Cistern 2

---

190. *SS III*, Fig. 44:1.   191. *SS III*, p. 238.
192. *Tarsus I*, No. 117.
193. Amphora were also occasionally reeded. Cf. *Tarsus I*, No. 117.
194. D 29 and E 67.
195. *SS III*, Fig. 44:2—6. This does not deny that undecorated kantharoi occur in post—200 B.C. contexts. Cf. *SS III*, pp. 241—42.
196. The kantharos is distinguished from the skyphos by its pedestal base.
197. Cf. *Tarsus I*, pp. 159—60. Nos. 106—108 and Fig. 125:D and E are from the LHU.
198. C 12, D 28, E 62, 63, 66, 69.
199. C 13, 14.
200. *TCHP*, pp. 450—51; C 15; D 30—32; E 70—73.

at Samaria.[201] Each of the four examples from Group E is of a different shape. Another form with a profile between two of the forms from E comes from Corinth and therefore dates before 146 B.C.[202] It is decorated by the West Slope technique and apparently had a hollow handle. The Corinth example shows that it is impossible to consider the E forms characteristic only of the end of the second century B.C., and Thompson himself makes no attempt to trace a development.

Megarian bowls. — The Agora evidence on the development of Megarian bowls may be briefly sketched since it has only somewhat tenuous chronological import for the Corpus evidence from Samaria. Waagé and Mrs. Crowfoot have concluded that most of the Samaria Megarian ware probably came from Antioch, although Delian and Spartan type sherds and a mold indicating local manufacture were found at Samaria.[203] This means that the value of the Agora evidence depends upon the amount of standardization in the decentralized Megarian industry.[204] Evidence for both standardization and local variation is brought to light at the Agora, but a precise judgment must await a more detailed examination of Megarian ware from well-dated contexts at a number of sites.

Thompson's analysis of the chronological development of the decorative motifs at Athens[205] indicates that the type with a register of plant motifs around the bottom rosette surmounted by a register of figures or other ornament occurs in the last half of the third and the second centuries B.C. Just before the middle of the second century B.C. the long petal decoration appeared and soon became predominant.[206] The former class is the most common type at Samaria, but the latter is not represented.[207] Another type that Thompson places with the earlier examples of the former class and which also occurs in an unstratified context at Samaria is the imbricated leaf motif.[208] The pineapple or nodule imbrication type[209] is dated toward the beginning of the second century B.C. on the basis of the limited Agora evidence, but at Tarsus the type occurs in the top level of the MHU and the LHU.[210] The LHU bowls indicate the continuation of this type through the second century B.C., which is at least a tenuous indication that the Samaria sherd of this kind need not be dated before 150 B.C.[211]

---

201. *Tarsus I*, Fig. 189:A. Corpus 228. A.
202. Oscar Broneer, *The South Stoa and its Roman Successors* (Corinth, Vol. I, Part IV; Princeton, 1954), p. 29; Fig. 7; Pl. VII:3. Cf. *TCHP*, Fig. 92:E 72–73.
203. *SS III*, pp. 272–73.   204. Cf. *Tarsus I*, p. 163.
205. *TCHP*, pp. 457–58.
206. This type is frequently referred to as the *à godrons* class, a term used by F. Courby, *Vases grecs à reliefs* (Paris, 1922), p. 329.
207. *SS III*, p. 273.
208. *TCHP*, pp. 456–57. Cf. *SS III*, Fig. 62:2 and 63:7.
209. The identity of the Athens "nodules" and the Samaria "pineapple" bosses is assumed by Mrs. Crowfoot (*SS III*, p. 275, Fig. 62:1), but photographs by which an independent judgment can be reached are not published. The drawings differ slightly. Cf. *TCHP*, C 29, 53, with *SS III*, Fig. 62:1.
210. *Tarsus I*, No. 144 and Fig. 129:D respectively.
211. *SS III*, Fig. 62:1. The irregularity of the imbrication of *Tarsus I*, Fig. 129:D, probably indicates a date later than *Tarsus I*, No. 144.

Regarding other developmental characteristics mentioned by Thompson, such as decline in glaze quality, development of a shallower bowl with flatter bottom, and the late careless attachment of the lip,[212] nothing more need be said than that none of the Samaria fragments possess characteristics that are clearly early. A dating after 150 B.C. would not contradict Thompson's criteria. The same may be said of the decorative motifs (in light of the Tarsus evidence), and the absence from Samaria of the long petal motif, probably of Athenian inspiration,[213] is related to conditions of trade in the Near East where it was also manufactured.[214]

Lamps.—Tarsus lamp Groups III and VI are much more closely related to Palestinian types than are any Agora lamps.[215] On the other hand, some lamps from Vault Cistern 2 at Samaria seem to be closer to the Agora type with *à godrons* decoration than to any lamps from Tarsus.[216] This type first appears in Group D and is common in E.[217] The relationship is obvious, and the date of the predominant context of the Vault Cistern 2 lamps is not much later than that suggested for the Agora evidence.

Kitchen ware.—The "plain ware" pitchers and jars do not have a close relation to Corpus types. The fact that the upswept handle is not found in Groups C—E but does occur in Groups A and B agrees with the contention above for a third century date for this form.[218]

In contrast, the cooking vessels present a range of forms very similar to those found in Palestine.[219] The globular type is clearly represented in Groups C and D, the deep lid type with vertical handles by an example from D, the deep lid type with horizontal handles by an example from C, and the shallow lid type by examples from C—E.[220] The lack of standardization within these groups makes tracing a chronological development difficult. The development toward a more horizontal rim in the shallow vessels has already been rejected, and even if the limited Agora evidence establishes such a trend there it need not be accepted for Palestine. Likewise, it cannot be ascertained whether the development of the more angular profile on the Athens vessels is paralleled in Palestine. Lids have flat to slightly convex shape.[221] Thompson, on

---

212. *TCHP*, pp. 452—55.   213. *TCHP*, p. 459.
214. Cf. *Tarsus I*, pp. 163—65.
215. The development of the Agora lamps, C 54—57 and E 89—96, which are related to Tarsus Group III, is not reflected in the Tarsus evidence. The "contracted top" seems an obvious development at Athens, but all the Tarsus examples could be considered of this type (*Tarsus I*, Fig. 93 and 94:32). The development of a longer spout is based, apparently, on E 90, but no other examples from E necessarily have a longer spout than C 57. *TCHP*, p. 462.
216. Corpus 83.2. B—D. The corresponding group from Tarsus, Group IX, is poorly represented, and the examples belong to a different variant of this type.
217. D 56—59 and E 97—114, 116.
218. A 51—52 and B 12.
219. C 69—75, D 64, 70—76, E 117, 118, 139—150.
220. Cf. respectively C 69 and D 71; D 70; C 70; Fig. 121:C 73—75, D 72, E 141, 145.
221. E 146—149.

subjective typological grounds, thinks that tall braziers were introduced to Athens about 200 B.C.,[222] but the chronological relation between examples from Groups D and E and the unstratified Samaria example is unclear.[223] In summary, the Palestinian and Agora cooking vessels show a close kinship, but neither adds to the chronological precision of the other.

There were a large number of deep basins (lekanai), but this type is not clearly represented in the Corpus.[224] The mortar of the type common at Tarsus and Palestine is represented by only one example at the Agora.[225] Blister ware[226] and gray ware[227] are not found in the Corpus. "Pergamene" ware has been discussed above.

Fusiform unguentaria occur in Groups A—E and Thompson dates their use at the Agora from the end of the fourth into the first century B.C.[228] He suggests a number of chronologically significant features. First may be mentioned the sharply defined shoulder which is considered early. At Tarsus, where there were sharper shoulders than any published from the Agora, this was considered a late feature (HRU), but this view has been rejected above.[229] Second is the careless workmanship especially obvious in the formation of the foot without differentiation which is held to be a late characteristic. The ring-footed examples from Group F make this an unsatisfactory criterion.[230] Third is the development from a bulbous to a very thin body between C and D—E supported by two published examples from each of the three groups. Thompson states that "stout specimens may occur late, [but] with these other criteria in mind one need not be deceived in their date." Yet, when other criteria are rejected and the bulbous examples from Group F just cited are considered, this criterion is not useful. Accordingly, there is no published evidence from the Agora which confutes conclusions reached above about fusiform unguentarium development.[231]

Athenian Agora—Roman Period

Although a separate treatment of the Roman deposit from the Agora might prove somewhat repetitious, it seems justified because the Roman pottery is discussed by a different author working after an additional quarter-century of advances in the precision of archaeological technique and methodology and a multiplication of available evidence. It is fortunate that this study became available just as the writer had completed his survey of non-Palestinian materials significant for the Palestinian Corpus.

Any evaluation of Robinson's study must remain somewhat tentative since the typological section is still unpublished and *SS III* became available after *Agora V* was completed.[232] However, two fundamental observations appear in order. First, the

---

222. *TCHP*, p. 468.
223. D 76, E 150. *SS III*, Fig. 60.
224. The development toward a more sharply bent-down rim (*TCHP*, p. 470) is not supported by the evidence. Fig. 122:A 78 and B 40 are as turned-down as any later examples. *Tarsus I*, Fig. 182:87, is a close parallel to *TCHP*, Fig. 122:A 77, but is probably to be dated about 150 B.C.
225. Cf. E 124 with *Tarsus I*, Figs. 184 and 190 and with Corpus 41. G, J, K.
226. A 68, C 78.
227. E 154—158.
228. *TCHP*, pp. 472—74.
229. Cf. n. 41 *supra*.
230. Cf. *infra* at n. 248.
231. Cf. p. 62 and n. 41 *supra*.
232. *Agora V*, p. vi.

methodology of Thompson has been followed by Robinson without significant alteration. Secondly, despite Robinson's views, the chronological precision of the Agora evidence, at least that from Groups F, G, H, M I, and M II, is sharpened by a comparative study of evidence available elsewhere in the Eastern Mediterranean.

The first observation indicates that the criticisms of Thompson's methods are also applicable here. Details are presented in the analysis of individual deposits below. The second observation is a reaction to Robinson's assumption (which is set forth as a "fact") that "the Agora pottery itself must serve as the basis for establishing the chronological and typological sequence of most of the ceramic output of the eastern Mediterranean in Roman times."[233] A detailed examination of his evidence makes this an unwarranted assumption. In none of the deposits studied is there a group that independently contributes toward the development of a precise absolute chronology, for no deposit is so homogeneous that individual forms can be dated independently with confidence. Further, the fact that a more precise chronology for some of the Agora groups can be proposed from a comparative study puts other sites at least on a level with the Agora in supplying the basis for a ceramic chronology of the Eastern Mediterranean in Roman times. It is difficult to understand what Robinson considers the peculiar difference in the "nature" of Athens as compared with Tarsus and Antioch which makes the Agora evidence more fundamentally significant for ceramic chronology.[234] The deposits and levels at the Agora have the same limitations of chronological precision as those at Tarsus. They are certainly no more homogeneous than those from Tarsus. The fact that items which "do not belong" to a given deposit are not eliminated in the Tarsus publication, as they are by Robinson, would seem to be to the greater credit of the Tarsus excavators.[235] Robinson realizes that there is no relation between quantity and chronological significance, but his multiplication of rather imprecise data does not lead to greater precision.[236] The lack of historical correlation at Tarsus might be stressed, but at the Agora only a single historical correlation is suggested for the period here studied.[237] In the following discussion of the deposits, the principle applied to the Hellenistic Agora evidence is still applicable. The evidence is helpful where it confirms and supplements the Corpus, but the kind of evidence presented is not strong enough to force significant alterations in it.

Group F. — This group comes from the upper filling of a cistern on the north slope of the Areopagus. The distribution of fragments of individual vases through the fill indicates that the fill was dumped there at one time. Robinson dates the group in the last three quarters of the first century B.C. and states that there is no evidence of

---

233. *Agora V*, p. v.
234. Cf. his remarks, *Agora V*, p. 1.
235. Cf. *infra*, esp. the discussion of Group F.
236. The inclusion of Group H in his study might be justified on the ground of its being the best evidence available from the Agora for the chronology of the late first and early second centuries A.D., but even this is questionable. When such a "floating deposit" is used in arguments for settling the chronology of other groups, the chronological issue is merely confused. Cf. *Agora V*, pp. 46, 83.
237. The debris of Group E may be related to the sacking of Athens *ca.* 86 B.C. Cf. p. 72 *supra*. Note that this relation is only suggested and the deposit probably contains later material.

later intrusion with the possible exception of the single Samian piece.[238] However, the fill did contain intrusive Hellenistic sherds which have been eliminated if they "can be shown by analogy with datable Hellenistic material to be Hellenistic intrusions into the dump heap from which this upper filling was obtained."[239] The *terminus post quem* is supported by the unpublished pottery in a lower level of the cistern which Edwards dates to the "very early" first century B.C.; this is interpreted as indicating that the cistern went out of use about the time of Sulla's attack in 86 B.C.[240] The absence of Arretine ware, which was becoming more common in Athens in the last decade B.C., indicates to Robinson a *terminus ante quem* of near the turn of the era. Coins included two dated about 88 B.C. and one dated about 50 B.C.[241]

A detailed examination of the published sherds indicates that there is indeed material from near 100 B.C. and from the last quarter of the first century B.C., but there are no forms which must be dated about 85—25 B.C. with the possible exception of a Knidian stamped amphora handle, which is no more precisely dated than "1st century B.C., subsequent to Sulla's sack of Athens."[242] This can be observed in the case of the Eastern Sigillata A forms. These belong with Samaria's Roman Ia group rather than with those groups which predate the building of the Temple of Augustus (pre-Gabinian, Roman I, and Vault Cistern 2).[243] The single piece of Samian ware, F 15, need not be considered intrusive, but may well indicate its initial appearance at the turn of the era. The West Slope bowls, F 16 and 17, fit a date in the last quarter of the first century B.C. The form is a development over the West Slope bowls, E 62 and 63, as Robinson states, and is related to a form that occurs in Samian, Eastern Sigillata A, Arretine, and possibly local Attic wares in contexts near the beginning of the Christian era.[244] The presence of "brittle," "thorn," and barbotine wares, F 18—25, also indicates a date late in the first century B.C. These wares occur at Tarsus beginning in the HRU, but Miss Jones considers these occurrences doubtful and places their first certain provenience in the first century A.D. If their occurrence in the HRU is authentic, the few fragments suggest the general introduction of the ware

---

238. *Agora V*, p. 10 and n. 6. 239. *Agora V*, p. 11.
240. *Agora V*, p. 10. 241. *Agora V*, p. 10, n. 5.
242. *Agora V*, p. 20, F 96.

243. The closest parallel to F 1 is Corpus 253.4.G from Roman Ia. F 1—3 do not have the generally thinner ware and lighter foot with outside grooved attachment of the earlier examples; F 3 has the instepped foot that first occurs on one of the ten smaller examples of this type from Vault Cistern 2, Corpus 253.1.G. The hemispherical bowls, F 6—11, appear to have less clearly grooved foot attachments and seem to be even heavier than the Roman Ia examples, Corpus 251.2.B. F 12—14 are similar to *Tarsus I*, Fig. 188:290, from the HRU, but the flatter floor indicates a slightly later date or a slightly different form. F 5 has a parallel in *Tarsus I*, Fig. 188:252, from the HRU, but evidence for tracing the development of the form is insufficient. It will be remembered that the *terminus ante quem* of the HRU has been set at ca. 25 B.C.

244. Cf. references cited in *Agora V*, p. 25. The Eastern Sigillata A form first appears in Roman Ia at Samaria (Corpus 251.6.A) and in the Roman Fill at Tarsus (*Tarsus I*, Fig. 194:417). The contexts of the Samian, Pergamene, and local Attic varieties would tend to exclude a date before the last quarter of the first century B.C.

just before 25 B.C., and a similar date is thereby indicated for Athens.[245] The gray ware examples, F 26—27, also leave no indication of a date in the middle of the first century B.C., but their dating is obscure.[246]

Besides the evidence from the fine imported wares, the unguentaria and the lamps also indicate a date about 25-0 B.C. for the F deposit. The piriform unguentarium, F 50, is not known to occur before 25 B.C., and its occurrence with the ring-footed fusiform unguentarium, F 48, fits this date well. This fusiform unguentarium, supported by parallels cited from Ornavasso,[247] completely substantiates the view held throughout the study that there has not been evidence to support a purported development toward a less bulbous unguentarium.[248] Lamp F 96 can be attributed to pre-Sullan material, but lamps F 98—104 can be dated in the last quarter of the first century B.C. No close parallels to F 102—103 have been found in the Christian era, and F 104 first appears in the Augustan Period.[249]

A more difficult problem to deal with is that of the "Miscellaneous Glazed and Non-Glazed Wares," F 28—47. The problem results from the fact that Robinson has not consistently applied his principle of excluding material closely parallel to earlier Hellenistic material. His procedure is certainly understandable in the case of the small, shallow, ring-based bowls, F 35—43, and possibly also in the case of the bowls with pushed-up horizontal handles, F 29—32. The latter are "very similar" in shape and

---

245. The isolated occurrences of barbotine ware in second century B.C. contexts (cf. *Agora V*, p. 12, n. 13) should be considered dubious. D 79, from a displaced fill, certainly proves nothing; this is an illustration of Robinson's use of Thompson's methodology which has been criticized above for relying too heavily on the homogeneous nature of each deposit.

246. F 26 has a Tiberian parallel while F 27 is perhaps to be dated with the pre-Sullan material as are two similar but larger plates. Cf. *Agora V*, p. 13.

247. *Agora V*, p. 15 under F 50.

248. Cf. *TCHP*, p. 472. *Tarsus I*, pp. 171—72. *Cyprus IV*, p. 79. Chap. IV, n. 45. This does not deny that *ca.* 150—50 B.C. unguentaria of nearly spherical form were produced. The ring-footed unguentarium, F 49, with its lack of the cylindrical stem above the foot could be considered transitional. A piriform unguentarium from Smyrna with a prominent ringed foot might also be transitional. It unfortunately does not come from a chronologically significant context. Cf. Siegfried Loeschcke, "Sigillata-Töpfereien in Tschandarli," *Mitteilungen des kaiserlich deutschen archäologischen Instituts, Athenische Abteilung*, XXXVII (1912), Abb. 10:7. Both of these, however, could be a "local" imitation of the unguentarium forms.

249. Cf. *Agora IV*, p. 140, and *Broneer*, p. 78. A word of caution is in order regarding the use of the lamps of *Agora IV* for dating purposes. Many of the types are dated primarily on the basis of ceramic contexts such as those under discussion and therefore cannot be used as independent dating evidence. The contexts for which no evidence is published in *Agora V* (from which many of the lamps come) are quite probably of no more independent chronological significance than the groups studied. Undoubtedly, Robinson has chosen the most significant groups for publication (*Agora V*, p. 2). The dates of Broneer should certainly also be consulted, even if at times his dates must be changed on the basis of the Agora evidence. *E.g.*, *Agora IV*, Type 35B is classified in Broneer's Type XII which is given a *terminus ante quem* of the early second century B.C., although Type 35B is probably dated correctly by Howland as late second to late first century B.C. (*Agora IV*, p. 111).

fabric to D 17 and 18.[250] Fragments of these vessels also occur in E.[251] The type is not excluded by its Hellenistic affinities, presumably, because at least five examples of it occur also in Group G.[252] Similarly F 35—43 are closely related in form and ware to the plate which was very common in the latest Hellenistic group, E 1—17. These vessels also occur in G.[253]

Robinson, on the basis of the evidence just cited, suggests that this bowl with unusual handles persists for nearly two centuries with only slight variations. A more plausible interpretation might seem to be that the earlier forms are contained in later deposits. The following reasons can be adduced to support this interpretation. First, it is consistent with Robinson's method of excluding material with close Hellenistic affinities. This is consistent with the principle used in this study in dealing with typical fills of this period which contain earlier material, namely, that only the new forms or developments in a given deposit are significant. Secondly, it would better agree with his observation of a "sharp break" in ceramic technique and form about 86 B.C.[254] Thirdly, it would eliminate the rather anomalous situation of a very unusual form continuing unchanged through two centuries when none of the other forms are static.[255] Fourthly, it is more realistic about the limited homogeneity of the displaced deposits in question.

The jug, F 44, can be included with the pre-Sullan group on the basis of its parallels in D, E, and at Ornavasso as cited by Robinson.[256] The jug, F 45, with its first century A.D. parallels should not be dated before 25 B.C.[257]

Some of the examples of household and cooking ware might also be considered pre-Sullan[258] while others have affinities with other vessels from the end of the first century B.C. or the first century A.D., or show development over earlier forms.[259]

The negative evidence may be of little or no significance, but it can also be mentioned. There are no examples of the earliest Eastern Sigillata A forms, but it might be argued that exportation to Athens did not begin with the earliest forms. The absence of "Megarian" type bowls, not uncommon in E, may indicate at least that the deposit must postdate 50 B.C., since, even if they were no longer available in Athens after 86 B.C., the complete absence of fragments would not be expected immediately.

---

250. *Agora V*, p. 13. The similarities here cited do not appear to be consistent with Robinson's reference to a "sharp break in pottery styles occurring after the sack of Athens by Sulla's troops," and his contention that there is a marked decline in glaze and clay of vessels which postdate 86 B.C. Cf. *Agora V*, p. 2.

251. E 52—53 and parts of two other such bowls.
252. G 51—52 and at least three examples from Layer II in storage.
253. G 82—84 and more than ten similar plates.
254. Cf. n. 250 *supra*.
255. Only the common small bowl with incurved rim appears to be an exception.
256. *Agora V*, pp. 14—15.   257. *Agora V*, p. 15.
258. F 55, 58, 59, 63, and 78. Cf. F 59 with B 12, which is twice as large, however.
259. F 60—62, 64—66, 69—71, 73, 76, 83—85. The similarities between F 60—61 and Corpus 45.1. A—B are striking. This appears to have been a rather standardized form throughout the Roman Empire.

Their absence, however, could be fortuitous since the form occurs in sigillata ware in Roman Ia at Samaria.[260]

The numerous parallels to first century A.D. materials might suggest extending the date of the deposit into the Christian era. Robinson prefers not to do this because of the absence of Arretine ware.[261] The absence of the common first century A.D. Eastern Sigillata A forms and stamps which do occur in the G Layer II deposit appears to be even more significant. However, since the deposit is displaced, there cannot be absolute certainty that there are not at least a few sherds that should be dated in the early years of the Christian era. Likewise, it cannot be absolutely certain that none of the sherds should be dated between 86 and 25 B.C., but in our present state of knowledge none of the vessels included in Group F can be placed there with confidence.

Group G.—Group G comes from a cistern filling divided into three layers. Layer I, located immediately over the floor, is "perhaps" debris accumulated while the cistern was in use.[262] It contained "pottery and lamps of the early first or even of the second century B.C.," and subsequently, "perhaps" following the 86 B.C. destruction, went out of use.[263] Actually, the evidence for dating this layer rests on a sigillata cup, a jug of thorn ware, and a lamp.[264] Howland dates the lamp type by a parallel from just after 86 B.C. and by the "finding place of 521 [=G 3]."[265] The two pottery vessels, however, do not indicate the 150—75 B.C. date suggested, and, in fact, could better be dated with Layer II, especially since there is no certain evidence for the existence of Eastern Sigillata A or thorn ware before 25 B.C. at the Agora. This means that the cistern could well have been used until the debris of Layer II was dumped into it. Robinson's labelling of Layer I "early 1st century B.C." is therefore a striking example of the weakness of the chronological foundation on which he claims the Roman ceramic chronology of the Eastern Mediterranean must rest.

In contrast, Layer II appears to be a rather homogeneous deposit which is correctly dated. The dating is based on the latest coin (dated A.D. 26—37), the pottery, and the lamps.[266] Robinson suggests that "there seems to be no reason for bringing the

---

260. Corpus 158.H. It also occurs in first and second century A.D. contexts at Tarsus, *Tarsus I*, pp. 177—78.

261. Arretine ware does appear in contexts predating the first century A.D. Cf. Corpus 354.2.A. August Oxé, *Arretinische Reliefgefässe von Rhein*, Heft V of *Materialien zur römisch-germanischen Keramik* (Frankfurt, 1933); *Frühgallische Reliefgefässe von Rhein*, Heft VI (Frankfurt, 1934), *et passim*.

262. Group C is discussed in *Agora V*, pp. 22—23.

263. *Agora V*, p. 22.

264. G 1—3. Robinson does not consider two other lamps from the deposit of chronological significance.

265. *Agora IV*, p. 126.

266. The precise reasoning by which Robinson arrives at absolute dates for his deposits is not entirely clear. He states that coins "have proved chiefly of negative value in confirming the chronology" (*Agora V*, p. 1, n. 4). From the discussion (p. 2) it seems that a study of the groups in question led to their placement in a relative sequence after 86 B.C. mainly from typological considerations. The coin in this deposit certainly is related to the *terminus ante quem*, and the results of other excavations, of which very few are cited, must have been at least an indirect influence in the absolute dating.

pottery of Layer IIb much beyond the time of Tiberius."[267] Analysis of the pottery presents no evidence against dating Layer II about A.D. 0—37.[268]

The dating of Layer III is somewhat confusing. The layer is dated by ceramic parallels in Groups J and M Layer III. The J deposit does not predate A.D. 138 and M Layer III is dated in the second half of the second century A.D., but the G Layer III deposit is dated late first to early second century A.D.[269] A somewhat earlier typology might be implied, but no development toward the J and M Layer III examples is mentioned in the catalogue or is apparent in an examination of the forms; the parallels cited seem to be very close. In addition, G Layer III contains numerous parallels to G Layer II, F, and even some to K and L, as well as a Thasian and three Knidian stamped amphora handles which Miss Grace dates before 86 B.C.[270] In the light of this evidence, G Layer III does not appear to be a very reliable group for dating purposes. The Layer II-III group is of little significance for similar reasons.[271]

Group H.—Of the 27 catalogued pottery vessels and lamps of Group H, twelve vessels and two lamps have parallels to G II as cited by Robinson.[272] Two vessels and an amphora fragment seem to be clearly later in date while a fragment of Attic black-figured ware and a Thasian (?) stamped amphora handle are certainly earlier.[273] Robinson considers Group H a "floating" deposit between Groups G and J, and dates it A.D. 100—150. The group could as well be considered a deposit contemporary with G Layer II with intrusions, if it is to be considered a closely dated group at all. Robinson recognizes the insignificance of the deposit when he states that "the Agora has so far yielded little evidence for establishing an exact chronology of the pottery of the late first and the second century after Christ."[274]

Group M.—Group M provides one of the few significant "stratified" deposits from the Agora.[275] It consists of debris from a well that was apparently in continuous

---

267. *Agora V*, p. 23, n. 3. Layer II was divided into Layer IIa and IIb, but this arbitrary division was abandoned in final publication.

268. The catalog of G 8—165 cites abundant chronological evidence for this dating. Only a few observations seem in order. The Eastern Sigillata A definitely belongs to the early first century A.D. Note the parallel to G 9 in Corpus 253.1.M and the fact that the plate with vertical sides (G 11) and the flanged hemispherical bowl (G 13, 14) just begin to occur in late first century B.C. contexts at Samaria and Tarsus. The occurrence of Samian and Arretine ware, the latter with precise chronological parallels at Haltern, is of crucial importance. Cf. the parallel to G 54 in Corpus 354.2.A from the turn of the era. The single fusiform unguentarium (G 96) among "many" piriform fragments is a strong indication that the former had practically fallen into disuse by the Christian era at Athens as at Tarsus and Haltern. The problems connected with G 51—52, 82—84 have been discussed above. A similar problem is involved in G 112 // F 78 // E 140. None of the lamps, G 127—158, need be dated outside A.D. 0—37, and Robinson's rejection of Miss Perlzweig's view that G 141 and 143—146 postdate A.D. 50 is in order (*Agora V*, p. 23, n. 3).

269. *Agora V*, p. 22.   270. *Agora V*, p. 43.
271. G 213—228.
272. *Agora V*, pp. 47—49. H 2—9, 11, 17, 30, 31, and lamps H 21, 22.
273. H 14, 15, 20, and p. 49.   274. *Agora V*, p. 46.
275. Robinson correctly states that a continuous accretion of material in a well does not properly constitute statification. *Agora V*, p. 82.

use from the first through the late sixth centuries A.D.[276] Unfortunately, only the first two layers are of significance for the period under study. Layer I, with fourteen pottery vessels and six lamps, is dated to the middle of the first century A.D. The dating is based on a coin from between A.D. 0–50, similarities of the pottery to that of G Layer II, and the absence of western sigillata forms that occur in G II.[277] The last argument seems very tenuous since Arretine ware was never very common and the deposit is small; besides, well deposits are known for their lack of fine wares. The group may therefore be considered contemporary with Group G Layer II. This is especially indicated by three lamps and another in storage parallel to a G form for which there is no evidence after the earliest years of the Christian era.[278] The plump variant of a piriform unguentarium may be noted. It has parallels at ʿAlâyiq and in the Roman Fill at Tarsus,[279] both contexts of the first half of the first century A.D.

M Layer II is dated to the end of the first and the first half of the second centuries A.D. Two jars dated A.D. 112 and 131[280] indicate the horizon of this deposit. From parallels cited, this deposit dates between G II and M III, the latter belonging to the second half of the second century A.D. The group is largely beyond the chronological scope of this study although a cursory examination casts some doubt on the homogeneity of the deposit.

In conclusion it may be reëmphasized that far from being normative material for Eastern Mediterranean ceramic chronology, the dating of the Early Roman deposits published in *Agora V* must be refined in light of evidence from Palestine and Tarsus. Even if the repertory of forms from Athens is more satisfactory, the Roman pottery of the Eastern Mediterranean from the first centuries B.C. and A.D. receives more of its chronological precision from Samaria and Tarsus than from Athens. The Agora does provide two groups that can be dated with some confidence, after revision, to the last quarter-century B.C. (F) and the early first century A.D. (G Layer II).

Lamps from Corinth and Athens

Howland's study of Agora lamps has been frequently mentioned in the previous section, and a brief evaluation of its chronological significance seems in order here. The comparable treatment of Corinthian lamps by Broneer may be conveniently considered at the same time. The work of Broneer had been an unrivaled classic until the recent appearance of *Agora IV* which henceforth will be used at least as widely as Broneer's work. Indeed, one of Howland's purposes was "to furnish a reliable guide for archaeologists who may be able to use these types of lamps as criteria for dating deposits on other sites, wherever they may be in the Mediterranean area."[281] These works are used to date lamps in such a fashion that the lamps are given independent chronological

---

276. *Agora V*, pp. 82–84. 277. *Agora V*, p. 85.
278. M 15–17 and G 130. Cf. *Agora IV*, Types 35B, 54B, 54C, and *Broneer*, pp. 65–66.
279. M 8 // Corpus 92. E and *Tarsus I*, Fig. 202:732.
280. M 45–46. Cf. Mabel Lang, "Dated Jars of Early Imperial Times," *Hesperia*, XXIV (1955), pp. 279–85. Note Catalogue Nos. 8 and 14.
281. *Agora IV*, p. v.

significance, similar to that of coins and stamped amphora handles, in dealing with deposits inside and outside Palestine. An evaluation of their limitations as chronological indicators is therefore crucial. Three subjects will be considered: the advances in chronological precison in *Agora IV*, the methodological limitations of the studies, and the application of their chronology to Palestinian material.

Broneer's study cannot henceforth be used without consulting *Agora IV*. The *Agora IV* corpus is much larger and more varied and fills the 146—44 B.C. gap at Corinth. The number of closed deposits from which the lamps come exceeds 1200.[282] The types distinguished by Broneer are frequently rearranged or divided. Many of Broneer's dates have to be revised considerably.[283]

Nevertheless, one might still have some reservations about describing *Agora IV* as a major advance in chronological precision for Greek and Roman lamp dating. This is because the methodology of Broneer has been substantially followed by Howland. This methodology is summarized as follows:

> The dating suggested for the Agora types is thus in almost all cases based on two considerations: first, the circumstances of finding, where the piece comes from a closed or closely dateable deposit; and second, the stylistic relationships between the types and sub-types themselves.[284]

Sometimes it seems that the second consideration takes precedence over the first in the dating of specific types. This may be deduced from the fact that *termini* assigned a given type are not always the earliest and latest of the loci in which they occur although Howland states that "the dates assigned to the individual types are the maximum over-all dates."[285] As pointed out in the discussion of Thompson's Hellenistic groups from the Agora, "developments" attributed chronological significance which are not based on empirical evidence tend to be highly subjective and are regarded as of doubtful chronological value in this study.[286] Fortunately, dated find spots are involved in nearly every type though frequently the less common types are found in only one or two dated contexts.

However, the examination of the groups selected by Robinson as of normative significance does not show that the dates assigned these deposits are above dispute. The dating of the deposits which fix the lamp chronology is based on internal (such as finds of pottery) and external (such as the relation to buildings of known date) evidence. The *Agora V* groups provide the evidence necessary for checking some lamp contexts,

---

282. *Agora IV*, p. 2.

283. *E.g.*, Broneer's Type XII (end of the third to early second century B.C.) is represented in Howland's Types 32, 33A, 34A, 35A, and 35B, which range in date from the late second quarter of the third to the late first century B.C. Broneer, p. 53. *Agora IV*, pp. 99—111.

284. *Agora IV*, p. 2.

285. *Ibid.* To illustrate, the *termini* of Type 44C indicated by find spots are from the beginning of the Christian era into the first half of the second century A.D., but the type is dated ca. A.D. 0—50. *Agora IV*, pp. 141—42.

286. Datings based exclusively on typological relationship, as, *e.g.*, Type 47A, are therefore not considered significant.

but in most cases the dates must be accepted without published evidence.[287] If the uncritical assumption of the homogeneity of the groups is also involved in the dating of the unpublished material, especially those dates assigned lamps on the basis of one or two dated find spots should be used with caution.

An illustration of the limited strength of evidence upon which a number of types are dated is provided by Type 44.[288] Type 44A is given the same date as that assigned by Robinson to Group F, about 75—0 B.C. This dating is based on two lamps of Type 44A from that group and the stylistic similarities to Type 49A (about 125 B.C.—A.D. 25) and 49B (early years of the first century A.D.). Most of the group F pottery has been redated in this study to the last quarter of the first century B.C., and the typological relations to Type 49A and B are so imprecise that they can, at most, indicate very broad dating limits. Type 44B is dated to approximately the first century B.C. on the basis of "some" stylistic similarities to Type 51A and on the finding place of the only inventoried example, a dumped well filling dated to the turn of the era. Type 44C is considered a later variant of Type 44A on typological grounds. It is dated to the first half of the first century A.D. although found in contexts from Augustan times through the first half of the second century A.D. Type 44D is dated in the first century A.D., especially its second quarter; find spots date from the first to the early second century A.D.[289] Type 44A could be dated either before 86 B.C. or, more probably, in the last quarter of the first century B.C. according to the analysis of Group F above. Type 44B—D can hardly be dated with confidence within a century on the basis of the few examples, the wide chronological spread of their contexts, and the tenuous chronological significance of the typological relationships cited.

In considering the chronological value of these lamp typologies for Palestine and other sites rather remote from Greece it is in order to recall the observations of Misses Goldman and Jones that each site has a slightly different set of lamp types.[290] The exigencies of trade determine which of the imports are found at a given site, and local preferences determine those to be copied. The "developments" at one site will not necessarily parallel those at another. The possibility of chronological disparity of similar forms in different geographical areas must also be considered. A striking illustration is provided by two lamps from the writer's Palestinian collection. One incorporates both "early" and "late" features of Broneer's Type XVIII: the ribbed decoration, which is "the simplest and undoubtedly an early form of rim decoration," and the triangular nozzle, which he considers late.[291] The other combines both the "early" plain disc and the "late" flat base of his Type XXII.[292] Either there is a difference in the chronological development of the lamps at the two sites, or his criteria of development are incorrect.

---

287. In the case of Corinth the publication of the pottery by G. Roger Edwards is still forthcoming. Cf. *Corinth I*, Part IV, pp. vi, vii.

288. *Agora V*, pp. 140—43.

289. Note that Group G Layer II is divided into two separately dated groups. This has been set aside as questionable by Robinson. Cf. n. 267 *supra*.

290. *Tarsus I*, p. 84.   291. *Broneer*, p. 64.

292. *Broneer*, p. 77.

In conclusion, it appears that lamps from Syria and Palestine will gain little in chronological precision from their Athenian and Corinthian parallels. The broad dating of lamps from unclear or imprecise contexts will, however, be aided by the Corinthian and Agorian typologies. It should be emphasized that each date assigned a lamp type must be evaluated for its individual merits. Only infrequently will such individual evaluation lead to a lamp dating that can be considered a precise independent datum in dealing with the chronology of a given Palestinian deposit. Because of its rather limited value to the Palestinian Corpus, such a detailed evaluation is beyond the scope of this study.

Antioch

With the published material from Antioch[293] the line between primary and secondary archaeological evidence is reached. Nearly all the Antioch material is of the latter category; it must be dated by comparative material from other sites. In the Antioch publication there is an almost complete lack of observed stratification or even closely dated loci.[294] The contribution of the Antioch material to an understanding of Palestinian ceramic chronology is therefore minor, and precise chronological implications for the Corpus are rare. The dating of most of the Antioch forms must be based on comparative material and is therefore beyond the scope of this study. It should be noted that only "glazed" pottery is published.

Despite the lack of closely dated deposits Waagé has described a number of formal changes to which he attributes relative or absolute chronological significance.[295] The emphatic rejection of these developments by Miss Kenyon may well be repeated here.

> Waagé's suggestions as to dating and sequence of forms, as well as his division into "Hellenistic" and "Roman" "Pergamene" are on typological and subjective grounds alone. For instance, in a deposit which he uses (op. cit. p. 37) as "almost the only evidence at Antioch for the contemporaneity of specific Early Roman 'Pergamene' shapes" he stated that there is "an appreciable quantity of Late Hellenistic Red pottery as well", and "the several Augustan Arretine sherds and some of the fragments of the imported, unglazed eggshell ware are probably a little earlier than the bulk of the Early Roman 'Pergamene'". Conclusions as to contemporaneity, or otherwise, of shapes, drawn in this manner are obviously valueless as evidence.[296]

Note also Miss Kenyon's comment on the sharp distinction between the Hellenistic and Early Roman sigillata (together constituting Miss Kenyon's Eastern Sigillata A group) which Waagé has set forth as basic to a study of the ware.[297]

> Finally, the hard-and-fast distinction Waagé makes between Late Hellenistic Red (Hellenistic "Pergamene") Ware and Early Roman "Pergamene" (no alternative title is here suggested) is not justified.

---

293. *Antioch I-III, IV*, Part I.
294. *Antioch IV*, pp. 2, 15. *SS III*, pp. 282, 287.
295. Cf. *Antioch IV*, pp. 16–17, 22–28, 33–38.
296. *SS III*, p. 287.
297. *Antioch IV*, pp. 18, 19.

He admits that his two groups simply represent different sets of forms being produced at the same factory or factories at different times. The Samaria evidence makes it quite clear that use of the two sets of forms overlapped very considerably. Waagé actually quotes an example from the Harvard excavations (*HE*, p. 305, fig. 185. 4b) as a specimen of Early Roman "Pergamene" which comes from the Vault Cistern 2 (see below) with a mass of the forms of his "Hellenistic" group. He moreover apparently treats as irrelevant, though he refers to it, the Antioch evidence of association of the two sets of forms in the group from sector 16—P, which he uses as evidence of contemporaneity of his Early Roman "Pergamene" forms. The appearance or preponderance of the different forms has undoubtedly chronological significance, but it is confusing and misleading to make such a sharp break as to require a different name. As to the actual chronology, Antioch unfortunately provides almost no evidence, as little true stratification was observed.[298]

Despite these limitations a discussion of three Antiochene ceramic groups will prove instructive.

The sector 16—0 deposits. — This sector contained a "series of superimposed deposits . . . which fall within the half century 225—175 B.C."[299] The presence of at least four coins of Antiochus III (222—187 B.C.) and the absence of coins of Antiochus IV (175—163 B.C.) or Demetrius I (162—150 B.C.), common at the site, is given as evidence favoring a terminal date of 175 B.C. Miss Kenyon accepts this date,[300] but the fact that the upper levels contained Eastern Sigillata A "and a few later sherds"[301] makes it possible that material later than 175 B.C. is also involved in all levels if the deposit is taken as a unit. The *terminus a quo* is based on the observation that the pottery "does not seem to cover a very long range of time,"[302] although at least nine coins belong to kings predating Antiochus III.[303] Since coins which could well belong to Antiochus III occur near the bottom of the debris, since the pottery is relatively homogeneous, and because no stratification was recorded, Waagé's ceramic developments based on differences in sherds from arbitrary levels within the deposit must be ignored, and the deposit treated as a single unit.[304]

The fish plate forms show a closer relation to those from Tarsus than those from Athens or Palestine, but most striking is the number of such plate forms that have no

---

298. *SS III*, p. 282. Another patent example of Waagé's attempt to draw conclusions where evidence is lacking or to the contrary is his conclusion that it was the "Late Hellenistic Red Ware which . . . caused the potters at Arretium to change from the production of black to that of red pottery." He bases his conclusion on the "strong eastern influence" shown by the names of owners and slaves on the Italian ware (*Antioch IV*, p. 31). However, p. 20, it is stated that no specimens of sigillata are known from Italy, and, p. 33, that "until the Italian ware has been made the subject of a special study by itself . . . the accurate determination of its influence in the eastern provinces and the probable sequence of the derived forms there will remain obscure." Cf. the remarks of Howard Comfort, *Antioch IV*, p. 61.

299. *Antioch IV*, p. 15. 300. *SS III*, p. 219.
301. *Antioch IV*, p. 17. 302. *Antioch IV*, p. 16.
303. Cf. n. 312 *infra*. 304. Cf. *SS III*, p. 219.

precise parallels at any of the sites studied.[305] The range of incurved and outcurved rim bowl types at Antioch is similar to that at other sites. A tendency toward very sharply incurved rims at Tarsus[306] is not prominent at Antioch, Shechem, Samaria, Beth-zur, or the Agora. The hemispherical bowls with or without incised or painted decoration are apparently distinctly Antiochene since they have not been previously encountered in this study.[307] Lamps related to the Agora type with *à godrons* style decoration with parallels at Samaria and Tarsus also occur in this debris.[308]

The relationships just referred to, plus a number of others that might be specified, merely point to the extremely complex situation involved in attempting to develop comparative chronological criteria for Hellenistic Decorated Ware at widely scattered sites. Local differences and variants in the manufacture of the common types are apparently the cause of this complexity which makes the tracing of development impossible except at a site where precisely dated pottery is excavated.[309]

On the other hand, the situation is quite different when one examines the early Eastern Sigillata A forms at these same sites. As will be noted below, the range of forms and variants at each of the sites studied is nearly identical.

The sector 17—0 deposits.—About eighty per cent of the pottery from sector 17—0 belongs to Waagé's Late Hellenistic Red Ware.[310] This deposit contained

---

305. Type 17 (*Antioch IV*, Pls. I-II) with a groove inside the rim is also common at Tarsus (*Tarsus I*, Fig. 179:E, F, 39, 40), but does not occur in Palestine or the Agora. Type 14 also appears to have close similarities at Tarsus: 14k // *Tarsus I*, Fig. 179:G, which, however, is much larger. On the other hand, Type 10 appears to have its closest parallels in Corpus 153. L and N, and Type 12, although having no precise parallel, belongs to a class similar to Corpus 153. H, but it does not have a central depression. Types 13, 15, and 16 do not appear to have any close parallels in the material studied. The common Samaria type, Corpus 153. E (also found at Tarsus), as well as the variant occurring in third century contexts, *Tarsus I*, Fig. 178:D and E, is missing from the Antioch corpus.

306. *Tarsus I*, Fig. 180:68, H—N, 72.   307. Types 50—57.

308. Cf. Corpus 83.2. B—D and *Tarsus I*, p. 89, Group III, with *Antioch III*, Fig. 75:11d, 13c.

309. Even the commonly accepted criterion of "glaze" deterioration and the later tendency toward leaving the foot and part of the exterior of the vessel "unglazed" cannot be universally relied upon. Cf. the fifth and early fourth century B.C. bowls with incurved rim from Olynthus. David M. Robinson, *Excavations at Olynthus*, Part V: *Mosaics, Vases, and Lamps of Olynthus found in 1928 and 1931* (Baltimore, 1933), Pl. 176.

310. The statement, *Antioch IV*, p. 20, that the greatest concentration of sigillata occurs in Palestine and Syria could be misleading, for there are no deposits in Palestine where sigillata ware comprises anywhere near eighty per cent of the deposit. More applicable to Palestine would be Westholm's observation regarding the Soli temple area at Cyprus, that plain and coarse (kitchen and cooking) ware constitutes eighty per cent of the pottery. Cf. *Cyprus III*, p. 539. It can be noted in passing that another site with a deposit where sigillata preponderated is Dura, contrary to the statement of Waagé that only a small quantity of sigillata occurred there (*Antioch IV*, p. 20). This deposit contained "a scattering of earlier datable sherds amid a preponderance of early 'Pergamene' sherds and the local imitations both of it and of 'Attic' black glaze in similar copied shapes." (Mikhail Rostovtzeff et al. [eds.], *The Agora and Bazaar* [*The Excavations at Dura-Europos*, Preliminary Report of the Ninth Season of Work, 1935—1936, Part I; New Haven, 1944], p. 30.) The assumption that this "distribution is characteristic of the late second century" is entirely unwarranted, however, and the epigraphic evidence used to support this view needs reinterpretation (*ibid.*, pp. 30, 169—76). Unfortunately, this deposit is not included in the final publication of the pottery where the same chronological

coins ranging from Antiochus I to 36/35 B.C. with a coin of 49/48 B.C. at the lowest level.[311] With Waagé's Late Hellenistic Red Ware were a very few early and late Roman fragments which, together with a few glazed medieval sherds, are considered intrusive.[312]

The footed hemispherical bowls and the footed broad-floored plates with slightly incurved rims are the most common types at Antioch as is the case of early sigillata deposits at other sites studied.[313] Comparisons with the closely dated material at Samaria led Miss Kenyon to date the deposit to the middle of the last quarter of the first century B.C.[314] A somewhat later *terminus ante quem* than Miss Kenyon's might be suggested in view of the Roman Ia parallels, but if the Syrian origin of the ware be accepted, Miss Kenyon's date need not be lowered for the Antiochene deposit. A dating to the last quarter of the first century B.C. is indisputable.

In addition to the common broad-floored plates with or without horizontal rim, the main forms by which Miss Kenyon dated the deposit, were plates with turned-down decorated rim,[315] broad plates with offset rim,[316] the flat-floored plate with slight foot extending from everted side,[317] and the higher walled version of the common broad-floored plate.[318] The parallels to all these forms from Samaria or Tarsus confirm the dating of this deposit to the last quarter of the first century B.C.

The sector 16—P deposits.—The extended quotations of Miss Kenyon at the beginning of the discussion provide ample reason for not considering this deposit in detail. It is used as the primary source for defining Early Roman sigillata forms, but

---

assumptions about sigillata ware are repeated. Cf. Dorothy Hanna Cox, *The Greek and Roman Pottery* (*The Excavations at Dura-Europos*, Final Report IV, Part I, Fascicle 2; New Haven, 1949), pp. 7, 25, and *SS III*, p. 306. The writer has also noted deposits at Missis (ancient Mopsuestia near Adana) in which Eastern Sigillata A was predominant. This evidence alone strongly supports an hypothesis of Syrian origin of the ware, but details must await more precisely published evidence. The distribution of the ware (scarce in Aegean sites and unknown in Italy) is harder to explain by an Egyptian origin with distribution from Alexandria, where, incidentally, the ware is not nearly so plentiful. Cf. Pagenstecher, Band II, 3, pp. 100—118, where the collection described even includes many vessels not from Egypt.

311. *Antioch IV*, p. 27.

312. Deposits of this kind with coins ranging over several centuries and rather homogeneous pottery dating about the time of the latest coins seem rather characteristic of the period under study. Cf. the deposits at Shechem, Samaria, Tarsus, and Athens. This particular deposit clearly proves that the earlier coins do not necessarily show that there is corresponding early pottery in the deposit. In this deposit with over half the coins predating the first century B.C. no Hellenistic Decorated Ware is mentioned.

313. *Antioch IV*, p. 27 (Types 164 and 126). Unfortunately only photographs of the hemispherical bowls are published. The statement, *Tarsus I*, p. 174, that the hemispherical bowls were not in common use does not alter the fact that more of them are recorded in the Hellenistic Pergamene category than any other type (*Tarsus I*, pp. 233—34, Nos. 271—289).

314. See *SS III*, p. 287, for specific comparisons, primarily of the common broad-floored type with and without horizontal rim.

315. Types 101—102 // Corpus 253.2. A.

316. Type 137p // Corpus 253.5. A.

317. Type 143f // *Tarsus I*, Fig. 188:C (from oven over Roman Fill and the HRU).

318. Type 151f // *Tarsus I*, Fig. 188:270 (near the turn of the era).

the typology is not based on objective evidence. It is instructive to note that the forms which first appear in first century A.D. contexts at Tarsus or Samaria are also represented at Antioch. These are plates with vertical sides,[319] bowls with vertical rims,[320] the hemispherical bowls with elaborately profiled foot and rim,[321] and the flat-floored bowls with rather tall everted rims and ring bases.[322] Seven of these types occur in the 16—P deposit where there are also first century A.D. coins.[323]

Conclusion.—Besides the general chronological correlation of the Antiochene forms with the Corpus forms, the Antioch material is of no special importance for clarifying the problems of the chronological treatment of Hellenistic Decorated Ware and Eastern Sigillata A. As stated above, the variations in the treatment of the common fish plate, incurved-rim bowls, and outcurved-rim (angular) bowls appear to be primarily of local origin. Each site appears to have a number of unique variants. The Eastern Sigillata A forms also have a considerable number of variants, but all of them are found at several sites. This seems to apply to all the forms common in the first centuries B.C. and A.D. at the sites studied. It also implies that the close dating of the development of Hellenistic Decorated Ware forms must be based on local archaeological evidence while sigillata forms, to a much greater degree at least, can be dated from non-local comparative material. This does not mean that the general decline in the quality of the Hellenistic Decorated Ware is not similar at different sites nor that dating of identical sigillata forms in widely separated sites must be the same.

Cyprus

A detailed examination of the evidence from Cyprus tombs and strata for the period under study indicates that the rather scanty evidence makes no significant contribution to the precision of Hellenistic and Roman ceramic chronology of the Levant.[324] In fact, the chronology of local Cypriote pottery is largely dependent on the ceramic chronology of other Levant sites. Westholm acknowledges this when he states:

> It is needless to say that without the pioneer work of these scholars [Miss Jones at Tarsus, Waagé and Comfort at Antioch, Iliffe in Palestine, and Thompson at the Agora] it would not be possible for the present author to establish a classification of the Cypriote pottery from the Hellenistic and Roman epochs.[325]

---

319. Types 410—432 // Corpus 254.2.A // *Tarsus I*, pp. 241—42, Nos. 372—394. Cf. p. 39 *supra*.
320. Types 453—469 // Corpus 251.6.A // *Tarsus I*, p. 244, Nos. 412—419.
321. Types 470—473 // *Tarsus I*, pp. 244—47, Nos. 423—464.
322. Types 445—446 // *Tarsus I*, p. 249, No. 500. Cf. Corpus 252.2 with trumpet foot.
323. Types 426, 430, 453, 455, 457, 460, and 470. Cf. *Antioch IV*, p. 37.
324. Most of the sites involved are listed by Westholm, *Cyprus IV*, p. 72. Amathus Tombs 2 and 21, Ajia Irini Period 7, and possibly Mersinaki should be added to this list, for, although they are of little significance, they are no less significant than some of the other loci listed. Cf. *Cyprus II*, pp. 16, 119, 820; *III*, p. 394.
325. *Cyprus IV*, p. 72.

With an examination of the Cyprus pottery the major sources of evidence from outside Palestine for sharpening the chronological precision of the Corpus are exhausted. The inclusion of the Cyprus evidence is justified because a modest attempt has been made there to develop a ceramic typology and because much of its material is from tombs, a source not represented in the Corpus.

A few general observations about the Cyprus materials will make the specific analysis of the strata and tombs more intelligible. While the stratification is published in admirable detail even for the tombs and the location of finds is carefully noted, the methods of presenting and interpreting the ceramic evidence leave much to be desired. With the exception of *Cyprus III*, Figure 280, no smaller sherds are published in the extensive volumes of the Swedish Cyprus Expedition although reference is frequently made to groups of sherds which are considered homogeneous. In dealing with the classification and chronological significance of the pottery the dominance given surface treatment over form necessitates broad chronological divisions and results in confusion and error.[326] Further, when the forms belonging to a particular ware are discussed (especially *Cyprus III*, page 51 and following), it is frequently impossible to associate the verbal description with an example; it is obviously impossible to construct the form from the verbal description.

The only chronological development which Westholm claims to have clarified by the quite limited Cyprus evidence is based on a very dubious distinction into two series of forms. The lagynoi are divided into two groups, one of which is traced back to Cypro-Classical prototypes, while the other appears at the end of Hellenistic I (that is, near 150 B.C.), and "it seems to be impossible to ascertain the predecessor."[327] That this distinction is necessary is not at all clear; that different origins must be sought for forms that are very similar is not at all transparent.[328]

---

326. The broad divisions are Hellenistic I (325—150 B.C.), Hellenistic II (150—50 B.C.), and Roman I (50 B.C.—A.D. 150).

An illustration of the confusion involved is the case of two piriform unguentaria, *Cyprus II*, Pl. CXLVIII:5 and 8. These vessels are listed in separate groups in the classification table, *Cyprus II*, p. 118. One is classed as Roman Plain Ware and the other as Roman Red Ware because its neck is dipped in red "varnish." Confusion is compounded by the descriptions, *Cyprus II*, p. 117, where the former is called a bottle and the latter, a jug; moreover, the latter is called Roman Plain *Red* in the description. Another piriform unguentarium from the same tomb (No. 54) is classed as a Plain White Roman bottle, but it is classed with the Plain Red bottle in the chart.

A serious error is involved in the classification of the red wares. Westholm states that the Cyprus designations Red Lustrous and Mat Red Ware correspond to Samian and Pergamene Wares (*Cyprus IV*, p. 55). These classes obviously include Hellenistic Decorated Ware that is red or even partly black. Cf., e.g., the description of *Cyprus III*, Pl. XXXVII:8 which is classed as "Red Lustrous" and described as "Black mottled" (*Cyprus III*, p. 53). Form, ware, and context indicate that this vessel belongs to the Hellenistic Decorated Ware class. The form of *Cyprus III*, Fig. 280:18 and 20, classed as Red Lustrous II, indicate that these also are Hellenistic Decorated Ware, not "Pergamene."

327. *Cyprus IV*, p. 75. Cf. p. 65.
328. *Cyprus IV*, pp. 59, 65, 75. Cf. Fig. 23:2 with 3.

The methods used in interpreting the chronological significance of the classified evidence also need scrutiny. The whole methodology of dating evidence from tombs need not be discussed here, but two points can be made. In general, painstaking care is given to associating vessels with specific burials, and vessels not specifically associated with a burial are excluded from its context. This care, however, is forgotten at times. A lagynos is given a "fixed" date toward the middle of the second century B.C. by a lamp from the same tomb.[329] The dating of the lamp is not contradicted by evidence cited in this study, but that the tomb consists of a single homogeneous burial is not certain; another lamp does not belong to the second century corpus,[330] and originally the tomb from which it came was considered of a piece with the other third century tombs of Kountoura Trachonia.[331] Westholm also asserts that the pottery from Marion Tomb 9 can be divided into groups "by means of a careful study of the situation of the various burials in the tomb."[332] This is by no means true in every case. An examination of the diagram and description of the relation of the finds to the burials[333] does not make it obvious, for example, that Number 1 should belong to Hellenistic II and Number 2 to Hellenistic I. One suspects that the division is primarily typological as, for instance, Number 47 would probably be considered Hellenistic II except for the assumed development of fusiform unguentaria in this period.[334]

The use of numismatic evidence from the tombs is extremely judicious. The principle of dating by the lastest coins is followed, and the precariousness of dating pottery groups by isolated coins is recognized.[335]

A reinterpretation of the ceramic evidence from the Soli temple area is suggested below.

Tombs. — A list of Cypriote tombs with Hellenistic and Roman pottery is given in *Cyprus IV*, page 72; additions have been suggested above.[336] There is nothing in the pottery studied so far to contradict a date in the third century B.C. for the Kountoura Trachonia tombs, except that two of the vessels from Tomb 14 seem to belong to the first century B.C. typologically although a date in the second century is not absolutely excluded.[337] The Amathus tombs are no more helpful. Tomb 2 contained a

---

329. Kountoura Trachonia Tomb 14. Cf. *Cyprus IV*, p. 75.
330. Cf. *Cyprus I*, p. 458.
331. *Cyprus I*, pp. 459—60.
332. *Cyprus IV*, p. 72.
333. *Cyprus II*, Fig. 73:3 and pp. 206—208.
334. *Cyprus IV*, pp. 61, 65. That the more bulbous unguentaria can be considered *characteristically* early has been rejected above.
335. E.g., *Cyprus I*, pp. 459—60. The fact that a fill with rather homogeneous pottery can contain a good portion of coins a century or more earlier than the pottery (cf. n. 312 *supra*) emphasizes the need for caution in dealing with isolated coins from tombs.
336. Cf. n. 324 *supra*.
337. The lamp, *Cyprus I*, p. 458, No. 10, parallels Corpus 83.2, *TCHP*, D 56—59, E 97—114, 116, and *Antioch III*, Fig. 75:11d. The lagynos, *Cyprus I*, p. 458, No. 1, is parallel to the Agora E 73. Cf. *Cyprus IV*, p. 75.

few unpublished sherds dated to the first century A.D. and Tomb 21 three piriform unguentaria and other "Hellenistic-Roman Varnished and Plain Wares" which are not published.[338] From Idalion Tomb 1 come four lamps that indicate a pre-second century date for this tomb, and only coins remain from the post—200 B.C. period in Idalion Tomb 2.[339] No pottery from the tombs at Tsambres or Aphendrika necessarily post-dates 200 B.C.[340] At Marion Hellenistic pottery is reported from Tombs 1—3 (not illustrated) and vessels antedating the second century B.C. occur in Tombs 58, 60, and 61.[341]

Marion Tomb 9 is the most important of the Cyprus tombs for the purposes of this study. Even evidence from it is secondary; the pottery and glass in it must be dated comparatively. As noted above, Westholm revised the Hellenistic I dating of this tomb and now holds that many of the vessels belong to Hellenistic II.[342] That this division was made rather arbitrarily on typological grounds rather than by burial orientation has been suggested above. In fact, a sigillata bowl with downturned molded rim and a lamp suggest a date after rather than before 50 B.C., that is, in Westholm's Roman I period.[343] A molded glass bowl was found in the vicinity of these items; it probably dates from the same time and, in any case, cannot date before the first century B.C.[344] A lagynos has a parallel from the Agora which dates to the first century B.C. and could fit a date just after the middle of the century.[345] Further, those vessels that are dated to the earlier period by Westholm do not necessarily date any earlier than the vessels just mentioned. Two fusiform unguentaria[346] certainly fit Westholm's description of Hellenistic II unguentaria as having a body "shaped like a sphere or with a somewhat carinated thickening portion in the middle of the vase."[347] A flat-based, small incurved bowl fits much more naturally in a context just after 50 B.C. than before 150 B.C.[348] A jug displaying a rim with an inside shelf characteristic of

---

338. *Cyprus II*, pp. 116, 119.

339. *Cyprus II*, pp. 630, 634.

340. A few vessels from Aphendrika Tombs 33 and 36 could belong to the early second century B.C., but, if the groups are homogeneous, they belong to the latter part of the third century B.C. Cf. E. Dray and J. du Plat Taylor, "Tsambres and Aphendrika, Two Classical and Hellenistic Cemeteries in Cyprus," *Report of the Department of Antiquities, Cyprus*, 1937—1939 (Nicosia, 1951), pp. 30, 61, 63.

341. *Cyprus II*, pp. 186, 187, 189, 350, 364, 366. There is no Corpus evidence that would militate against dating the latter tombs to the third century B.C.

342. *Cyprus II*, p. 209; *Cyprus IV*, p. 72.

343. *Cyprus II*, p. 209, Nos. 36 and 37 respectively. No. 37 = *Cyprus IV*, Fig. 37:15. The earliest context of the bowl with turned-down molded rim is Vault Cistern 2 (Corpus 253.2.A), and the lamp is similar to lamps from Qumrân Ib (Corpus 84.A—D).

344. *Cyprus II*, p. 209, No. 33. Cf. *SS III*, pp. 403—404. For revised dating of the S 3 street cistern cf. Miss Kenyon's remarks, *SS III*, p. 285.

345. *Cyprus II*, p. 209, No. 45 = *Cyprus IV*, Fig. 24:34. Cf. *TCHP*, p. 405, E 73. If it is sigillata as stated, *Cyprus IV*, p. 79, it provides another indication of a post—50 B.C. date.

346. *Cyprus II*, p. 209, No. 45 = *Cyprus IV*, Fig. 24:34; *Cyprus II*, p. 209, No. 47 = *Cyprus IV*, Fig. 24:32.

347. *Cyprus IV*, p. 79.

348. *Cyprus II*, p. 209, No. 8 = *Cyprus IV*, Fig. 21:7. Cf. pp. 46—47 *supra*.

jugs in Palestine beginning in the second quarter of the first century B.C. is especially interesting.[349] Another jug has a twisted handle that also would better fit a first century B.C. date; at least there are no definite parallels known before 150 B.C.[350] These are hints that, in the absence of evidence to the contrary, *all* the pottery in Tomb 9 should be dated about the third quarter of the first century B.C. This dating is most doubtful in the case of the cooking pots which Westholm considers with his late group.[351] The necks are more everted than the typical pot of this period in Palestine; yet, the groove to receive a lid[352] is not present, and some room for local variation should be allowed. The tomb vessels do not appear to differ from those used by the living.[353]

Tomb 8 at Kurion, studied by McFadden, is also of only secondary significance since dating is primarily by ceramic comparisons. Burial 1 contained three lamps which are dated to the last half of the first century A.D.[354] With Burial 4 were two lamps which are dated to the Augustan period;[355] they belong to Tarsus Group XII dated to the first century A.D. Two jugs and a bowl are similarly dated.[356] Burial 5 contained similar pottery and probably is to be dated to the same period. In this group are an unstamped Rhodian amphora with sharply bent handle, two jugs also with sharply bent handles, a similar jug with a more arched handle, a small amphora, a lid with straight sides, and a piriform unguentarium.[357] These forms from Tomb 8 contrast sharply with the Marion Tomb 9 forms, and, because of the closely dated lamps, they can be placed, at least tentatively, in the first century A.D.[358]

Stratified evidence.—Only two sites produced evidence in this category. Kition Period 9—10 is termed Hellenistic.[359] From the published pottery it appears that the level is not closely dated.[360] Material from the third and second centuries B.C. occurs.[361]

---

349. *Cyprus II*, p. 209, No. 13=*Cyprus IV*, Fig. 22:9. Cf. Corpus 21.1.L, M, R.

350. *Cyprus II*, p. 209, No. 15=*Cyprus IV*, Fig. 24:2.

351. *Cyprus II*, p. 209, No. 22=*Cyprus IV*, Fig. 29:12. *Cyprus II*, p. 209, No. 38=*Cyprus IV*, Fig. 29:11.

352. For such a pot rim at Cyprus cf. *Cyprus IV*, Fig. 25:7, probably from a late third century B.C. context.

353. The forms can be conveniently noted in *Cyprus II*, Pl. XXXVIII:2. Drawings of many of the vessels (in addition to those cited above) are found in *Cyprus IV*, Figs. 22:8; 24:21, 22; 27:6, 14, 21; 28:1—4; 29:9, 10.

354. George H. McFadden, "A Tomb of the Necropolis of Ayios Ermoyenis at Kourion," *AJA*, L (1946), p. 464 and Pl. XXXVIII:28—30. Nos. 28 and 29 belong with Tarsus Group XVIII dated A.D. 50—100.

355. McFadden, *AJA*, L, p. 467 and Pl. XLIII:92—93.

356. McFadden, *AJA*, L, Pl. XLI:50—51 and XLII:82 respectively.

357. McFadden, *AJA*, L, Fig. 15:63, Pl. XL:48, XLI:49, XL:46, XLI:66, XLIII:90, and XLII:74 respectively.

358. The widest part of the jugs is lower; the piriform have replaced the fusiform unguentaria; lamps are of different types in the two groups.

359. *Cyprus III*, pp. 54, 72—75.

360. *Cyprus III*, Pl. XXXVII.

361. *Cyprus III*, Pl. XXXVII:5 likely belongs to the third century B.C., No. 7 probably to the early second century B.C., and No. 9 probably still later.

The lamps from the deposit are also probably of the third century B.C.;[362] at least no examples of such widely opened lamps occur in the Corpus. A coin of Tiberius also comes from Period 9, but it is considered intrusive.[363] Thus, the level is of little chronological significance especially since the mass of sherds from it is ignored except for a statistical treatment of the wares.[364]

From the Soli temples comes the only really stratified evidence from Cyprus for the period under study. The value of the evidence has been diminished by the scanty publication of the pottery and classification system within which it is published.[365] Omitting a criticism of the interpretation of Westholm, the following interpretation of the evidence presented in the ware diagram may be offered.[366] Red Lustrous and Mat Ware (which includes Eastern Sigillata A) does not appear in Temple A, but it does appear in the First Intermediate period (which follows a gap after Temple A).[367] Temple B was constructed just after 50 B.C. according to evidence from coins.[368] To correlate with Miss Kenyon's analysis of other sites,[369] this should be interpreted as indicating that sigillata began to appear in the First Intermediate shortly before the building of Temple B. It is instructive to note that the twenty-six entries of Red Lustrous Ware in the First Intermediate are all of the best type, Red Lustrous I. The large amounts of both black and red ware discovered in Temples B—D and the ensuing Second Intermediate constructions (which already postdate the first century A.D.) should probably be explained in terms of fills which incorporated older material and perhaps in part by the continued predilection of many Cypriotes for black ware. The discussion of forms related to each ware, however, makes the latter dubious since the forms involved practically disappeared at other sites before the beginning of the first century A.D., if one can judge from the verbal description and the few sherds represented.[370] Beyond this no further conclusions of significance for Palestinian or Cypriote ceramic chronology seem possible from the evidence available.

In conclusion a word of warning is in order even regarding the evidence from Marion Tomb 9 and Kurion Tomb 8 which appears more helpful than any other Cypriote evidence. It remains secondary material based upon absolute datings at other sites whose limitations have also been discussed. Any precise correlation between the forms involved and similar forms in Palestine must be considered tentative. The above discussion has shown that the Palestinian Corpus can make significant contributions to ceramic studies of the Cypriote excavations, but unfortunately it receives practically nothing in return.

---

362. *Cyprus III*, Pl. XXXVIII.   363. *Cyprus III*, p. 67.
364. *Cyprus III*, pp. 67ff.
365. *Cyprus III*, p. 511, Fig. 280, contains the only sherds of this period drawn by the Swedish Cyprus Expedition, and, as stated above, these are not usually related specifically to the typological discussion.
366. *Cyprus III*, p. 540.   367. *Ibid*.
368. *Cyprus III*, p. 542.   369. *SS III*, pp. 284—88.
370. *Cyprus III*, p. 511, Fig. 280:1—10.

CHAPTER V

AN ANALYSIS OF OTHER PALESTINIAN CERAMIC MATERIAL

According to the outline suggested in Chapter I two major tasks remain for this chapter and the next. One is an examination of the published ceramic material from Palestine that can be dated between about 200 B.C.—A.D. 70 and the other is the synthesis of the evidence presented in the form of a Palestinian pottery corpus. There are advantages to discussing either of these first. It has no doubt become obvious in the previous chapters that the writer has found it impracticable to ignore the Corpus either at a given stage as the argument develops or in the final form as it appears in Chapter VI. A presentation of the Corpus first would lead to a more intelligible analysis of the groups discussed in this chapter, and one interested in a careful analysis of any of the groups discussed below should familiarize himself with the Corpus beforehand. The Corpus is put last, however, because it is viewed as a summary of the entire study including the material presented in this chapter, and some of the groups discussed below do add slightly to the perspective of the Corpus.

Included below are pottery groups of known provenience from Palestine (including the Jordan Valley).[1] These are arranged alphabetically according to site. The name by which a site is designated is the one which the writer considers best known, but in many instances the designation is rather arbitrary.[2] Where possible the spelling is generally in accord with that of the 1956 edition of the *Westminster Historical Atlas to the Bible*.[3] A few sites where pottery of the period under study has been reported but not published are included if there is reasonable expectation that the reporting is

---

1. This implies that pottery from Transjordan beyond the Jordan Valley, Hellenistic or Early Roman pottery groups of unspecified provenience, and Hellenistic or Early Roman pottery groups assembled from the material discussed in this chapter are not included. *E.g.*: "Palestine Archaeological Museum Gallery Book: Persian, Hellenistic, Roman, Byzantine Periods" (Jerusalem, 1943), Nos. 810ff. (mimeographed); Department of Antiquities for Palestine, *Palestine Museum, Jerusalem: Bulletin No. 4*, 1927, Pls. VI—VII (reproduced in Albright, *The Archaeology of Palestine*, p. 148); Millar Burrows, *What Mean These Stones?* (New Haven, 1941), p. 169 and Fig. 34; P. S. P. Handcock, *The Archaeology of the Holy Land* (London, 1916), p. 263 and Figs. 79—82; H. Vincent, *Canaan d'après l'exploration récente* (Paris, 1907), pp. 346—47; Peter Thomsen, *Kompendium der palästinischen Altertumskunde* (Tübingen, 1913), p. 72 and Abb. 34. Older general speculations about the pottery are also ignored. *E.g.*: G. M. Fitzgerald, "The So-called Maccabaean Pottery," *PEF QS*, 1925, pp. 189—92; "'Maccabaean Pottery': A Rejoinder," *PEF QS*, 1926, pp. 84—90. Nelson Glueck's material from the Jordan Valley is also omitted (*v.* n. 186a *infra*).

2. An attempt to list all sites by their modern Arabic names was abandoned because many of these names are not commonly known.

3. G. Ernest Wright and Floyd V. Filson, *The Westminster Historical Atlas to the Bible* (Philadelphia, 1956).

accurate. Since a systematic survey of central and northern Palestine has never been completed, a comprehensive list of Hellenistic sites is not available.

Where possible, specific comparisons with the Corpus types have been made for the vessels and sherds of each group. The exactness of parallels varies, but an attempt has been made to be more strict in the use of the term parallel than is commonly accepted in the parlance of Palestinian archaeologists.[4] In some instances where the group was of little apparent significance the nearest Corpus comparison has been cited even though the parallel is not completely satisfactory. Where forms seemed unmistakably related but significant variants occur, the variants are noted in parentheses. Some will feel that the writer has erred in being too strict about what constitutes parallel material while others will consider certain comparisons cited as an overstretching of the term. The writer has attempted to be consistent and has cited those parallels that he considers significant for the chronological delimitation of the group in question.[5]

Although a few historical or cultural implications are alluded to in the following discussions, an attempt is made to treat these subjects, at least in a cursory way, in appendices. If there is any single impression that an examination of the following material will leave with the reader, it is probably the gross ignorance of ceramic chronology in the period under study up to very recent times.

Acre

Two Hellenistic tombs were discovered in the vicinity of Acre.[6] Only one piriform unguentarium has so far been published from this site.[7]

'Ain Shems

Only three jars and two lamps from the 'Ain Shems excavations belong to the period 200 B.C.–A.D. 70.[8] The jars come from Cistern 4 which also contained a hoard of eleven coins of Antiochus Epiphanes (175–163 B.C.). The lamps came from nearby on the same slope of the tell.[9] Wright assumed the association of the coin hoard and the jars and lamps and suggested a second century B.C. date for them.

---

4. Cf., e.g., the criticism of the Lachish typological publication *infra*.

5. In the period under study the repertory of common types is rather limited, but the amount of variation within each type is considerable. The amount of variation differs from type to type. *E.g.*, there are more variations in Lamp Type 83.2 than in Type 82; Lamp Type 81.1 is much more standardized in form than the Eastern Sigillata bowls, Type 253.1. Where the amount of variation is large some greater latitude in parallels seems permissible. Further, those variations that have been demonstrated to be of chronological significance should never be ignored, while failure to ignore certain other variations without known chronological significance would not only be pedantic but would tend to obscure some of the significant results of the study.

6. *IEJ*, IV (1954), p. 129.

7. *Kahane II*, Pl. 12:a // Corpus 92. D.

8. Elihu Grant and G. Ernest Wright, *Ain Shems Excavations (Palestine)*, Part IV (Pottery) (Haverford, 1938), Pl. LXIX:2 (=Pl. XLVII:19), 5 (=Pl. XLIX:8 and cf. 7). Elihu Grant, *Ain Shems Excavations (Palestine)*, Part II, (Haverford, 1932), Pl. L:24, 26.

9. Elihu Grant and G. Ernest Wright, *Ain Shems Excavations (Palestine)*, Part V (Text) (Haverford, 1939), pp. 16–17, 85, 146–47.

Either the hoard is not actually associated with the pottery or it is an extremely old hoard, for the jar forms can hardly precede 50 B.C. and a date in the latter part of the first century B.C. is also possible for the lamps.[10] The folded lamp (and possibly also the open one) could belong to the second century B.C., however.[11]

'Athlīt

Hellenistic occupation and burials at 'Athlīt continue into the second century B.C. according to Johns.[12] He mentions "red varnished" ware resembling *terra sigillata* and the presence of molded lamps as supporting this contention. There was also a second century B.C. coin.[13] The affinities with *terra sigillata* lose their chronological significance when it is recognized that Eastern Sigillata A was not introduced nearly as early as was generally believed when Johns wrote in 1932. Broneer's contention that molded lamps begin to appear about 200 B.C. is also refuted.[14] The second century coin was found in a tomb without second century B.C. pottery. Actually, only two of the published ceramic forms certainly belong to the period 200 B.C.–A.D. 70. These are a lamp and a piriform unguentarium from the mixed debris of Tomb L 21 B; they have parallels from near the beginning of the Christian era.[15]

Yet, one pottery group should be mentioned because it could date from the first years of the second century B.C. This group comes from Tomb L 24 which also contained earlier material.[16] One bowl is very similar in form to the common small bowl with everted rim in Hellenistic Decorated Ware.[17] The fusiform unguentaria could certainly belong to the early second century B.C., but the black design on the example illustrated could indicate an earlier date.[18] The bowl with incurved rim[19] is certainly ubiquitous in the second century B.C., but it also could come from the third

---

10. Grant and Wright, *Ain Shems IV*, Pl. LXIX:2 // Corpus 11.1.A; Pl. LXIX:5 // 12.1.C. Grant, *Ain Shems II*, Pl. L:24 // 81.1; Pl. L:26 // 81.2.

11. The many folded lamps from Beth-zur (*CBZ*, Fig. 41), which was virtually abandoned ca. 100 B.C., assure a second century date for this type.

12. C. N. Johns, "Excavations at Pilgrims' Castle, 'Athlit, (1932)," *QDAP*, III (1933), pp. 149, 147.

13. C. N. Johns, "Excavations at 'Athlit (1930–31)," *QDAP*, II (1932), p. 59.

14. Johns cites this opinion, *QDAP*, II, p. 98. Contrast, *e.g.*, Howland's Type 46C which dates to the last half of the third century B.C.

15. The lamp, *QDAP*, II, Pl. XXVI:619 // Corpus 83.2.A. The unguentarium, *QDAP*, II, Fig. 47=PAM 684 resembles Corpus 92.E.

16. *QDAP*, II, pp. 94ff.

17. *QDAP*, II, p. 95, Fig. 77 // Corpus 151.3, cf. esp. A. Contrary to the statement of Johns (*QDAP*, II, pp. 52 and 94–95) the shape does not have close affinities to any sigillata forms. Note that the parallel from the HFW at Samaria could belong with the third century elements of that deposit.

18. *QDAP*, II, p. 98 and Fig. 82=PAM 926. P. Kahane notes that this is the earliest context in which a fusiform unguentarium has been found in Palestine. *Kahane I*, p. 132.

19. *QDAP*, II, p. 51, Fig. 4 J // Corpus 51.1.

century. Likewise, the lamp[20] could belong in the latter part of the third century or beginning of the second century B.C.[21]

This evidence indicates that there is no published pottery from 'Athlît certainly of the second century B.C. although some of the pottery of Tomb L 24 might have been made just after 200 B.C.

Bethany

Aside from the early deposit in Cistern 61 discussed in Chapter III comparatively little of the published pottery from Bethany belongs to the period 200 B.C.—A.D. 70. None of the other loci with pottery from this period provide homogeneous groups. The fact that very little later Hellenistic Decorated Ware or early Eastern Sigillata A was recovered during the excavations correlates well with this observation.[22]

Saller has made an admirable attempt to segregate the pottery forms chronologically on the basis of a broad knowledge of the evidence available up to 1957. Unfortunately, a substantial portion of his judgments could be correlated only with subjective opinions about the dating of specific forms, and, where stratigraphical evidence was available, it was not usually given a higher value than subjective opinion. Despite this, most of the pottery to be related to the Corpus is presented in the "Late Hellenistic—Early Roman" groups.[23] Much of this material cannot be profitably discussed because it is (properly) published only by verbal description or because photographic reproduction is inadequate. Material attributed to this period because of its "predominant context" is also excluded if it has no parallels in the basic Corpus; in such cases the material may well belong with other elements of the context.[24] Material included in this period by dubious affinities in ware has also been ignored.[25]

Loci with more than isolated material from the period under study are 5, 10, 15, 65, and 69.[26] Parallels for lamps and an unguentarium date a pottery group from Locus

---

20. *QDAP*, II, Pl. XXXIV:907 = PAM 875. The profile parallels Corpus 83.1.A.
21. The parallels cited from Samaria (*HE I*, p. 320, Fig. 191:1 3a and Fig. 192:1 9a) are not close and, in any case, their contexts are not of precise chronological significance. No precise parallels of chronological significance for this lamp (or for the earlier forms of this lamp illustrated in *QDAP*, III, Pl. LIX:2) occur at Athens, Corinth, or in the Corpus. The nozzle of the former resembles those of Broneer's Type XXI, but he states that these lamps are made of the same clay as the Ephesus Type XIX, which he admits goes back to the early second century B.C. Cf. the discussion of Kahane, *Kahane I*, where a Delian parallel is cited. The dating suggested is based on subjective typological considerations, not empirical stratified evidence.
22. *Bethany*, pp. 262, 290.
23. *Bethany*, pp. 197ff., 222ff., et passim.
24. E.g., *Bethany*, p. 275 et passim.
25. Cf., e.g., *Bethany*, pp. 321—22.
26. Pottery coming from Loci 16 and 17 is frequently not distinguished. All the published material exclusively from Locus 17 is probably Persian (cf. *Bethany*, p. 258, No. 836; p. 252, Nos. 793, 794; p. 253, Nos. 735, 753—55). There are two lamps of Corpus Type 82 from Locus 16 (p. 165, Nos. 736, 737), and three others cited from Pits 16—17 may be from Locus 16 also (p. 161, Nos. 748, 750; p. 164, No. 746). The earlier phase of Locus 47 is attributed to the end of the Hellenistic or beginning of the Roman period (cf. p. 167, No. 2666; pp. 255—56, Nos. 2669, 2671; p. 293, No. 2690; p. 296, No. 2674), but the Corpus only assures such a date for the Herodian lamp spout (No. 2666 // 82.1). The only sherd published from Locus 70 possibly of second century B.C. date is a flask (p. 223, No. 4699). Because of the earlier material in the context and its gray ware, this sherd probably belongs to the third century B.C.

5 near the turn of the era if this group should be considered homogeneous.[27] This locus also contained material belonging to the pre-second century B.C. horizon of Columbarium 65[28] and the Byzantine period.[29] From the predominantly Late Roman Cistern 10 come sherds from the same horizon as the early deposit of Cistern 61.[30] Cave 15 contained fragments of a good parallel to a Beth-zur cistern jug, an open lamp, and a Herodian lamp.[31] A jug with pointed base and a bottle may also belong within the period under study,[32] but in this cave with remains from so many chronological periods each sherd must be dated independently. Most of the material from Columbarium 65 belongs to the Persian or Early Hellenistic Periods, but subsequent periods are represented down to medieval times.[33] Sherds representing jug, juglet, and cooking pot types probably belong to the latter part of the second century B.C. while fragments of small folded lamps may be from the same time or as much as a century later.[34] Locus 69 is described as containing Late Hellenistic and Roman sherds.[35] Actually the Hellenistic material published consists largely of Hellenistic Decorated Ware which by ware and form probably belongs to the latter part of the third century B.C.[36] The early first century A.D. seems an appropriate date for the piriform unguentarium and the early Eastern Sigillata A.[37]

Besides the material from the above loci only a few cooking pots and a jug have Corpus parallels.[38]

Bethel

W. F. Albright's earlier work at Bethel has recently been resumed by J. L. Kelso. His work has tended to confirm Albright's delimitation of three phases of oc-

---

27. *Bethany*, p. 161, Nos. 1932, 666, and 667 // Corpus 81.1; p. 167, Nos. 664 and 665 // 82.1; p. 229, No. 669 // 92.

28. *Bethany*, p. 226, Nos. 709, 708 (cf. *CBZ*, Pl. X:15 and n. 67 *infra*); p. 290, No. 714; p. 292, No. 675.

29. *Bethany*, p. 207, Nos. 706, 707.

30. *Bethany*, p. 293, No. 7256 // Corpus 21.1.P; p. 294, No. 7218 // 21.1.M; p. 167, No. 7269, 7270 // 82.1.

31. *Bethany*, p. 289, No. 7119 // Corpus 21.1.G; p. 159 and Fig. 33:2 // 81.1; p. 167, No. 7105 // 82.1.

32. *Bethany*, p. 225, No. 7108; p. 227, No. 7161.

33. For medieval material cf. *Bethany*, p. 250, Nos. 1457, 1453, 5139; p. 287, Nos. 5130–31.

34. *Bethany*, pp. 289–90 and Fig. 60, Nos. 5105, 5106, 5226 // 21.1.G; p. 292 and Fig. 38, No. 5117 // 32.1.A; p. 237 and Fig. 46, No. 5142, // 71.1.A; pp. 160–61, Nos. 5063–5066, 5072 // 81.1; p. 165, Nos. 5189, 5192, // 81.2. The large number of small folded lamps from Beth-zur assures a second century B.C. date for this type (cf. *infra*).

35. *Bethany*, p. 152.

36. *Bethany*, p. 255, No. 4731; p. 290, No. 5037.

37. *Bethany*, p. 229, No. 5061 // Corpus 92; p. 260, Nos. 4957, 4949, 4951–4954.

38. *Bethany*, p. 237 and Fig. 46, No. 5142 // 71.1.A; p. 241 and Fig. 46, No. 4538 // 71.1.N$_2$; p. 242 and Fig. 46, Nos. 4872, 5213, 3987 // 72.2; p. 294 and Fig. 59, No. 612 // 21.1.Q–R.

cupation between the fourth century B.C. and A.D. 69.³⁹ These periods are from the end of the fourth century B.C. to about 160 B.C., from about 135 to 63 B.C., and from about 4 B.C. to A.D. 70. Kelso has kindly made available to the writer drawings of Hellenistic and Early Roman pottery from the 1934 and 1957 campaigns. A study of this material indicates that Albright's datings are correct except that the earliest Hellenistic pottery belongs to the late third, not the fourth, century B.C. Until the pottery is published in detail no further comment seems profitable, but it is of significance that the material does provide independent confirmation of some of the distinctions made in the Corpus between earlier and later second century B.C. forms.

Bethlehem

A globular juglet from Shepherds' Field and a piriform unguentarium from a tomb at Bethlehem are reported by Bagatti.[40]

Beth-shan

The published Hellenistic and Roman pottery from Beth-shan is of very little significance for a variety of reasons. First, and foremost, no stratification was observed below the Byzantine buildings,[41] and the closest thing to observed stratification in these periods is the distinction between Hellenistic and Roman levels east of the Temple Area.[42] Further, information about the pottery published is not given consistently. Frequently provenience or ware description is lacking; slip, wash, varnish, and glaze appear to be at times confused;[43] parallels cited are often questionable.[44] Finally, the datings of some of the forms and developments have changed so radically in the thirty years since the Beth-shan publication was prepared that a great number of statements are now completely misleading.[45]

A few loci are worth brief attention. Rooms 1040 and 1041 are considered Hellenistic by Fitzgerald although Room 1041 contained an Iron II juglet.[46] The distinctive ware found in these rooms probably is Hellenistic, but most likely earlier than the second century B.C. The two levels east of the Temple Area can be roughly

---

39. W. F. Albright, "The First Month of Excavation at Bethel," *BASOR*, 55 (Sept., 1934), p. 24, and "The Kyle Memorial Excavation at Bethel," *BASOR*, 56 (Dec., 1934), p. 14. *V.* also J. L. Kelso, "Excavations at Bethel," *BA*, XIX (1956), p. 42; "The Second Campaign at Bethel," *BASOR*, 137 (Feb., 1955), pp. 5–10; and "The Third Campaign at Bethel," *BASOR*, 151 (Oct., 1958), pp. 3–8.

40. P. B. Bagatti, *Gli antiche edifici sacri de Betlemme* (Gerusalemme, 1952), p. 261 and *fot.* 106:5 // 31.1.C; p. 263 and *fot.* 107:5 // 92.C.

41. *Beth-shan III*, p. 39.

42. Even here, *e.g.*, *Beth-shan II, II*, p. 15 and Pl. LI:13, an obvious early Roman form is referred to as belonging to the Hellenistic level.

43. Cf., *e.g.*, *Beth-shan II, II*, p. 16.

44. The use of Galling's lamp classification is especially objectionable, *Beth-shan III*, p. 40.

45. A common Byzantine lamp type was considered Hellenistic (*Beth-shan III*, Pl. XXXVI:25 and p. 40) while the Herodian lamp was "also well-known in Byzantine times" (p. 40). Fitzgerald dates the lamp, Pl. XXXVI:2, to the early first century B.C. whereas it should be dated in the last half of the third century B.C. (cf. Howland Type 45). That "the transition to the general use of red-glazed ware" began about 250 B.C. (p. 39) is not supported by evidence now available.

46. *Beth-shan II, II*, Pl. LI:19.

dated to the second century B.C. and near the onset of the Christian era.[47] The *terminus ante quem* of the earlier level was probably 107 B.C., when Hyrcanus captured Beth-shan. The general paucity of Hellenistic Decorated Ware as compared with the amount of Eastern Sigillata A and related wares may indicate a *floruit* for Beth-shan after the Gabinian rebuild about 57 B.C.[48] A few other miscellaneous forms with Corpus parallels may be noted.[49]

Beth-shearim

Rhodian jar handles from the excavations are dated in the second century B.C.[50] Practically no pottery has yet been published so no further conclusions are possible.[51]

Beth-yerah

"Fine samples of Hellenistic household ware" are reported from houses overlooking the Sea of Galilee at this site.[52] Rhodian jars and coins indicate Ptolemaic occupation, but conclusions regarding second century B.C. occupation must await detailed reports and the publication of the pottery.[53]

Beth-zur

Included in the published Hellenistic pottery from the 1931 campaign at Beth-zur is the pottery considered post-exilic and pre-Roman.[54] Only rarely was it possible to distinguish between Persian and Hellenistic pottery.[55] Much of the pottery published[56] is not described in detail as to provenience or ware. It follows that this material is not of chronological significance for the Corpus, and only close parallels should be noted.

---

47. Belonging to the second century B.C. level are *Beth-shan II*, II, Pl. XLIX:40 // Corpus 71.1.A; L:4 // 151.3.B; L:5 // 353.2.A; L:11 // 151.5; L:19 // 151.4.B–C; L:20, 21 // 158; LI:11 // 91.2.B; LI:12 // 29.A (neck differs); and possibly LI:14 // 52.9.A (cf. *CBZ*, Pl. XIII:23, and *infra*, n. 67). To the Roman level belong *Beth-shan II*, II, Pl. XLIX:30 // Corpus 12.E; L:7, 8 // 53.H–N.

48. *Beth-shan III*, p. 38. Cf. *Beth-shan I*, p. 46. Hellenistic Decorated Ware and Eastern Sigillata A in *Beth-shan III*, Pl. XXXIV, with Corpus parallels are as follows: 1, 8 // 151.1; 2 // 151.3.A; 3 // 151.5; 6 // 153.1.J; 15, 16, 25, 29 // 251.2; 30 // 251.2a; 7, 9, 14, 18–21 // 251.6; 11 // 252.2; 28 // 253.1.J; 32 // 253.1.K; 23 // 253.1.L; 31 // 253.4.G; 22, 35 // 254.2.

49. *Beth-shan II*, II, Pl. LI:13 // Corpus 21.2.C; L:25, 30 // 65; L:26 // 82.1; LI:17 // 91.1. *Beth-shan III*, Pl. XXXVI:1 // Corpus 82.1.B; XXVIII:3b // 83.3; XXXIII:21 // 91.1.D; XXIV:39, 41 // 354.2.

50. N. Avigad, "Excavations at Beth She'arim, 1953: Preliminary Report," *IEJ*, IV (1954), p. 92; "Excavations at Beth She'arim, 1954: Preliminary Report," *IEJ*, V (1955), p. 211. Cf. B. Mazar, "The Eighth Season of Excavations at Beth She'arim, 1956," *BIES*, XXI (1957), p. 161, Fig. 4:23–24.

51. Mazar, *BIES*, XXI, Fig. 4:19, is a Megarian bowl, but lack of detailed description makes close dating impossible. The same is true of Fig. 4:16, which belongs with Corpus 151.3, and Fig. 4:20 and 21 (West Slope Technique). These are considered early Roman, but mere examination of the published forms suggests that a late Hellenistic date is more likely.

52. *IEJ*, III (1955), p. 132.

53. B. Maisler, M. Stekelis, and M. Avi-Yonah, "The Excavations at Beth Yerah (Khirbet el-Kerak) 1944–1946," *IEJ*, II (1952), pp. 166, 222–23. Cf. *IEJ*, V (1955), p. 273.

54. *CBZ*, p. 15, n. 7.

55. *CBZ*, p. 15.

56. *CBZ*, Figs. 33–42 and Pls. X–XIII.

Fortunately, after the 1957 campaign, some of the 1931 Hellenistic pottery was discovered in an attic of the American School of Oriental Research in Jerusalem and could be studied by locus and correlated with material of chronological significance from the 1931 Object Register available in the Palestine Archaeological Museum through the courtesy of Mr. Yusef Saad. Since the details of this analysis can make no independent contribution to chronological precision in dating Hellenistic pottery, their discussion here would be inappropriate. The few loci selected for discussion below are merely further illustrations of the effectiveness of the Corpus as a tool for isolating homogeneous pottery groups.

Although no chronologically significant objects were recovered from Locus 29, the thirty-eight potsherds available can belong (as a group) only to the latter part of the second century B.C. because of their close affinities with Beth-zur I. In addition to fragments of jars, jugs, bowls, and cooking pots[57] there were several sherds of the poorest quality of Hellenistic Decorated Ware. Accordingly, the "inn" with pillared animal stalls which comprised Locus 29[58] was in use in the latter part of the second century B.C.

Loci 41 and 43 "across the street" from the "inn"[59] contained pottery of the same horizon. Only fragments of a bowl[60] and very poor quality Hellenistic Decorated sherds remained from Locus 41. There were evidently two levels of occupation excavated in Locus 43. A third century B.C. level is indicated by coins[61] and a number of sherds with third century B.C. characteristics, especially some better quality Hellenistic Decorated Ware. An occupation level belonging to the latter part of the second century B.C. is indicated by a coin of Antiochus Euergetes (137—129 B.C.) and a number of pottery types.[62]

The two coins of Antiochus Epiphanes[63] and two Rhodian handle stamps dated 220—180 B.C.[64] from Locus 67 point to affinities with Beth-zur II. A number of sherds,[65] including some of heavier ware than is common in Beth-zur I, confirm a link with Beth-zur II and provide a dating for a locus within the citadel proper.[66]

---

57. Corpus types represented in this group include 11.2. C, 21.1. F—G, 51.1. B, 53. D, 71.1. C—D, 71.2, and 91.1.

58. *CBZ*, p. 19 and Fig. 8.   59. *Ibid.*

60. Corpus 53. D.

61. Coin Nos. 94, 420, and 458 from the 1931 Object Register.

62. Coin No. 177 from the 1931 Object Register. Pottery types: Corpus 21.1. F—G, 31.1. C, 53. D, and 71.2 (several sherds of each type).

63. Coin Nos. 589 and 658 from the 1931 Object Register.

64. Nos. 555 and 560 from the 1931 Object Register=*CBZ*, p. 54: A, 8 and B, 5.

65. Cf. Corpus 11.2. A and B, 21.1. A, 51.1. B, 71.1. F. *CBZ*, Pl. X:14, XI:10, and XIII:22 and 24 are from Cistern 67, and a parallel to Pl. XI:11 also occurred there. Cf. end of n. 67.

66. This locus also contained Iron II material. *CBZ*, pp. 22—23.

A substantial portion of the Hellenistic pottery published in *CBZ* belongs to the second century B.C., and there are a few vessels with their closest parallels in the first century B.C.[67]

---

67. This parallels the quantitative distribution of the coins from the 1931 campaign. *CBZ*, p. 70. A tentative examination of the remaining Hellenistic forms indicates that most of them belong to two periods. The earlier period, from exilic times to *ca.* 430 B.C., is represented primarily by sherds from the reservoir, Locus 44 (*CBZ*, Fig. 38: three of the incised fragments; Pl. X:15; XI:6). Although this locus contained later material (cf. pp. 29–31, 73–74 [No. 9], and Fig. 41), the pottery available to the writer from this locus appeared to be a homogeneous deposit probably belonging to the horizon of the fifth century B.C. Athenian drachma (p. 71, No. 2=1931 Object Register No. 96). The ware decorated by triangular incision has been reported from a late Iron II context at Ramat Rahel, but the ware of the Locus 44 examples is unparalleled in Iron II times. Cf. Aharoni, *IEJ*, VI, p. 143. There appears to be no ceramic (and little numismatic) material belonging to the century before the appearance of Alexander the Great. Pottery that probably belongs to the late fourth and third centuries B.C. includes Pls. XI:4, 9, 14; XII:2 (cf. Fig. 37), 9; XIII:8, 9. Pls. X:10 and XI:12 have no parallels in post-Iron II contexts.

Parallels to Corpus forms summarized in tabular form below are of the second century B.C. except where indicated otherwise. A few loci are dated if they contain a homogeneous pottery group and correlative coins.

Corpus Type	CBZ Reference	Observations
11.2.B	Pl. XII:8=Fig. 34	Locus 215
	Pl. XII:10, 11	Locus 50
21.1.A–H	Pl. XI:1, 2	
	Fig. 36:base and sherd above to the right	
	Fig. 37:first four sherds	
	Fig. 38:first sherd	
21.1.J–Q	Pl. XI:3	First century B.C. parallels; Fig. 36 sherd cannot be distinguished from examples of this type from Qumrân Ib.
	Fig. 36:sherd following globular juglet	
29.B	Fig. 36:first sherd	Locus 102
29.C	Fig. 36:sixth sherd left to right	
31.1.C	Pl. XII:3 (cf. Fig. 36: whole specimen and sherd)	
	Pl. XII:4	Locus 28
	Pl. XII:5	Locus 101
41.L	Fig. 38:third sherd	
51.1	Pl. XIII:14–21 (cf. Fig. 39, top)	Pl. XIII:20 from Locus 29, dated 140–100 B.C.
53	Pl. XIII:3–7, 10–13	
71.1.D	Pl. X:3, 8	Pl. X:3 has no handles.
71.1.G	Pl. X:2	Rim variant
71.1.J	Pl. X:6	Locus 204, 175–100 B.C.; rim variant
71.1.L	Pl. X:1, 5, 7	Locus 204, 175–100 B.C.; Pl. X:1 has two handles; first century B.C. parallels
72.1.D	Pl. XI:5	Locus 164; stance variant
72.1.J	Pl. X:4	Pl. X:4 is a deep type!
81.2	Fig. 41 (11 examples)	Few have rounded bases; parallels are of the first century B.C., but the history of the site demands a second century B.C. date for most of the numerous examples.

Little need be said of the Hellenistic pottery from Fields I and III of the 1957 campaign at Beth-zur. The material from these fields has been compared with that from the stratified deposits in Field II discussed in Chapter II and, being unstratified, is of no independent significance.[68] Except for Locus 279, sherds indicating occupation in the latter part of the second century B.C. were excavated only in Loci 282, 285, and 292 of Field III, and only Locus 282 offered a homogeneous pottery group of the Beth-zur I horizon. Other loci contained material related to Beth-zur II or slightly earlier. Sherds belonging to the third century or Persian Period were rare.

A few individual vessels should be mentioned. A lid with vertical sides[69] came from Locus 282. Since the Hellenistic pottery of this locus formed a homogeneous group belonging to the latter part of the second century and the ware of the lid indicates a date definitely earlier than Qumrân Ib,[70] this type of lid must have been in use by the end of the second century B.C. The large store jar from Locus 283[71] also probably belongs with its homogeneous context to the early second century B.C. A folded lamp[72] should be mentioned because it comes from a context that indicates a date early in the second century B.C.

Caesarea

Hellenistic ruins and pottery and a large public building of the Herodian Period with *terra sigillata* and Augustan coins are reported.[73]

Dothan

A Hellenistic level over five feet in depth is reported from the "acropolis" at Dothan, and the excavator suggests a settlement between 300 and 100 B.C.[74] Since

83.1	Fig. 42 (second column)	
83.2	Fig. 42 (third and fourth columns)	
91.1.A–S	Pl. X:14=Fig. 39:left	Illustrated in the Corpus
91.1.C	Pl. X:16	Locus 183
91.1.B–S	Pl. X:13	Illustrated in the Corpus; cf. 91.1.D
91.2.B	Pl. X:12	Locus 28; first century B.C. parallels
151.4	Fig. 39:two sherds right center	
153.1.H	Pl. XIII:1=Fig. 40:lower left	
	Pl. XIII:2	
158	Fig. 33:2	Locus 28

Not included in the table are the miniature vessels of Pl. XIII:22–26. Since Pl. XIII:22 and 24 come from a context containing much material from the first half of the second century B.C. (cf. n. 65), at least these two miniatures could belong to this time. Cf. *Beth-shan II, II*, Pl. LI:14, and *HE I*, Fig. 181, neither of which are chronologically helpful.

68. Cf. also the discussion of Locus 279, pp. 49–50 *supra*.
69. No. 1906 // Corpus 62.B.
70. The Qumrân Ib ware is much harder and more finely levigated.
71. No. 1922 // *CBZ*, Fig. 34, and Corpus 11.2.B.
72. No. 1260 // Corpus 81.2.
73. *IEJ*, VI (1956), p. 260.
74. J. P. Free, "The Excavation of Dothan," *BA*, XIX (1956), pp. 47–48. Cf. J. P. Free, "The Second Season at Dothan," *BASOR*, 135 (Oct., 1954), p. 15.

Roman sherds are only reported "at the top" of the acropolis[75] and do not indicate a general settlement of the tell, this site can probably be added to the considerable number of sites which were abandoned between about 150 and 40 B.C.

Elusa

A Hellenistic cemetery is reported.[76]

En-gedi

In the En-gedi area a cave in the Wâdi es-Sudeir was discovered near the top of a cliff. It contained pottery of several periods including Hellenistic and Roman. Two of the sherds from the cave have Corpus parallels.[77]

Gezer

The extremely confused state of the Gezer publication makes it necessary to deal with the published material without serious attention to the chronological discussion and classification of the text.[78] The separation and analysis of Hellenistic pottery at the site has never been attempted in detail. A cursory examination indicates that much of it belongs before 200 B.C., and all that is attempted here is the delimitation of the second century B.C. material. This material is not published by group or locus because there was no good group for the later ware of the Hellenistic Period.[79] This means that the only significant result of this analysis can be the determination of the date of Gezer's abandonment by an analysis of the latest pottery from the tell.

The problem of the date of abandonment has been reopened by the recent discovery by Y. Yadin that Macalister's "Maccabean" gateway (and, thus, his Maccabean fortress) is actually Solomonic.[80] This makes unnecessary the hypothesis of Macalister that there was a Syrian reoccupation shortly after Simon's capture of the city in 143 B.C. This hypothesis was necessary to account for the "Syrian Bath" that was erected over what was thought to be Simon's fortress.[81]

An examination of the ceramic evidence indicates that there is no compelling reason to date any of the material from the tell after 143 B.C.[82] A very few vessels

---

75. J. P. Free, "The Third Season at Dothan," *BASOR*, 139 (Oct., 1955), p. 5.

76. *IEJ*, IV (1954), p. 50.

77. Y. Aharoni, "Archaeological Survey of 'Ein Gedi," *BIES*, XXII (1958), p. 43, Fig. 14:5 // 71.1.D; Fig. 14:7 // 12.E.

78. In *TBM III*, p. 143, Albright refers to the fact that Gezer Iron II pottery was dated to the Persian or even the Hellenistic Period.

79. *Gezer II*, p. 226.

80. Y. Yadin, "Solomon's City Wall and Gate at Gezer," *IEJ*, VIII (1958), pp. 80—86. Cf. Y. Aharoni, "The Date of Casemate Walls in Judah and Israel and Their Purpose," *BASOR*, 154 (Apr., 1959), pp. 35—39, esp. p. 36.

81. *Gezer I*, pp. 37, 209—223, 228. On p. 37 Macalister admits that there is no literary evidence for a Syrian occupation after Simon's destruction in 143 B.C.

82. The provenience of much of the material in the *Gezer III* plates is unspecified, and some of it may be from tombs. In any case, the following observations may be made. The folded lamps, *Gezer II*, Fig. 368, do not have second century B.C. Corpus parallels, but cf. the remarks about this form in the discussion of Beth-zur, *supra*, n. 67. There is no evidence for limiting the provenience of the form to the

indicate that there was some later use of Gezer tombs.[83] Accordingly, the "Syrian Bath" was probably destroyed by Simon, and his resettlement of Gezer with Law-observing Jews must have consisted of a small community which lasted only a short time.

Hazor

Yadin has been hesitant about dating Stratum I at Hazor although in one place he attributes it to the second century B.C.[84] Some of the published material from Stratum I has close affinities with Persian Stratum II as the excavators recognize.[85] The affinities with Stratum II are much closer than with the second century B.C. material of the Corpus. Therefore, a second century date for the "Hellenistic" citadel is probably excluded.

Jaffa

A Hellenistic level and building remains are reported.[86] Nearby a line of small Hellenistic (Maccabean?) forts along the Yarkon River has also been discovered.[87]

---

last third of the second century B.C. The Megarian bowl fragments, *Gezer III*, Pl. CLXXVII:1–13, appear to be similar to those from the PHFW at Samaria (Corpus 158.A–B). They were not introduced at Samaria until after 150 B.C. (cf. p. 33 *supra*); the examples from Gezer may be from a recently introduced form, but it is not impossible that they were introduced at Gezer before 150 B.C. since they occur earlier elsewhere (cf., *e.g.*, p. 66 *supra*). Pl. CLXXVII:18 (black glaze) // 353.1.A (may be third century B.C.). Pl. CLXXX:6 // 71.1.B. Pl. CLXXX:8 // 71.1.A. Pl. CLXXXI:7 // 53.B. Pl. CLXXXI:10 // 91.1 (?). Pl. CLXXXI:11 // 31.1.C. Pl. CLXXXI:15 // 51.1.A (parallel not exact, but this type is not significant for chronological precision). Pl. CLXXXIII:3 // 83.1.A. The lamps with ray motif in the Corpus come from the first century B.C., but those from Gezer (and related types) display earlier characteristics and need not postdate 143 B.C. Note the sheaths of Pl. CLXXXIII:10, 11, 13, 14, and 22, and the well-developed "S" knob on the right in Pl. CLXXXIII:7, 16–19. Cf. *Broneer*, p. 64.

To be sure, 1 Macc. 13:43–53 mentions Simon's resettlement, but there is no indication of the number of settlers or how long this community lasted. The Gezer boundary inscriptions, which Cross wants to date *ca.* A.D. 50–70, do not necessarily imply communal occupation of the mound at that time. Cf. Frank M. Cross, Jr., "The Oldest Manuscripts from Qumran," *Journal of Biblical Literature*, LXXIV (1955), p. 163, n. 34. The same is true of the Gezer seal, which is likely of the same date. Contrast the dating, of N. Avigad, "Epigraphical Gleanings from Gezer," *PEQ*, 1950, p. 49.

83. Tomb 8 contained three Herodian lamps (Pl. LXIX:9 // 82.1.B) in addition to several Byzantine lamps (*Gezer I*, p. 307). Note, incidentally, the typical Herodian lamp classified with pottery of the Arab Period (Pl. CLXXXIX:1)! That this admittedly "Hellenistic" form is actually Arabic because the top is "rather flatter" than the Hellenistic form is hardly credible (*Gezer II*, p. 229). Pl. LXXXIII:31 is another lamp that may belong to the first century B.C. (cf. Corpus 83.2.A) from Tomb 58 (*Gezer I*, p. 324). Tombs 103 and 227 contained pottery probably of the first half of the second century B.C. Pl. XCVII:1–5 // Corpus 83.1.A. Pl. XCVII:7 // 91.1.D. Pl. CVII:20 // 51.1. Cf. *Gezer I*, pp. 340–42 (Tomb 103) and 386 (Tomb 227).

84. Y. Yadin, "Excavations at Hazor, 1956: Preliminary Communique," *IEJ*, VII (1957) p. 121. Cf. Y. Yadin, "Excavations at Hazor, 1955: Preliminary Communique," *IEJ*, VI (1956), p. 125; "Excavations at Hazor, 1957: Preliminary Communique," *IEJ*, VIII (1958), pp. 4, 7.

85. *Hazor I*, Pl. LXXIX:1–16 and pp. 63–64.

86. *IEJ*, VI (1956), p. 259; cf. *IEJ* III (1953), p. 132.

87. *IEJ*, I (1950–51), p. 249.

Jericho

A few vessels from the early German excavations indicate some use of the tell in the second and/or first centuries B.C.[88] The publication of the vessels is not precise enough to make it possible to suggest a more exact date. Since no provenience is given, they may merely indicate burials in the vicinity of the tell. Early Roman burials of the Qumrân II horizon are also reported by Miss Kenyon in her excavations at Jericho.[89]

Jerusalem and environs

Three pottery groups from Jerusalem of some corroborative chronological significance for the Corpus have been discussed in Chapter III. There remain a number of small published groups which seem to make no independent contribution to the chronological precision of the Corpus and which are not of enough importance *per se* to merit individual treatment in this study. Some of these groups come from small excavations at Jerusalem, but most of them come from the ossuary *kokhim* which honeycomb the hillsides around Jerusalem.

Some of the pottery forms from the latter have been subjected to a detailed study by P. Kahane in connection with his investigation of the problem of the "Hellenization of Jewry in the Herodian Period."[90] A criticism of the implications drawn for the process of Hellenization in the Herodian Period may be found in Appendix A, but certain observations are in order at this point on some of the chronological conclusions reached in Kahane's study. Basically, they are derived from a methodology comparable to that of Thompson at the Agora which has been criticized above.[91] The extensive search for parallels to the ossuary pottery types has not been accompanied by a systematic, critical evaluation of the dates assigned the parallel forms. While the broad dating of forms on this basis is in general agreement with the empirical evidence presented in this study, the following points should be noted. The globular cooking pot (Kahane's Type A), which Kahane considers one phase in the development of the common Palestinian cooking pot from Late Bronze to Arab times, shows a definite development near the turn of the era.[92] Kahane's cooking pot Type B needs reinvestigation in the light of evidence that this type does occur in other contexts than ossuary tombs[93] and the fact that there were at least three types of open cooking pots,[94] one of which was

---

88. Ernst Sellin and Carl Watzinger, *Jericho* (Leipzig, 1913), p. 148 and Abb. 174:J.4 // Corpus 151.9; p. 148 and Abb. 176:J.8 // 158; p. 148 and Blatt 40:J.6 // 91.1; J.9 // 83.2; p. 161 and Blatt 43:11b // 71.1; p. 141 and Abb. 151 // 81.2.

89. Kenyon, *Digging Up Jericho*, p. 264.

90. Three installments of the study, entitled "Pottery Types from the Jewish Ossuary-Tombs around Jerusalem," have appeared (*Kahane I-III*). Cf. *Kahane I*, p. 126, for the statement of the author's purpose.

91. Pp. 71—72 *supra*. Kahane considers Thompson's work a "model as regards the well-balanced treatment of details (in the catalogue) and of the general problems (in its summary)." *Kahane I*, p. 127.

92. Pp. 19—20 *supra*.

93. Corpus 72.2. Cf. references cited. The example from the North Wall of Jerusalem was published some years before Kahane's study!

94. Cf. Corpus 72.1—3.

not uncommon in the third and second centuries B.C. Though this type of cooking pot was not used as commonly as Type A, there is no reason why it must be considered "independent to a great extent of local ceramic tradition."[95] Precise parallels to the sharp-shouldered Type B occur only in first century A.D. contexts in the Corpus, but this may be due to the limited extent of chronologically significant material available. It is also possible that this form is a first century A.D. type developed from the earlier shallow cooking pots.[96] In any case, there is no evidence outside Palestine to support a non-Palestinian origin.[97]

The chronological treatment of the piriform unguentarium variants[98] is open to serious question. The claim that variant b[99] has early exemplars at Chatby and 'Athlît is extremely tenuous. There is no empirical evidence that necessitates the dating of all tombs at the Chatby cemetery to the early third century B.C. and before, and, regarding the example from 'Athlît Tomb L/21 B, Kahane admits that "we do not have any external evidence as to its date."[100] Kahane thinks that variant a (which is very similar to variant b) occurred sometime "during the second half of the first century B.C."[101] The Corpus indicates that there is no certain evidence for the occurrence of this type before the Christian era.

The *kokhim* pottery from the Dominus Flevit excavation deserves at least passing mention. It is published in some detail typologically.[102] It is possible that if the pottery had been published by *kokhim*, earlier and later characteristics might have been distinguishable. In present form only a few vessels are published from any single *kokhim* complex. Five types of vessels from *Kokhim* Complex 65—80[103] have first century A.D. parallels and may well be dated to the middle of the first century A.D., but to be assured of this the publication of a larger group of vessels would be necessary.[104] The problem of the dating of the pottery from Cave 151[105] cannot be solved here. Suffice it to say that none of the forms belong to the period under study.

---

95. *Kahane I*, p. 131.   96. Corpus 72.1.
97. The supposition of a metallic prototype is rejected in Appendix A, n. 42.
98. *Kahane II*.   99. *Kahane II*, Pl. 12:b.
100. *Kahane II*, p. 179.
101. *Kahane II*, p. 179. As evidence from outside Palestine for dating this type, examples from a tomb at Priene and the fort at Haltern are cited. The chronological significance of the Priene group is indicated by the fact that Kahane himself sees fit to alter the date. It is difficult to see how the placing of the Priene example alongside the Haltern example as chronological indicators can be justified. Only Haltern provides independent empirical evidence. *Kahane II*, pp. 179—80.
102. P. B. Bagatti e J. T. Milik, *Gli scavi del "Dominus Flevit,"* Parte I (Gerusalemme, 1958), pp. 110ff.
103. *Ibid.*, pp. 6ff. The vessels from this complex are illustrated in Figs. 25:8; 30:22, 24; 31:7—8; 32:16, 17, 19, 20, 23. Corpus types represented are 82.1.A, 92.C, 72.2.A, 51.1.G, 54.2.G.
104. That there was a great mass of pottery recovered in the excavation is indicated by the reference to ninety-five Herodian lamps, *ibid.*, p. 117, and eighty-six examples of piriform unguentaria, *ibid.*, p. 133.
105. *Ibid.*, p. 122, Fig. 27.

Even exclusive of the Jerusalem groups discussed in Chapter III, a large number of pottery types with Corpus parallels occur in the Jerusalem environs.[106]

---

106. These parallels are summarized in the following table:

Corpus Type	Reference
11.1. A	*Gli scavi del "Dominus Flevit,"* Fig. 28:1.
	P. B. Bagatti, "Scoperta de un cimitero Guideo-Cristiano al 'Dominus Flevit,' (Monte Oliveto-Gerusalemme)," *Liber Annuus*, III (1952–53), p. 176.
	E. L. Sukenik, "The Earliest Records of Christianity," *AJA*, LI (1947), p. 362, Fig. 6:1 (with neck as 12.E!), 2.
11.2. F	R. W. Hamilton, "Note on Excavations at Bishop Gobat's School, 1933," *PEF QS*, 1935, p. 143, Pl. VI:3, 4.
12. C	*Ibid.*, Pl. VI:11.
12. D	Sukenik, *AJA*, Fig. 6:9.
	L. Y. Rahmani, "A Jewish Tomb on Shahin Hill, Jerusalem," *IEJ*, VIII (1958), p. 103, Fig. 2:11.
12. F	Sukenik, *AJA*, Fig. 6:8.
21.1. F	Sukenik, *AJA*, Fig. 6:3.
21.1. L–M	Hamilton, *PEF QS*, 1935, Pl. VI:5, 17.
29. C	F. J. Bliss and A. C. Dickie, *Excavations at Jerusalem* (London, 1898), Pl. XXV:6.
	R. A. S. Macalister and J. G. Duncan, "Excavations on the Hill of Ophel, Jerusalem, 1923–1925," *PEFA*, IV (1923–25), p. 186.
29. G	Hamilton, *PEF QS*, 1935, Pl. VI:16.
31.1. A	*Gli scavi del "Dominus Flevit,"* Fig. 30:1.
31.1. C	Sukenik, *AJA*, Fig. 6:12.
	Excavations at Jerusalem, Pl. XXV:4.
	E. L. Sukenik, "Jewish Tombs in the Kedron Valley," *Kedem*, II (1945), pp. 23–31, Pl. 3:1 (second vessel).
	Hamilton, *PEF QS*, 1935, Pl. VI:1, 13.
	Macalister and Duncan, *PEFA*, IV, p. 186. Note the curious description!
	S. J. Saller, *Discoveries at St. John's, 'Ein Karim, 1941–1942* (Jerusalem, 1946), Pl. 35, 1:1 and 2.
	C. Clermont-Ganneau, *Archaeological Researches in Palestine during the Years 1873–1874* (London, 1899), I, p. 382.
	Kahane III, Pl. 4:2.
31.2. A	Sukenik, *AJA*, Fig. 6:14.
	Sukenik, *Journal of the Jewish Palestine Exploration Society*, Fig. 8 (first vase, upper row).
	Excavations at Jerusalem, Pl. XXVI:30.
	Kahane III, Pl. 4:1.
38. A–S	*Gli scavi del "Dominus Flevit,"* Fig. 30:22 (illustrated in Corpus).
	Excavations at Jerusalem, Pl. XXV:9.
	Bagatti, Fig. 24:10.
38. B–S	*Gli scavi del "Dominus Flevit,"* Fig. 30:26 (illustrated in Corpus).
	Sukenik, *Journal of the Jewish Palestine Exploration Society*, Fig. 8 (second vase, upper row).
51.1. G	Sukenik, *AJA*, Fig. 6:11 (concave base).
	Excavations at Jerusalem, Pl. XXVI:32.
	Bagatti, Fig. 24:3.
	Gli scavi del "Dominus Flevit," Fig. 32:17, 18.

Corpus Type	Reference
51.2.A	Rahmani, Fig. 2:8.
54.2.G	*Gli scavi del "Dominus Flevit,"* Fig. 32:19.
54.2.H	*Ibid.*, Fig. 32:20.
71.1.B	Sukenik, *AJA*, Fig. 6:6, 7.
	Gli scavi del "Dominus Flevit," Fig. 31:2, 5.
71.1.C	*Ibid.*, Fig. 31:1.
71.1.D	*Ibid.*, Fig. 31:3.
71.1.K	Bagatti, Fig. 24:1.
71.1.N$_1$	*Gli scavi del "Dominus Flevit,"* Fig. 31:4.
	H. Vincent, "Chronique, IV. Fouille a l'Angle N.—O. de Jerusalem," *RB*, X (1913), p. 102.
71.1.N$_2$	Sukenik, *AJA*, Fig. 6:4.
	Excavations at Jerusalem, Pl. XXV:2.
	Sukenik, *Kedem*, Pl. 3:1.
	Gli scavi del "Dominus Flevit," Fig. 31:6.
	Archaeological Researches in Palestine, p. 382.
	Rahmani, Fig. 2:7, 9.
71.1.P	Hamilton, *PEF QS*, 1935, Pl. VI:10.
72.2.A	Sukenik, *AJA*, Fig. 6:5.
	Hamilton, *PEF QS*, 1935, Pl. VI:9.
	Gli scavi del "Dominus Flevit," Fig. 31:7, 8.
	E. L. Sukenik, "A Jewish tomb-cave on the slope of Mt. Scopus," *Journal of the Jewish Palestine Exploration Society*, 1934–1935, p. 70, Fig. 8 (lower left).
81.1.A	*Excavations at Jerusalem*, Pl. XXV:3.
	Gli scavi del "Dominus Flevit," Fig. 25:1.
81.2.A	*Excavations at Jerusalem*, Pl. XXV:5.
	Rahmani, Fig. 2:5.
82.1.A	*Gli scavi del "Dominus Flevit,"* Fig. 25:8 (p. 118: 8 examples).
	Sukenik, *AJA*, Pl. LXXXV A (lower left).
82.1.B	*Gli scavi del "Dominus Flevit,"* Fig. 25:7 (p. 117: 95 examples; cf. *Liber Annuus*, III, p. 177).
	Sukenik, *AJA*, Pl. LXXXV A (upper right and central fragment).
	Hamilton, *PEF QS*, 1935, Pl. VI:14.
	Rahmani, Fig. 2:10.
82.1.C	*Gli scavi del "Dominus Flevit,"* Fig. 25:6.
82.1.D	Sukenik, *AJA*, Pl. LXXXV A (lower right).
83.1.A	*Excavations at Jerusalem*, Pl. XXVI:26 (spout more triangular).
83.2.D	Sukenik, *AJA*, Pl. LXXV A (upper left; ray design variant).
	Gli scavi del "Dominus Flevit," Fig. 25:3–5 (various designs).
91.1	Sukenik, *Kedem*, Pl. 3:1 (last fragments).
	Macalister and Duncan, *PEFA*, IV, p. 185.
	"Model of a Columbarium: An Alleged Model of a Sanctuary from the Garden-Tomb Grounds," *PEF QS*, 1924, p. 144, Fig. 2.
	Gli scavi del "Dominus Flevit," Fig. 30:18–20.
	Rahmani, Fig. 2:3, 4.
91.2	*Excavations at Jerusalem*, Pl. XXV:11 (possibly 91.1).
	Hamilton, *PEF QS*, 1935, Pl. VI:2, 15.
	Macalister and Duncan, *PEFA*, IV, p. 185.
	Discoveries at St. John's, 'Ein Karim, p. 69.
	Sukenik, *Journal of the Jewish Palestine Exploration Society*, Fig. 8 (fifth vase, upper row).

Kadesh-naphtali

A Hellenistic stratum is reported.[107]

Khirbet 'Alyata

De Vaux reports a continuous series of sherds from Iron Age to Byzantine at this site. The Roman period is well represented.[108]

Khirbet et-Tuleil

A "stratum" containing Persian and Hellenistic potsherds without associated construction is reported.[109]

Lachish

This is not an appropriate place for a general critique of the methods of analysis and presentation of archaeological evidence exhibited by the Lachish volumes. Pertinent are a few general observations on the dating of certain Hellenistic pottery forms and its underlying methodology. These emphasize the limitations placed upon the subsequent analysis of the *Lachish III* Hellenistic material.

The typological discussion of the Iron Age pottery from Lachish[110] includes attributions of certain pottery forms to the second century B.C. There is no independent evidence from Lachish to establish a conclusive second century B.C. date for any form, and where parallels are cited they are not usually close enough to suggest contemporaneousness and are not often of independent chronological significance. For instance, Types 340 and 341 from Cave 515 are dated to the second century B.C. "judging

Corpus Type	Reference
92. B	Sukenik, *AJA*, Fig. 6:15.
92. C	*Ibid.*, Fig. 6:13.
	Excavations at Jerusalem, Pl. XXV:10.
	Bagatti, Fig. 24:9.
	Gli scavi del "Dominus Flevit," Fig. 30:24, 25 (more bulbous).
	D. C. Baramki, "An Ancient Tomb Chamber at Wa'r Abu es-Safa near Jerusalem," *QDAP*, IV (1935), Pl. 80:10.
	Sukenik, *Journal of the Jewish Palestine Exploration Society*, Fig. 8 (third and fourth vases, upper row).
92.D	*Gli scavi del "Dominus Flevit,"* Fig. 30:21.
	Baramki, *QDAP*, IV, Pl. 80:11.
92. F	*Gli scavi del "Dominus Flevit,"* Fig. 30:23.
151.1. E	*Ibid.*, Fig. 32:15, 16.
151.4. A	*Ibid.*, Fig. 32:21 (?), 22 (?).

Note, finally, a fragment of Eastern Sigillata A (Hamilton, *PEF QS*, 1935, p. 143, Pl. VI:7) which is a molded rim of a flat plate similar to Tarsus Nos. 252–253 discussed in Chap. IV, p. 69 and n. 124.

107. *IEJ*, III (1953), p. 263.

108. R. de Vaux, "Notes archéologiques et topographiques," *RB*, LIII (1946), p. 266. De Vaux refers to other sites with Roman pottery, but it is not certain that any of it can be dated as early as the first century A.D.

109. *IEJ*, IV (1954), p. 127.

110. *Lachish III*, pp. 257ff.

from the associated pottery."¹¹¹ Actually Cave 515 contained nothing that could be dated with certainty to the second century B.C.¹¹² The only other pottery form besides 340 and 341 was a "Mesopotamian" lamp of Type 138 which occurs as early as the sixth century B.C.¹¹³

The cooking pot analysis is quite confused.¹¹⁴ Belonging to the flared neck class are Type 460 which certainly predates the second century B.C., Type 691 which could belong to the early second century B.C., Type 446 from near the end of the second century B.C., and Type 692 which is Byzantine unless the ribbing is exaggerated in the drawing.¹¹⁵ At least such sharp ribbing is unknown in Late Hellenistic and Early Roman times. It is stated that Type 692 came from a fourth-second century B.C. building, but it will be shown that there is no proof of fourth-third century remains in the building and there are post-second century B.C. remains. The cooking pots with straight neck are dated about 450–300 B.C. because of the contexts in which they were found.¹¹⁶ However, Types 688 and 695, for example, are certainly to be dated after 300 B.C., probably to the second century B.C. by comparisons with the Corpus.

These examples point up two major weaknesses in the Lachish methodology. First, there is an attempt to deal chronologically with broad types of vessels without reference to their chronologically distinct features.¹¹⁷ Secondly, objects of known date are used to determine the dating of other material from the same context when its homogeneity is doubtful. This procedure would be dubious solely on the ground that most of the debris from Hellenistic levels in Palestine consists of imported fills. But when any chronological opinion is uncritically accepted for parallels (which are frequently, to say the least, inexact) and when Lachish pottery groups dated in this manner are used to date other Lachish groups, no precise chronological conclusion can possibly be reached. In terms of the purposes of this study, therefore, the typological discussions can be ignored.

In any case, there are a number of Lachish loci that contain pottery forms belonging to the second century B.C. The Solar Shrine is a very doubtful case. Miss Tufnell cites the opinion of Miss du Plat Taylor that the small amount of pottery from this

---

111. *Ibid.*, p. 304.

112. Cf. the list of the objects, *ibid.*, p. 221. Note that the tomb is purported to have been "in frequent use between *ca.* 2000–100 B.C."

113. Wright so dated Tomb 14 at 'Ain Shems where a lamp of this type was found. *Ain Shems V*, pp. 78, 145.

114. *Lachish III*, p. 311.

115. Note also that there is a contradiction between the text and the plates: *Lachish III*, p. 311, states that ribbing reaches "up to the neck" whereas Pl. 104:692 shows the neck (left side only!) ribbed also.

116. *Ibid.*, p. 311. Note the indiscriminate citing of parallels for the class as a whole with dates ranging from 650 B.C. to the fourth century A.D.

117. The details of a form are often obscure even in the drawings of Types 1–492. A striking example is provided by two cooking pots from Tomb 217 (*Lachish III*, p. 202, Fig. 24:16 and 18) which are both assigned to Type 464 although they exhibit chronologically distinguishing features (cf. pp. 19–20 *supra*).

building belongs to the last half of the second century B.C.[118] A date after 150 B.C. is unlikely for any of the pottery types from the Solar Shrine. Parallels from the first half of the second century B.C. could be cited for Types 67, 111, 130, and 376,[119] but Type 465, and possibly 130, do not occur after 200 B.C. Since Types 67 and 111 were found inside jar Type 465 and since it seems that the quality of the Hellenistic Decorated Ware is better and the forms somewhat carefully made, all the pottery from the Solar Shrine could belong to the third century B.C.[120] Since the debris is quite mixed and nothing is definitely associated with the floors, no precise conclusions can be reached regarding the date of construction and use of the building.[121]

South of the Solar Shrine is a building referred to in the publication as R/Q/S. 15/16:10—21.[122] Miss Tufnell avers that the building was in use from the fourth through the early second centuries B.C. on the basis of "fourth-to-third-century forms in the rooms" and a coin of Antiochus Epiphanes.[123] The pottery in the building was a mixture of Iron II, Persian, and Hellenistic forms.[124] One can postulate that if the material above the floors could be segregated it would consist of the Hellenistic forms which can be attributed to the second and first centuries B.C. by Corpus parallels.[125] Parallels from the latter part of the second century B.C. predominated, and the writer is left with the impression that if accurate drawings were available for all the forms represented in this group and if the Corpus were more complete, the group might be dated about 150—100 B.C. Pre-Hellenistic pottery probably comes from beneath the

---

118. *Lachish III*, p. 142.

119. Cf. Corpus 153.1.B, 151.4.B, 151.1.D, and 91.1 respectively.

120. This includes unpublished fragments of a carinated bowl of Hellenistic Decorated Ware from Room 103 and a piece of West Slope Ware in Room 109 or 110.

121. The pottery types from Court 106 are from the end of Iron II, so that the building was probably built on debris resulting from the 588 B.C. destruction. The latest object from the building appears to be a Tyrian coin of 47 B.C. (*Lachish III*, p. 413, No. 43), but this only indicates that debris was dumped in this area subsequent to that date. There were also two third century B.C. and a second century B.C. coin from the building (*Lachish III*, pp. 412—13, Nos. 6, 36, 39). The Mesopotamian lamp from Room 103 should also be noted (cf. n. 113 *supra*).

122. *Lachish III*, pp. 146ff. and Pls. 108 and 123.

123. *Ibid.*, p. 148.

124. Iron II Types include 75, 79, 152, 391, 401, 468, 474, 501 (four examples), 511, 539, 540, 555, 602, 635, and 665. Some of these forms undoubtedly continue into the Persian Period, but definitely Persian are Types 138, 510, and 568.

125. Types 10, 127, and 583 (flat bases!) // Corpus 151.1.C and cf. 51.2.B—C. Types 67 (two examples in the building and one just outside in Locus 20) and 562 // 153.1.B. Types 59 and 60 // 53. H—L. Type 111 // 151.4. Type 130 (three examples) // 151.1, but shape nearer 51.1.G, except for ring base. Type 136 // the form of 83.2.A. Type 139 can perhaps be considered an earlier form of Corpus 84. Type 175 // the form of 71.1.L. Type 349 // rim of 31.1.B. Type 376 // the base, 91.1.D. Type 395 // 65.A. Type 515 // 11.2.F. Type 527 // 11.3.E rim. Type 534 // 11.2.D. Type 535 // 11.2.A. Type 658 is perhaps a slightly later form of 83.1.A. Type 679 // 29.B. No parallels have been cited for Types 407, 486, 514, and 670, but none of them are necessarily suggestive of a fourth or third century B.C. date. The lagynos fragment, Type 670, has good parallels in Athens Group E (110—75 B.C.). In short, the fourth and third century B.C. forms mentioned by Miss Tufnell do not exist.

floors since it seems unlikely that a building so poorly constructed would have been built two centuries before the time indicated by its occupation debris. There is no evidence that this building was in use in the fourth and third centuries B.C. It was probably constructed in the second century B.C.

Immediately south of this building is the Great Shaft which contained mixed debris from Early Bronze to Arab times.[126] The south wall of the building was reinforced possibly after part of the building had slid down the slope of the shaft depression. This could account for the presence of second century B.C. pottery forms in the shaft. This seems more likely than that the depression served as a refuse pit for the occupants of the adjacent building. Such use could have been expected to have a fairly homogeneous level of pottery with parallels from the building, but this was not the case. The second century B.C. forms were mixed with sherds from Early Bronze to Arab times throughout the upper filling of the shaft.[127]

Miss Tufnell suggests that the Gatehouse (G. 18:25—33) was falling into disuse in the third quarter of the third century B.C.[128] A Rhodian stamp attributed to this time suggested this date. While Types 535, 679, and 695 occur in the Corpus, their exact character cannot be recovered in the publication, and, in any case, the development of the forms has not been so precisely traced as to exclude the possibility of a third century B.C. date. Thus, nothing contradicts the dating suggested by Miss Tufnell.

Two tombs from Lachish belong to the period under study. Many of the forms from Tomb 217 have parallels in the Corpus from the second and first centuries B.C.[129] Other forms not represented in the Corpus also probably belong to the same period.[130]

---

126. *Lachish III*, p. 163.

127. Types 138, 376, and 562 from building R/Q/S.15/16:10—21 also occur in the shaft. In addition, Types 382 and 672 // Corpus 91.1 and Type 582 // 151.1.E. It may be noted that the bottom of the shaft contained late Iron II forms (Types 254, 280, 649), but also types hardly earlier than the third century B.C. (Types 68 and 673)! (Note especially the "green slip" of Type 68; cf. Chap. III, n. 263.) These make it possible to postulate that the shaft was carved out, not at the end of Iron II as Starkey thought, but in the third century B.C. The upper part of the shaft can then represent debris from a slide into the shaft in the second century B.C.

128. *Lachish III*, p. 150.

129. The tomb group is drawn in *Lachish III*, p. 202, Fig. 24. Fig. 24:1, 3, and 4 // Corpus 151.1; two of the examples are deeper and all three seem to belong typologically between examples with a more pronounced ring base (151.1.A—D) and those with a concave base (151.1.E—G). Fig. 24:2 (flat base) // 151.1.E. Fig. 24:5 (3 examples) // 151.4.A. Fig. 24:6 // 151.3.F. Fig. 24:8 // 53.H. Fig. 24:14 (with band of red slip just above mid-body) // 21.1.M. Fig. 24:16 // 71.1.N$_1$. Fig. 24:17 // 71.1.A. Fig. 24:18 has similarities to both 71.1.B and C. Fig. 24:19 // 91.1.C.

130. Except for a crater and an unusual "beaker" fragment in Hellenistic Decorated Ware (Fig. 24:7), these are all jugs or juglets which are represented in the Corpus by only a limited number of forms. They seem to belong to a horizon similar to that of Marion Tomb 9 at Cyprus which has been dated ca. 50—25 B.C. (pp. 96—97 *supra*). Cf. Fig. 24:13 with *Cyprus II*, p. 208:23=*IV*, Fig. 28:2. Cf. Fig. 24:10 with *Cyprus II*, p. 208:15=*IV*, Fig. 24:2, and with Corpus 31.2.A. Fig. 24:15 may belong with the bases of Corpus Type 28 and indicate a large jug form of the second century B.C. Type 403 may similarly be a crater of the second century B.C., and in that case would fill in a gap in the Corpus. Fig. 24:13 shows the same tendency to flatten the ring base as Fig. 24:5. These observations do not give precise data, but they do indicate a similar period. The evidence is not conclusive, however, and, since the period in question is greater than a century, the forms are not added to the Corpus.

The repertory of forms indicates that the tomb was in use for at least 150 years.[131] Tomb 1009 is dated about 450 B.C., but the three pottery types represented in it have parallels in the second century B.C.[132]

Makmish

An abandoned Persian sanctuary at this site was used as an open-air cult place in the Hellenistic period. This Hellenistic phase is dated to the third and second centuries B.C. by pottery and coins.[133]

Masada

No pottery has yet been published from the survey of the Herodian fortress of Masada in 1955–1956.[134]

Megiddo

Out of all the published Megiddo pottery only three vessels from tombs have Corpus parallels.[135]

Nahariyah

Hellenistic and Roman pottery is reported from the surface level.[136]

Pella

Hellenistic and Roman remains are reported, but not distinguished, in a preliminary sounding. Two vessels labeled Hellenistic-Roman are published by photograph.[137]

El-Qubeibeh and Khirbatani

Bagatti has recovered coins from the third century B.C. to the fifth century A.D. in excavations at Qubeibeh. Hellenistic and Roman sherds including *terra sigillata* are reported.[138]

---

131. None of the vessels would seem to require a date much before *ca.* 150 B.C., the time when the transition to flat bases was in process for the Hellenistic decorated bowls with incurved rim (cf. p. 30 *supra*). At the other end, the earliest parallel to Fig. 24:16 is from Roman Ia at Samaria (20 B.C–A.D. 20) except for a similar form from Trench A at Qumrân which is not necessarily to be dated 50–31 B.C.

132. *Lachish III*, p. 238. Types 376 and 382 // Corpus 91.1. Type 664 // 31.1.B.

133. *IEJ*, VIII (1958), p. 276; X (1960), pp. 92, 93, 96.

134. M. Avi-Yonah *et al.*, "The Archaeological Survey of Masada, 1955–1956," *BIES*, XXI (1957), pp. 9–77. The English version is found in *IEJ*, VII, (1957), pp. 1–60. P. 12 mentions Hellenistic and Roman pottery.

135. P. L. O. Guy, *Megiddo Tombs* (Chicago, 1938), Pl. 42:31 from Tomb 219 // 91.1.C. Pl. 172:9 is from Tomb 76 A and a similar lamp was found in Tomb 47 // 83.1.A. Cf. pp. 87 and 127.

136. M. Dothan, "The Excavations at Nahariyah: Preliminary Report (Season 1954/1955)," *IEJ*, VI (1956), p. 18.

137. Funk and Richardson, *BA*, XXI, p. 90, describe the locus in which the vessels were found together with "Hellenistic Pergamene" ware. Fig. 4 is a jar that seems to be a good parallel to Corpus 11.2.F from Qumrân Ib. This vessel probably belongs with the "Hellenistic Pergamene," but the other, Fig. 1, is of a much later period, as the base and handle indicate.

138. P. B. Bagatti, *I monumenti di Emmaus el-Qubeibeh e dei Dintorni* (Gerusalemme, 1947), pp. 101, 198, and *fot.* 48:1–13 and 67:1. The photographs make it difficult to make comparisons, but according to descriptions, Corpus Types 41, 53, 82.1, and 83.2.A are certainly represented.

Qumrân Caves and 'Ain Feshkha

Since no coins were found in the caves and no stratification was observed,[139] any dating of the pottery from the caves depends on a correlation of the forms with Qumrân Ib or II.[140] A similar situation obtains at 'Ain Feshkha. "Pour déterminer la céramique attribuable à la Période I, on s'est guidé sur la comparison avec Khirbet Qumrân."[141] While the pottery having closest affinities with Qumrân Ib was generally found at a lower level than that belonging with Qumrân II, the distinction is not based primarily on empirical stratified evidence.[142] A correlation of the pottery groups from the caves and 'Ain Feshkha indicates that they contribute hardly any new forms or variations to the ceramic types from Qumrân Ib and II.

De Vaux attributes most of the pottery from Qumrân Cave I to the Qumrân II horizon, but of a few vessels he concludes: "Nous continuons de penser qu'elles se rattachent à une tradition hellénistique."[143] To the Hellenistic group De Vaux attributed the two jars with handles and the loop-handled lamps with long spouts.[144] De Vaux's assignment of the lamps to this group is a striking illustration of his good judgment, for the campaigns which unearthed Qumrân Ib and produced from it parallels to these lamps had not yet taken place.[145] Similar confirmation has not been forthcoming for the cylindrical jars with handles, but the fact that so few large jars have been recovered from Qumrân Ib could explain this. In any case, the Egyptian parallels cited[146] are not close enough to aid in a precise dating, and the assignment to Ib must remain tentative. Evidence indicates that the flat plates, like the lamps, belong to the Qumrân Ib horizon.[147] The loop-handled lamps with bowed spout, which De Vaux considers imported,[148] may also belong to the earlier group. The remaining forms have parallels in Qumrân II.[149] Note especially the form of the cooking pot which could not precede the first century A.D. Paralleling this ceramic analysis, paleographic study has led to

---

139. *Caves*, p. 553. Cf. R. de Vaux, "Les manuscrits de Qumrân et l'archéologie," *RB*, LXVI (1959), p. 104.

140. There seems to be no reason for postulating that the caves might have been occupied during the gap between Qumrân Ib and II.

141. *Feshkha*, p. 247.

142. *Feshkha*, pp. 237, 244, 247–48.

143. In *DJD I*, p. 12. Cf. his preliminary report, "La grotte des manuscrits Hebreux," *RB*, LVI (1949), p. 587, where he originally suggested a dating in the second century B.C.

144. *DJD I*, Fig. 2:10, 12; 3:4, 5.

145. Corpus 84; cf. *Rapport III*, p. 551.

146. *DJD I*, p. 9. With these jars De Vaux considers E. L. Sukenik (ed.), *The Dead Sea Scrolls of the Hebrew University* (Jerusalem, 1955), Fig. 6, second jar.

147. *DJD I*, Fig. 2:2 and p. 10, where De Vaux states that parallels were not found in the first campaign at the Khirbet which brought to light Qumrân II debris. Cf. p. 19 *supra*.

148. *DJD I*, Fig. 3:1 and p. 11.

149. *DJD I*, Fig. 2:1, 3 // Corpus 51.7. A. Fig. 2:4–9, 3:6–8 // 62. Fig. 2:11, 3:9–11 // 14.1. B. Fig. 3:2 // 71.1. N_2. Fig. 3:3 // 31.1. E. Sukenik, *The Dead Sea Scrolls of the Hebrew University*, Fig. 6, first jar // 14.1. B and lids // 62. Carl H. Kraeling, "A Dead Sea Scroll Jar at the Oriental Institute," *BASOR*, 125 (Feb., 1952), p. 1, jar // 14.1. B and lid // 62.

the conclusion that both the Hasmonean (150—30 B.C.) and the Herodian (30 B.C.—A.D. 70) periods are represented in the Cave I manuscripts.[150]

Exploration in the region of Qumrân revealed twenty-five more caves with pottery like that of Cave I and the Khirbet.[151] Most of the pottery consisted of jars (over a hundred) and lids (about seventy), but there were twenty other pieces.[152] One would expect that most of this pottery would belong to the period just before the final abandonment of the caves in A.D. 68, and parallels to Qumrân II pottery support this contention. One of the few caves with more than isolated forms published in the preliminary report is Cave 8 (=MSS Cave III) where the copper scroll was discovered. All the forms from this cave have close parallels in Qumrân II.[153] The pottery is therefore contemporary with the copper scroll which, from considerations of paleography, is "scarcely earlier than the middle of the first century A.D."[154] Except for Cave 29, similar parallels can be suggested for the published pottery of the other caves.[155]

The loop-handled lamp from Cave 29, like the similar lamps from Cave I, belongs to the Qumrân Ib horizon.[156] One of the large jars from Cave 29 has a short everted neck which is not characteristic of jars of this type from Qumrân II, and it is possible that it is contemporary with the lamp.[157] The other material from this cave has Qumrân II parallels, but evidence does not exclude the possibility that all the pottery from Cave 29 may be of the Qumrân Ib horizon.[158]

The Qumrân II conspectus of forms provides close parallels for most of the 'Ain Feshkha forms presented in the preliminary report.[159] These forms are attributed to Period II which is considered contemporary with Qumrân II. The only form from Period II without published parallels in Qumrân II is Fig. 2:6, which cannot be certainly attributed to this period by its context. Forms attributed to Period I (contemporary with Qumrân I) are presented from Loci 21—22 and debris outside the north wall of the main building. The forms from Loci 21—22 have parallels from Qumrân Ib or

---

150. Cf., e.g., Cross, p. 89, where 1QS is attributed to the earlier and 1QM to the later period.
151. *Caves*, p. 541.   152. *Caves*, p. 552.
153. *Caves*, Fig. 1:1, 2 // 14.1.C. Fig. 2:1 // 14.1.A. Fig. 2:7 // 14.1.B. Fig. 3:2, 5, 9, 10 // 62. Fig. 4:1 // 32.2.A. Fig. 4:2 is a jug with parallels illustrated from Qumrân III (21.2.C). Its occurrence in this cave, which was abandoned by A.D. 68, confirms it as a Qumrân II form.
154. Cross, p. 17, n. 29.
155. *Caves*, Fig. 1:4, 8 // 14.1.B. Fig. 1:10 // 14.2.A. Fig. 2:3 (with four pierced ear handles) // 14.1.C. Fig. 2:4 // 12.D. Fig. 2:5 (two pierced ear handles; illustrated in the Corpus) // 11.1. Fig. 1:3, 7, 9; 3:3, 6, 7 // 62. Fig. 4:3 // 71.1.N. Fig. 4:5 // 82.1.B. Fig. 4:7 // 51.8.C. Fig. 4:8—10, 13 // 51.1.L. Fig. 4:11 // 51.7.A. Fig. 4:12 (exterior rim thickened) // 51.2.K.
156. *Caves*, Fig. 4:4 // 84.
157. *Caves*, Fig. 2:6 (illustrated in the Corpus) // 14.1.
158. *Caves*, Fig. 1:6 // 14.1.A. Fig. 2:2 // 14.1.B. Fig. 1:5; 3:1, 4, 8 // 62. Fig. 4:6 (larger) // 51.1.J.
159. *Feshkha*, Fig. 1:1 // 12.D. Fig. 2:1 (illustrated in the Corpus) // 31.2. Fig. 2:2 // 92. Fig. 2:3 // 82.1.A. Fig. 2:4 // 92.C ('Alâyiq). Fig. 2:5 (base slightly flattened) // 31.1.E. Fig. 2:7 (decorated) // 51.1.J—M. Fig. 2:8 (possibly from Period III), 12 // 54.2.G. Fig. 2:10 // 54.2.H. Fig. 2:11 (shallower) // 54.2.K. Fig. 2:13, 14, 16 // 51.2.K—L. Fig. 2:18 // 51.8.C. Fig. 2:20 // 52.2.E. Fig. 2:15 // 29.E (Qumrân Ib). Fig. 2:19 // 72.2.B.

slightly later deposits,[160] but some of the forms from north of the building are more probably to be associated with Qumrân II.[161] De Vaux assigns these forms to Period I because he associates the debris north of the building with a cleaning operation after the abandonment in the last decades of the first century B.C. He cites a similar situation in Loci 130 and 134 at the Khirbet.[162] However, there is no proof that some debris contemporary with the return and subsequent to it was not also associated with this deposit.[163]

It seems appropriate to mention at this point briefly the reasons for excluding the pottery of Qumrân III and the Wâdi Murabba'ât.[164] The limited amount of material for the period after A.D. 70 available from these groups is not supplemented by any other material so precisely dated, and these groups would not provide a significant Corpus. Obviously the limits of the period under study were also dictated by practical considerations.

Ramat Rahel

In 1931 a cave burial was discovered which contained a small pottery group datable to near the turn of the era.[165] An excavation in 1954 unearthed Persian-Hellenistic-Early Roman remains, designated "stratum IV" and dated from the fifth century B.C. to A.D. 70.[166] Published in the preliminary report is a plate with some "Attic" ware and figures with other pottery. The "Attic" ware appears to belong to a pre-second century B.C. horizon, but most of the rest of the pottery has Corpus parallels.[167]

---

160. *Feshkha*, Fig. 1:2 (Period I?) // 11.1.A (Samaria Roman Ia). Fig. 1:3 // 12.C (earliest fragment from Jerusalem, Tyropoeon Valley). Fig. 3:1 (illustrated in the Corpus) // 62. Fig. 3:4 // 53.J. Fig. 3:8, 9 // 51.8.A. Fig. 3:13, 14 // 11.2.F. Fig. 3:17, 18 // 52.2.E (Qumrân II development). Fig. 3:21 // 52.2.B.

161. *Feshkha*, Fig. 3:2 (shallower) // 54.2.H. Note that the only first century B.C. example which has sides as closely approaching the vertical as the Feshkha bowl is from Trench A which may also belong with Qumrân II. Fig. 3:5 // 92.C. No piriform unguentaria have been discovered in contexts assuredly as early as Qumrân Ib. Fig. 3:15, 16 are more likely of Qumrân II horizon (// 11.2.G). Other forms could be from Period I: Fig. 3:3, 6 // 53.H–L which do not occur in the first century A.D. Fig. 3:7, 10 // 51.8.A. Fig. 3:11, 12 // 11.2.F. Fig. 3:19 // 51.2.G. Fig. 3:20 // 15.A, which De Vaux now hesitates to attribute to Qumrân II (*Feshkha*, p. 248). This form may belong to either Qumrân Ib or II horizon, or to both.

162. *Feshkha*, pp. 247–48.

163. Cf. pp. 51–52 *supra*.

164. *Rapport II*, pp. 217, 226–28, and R. de Vaux, "Les grottes de Murabba'at et leurs documents," *RB*, LX (1953), pp. 255–60.

165. The pottery is shown in M. Stekelis, "A Jewish tomb-cave at Ramath Rachel," *Journal of the Jewish Palestine Exploration Society*, 1934–35, p. 28:1–12. If the group is relatively homogeneous, as is likely, a date *ca.* 25 B.C.–A.D. 25 is indicated by the presence of a fusiform unguentarium (28:7 // 91.2.B) and three piriform unguentaria (28:1 // 92.C; 28:2–3 // 92.A). The form of the cooking pot favors the same date (28:8 // 71.1.N_1). Except for the unusual cup (28:9), the rest of the forms have parallels from slightly earlier contexts: 28:4–6 // (?) 82.1.B; 28:10 // 53.H; 28:11 // 38.B–S; 28:12 // 31.2.A.

166. Aharoni, *IEJ*, VI, pp. 102–11, 137–57. On the designation of these remains as "stratum IV," cf. p. 8 *supra*.

167. For the "Attic" pottery *v.* Aharoni, *IEJ*, VI, p. 137 and Pl. 13:C. Parallels to Figs. 7 and 8, pp. 138–39, follow. 7:1 // 53.L. 7:2–3 // 51.1.H. 7:4 // 11.3.H. 7:5 // 31.2.A. 7:6 is a miniature vase which may also belong within the period; cf. n. 67 *supra*. 8:1 // 81.2.A. 8:2 // 81.1.A. 8:3 // 83.1.A. 8:4–5 // 83.2.A. 8:2 (below) // 34.A. 8:4 (below) // 33.A. 8:6–7 (below) probably belong with mortaria of Corpus Type 41.

Some of the parallels are from the first half of the second century B.C. (Fig. 8:3 and possibly also Fig. 7:6 and Fig. 8:6—7), but most are from the same horizon as the tomb group. Accordingly, at least minor occupation is indicated at this site in the early second century B.C. and near the turn of the era.

Râmet el-Khalîl

Important Maccabean and Herodian remains were uncovered at this site.[168] Unfortunately the recently published final report of the excavations paid no significant attention to the pottery of these periods.[169]

Rubin River area

Hellenistic and Roman pottery is reported from the territory around the mouth of the Rubin River. A map designates Yavneh Yam, Yammah, Tell Ghazza, Nebi Rubin, and Tell es-Sultân as Persian-Hellenistic sites.[170]

Saffûriyeh

There is evidence of occupation beginning in the first century B.C., but no pottery is published.[171]

Samaria

The chronologically significant material of both the Harvard and the Joint Expeditions at Samaria has been discussed in detail in Chapter III. It is necessary at this point only to present that ceramic material from chronologically ambiguous contexts that has parallels in the Corpus. A few remarks are in order regarding these contexts and the nature of their pottery.

No effort expended in this study was less rewarding than the detailed analysis of the loci described in *HE I*. With the exception of Vault Cistern 2 none of the other pottery groups from this excavation provided any independent chronological evidence for the period under study, either because the number of significant objects (coins, lamps, stamped jar handles, and pottery) were too few, or because a locus with a significant quantity of material inevitably represented a broad chronological span.[172] It still appears likely that if access could be gained to the pottery in Istanbul (which according to oral report has never been uncrated), first hand study of the material by loci with special attention to the latest materials in each group would make substantial contributions to the Corpus here developed. The results of the rather fruitless investigation of the *HE I* published groups do help to emphasize the thorough disruption of stratification by the

---

168. F. M. Abel, *Géographie de la Palestine*, I (Paris, 1933), p. 453. Albright, *The Archaeology of Palestine*, p. 156.

169. E. Mader, *Mamre: die Ergebnisse der Ausgrabungen im Heiligen Bezirk Râmat El-Halîl in Südpalästina, 1926-1928* (Breisgau, 1957), cf. esp. Plan 1.

170. M. Dothan, "An Archaeological Survey of the Rubin River," *IEJ*, II (1952), p. 112.

171. L. Waterman, *Preliminary Report of the University of Michigan Excavations at Sepphoris, Palestine, in 1931* (Ann Arbor, 1937).

172. The best examples of the latter are the following deposits from Strip 3: Street Cistern, Street, a, b, and c.

Hellenistic and Roman building operations on this site, a situation typical of other sites in Palestine examined in this study. This situation has made the extraction of chronologically significant evidence from Samaria a challenge to the ingenuity of some of Palestine's best archaeologists.[173]

This ingenuity has been displayed by Miss Kenyon in *SS III* as indicated in Chapter III. An examination of the General Lists of Hellenistic Pottery and Terra Sigillata shows that the evidence from Samaria has more precise chronological significance than all the comparative material so laboriously gathered by Mrs. Crowfoot.[174] In fact, this precision seems only to be matched in the dating of Western Sigillata wares at Rhenish and other Roman campsites. The Hellenistic General List merely gives a slightly broader view of some of the variations in decoration and form of Hellenistic Decorated Ware. That none of these can be added with confidence to the Corpus is no great detriment.[175] The analysis of Megarian bowls outside of chronologically significant contexts does not reveal any fragments from the same molds as those represented in the Corpus, so none of this material may be assigned precise dates except insofar as this is possible in terms of ware, form, and decorative motif.[176] With regard to the Terra Sigillata General List, the additional material is of greater scope, but little of it can be considered certainly earlier than A.D. 70 except on the strength of parallels, especially with Tarsus and Athens forms. It has been considered best to withhold such forms from the Palestinian Corpus until independent chronological evidence from Palestine is available.[177]

Much of the published pottery from *HE I* and *SS III* has fairly close Corpus parallels.[178]

---

173. In dealing with the Corpus parallels to *HE I*, the most immediate difficulty appears to be the thickness of the ware in the drawings. A thorough study of the material leads almost inevitably to the conclusion that it has been frequently exaggerated in the drawings, although this conclusion is advanced with some hesitancy. For example, none of the piriform unguentaria of the first century A.D. have ware as thick as *HE I*, Fig. 179a or bases as thick as Fig. 179:b. The ware of the cooking pots in Fig. 176 is represented as being thicker than the average ware of cooking pots from Iron II to Roman times.

It should also be noted that some of the Hellenistic and Early Roman imported ware in *HE I* can be dated by evidence outside Palestine discussed in Chapter IV. Cf., *e.g.*, *HE I*, Fig. 183:21a with pp. 76–77 *supra*.

174. *SS III*, pp. 235ff. and 306ff.

175. As with *HE I*, much of the late Hellenistic imported ware of *SS III* can be dated by evidence outside Palestine discussed in Chap. IV. Cf. esp. *SS III*, Fig. 43–47.

176. *SS III*, pp. 272ff. On the limitations of these methods *v*. pp. 77–78 *supra*.

177. Mrs. Crowfoot's Forms 8 (two shallow types), 18a, and 24 undoubtedly occur in the first century A.D. although they are not represented in the Corpus. Cf. *SS III*, pp. 327–28, 338–39.

178. Table of Corpus parallels from Samaria:

Corpus Type	Locus	Reference
11.1.A	S7–365 Cistern 1	*HE I*, Fig. 175:3976 (pre-Herodian deposit, p. 80).
11.2.F	Basilica Cistern 3	" " " 160:3 (acknowledged as possibly of later date than most of the material from Basilica Cistern 3, p. 284).
11.2.F–G	S1–Cistern 8	*HE I*, Fig. 175:1487, 1488.

Corpus Type	Locus	Reference
21.1.G	S1—Square Cistern 8	HE I, Fig. 177:7a (base more angular).
21.1.R	S7—Cistern 3	" " " 177:7e.
29.B	S2—Corner Cistern	" " " 183:30a.
31.2.A	S9—Cistern 1	" " " 183:27b.
	S1—Cistern 8	" " " 183:27a.
51.1.B	Dc	SS III, Fig. 56:9.
	Dg	" " " 56:10.
	Bk	" " " 56:11.
53.B	S4—404 sub	HE I, Fig. 154:1 (listed as Israelite: 900—700 B.C.).
53.C	Qd	SS III, Fig. 56:1.
53.D	Dc	" " " 56:5 (no central depression).
53.J	Dn	" " " 56:4.
71.1.A	S1—Cistern 8	HE I, Fig. 176:2a.
	S7—Cistern 4	" " " 176:2d.
71.1.C	S1—Cistern 7	" " " 168:14a (may have Byzantine ribbing, but is certainly not as early as 300 B.C. which is given as the *terminus ante quem* for the deposit, pp. 62, 284—85).
71.1.H	L.T. 1 c	HE I, Fig. 176:2g.
81.2	S10—d	" " " 187:5a.
91.1.C	S11—z	" " " 178:5 (?).
	S3—street	" " " 178:7.
91.1.D	H.S. 1	" " " 178:9.
	S8—816	" " " 178:10.
	S2—III 59 sub	" " " 178:11 (pre-Herodian deposit, HE II, p. xxii).
	L.T. a W	" " " 178:12.
91.2.A	S3—street	" " " 178:6.
	H.S.	" " " 178:8.
92.C	Samarra C	" " " 179:b.
92.D	N.G.T. 4	" " " 179:a.
128.B	Qx	SS III, Fig. 58:4 (smaller).
151.1.A	Qb	" " " 49:7.
	Qc	" " " 49:8 (other examples from Qb, Qn, Qy N).
	Qy S	" " " 49:12 (other examples from Qy and Qn).
151.1.B	S1—III	HE I, Fig. 174:48 (pre-Herodian level, cf. HE II, p. xxii).
	Qy N	SS III, Fig. 49:14.
151.1.C	Qb	" " " 49:15 (other examples from Qy N and Qb).
151.1.E	S3—Corner Cistern	HE I, Fig. 174:45 (flat base).
151.1.F	S2—47	" " " 174:51 (v. p. 304, 34.a).
151.2.A	Qn	SS III, Fig. 53:3.
151.3.B	—	" " " 48:6.
151.3.C	Qb	" " " 48:7.
151.3.D	Qb	" " " 48:8.
151.3.F	S10	HE I, Fig. 174:43.
151.4.A	Bb	SS III, Fig. 57:2 (14 other examples from Da, Dc, Dg, Dj, Bz, Qf, Qn, Qy, Td, and S).
151.4.B	Qe	SS III, Fig. 57:1.
151.5.A	Td	" " " 46:5.
	Dj	" " " 46:6.
153.1.A	S7—755 N	HE I, Fig. 174:39 (probably pre—200 B.C. as Corpus example).

Corpus Type	Locus	Reference
153.1.B	S8	HE I, Fig. 174:34.
	S3 — Street Cistern	" " " 174:36.
	Td	SS III, Fig. 54:8.
	Bb	" " " 54:9.
	Qb	" " " 54:10.
153.1.C	?	" " " 54:14.
153.1.E	Qb	" " " 51:5 (no central depression).
153.1.F	S7 — 755	HE I, Fig. 174:29 (possibly pre — 200 B.C.).
	S9 — 901 c sub	" " " 174:30 (possibly pre — 200 B.C.).
	Qn	SS III, Fig. 51:6 (possibly pre — 200 B.C.).
153.1.G	Qb	" " " 51:8.
153.1.H	Qb	" " " 55:2, 4.
	Qy N	" " " 55:8.
	Qy S	" " " 55:14.
153.1.J	Trench F	HE I, Fig. 174:33.
	S2 — 7	" " " 174:10.
	Bc	SS III, Fig. 54:11.
	Da	" " " 55:10.
	Td	" " " 55:11.
153.1.K	Dc	" " " 55:17.
153.1.L	S10 — a	HE I, Fig. 174:40 (smaller).
	Dg	SS III, Fig. 54:6 (other examples from Dc, Dl, Bz, Qy).
153.1.N	Qb	" " " 55:7.
153.1.Q	?	" " " 54:20.
153.9.A	Qn	" " " 59:1 — 5.
	?	" " " 39:7a, b (attributed to both Qy and Qn on p. 270).
158.A	?	HE I, Fig. 173:19 (cf. p. 307).
228.A	Qb	SS III, Fig. 82:2 (rim variant; other examples from Da, Dc, Dj, Dk, Do, Qa, Qc, Qh, Qn).
228.B	S10 — d	HE I, Fig. 185:15a.
	Qn	SS III, Fig. 82:3.
251.2.A	Dc	" " " 80:2 (other examples from Dn, Bn, Dc, Dd.)
	Ba Cistern	" " " 80:6 (other examples from Tc, Dd, G).
	Dd	" " " 80:7.
	Qa	" " " 80:8.
251.2.B	Dc	" " " 80:1 (33 other examples in Dc; two larger examples from Dc, Dl).
251.2a.B	S10 — d	HE I, Fig. 185:8e.
	Qn	SS III, Fig. 80:10.
251.2b.A	—	" " " 80:18 — 22 (proveniences respectively Qy, Qn, Dd, Qx, Dc).
251.6.A	Zd	SS III, Fig. 81:6 (lower base and plainer).
252.2.A	Qe	" " " 81:1 (floor variant; other examples from Qn).
252.2.B	Qf	" " " 81:2.
253.1.B	Dg	" " " 73:7 (other examples from Dg, Dc, Dj, Dl).
	Dc	" " " 73:8 (other examples from Dk, Dg, Qg).
253.1.D	Dd	" " " 73:3 (other similar vessels from Dg, Qb, Qe).
	Dc	" " " 73:10 (another smaller example from Dc).

Shechem

Besides the material from the Hellenistic House discussed in Chapter III, pottery of the second century B.C. in the first three Drew-McCormick campaigns belongs entirely to surface-contaminated groups. Sherds of the second century B.C. have been recorded in the East Gate area, in Field VII in the central part of the mound, and in Field III at the northeast edge of the city.[179] Reference to the earlier German excavations is not necessary since attention was not given to ceramic evidence.[180]

Corpus Type	Locus	Reference
253.1.G	Dc	SS III, Fig. 73:4 (other examples from Dc, De, G—wall N. of Mosque).
	Dc	SS III, Fig. 73:12 (step base: Db, Dg, Dl, Qn; plain base: Dd, Dc, Dk, Qg, Qn, Qb).
253.1.H	Qe	SS III, Fig. 73:9 (another example from Dg).
	Dc	" " " 73:11 (two larger examples from Dc and Dg).
253.1.M	Te	" " " 79:5 (other similar examples from G, Qf, Qb=Roman I, Qn).
	Db	SS III, Fig. 79:6 (other examples from Dg, Qn).
253.2.A	Dg	" " " 78:8 (other example from Dd).
253.3.B	Dg	" " " 79:1 (other examples from Dg, Dc, Do).
253.4.A	De	" " " 73:1 (two examples from Dg).
253.4.D	S5−b	HE I, Fig. 185:18b (only similar).
	Dd	SS III, Fig. 73:2 (other examples from Da, Qe, Qn, Dc).
253.4.G	Basilica Trench A	HE I, Fig. 185:3a (flat floor).
	Dg	SS III, Fig. 73:14 (flatter floor, narrower base; another example from Qf; cf. HE I, Fig. 185:3a).
253.5.A	Bz	SS III, Fig. 77:1 (other sherds from Dc, Dd, Dg, Qk, Qn, Qy, Bp, Bb, T; in black glaze from Dx, Qx).
253.6.A	Dl	SS III, Fig. 77:3 (base and rim variant).
	Bb	" " " 77:4.
254.2.A	Qg	" " " 79:14.
	Da	" " " 79:15.
	Qc	" " " 79:16.
254.2.B	Qg	" " " 79:13 (additional interior ridge and XAPIC stamp).
345.1.A	S8−882	HE I, Fig. 175:17 (probably third century B.C.).
	Dl	SS III, Fig. 45:1.
	Dg	" " " 45:2.
353.1.A	S6−g	HE I, Fig. 173:1 (possibly third century B.C.).
	H.S. 2	HE I, Fig. 173:2 (possibly third century B.C.).
	Qa	SS III, Fig. 47:2.
353.2.A	Qn	" " " 47:9, 10.

179. These observations are based on the writer's study of the 1956, 1957, and 1960 campaign material made available through the courtesy of the Drew-McCormick Expedition. The important Shechem evidence has been summarized by Lawrence E. Toombs and G. Ernest Wright, "The Third Campaign at Balâtah (Shechem)," *BASOR*, 161 (Feb., 1961), esp. p. 48. The more popular summary (Edward F. Campbell, Jr., "Excavation at Shechem, 1960," *BA*, XXIII [1960], p. 104) tends to overrate the Shechem evidence. Certainly the third century B.C. typological development has been clarified by the Field VII Shechem stratification, but the dating of the second century B.C. Hellenistic deposits of Field II was only possible in light of Beth-zur and Samaria evidence.

180. Cf. G. Welter, "Stand der Ausgrabungen in Sichem," *Jahrbuch des deutschen archäologischen Instituts*, 1932, pp. 290−315.

Shiloh

A "considerable" Hellenistic settlement is reported, primarily on ceramic evidence, but no pottery has been published.[181]

Silet edh-Dhahr

The cave in the vicinity of Silet edh-Dhahr excavated in 1949 under the auspices of the Jerusalem School of the American Schools of Oriental Research produced primarily Byzantine material, but a piriform unguentarium and several Herodian lamps indicated that some burials were made in the first century A.D.[182]

Tell Abû Hawâm

Hellenistic and *terra sigillata* sherds are reported from "Stratum I" (surface) but no material is published. Only a fusiform unguentarium, designated from Stratum II (mostly Persian), has Corpus affinities.[183]

Tell ej-Judeideh

Bliss and Macalister report a few "Seleucidan" types from the surface of the tell.[184] Some of these were presumably of the second century B.C.

Tell el-Fâr'ah (North)

Evidence from De Vaux's extensive operations indicates that this site was abandoned during the period under consideration. The two forms with parallels in the second century B.C. merely indicate sporadic use of the site.[185]

Tell el-Fâr'ah (South)

From the pottery published in *CPP* and *Beth-pelet II* it seems certain that the important Persian occupation here, like that at nearby Tell Jemmeh, was followed by a period of abandonment. At least, with the possible exception of two lamp forms,[185a] there is no ceramic evidence of occupation in the second and first centuries B.C. From

---

181. Hans Kjaer, "The Danish Excavation of Shiloh," *PEF QS*, 1927, p. 207; "The Excavation of Shiloh, 1929," *Journal of the Palestine Oriental Society*, X (1930), p. 109.

182. O. R. Sellers and D. C. Baramki, *A Roman-Byzantine Burial Cave in Northern Palestine* (Supplementary Studies, Nos. 15–16, of *BASOR*; New Haven, 1953). Fig. 30:17 // 92. C. Fig. 33:156 // 82.1. D, 269 // 82.1. B, 341 // 82.1. C. The handled and the decorated specimens (Fig. 33:291 and 34:315) may be later as the excavators suggest (pp. 32–33), but this is not necessarily the case. Cf. the decorated example in the Corpus, 82.2. A from Qumrân Ib. The parallels cited do not provide empirical evidence for close dating.

183. R. W. Hamilton, "Tall Abu Hawam: Interim Report," *QDAP*, III (1934), p. 78. Pl. XXIIIa:4 // 91.1. D. Cf. R. W. Hamilton, "Excavations at Tell Abu Hawâm," *QDAP*, IV (1935), p. 14, where Hellenistic lamp sherds, Rhodian jar handles, and "Samian ware" are reported from the surface.

184. Frederick Jones Bliss and R. A. S. Macalister, *Excavations in Palestine during the Years 1898–1900* (London, 1902), p. 74.

185. R. de Vaux, "Les fouilles de Tell el-Far'ah près Naplouse: Sixième campagne, rapport préliminaire," *RB*, LXIV (1957), p. 573, Fig. 7:3 from Grotte T // Corpus 51.1. B. R. de Vaux, "La troisième campagne de fouilles a Tell el-Far'ah, près Naplouse: Rapport préliminaire," *RB*, LVIII (1951), pp. 417 and 419, Fig. 12:9 // Corpus 91.1.

185a. E. MacDonald, J. L. Starkey, and G. L. Harding, *Beht-pelet II* (London, 1932), Pl. LXXXVIII:5 // Corpus 83.1. A and 11 // 83.2. A.

the Roman levels (or slightly below) at the south end of the tell come a number of forms that suggest a Qumrân II horizon, but these are mixed with later material.[186]

Tell el-Fukhâr

At this tell one kilometer southwest of Tell Deir 'Allâ Glueck reports "large quantities of sherds, most of which are Byzantine, and the rest mediaeval Arabic."[186a] In a surface exploration of this tell on 7 February 1961 the writer examined hundreds of surface sherds. With one possible exception, all the sherds could be dated within the period 50 B.C.—A.D. 70. This is just one example of the errors that could be involved in the Hellenistic attributions of Glueck in his survey of Transjordan. In light of the very primitive knowledge of Hellenistic and later pottery at the time of his explorations, it seemed wise not to include his Jordan Valley "Hellenistic" sites in this study.

Tell el-Fukhkhâr

A Hellenistic-Roman necropolis is reported at the foot of this tell near Acre.[187]

Tell el-Fûl

Only one cooking pot from the period under study was illustrated from W. F. Albright's sounding at Tell el-Fûl in 1922, but the publication of his 1933 excavation does contain forms which may be assigned to second century B.C. and first century A.D. horizons.[188] Unfortunately, the dating of the pottery in the latter publication is based on subjective typological considerations, and the chronological significance of parallel material is not discerned. As a result, pottery dated to the second half of the fourth and third centuries B.C. can be assigned to Iron II, the second century B.C. (suggesting,

---

186. Qumrân II horizon: *ibid.*, Pl. LXXXIII:18G10 and 22H10 similar to *Agora V*, G 13—14 (A.D. 0—37); Pl. LXXXIV:32E7 // Corpus 71.1.N₁ (neck variant); Pl. LXXXVI:48X5 // 12.D; Pl. LXXXVII:53Z1¹ // 33. A—B; Pl. LXXXVIII:2, 4 // 82.1; 6 shape similar to 82.2; 8 // 85. A. Later material: Pl. LXXXIV:32S9, 37E6, 37X5; LXXXVI:48C3, 48C5; LXXXVII:53Z1, 65W8, 67M; LXXXVIII:7, 9. Other published first century A.D. forms include Pl. LXXXVI:48X1 // 12.D and LXXXVIII:1 // 82.1.B from tombs; LXXXVIII:3 // 82.1 from the fort of Vespasian at the north end of the tell; cf. Flinders Petrie, *Beth-pelet I* (London, 1930), pp. 20—21 and Pl. LXI.

186a. Nelson Glueck, "Explorations in Eastern Palestine, IV" *AASOR*, XXV—XXVIII (1945—49), p. 312.

187. *IEJ*, I (1950—51), p. 249.

188. W. F. Albright, "Excavations and Results at Tell el-Fûl (Gibeah of Saul)," *AASOR*, IV (1922—23), Pl. XXIV:3 (one handle) // Corpus 71.1.C. L. E. Sinclair, "An Archaeological Study of Gibeah (Tell el-Fûl)," in *AASOR*, XXXIV—XXXV (1954—56), appeared in 1960. Since the pottery attributed to Period IV is "not homogeneous" (p. 37) and includes Iron II and Early Roman forms, the group comes from mixed fill(s) or is not derived from empirical stratigraphy.

Period IV pottery that belongs to the end of Iron II (or slightly later) includes Pl. 23:3 (cf. *AASOR*, XXXIV—XXXV, p. 38 with pp. 41ff. *supra*); Pl. 23:5 (cf. *SS III*, Fig. 12:9, from Period VIII); Pl. 23:9, 10, and 12 (an examination of the Tell el-Fûl pottery in the Jerusalem School [which was not used first-hand by Sinclair in his study] indicates that the ware of these vessels is in the Iron II tradition of holemouth and "neckless" jars, not Hellenistic); Pl. 23:15—16 (cf. discussion of "neckless" jars and the many Beth-zur III [end of Iron II] parallels cited in the final publication of the 1957 campaign in a forthcoming *AASOR*); Pl. 25:3 (considered as belonging to Periods I-II in the 1922 sounding, *AASOR*, IV, p. 12

as Albright thought already in 1922, that the Period IV fortress was Maccabean), and the first century A.D.

Tell el-Qasîleh

The dating of Strata V and IV at Tell el-Qasîleh was originally set at the third to first centuries B.C. and the Herodian Period respectively. After some vacillation during the second campaign, the original dates were reaffirmed in the third season of excavation.[189] However, the few pottery fragments so far published from "Stratum V" seem to belong to the date assigned to "Stratum IV."[190] Any conclusions must await final publication.

Tombs of the Hellenistic period from the vicinity of Tell el-Qasîleh have also been reported. One was dated to the first half of the first century B.C., but it was later revised to a more general attribution to the Hellenistic period.[191] Some tombs published by J. Kaplan contained, together with other remains, three fusiform unguentaria and a lamp with the ray motif which have Corpus parallels.[192] The parallels probably indicate that these tombs were in use in the second and first centuries B.C.

and Pl. XXXVIII:1–4; the description of the ware is obviously *not* Hellenistic; contrast *AASOR*, XXXIV–XXXV, p. 40); Pl. 25:4 (stratified Iron II parallels from Shechem); Pl. 26:14–16 (cf. discussion in 1957 Beth-zur final report).

Pottery belonging to the earlier or later second century B.C. horizon includes Pl. 17:1 // Corpus 83:1; Pl. 17:2–3 // 81.2; Pl. 17:4–5 // 81.1 (suggesting that this form, like Corpus 81.2, is extant in the second century B.C.); Pl. 24:1–9, 28 and 25:2 // 11.3; Pl. 24:14, 15, 20, 21, 24–27 // 11.2.A–D; Pl. 25:7 // 71.1.C–D; Pl. 25:9, 10, 14, 15, 18–20, 22 // 21.1.A–H; Pl. 25:21 // 14.1; Pl. 26:1–3 // 29.A–D; 26:4 (no Corpus parallel but two examples in the writer's private collection are from a small group probably belonging to the early second century B.C.); Pl. 26:5 // 53.B.

First century A.D. forms include Pl. 24:10–13, 16, 18, 19, 22, 23 // Corpus 11.2.G or 12; Pl. 24:17 (?) and Pl. 25:8 and 11 // Corpus 13; Pl. 25:6 // 71.1.N_2; Pl. 25:17 (only published sherd assigned to Period V) // 12.D.

Some of the second century B.C. forms as well as some assigned to the first century A.D. could belong to the first century B.C., but no forms necessarily belong there. The absence of sigillata also suggests a gap in the first century B.C. and slightly later. In accordance with the principle that pottery tends to represent the end of an occupational period, most of the first century A.D. group probably belongs to the third quarter of the century, before the site was destroyed or abandoned about A.D. 70.

In summary, then, there is no reason to assign any of the Period IV pottery to the time suggested by Sinclair. An attempt to date Hellenistic forms and even to redate Shechem Hellenistic strata on the basis of photographs of sherds without knowledge of their stratification (*AASOR*, XXXIV–XXXV, p. 37, n. 6, and cf. p. 45, n. 44) is typical of the inflated, muddled discussion of the Tell el-Fûl pottery, a detailed criticism of which would not be useful.

189. B. Maisler, "The Excavations at Tell Qasile: Preliminary Report," *IEJ*, I (1950–51), p. 67, 216, and 218.

190. *Ibid.*, p. 213, Fig. 14:c from "Stratum V" is Eastern Sigillata A with a XAPIC stamp that the excavator admits (p. 215) is of the first century A.D. Fig. 14:g also belongs to the first century A.D. (cf. Corpus 12.D). On the other hand, Fig. 14:e is possibly of the third century B.C. since it is probably of better workmanship than the second century B.C. Hellenistic Decorated Ware.

191. *IEJ*, VII (1957), p. 265. Corrected, *IEJ*, VIII (1958), p. 135.

192. J. Kaplan, "Excavations of Tombs near Tell Qasile in 1957," *BIES*, XXII (1958), p. 97. Pl. X,9:1, second vessel // Corpus 91.1.D; third vessel // 91.2.B; fourth vessel // 91.1. Pl. X,9:2, second lamp (left to right) // 83.2.C.

Tell en-Nasbeh

A number of Tell en-Nasbeh tombs contained small ceramic groups with Corpus parallels. Tomb 2 contained a Herodian lamp, but the other two lamps from this tomb are of a later date.[193] Tomb 3 contained a fusiform unguentarium that could belong to the second century B.C., but it probably dates with the rest of the Hellenistic material from that tomb which seems to belong to the third century B.C.[194] C. C. McCown states that Tomb 4 "belongs to Hellenistic-Roman times, but may have some later vessels";[195] actually, the only possible evidence of use before A.D. 70 is a Herodian lamp.[196] In addition to much later material, Tomb 6 contained three whole and seven fragmentary lamps[197] and a fragment of a globular juglet probably of the first century A.D.[198]

Tomb 8 contained two Herodian lamp spouts, five cooking pot fragments belonging to the Qumrân II horizon, and a jug fragment which has a parallel in Qumrân Ib; the latter type, however, is not well represented in the Corpus and may also occur in the first century A.D.[199] Tomb 14 contained three examples of the Herodian lamp and a cooking pot fragment also of the Qumrân II horizon in addition to Iron II and Byzantine material.[200] From Tomb 15 came a third century B.C. coin, pottery of the Qumrân II horizon, and a Byzantine lamp.[201] This tomb, incidentally, provides a striking illustration of the precarious nature of numismatic evidence from tombs. None of the pottery belongs to the time of the coin. Forms from Tomb 18 also have parallels in Qumrân II.[202] Tombs 57 and 59 contained fragments of piriform unguentaria;[203] Tomb 71 had pottery of Qumrân II horizon.[204]

---

193. Cf. *TN I*, p. 110. S 1648 // Corpus 82.1.B. S 1652 has not been found in contexts predating A.D. 70, and S 1660 is a typical Byzantine "rayed" lamp.
194. W. F. Badè, *Some Tombs of Tell en-Nasbeh Discovered in 1929* (Berkeley, 1931), pp. 31–43. Pl. XIII:7 // Corpus 91.1. Cf. *TN I*, pp. 102–104. The dating of the Hellenistic material in Tomb 3 as 300–100 B.C. should probably be corrected to 300–200 B.C., but the establishment of this date depends on the discovery of evidence that the fusiform unguentarium was in use in Palestine before 200 B.C. as it was elsewhere in the Near East. Cf. *TN I*, p. 104; p. 101 *supra*; and *Kahane I*, pp. 131–39.
195. *TN I*, p. 104.   196. S 1648 // Corpus 82.1.B.
197. Cf. *TN I*, p. 110. Lamps, S 1648 // Corpus 82.1.B and Fig. 22:5 // 82.1.D.
198. Cf. *TN I*, p. 112 and Fig. 22:16 // Corpus 31.1.E.
199. *TN I*, p. 109 and Fig. 21:10–16. The lamps, S 1648 // Corpus 82.1.B. Fig. 21:11, 13 // 72.1.K. Fig. 21:12 // 21.2.B. Fig. 21:14 // 72.1.B. Fig. 21:15 // 71.1.N$_2$. Fig. 21:16 // 71.1.P ('Alâyiq).
200. *TN I*, pp. 104–105, and Fig. 21:1–9. S 1648 // Corpus 82.1.B. Fig. 21:6 // 71.1.N$_2$. Here, as in the case of Tomb 4, McCown refers to Hellenistic-Roman use when there is no evidence for Hellenistic use.
201. *TN I*, p. 110 and Fig. 21:17–22. The pottery forms with Qumrân II affinities are Fig. 21:19 // Corpus 82.1.B, Fig. 21:21 // 31.1.D$_5$, Fig. 21:22 // 12.D. In the last parallel the rippling of the Tomb 15 example may indicate a date somewhat after Qumrân II, but the suggestion that this jar may date as late as the sixth century A.D. is based on a confusion of rippling and genuine Byzantine ribbing, if the drawing is accurate.
202. *TN I*, p. 107 and Fig. 22:1–4. The tomb is designated "Roman (?)," but there is no doubt that the sherds belong to the early Roman period. Fig. 22:1 // Corpus 71.1.N$_2$. Fig. 22:2 // 72.1.K. Fig. 22:4 // 12.D. The lamp S 1652 is not represented in the Corpus and may indicate that the group belongs slightly after Qumrân II (cf. n. 205, *infra*).
203. *TN I*, p. 106. S 1735 // Corpus 92.C. This is called a Hellenistic type, but occurrence even before the Christian era has not been established.
204. *TN I*, pp. 109–110 and Fig. 71:23–24. S 1648 // Corpus 82.1.B. Fig. 21:23 // 71.1.P.

It should be noted that material from these tombs has parallels with the latest material in the Corpus, and the ware of the two large jars from Tombs 15 and 71 may indicate a later date.[205] Except for tomb material, the only forms that are catalogued in *TN II* which belong to the period 200 B.C.–A.D. 70 are S 298, 592, 686, 1567, 1643, 1644, and 1734.[206] The first three occur in surface debris, the fourth is given a provenience "Roman tower on top of mound (?)," the fifth and last are from mixed cistern deposits, and the sixth is obviously intrusive in level I.[207] Thus, only sporadic surface occupation at Tell en-Nasbeh is indicated for the period under study.[208]

The extensive typological series of *TN II* provides opportunity to note that the pottery of the period under study is quite easily distinguished from the forms of those ceramic periods represented at Tell en-Nasbeh. The only exceptions are a few jar and bowl rims.

Tell en-Nasbeh also provides some evidence of use in refuting the contention that "Herodian" bow-spouted lamps occur as late as Byzantine times.[209] The groups of tombs described as "Tombs predominantly Byzantine" and "Tombs characterized by 'Rayed' Lamps" contained no bow-spouted lamps.[210]

Tell Jemmeh

This site, which Petrie mistakenly identified with Gerar, had important Persian remains, but it appears to have been abandoned before 200 B.C. The only published pottery forms with Corpus affinities are a fusiform unguentarium and a few bowls and jugs.[211] None of these forms demand a date after 200 B.C.

Tell Sandahannah

A Sidonian colony was founded at Tell Sandahannah (Marisa) near the middle of the third century B.C. It apparently flourished until the site was razed by the Parthians in 40 B.C. There is no certain evidence of occupation after this time. Unfortunately, the pottery from Tell Sandahannah is published *en masse*, and it is impossible to make any independent chronological distinctions within this period.

Much of the published pottery has Corpus parallels and most of the rest of the material is known to belong to this general period from parallels at sites outside

---

Fig. 21:24 // 12.D. Both these are also more rippled than Qumrân II examples and may be of a somewhat later date.

205. Cf. Chap. III, n. 333.

206. S 298 // Corpus 11.2.G. S 592 // 21.1.H. S 686 // 21.1.M. S 1567 // 254.2 (perhaps heavy floor indicates a date after A.D. 70). S 1734 // 91.1.D.

207. Cf. the pottery descriptions, *TN II*, pp. 129ff.

208. With this the numismatic evidence agrees; cf. *TN I*, p. 174.

209. Cf., *e.g.*, Crowfoot and Fitzgerald, *PEFA*, 1927, p. 90.

210. *TN I*, pp. 112–22.

211. F. Petrie, *Gerar* (London, 1928), Pl. LXII:W181 // Corpus 91.1.B. Much of the Tell Jemmeh pottery is also published in *CPP*. The pottery drawings not specified from other sites are from Tell Jemmeh (*CPP*, p. 5). The drawings are unsatisfactory and make close comparisons difficult. Some of the forms have Corpus parallels (*e.g.*, 2C8–9, 22T–X, 37H2, 53W–X), but it is not certain that these examples are to be dated after 200 B.C. For the early dating of the fusiform unguentarium *v.* n. 194 *supra*.

Palestine.²¹² The earliest date mentioned in the inscriptions in the famous painted tombs is 196 B.C., but it is recognized that the inscription was written some time after the construction and decoration of the tomb.²¹³ From Tomb V came three small bowls that could be contemporary with the inscription.²¹⁴

The Eastern Sigillata A ware²¹⁵ presents a difficult problem. If it were certain that there was a complete abandonment of the tell in 40 B.C., provenience here would indicate the earliest context for a number of Eastern Sigillata A forms, and considerable evidence points in this direction. Of the rest of the published pottery (especially the lamps) there is no form which must postdate 40 B.C. Most of the sigillata forms have parallels in Vault Cistern 2 or Roman I at Samaria and therefore are attested before 25 B.C., and the excavators claim homogeneity for the entire sigillata group.²¹⁶ However, this last observation is inaccurate according to the observations of Mrs. Crowfoot.²¹⁷ She also noted that the sigillata group "came from just outside the inner wall of the city."²¹⁸ Four of the forms are not represented in the Corpus, and it is difficult to date two of these as early as 40 B.C.²¹⁹ Thus, it is not impossible that this sigillata cache may be attributed to a patrician's house which could have existed at the site after the 40 B.C. destruction. While such an hypothesis appears to have the weight of evidence

---

212. The material is found in Bliss and Macalister, *Excavations in Palestine*, Pls. 58—64. For the dating of the lagynoi, Pl. 59:1—4, to this period v. pp. 76—77 *supra*. The "Ephesus" lamps, Pl. 63:2, 8—13, probably occur throughout this period (Corinth Type XIX, cf. *Broneer*, pp. 66—70), and the "Knidian" lamp, Pl. 63:7, also is attributed to the earlier part of the period (Corinth Type XIII; cf. *Broneer*, pp. 53—54).

213. J. P. Peters and H. Thiersch, *Painted Tombs in the Necropolis of Marissa (Marêshah)* (London, 1905), p. 80. The suggestion of construction ca. 200 B.C. is the lowest possible date, and it may well have been several decades earlier.

214. F. M. Abel, "Chronique, I. Tombeaux récemment découverts à Marisa," *RB*, XXXIV (1925), p. 274, Fig. 3. The two upper bowls // Corpus 51.1.B, and the pinched bow handle fragment // 151.4.A.

215. Bliss and Macalister, *Excavations in Palestine*, Pl. 61.

216. *Ibid.*, p. 128.

217. *SS III*, p. 349, mentions ware ranging from dark buff to cream.

218. *SS III*, p. 349.

219. Pl. 61:1 has parallels in *HE I*, Fig. 185:2r from S11—z and *SS III*, Fig. 73:15, 17 from Dc (with other examples from Dc and Dd). All three contexts (S11—z, Dc, and Dd) contained first century B.C. sigillata. Cf. *HE I*, p. 306, 6i and *SS III*, p. 307. Pl. 61:21 is related to Pl. 61:2 which has a parallel in Vault Cistern 2. Thus, a date before 40 B.C. would be quite possible for Pl. 61:1 and 21. Pl. 61:9 and 11 present difficulty because their sharp angularity is not found in sigillata forms known to predate 25 B.C. A parallel to Pl. 61:9 comes from Dg (*SS III*, Fig. 81:4) and bases which may be of this type come from Dd. Both of these contexts did contain sigillata of the first century B.C. Pl. 61:11 is similar to *SS III*, Fig. 79:8, from two contexts (Db and Qy) which also contained first century B.C. pottery. Cf. the table of Samaria Corpus parallels, n. 178 *supra* (*e.g.* under Corpus 253.1.G and 253.5.A). While all four forms occur in contexts with first century B.C. material, none of them is empirically demonstrated as belonging before 25 B.C. Especially the last two cannot be confidently dated before 40 B.C. on the basis of their provenience in the Tell Sandahannah group (which lacks adequate contextual description) because of the typological consideration mentioned above.

against it, it seems wise to withhold these forms from the Corpus until additional evidence establishes their date beyond question.

The variety of jugs, juglets, and bottles on Plates 58 and 59 no doubt indicates gaps in the Corpus in these categories. A number of examples, however, probably belong to the third century B.C., and others may represent Sidonian influence. The Corpus parallels range in date from about 200 to 25 B.C.[220]

Tell Ta'annak

Sellin reports no Seleucid pottery, and only two *terra sigillata* sherds from the surface.[221]

Tell Zakarîyeh

Tell Zakarîyeh was one of the four Shephelah tells excavated by Bliss and Macalister between 1898 and 1900. He reported a small quantity of "Seleucidan"

---

220. Corpus parallels from Tell Sandahannah illustrated in Bliss and Macalister, *Excavations in Palestine*, are listed in the table below:

Corpus Type	Reference
21.1.M	Pl. 59:7
29.D	" 58:11
51.1.A	" 60:26 (flat base)
51.1.B	" 60:24
51.1.C	" 60:27, 29
51.2.B	" 60:25
51.2.G	" 61:23, 24
53.B	" 61:20 (deeper)
71.1.L	" 58:10
81.1.A	" 66:11 (a ring of similar lamps)
83.2	" 62:4, 5, 7—10
91.1	" 60:6—8, 11
91.2	" 60:9, 10
151.1	" 60:30—35 (the examples resemble those from Lachish Tomb 7; they are generally deeper than the Corpus examples and the foot belongs typologically between 151.1.A—D and E—G)
151.1.D	" 61:27 (foot variant; probably pre-second century B.C.)
151.3.E	" 60:38 (smaller)
151.3.F	" 60:37
151.3.G	" 61:10 (classed with Eastern Sigillata A, but dubious)
153.1.H	" 61:26
158.H	" 61:19
251.2.B	" 61:8
251.2a.A	" 61:7 (foot variant)
253.1.B	" 61:12, 13
253.1.D	" 61:3
253.1.E	" 61:14
253.1.F	" 61:4
253.1.K	" 61:5, 16
253.2	" 61:2
253.3.A	" 61:6

221. E. Sellin, *Tell Ta'annek* (Wien, 1904), p. 91.

types, but the pottery of Tell Sandahannah of this period was selected for publication. However, a few sherds from Tell Zakarîyeh published with the "Jewish" pottery have Corpus parallels from the second century B.C.[222]

Tulûl Abû el-'Alâyiq

Kelso reports a few Hellenistic sherds associated with the Hellenistic construction "likely the work of Bacchides," but none are published.[223] Much of the Roman pottery belongs to the same horizon as that from the building published by Pritchard and discussed in Chapter II. The Roman pottery is divided into thirty-eight types, primarily on the basis of ware but also considering form and decoration, and abundant comparative material is cited in the discussion. Yet, since provenience or stratification of the published sherds is not specified and the Early and Late Roman forms are lumped together, all that can be attempted here is an identification of those forms which from Corpus parallels belong substantially to the first half of the first century A.D.[224]

---

222. Bliss and Macalister, *Excavations in Palestine*, p. 74. Cf. Fig. 48 // Corpus 81.2.A. Pl. 49:9 // 21.1.F; 54:6 // 71.1.C; 54:7 // 71.1.D; 54:8 // 71.1.F.

223. J. L. Kelso and D. C. Baramki, "Excavations at New Testament Jericho and Khirbet en-Nitla," *AASOR*, XXIX–XXX (1949–1951), p. 7.

224. Forms such as the plate, Pl. 23:A80, the lamp, Pl. 14:A6, and the cooking pot, Pl. 23:A173, do not appear as late as Qumrân II. Corpus parallels to the Kelso and Baramki material, indicating a preponderantly first half of the first century A.D. horizon, follow.

Corpus Type	Reference
11.1.A–S*	Pl. 24:A179
11.2.G	" 24:X84, A118
11.3.H	" 24:A243
12	" 24:X60, X72
13.A	" 22:A241 (rim and handle developments beyond the first century B.C. parallel)
13.C	Pl. 22:A238
14.1	" 23:A115
15.A–B	" 23:X80
19.C	" 24:X61
21.1.Q–R	" 22:X21; 24:A26
21.2.C	" 22:A407; 24:X77
29.E–G	" 25:X33, X36, A208, A244, A429
31.1.D–F	" 24:X22, A137
31.2.A–S*	" 24:A75 (base variant)
32.1	" 24:X23, A45
32.2	" 24:A46 (base variant)
34	" 23:X26, A248
38.A–S*	" 24:A74
45.1	" 22:A119, A120, X3, X5, X59, X93, X136, A174
51.1.H–M	" 23:A20, A38, A79, A88, A91, A92, A97, A100, A136
51.7	" 23:A71
53.H–L	" 23:A80, A81, A82, A168, A138
54.2.A–C	" 23:A209 (form more similar to 54.1.A–B)
68.B	" 25:A5–A213 (additional "flower pot" forms that could be added to the Corpus)

Zâharîyeh

Saller has published a few vessels from Zâharîyeh which indicate some use of the site in the first century B.C.[225]

Corpus Type	Reference
71.1.K$_2$	Pl. 23:A173 (body as 71.1.N$_1$)
71.1.P—Q	" 23:X54
72.2.A—B	" 23:A172, A415, X4, A171
82.1.B	" 14:A4
83.2	" 14:A6
92.A—D	" 24:X96, X131, X63, A246
251.2.B	" 22:A103 (base variant), A108
251.6	" 22:A40 (later development), A105, A472, A41 (?)
253.1.L—M	" 22:A106, A77, A104
254.2.B	" 22:A471

225. S. Saller, "Ez-Zahiriyye in the Light of Ancient Pottery," *Liber Annuus*, VII (1956—57), pp. 56—61. Fig. 1:20 // Corpus 151.1 (deeper than examples in Corpus). Fig. 1:21—23 // 91.1. Fig. 2:24 // 83.2.A. Fig. 2:25 // 82.1.B.

CHAPTER VI

A CORPUS OF PALESTINIAN POTTERY, 200 B.C.—A.D. 70

The Corpus presented in this chapter has two main purposes. First, it attempts to summarize what has been discovered about the chronology of Palestinian pottery in the period under study, and, secondly, it attempts to provide a useful handbook of Late Hellenistic and Early Roman ceramic forms that will be of use to a Palestinian field archaeologist. Both of these purposes imply that the Corpus dare not be too lengthy and detailed, for inability to produce a clear and precise summary would indicate a deficient analysis of the material and would be of little use to an archaeologist in the field. On the other hand, the Corpus types could be so broad and general that they would be of little or no chronological significance. The Corpus is the result of an effort to avoid both extremes. In those decisions regarding format or extent of the Corpus that were difficult to make, error in the direction of too much detail was preferred with the thought that a further generalization is much simpler than the refinement of a more general analysis.

Delimitation of Corpus Material.—Instead of attempting to include all forms which might occur in the period, only those forms which can be dated with some precision are included. Most of these forms are attested in strata dated by non-ceramic evidence. A few forms are added from sealed loci where their homogeneity has been established by the stratified evidence, or when it has been possible to isolate the latest types in a series of independently dated fills. The attempt is made to take the illustrated Corpus forms from stratified groups whenever practicable. As a rule, when forms from sealed loci are illustrated, it is because the forms are not attested in the stratified groups or because the sealed locus contained a more complete specimen.

The Corpus as described above is supplemented by a very few forms or variations. These are all marked with an S; see, for example, 38.A—S and 38.B—S. These forms are included because they commonly occur with small pottery groups (for example, ossuary tomb groups) that in other respects belong to the period under discussion. These forms should be accepted with some reservation. They cannot be dated closely with any confidence since the groups to which they belong are so small or for other reasons.

An examination of the material in Chapters IV and V suggests that a number of forms of several types are missing from the Corpus because of the limited evidence available. The classes that seem to be especially weak (beginning with the weakest) are lamps, jugs, juglets, and unguentaria. Rather than attempting to fill out these classes from less trustworthy evidence, it seems best to await new material.

Originally, an attempt was made to use some of the groups discussed in Chapter V to expand the Corpus. This attempt was abandoned because the "evidence" from these groups results from subjective typological comparisons and analyses which should not be placed on the same level with the evidence from Chapters II and III presented in the Corpus. It was felt that the multiplication of such comparisons and of subjective opinions regarding the dating of the various groups is precisely what has led to the confusion which has prevailed until quite recently in this period. Some significant conclusions may have thereby been excluded, but, with few exceptions, it is impossible to segregate these from conclusions whose significance is dubious. Some of the least dubious have been noted in the supplementary (S) forms in the Corpus.

Instead of the original plan, under each type are listed alphabetically the sites discussed in Chapter V at which the forms occurred. This brings together the published evidence on the provenience of each type; turning back to Chapter V will provide the pertinent reference to any context that an investigator might consider worthy of examination. The sites in Chapter V are discussed alphabetically except 'Ain Feshkha, which is treated with the Qumrân caves.

Validity and Reliability of the Corpus. — If the Corpus is to be used as a chronological tool, attention must be given to its validity and reliability. The validity is concerned with the ability of the Corpus to measure what it purports to measure. The Corpus purports to measure the actual ceramic development, not, for example, the subjective idealization of typological development. The methodology adopted in the study has attempted to assure the validity of the study. The framework of the Corpus is provided by pottery groups dated independent of ceramic evidence and the developments observed are empirically described. The Corpus is supplemented by actual ceramic data, and general descriptions of typological development are limited to descriptions of the empirical evidence. No attempt is made to describe transitions from one form to another or developments of forms which are not at the same time descriptions of actual ceramic data. Where subjective opinions of development without evidential support have been observed, they have been rejected. In the analyses in Chapters III-V the validity of the original Corpus framework has been confirmed by its ability to measure ceramic development in the period under study, that is, to identify homogeneous groups and establish dates for them. Frequent independent correlations with these dates from literary or non-ceramic evidence provide additional independent confirmation of their validity.

The reliability of the Corpus refers to the consistency and precision with which it measures. In a sense the reliability of the Corpus has not been adequately checked. Only if two or more researchers working independently on the basis of the Corpus can arrive at similar datings for specific groups, is there any check on the reliability of the Corpus. Needless to say, access to the pottery itself and the experience of the researcher will materially affect the reliability of his conclusions. In a more basic sense, however, the reliability of the Corpus has been established. The chronological conclusions regarding the dating of groups in Chapters III-V have consistently agreed with datings provided by independent, non-ceramic evidence such as literary references to the history of the site, numismatic evidence, and epigraphic remains. The extent of this reliability or the preciseness of the Corpus as a measuring tool, of course, leaves much to be desired. The lack of evidence or very limited evidence on a number of the ceramic types of this period makes precision impossible. Those types represented by a single example, for instance, need not even be dated through the entire period of the context indicated. Yet, other types can be dated more closely and certain forms can be dated confidently within half a century. When a number of these forms occur together, groups may be dated within a quarter century,[1] and any attempt to date groups more closely than this by ceramic evidence alone would not be judicious.

Method of Presentation. — Undecorated ware has been separated from decorated ware. Types numbers below one hundred refer to undecorated ware.[2] Types 101—199 refer to Hellenistic Decorated Ware, types 201—299 to Eastern Sigillata A, and types 301—399 to other miscellaneous wares (West Slope Technique, Pompeian Red Ware, and Arretine Ware). The order of the types varies from publication to publication and from one geographical area to another. The order followed in the Corpus presents what are at times called "closed" types first, the jars (11—19), the jugs and flasks (21—29), and the juglets, bottles, and vases (31—39). Then follow "open" types, the mortaria and craters (41—49) and bowls, cups, and plates (51—59). The "kitchen" ware is completed with a miscellaneous class of lids, stands, and funnels (61—69). The cooking ware follows in types 71—79. Types 81—89 are reserved for lamps, and 91—92 for unguentaria. This last group is separeted from the bottles in types 31—39 in many non-Palestinian classifications,[3] but this separation has not generally been made in Palestinian publications. Unlike other "kitchen ware," precise parallels to the unguentaria are found throughout the Graeco-Roman world. Accordingly, unguentaria should not be lumped with local undecorated ware.[4]

Where possible forms in types 101—399 correspond numerically to similar forms in undecorated ware. For example, the undecorated bowl with incurved rim is type 51.1; the bowl with incurved rim in Hellenistic Decorated Ware is type 151.1. In this way local kitchen ware provides the framework from which imported pottery is viewed. This seems justified by the preponderance of local kitchen ware at all Palestinian sites studied.

Method of Use. — A few words of caution are in order in regard to the use of the Corpus. An excavator discovering a sizable group of forms with close Corpus parallels of similar date can tentatively date that group, but before final conclusions are

---
1. Cf. p. 25 *supra*.
2. An exception is made in the case of common undecorated forms that are occasionally decorated. Cf. Chap. V, n. 159 under Fig. 2:7.
3. Cf., *e.g.*, TCHP, pp. 472—74.
4. It might be suggested that the bottle of Corpus type 38. A—S and 38. B—S should be considered with the unguentaria, but it does not have the widespread provenience of the piriform and fusiform unguentaria and seems to be related to Corpus type 31.2. A. Cf. *Kahane III*, pp. 51—52.

drawn, relationships in ware, paste, and firing should be checked. Attention must be given to the relative sizes of the vessels compared. Centimeter scales are provided for Corpus drawings where these are available, but vessels included are drawn to different scales.[5] The full range of variation in a given type is not always presented in the Corpus, and the original publications may yield more precise parallels. In this connection the remarks about method of selecting parallels made at the beginning of Chapter V should be recalled. At times the original publication also includes photographs which are helpful. In short, what is stressed here is that the Corpus can serve as a helpful preliminary tool, but where precision is needed the Corpus is no substitute for the original publication, and even consultation of the original publication is no substitute for an examination of the pottery itself.

Reference to a few detailed points may also be helpful. Observations listed under the types are not meant to be definitive. Notations of typological development are given only where these are not easily observed in the illustrated (*) examples. It should be kept in mind (as noted specifically with certain vessels) that the Samaria HFW did contain pre – 200 B.C. material, and Qumrân Trench A probably contained a few vessels from the turn of the era. The dates 200 B.C. and A.D. 70 merely represent the *termini* of the period studied and *not* necessarily the *termini* of the forms. The dates mentioned in the Corpus are not to be considered definitive; they represent the dates in which the type has occurred according to the limited evidence available. The limited extent of the evidence should be noted throughout the Corpus, as, for example, the fact that all the bowls of type 52 come from Qumrân. Finally, the numbers listed for pottery from Beth-zur and Shechem are Pottery Registration Numbers. They refer to material as yet unpublished.

---

5. Some of the plates in *SS III*, it will be noted, have no indication of scale.

CORPUS OUTLINE

11 – 99 Undecorated Wares

11 – 19 Jars
    Type 11. Large Cylindrical to Bag-shaped Jars with Rounded Base
        11.1 Simple rim
        11.2 Squared rim
        11.3 Rounded rim
        11.9 Miscellaneous parts of large jars
    Type 12. Large Bell-shaped Jars
    Type 13. Large Inverted Ovoid Jars with Ring Base
    Type 14. Large Cylindrical Footed Jars
        14.1 Angular to rounded shoulder
        14.2 With shoulder ledge
    Type 15. Small Cylindrical Footed Jars
    Type 19. Miscellaneous Jars

21—29 Jugs and Flasks
    Type 21. Large Jugs
            21.1 Wide neck
            21.2 Narrow neck
    Type 28. Miscellaneous Jugs and Fragments
    Type 29. Flasks

31—39 Juglets, Bottles, and Vases
    Type 31. Globular Juglets
            31.1 Round base
            31.2 Flat base
    Type 32. Spherical, Straight-necked Juglets
            32.1 Round base
            32.2 Flat base
    Type 33. Elongated Piriform Juglets
    Type 34. Wide-mouthed, Squat Juglets
    Type 38. Miscellaneous Bottles and Vases
    Type 39. Miscellaneous Fragments

41—49 Mortaria and Craters
    Type 41. Mortaria
    Type 45. Craters
            45.1 Large, without handles
            45.2 Small, without handles
            45.3 Large, with two handles
    Type 49. Miscellaneous Craters

51—59 Bowls, Cups, and Plates
    Type 51. Small Deep Bowls
            51.1 Incurved rim
            51.2 Hemispherical
            51.6 Vertical rim
            51.7 Incurved sides with everted rim
            51.8 Everted rim or sides
    Type 52. Cups
            52.1 Inverted to vertical sides
            52.2 Everted sides
            52.9 Miscellaneous cups
    Type 53. Shallow Bowls and Plates
    Type 54. Shallow Bowls with Vertical Sides
            54.1 Large
            54.2 Small

61–69 Lids, Stands, and Funnels
    Type 61. Shallow Lids
    Type 62. Lids with Vertical Sides
    Type 63. Miscellaneous Lids
    Type 65. Stands
    Type 68. Funnels

71–79 Cooking Pots, Pans, and Braziers
    Type 71. Globular Cooking Pots
        71.1 Without lid device
        71.2 With lid device
    Type 72. Shallow Cooking Pots
        72.1 With lid device
        72.2 With shoulder
        72.3 Simple rim
    Type 78. Frying Pans

81–89 Lamps
    Type 81. Small Folded Lamps
        81.1 Open
        81.2 Closed
    Type 82. Bow-spouted ("Herodian") Lamps
        82.1 Undecorated
        82.2 Decorated
    Type 83. Delphiniform Lamps
        83.1 Plain
        83.2 Ray motif
        83.3 Volute motif
    Type 84. Loop-handled Lamps
    Type 85. Molded Lamps with Slight Nozzle

91–92 Unguentaria
    Type 91. Fusiform Unguentaria
        91.1 Heavy ware
        91.2 Thin ware
    Type 92. Piriform Unguentaria

101–199 Hellenistic Decorated Ware

121–129 Jugs and Flasks
    Type 128. Miscellaneous Jugs

131–139 Juglets, Bottles, and Vases
    Type 139. Miscellaneous Fragments

151—159   Bowls, Cups, and Plates
    Type 151.   Small Deep Bowls
            151.1   Incurved rim
            151.2   Hemispherical
            151.3   Outcurved rim
            151.4   Pinched handle
            151.5   Skyphos
            151.9   Miscellaneous fragments
    Type 153.   Shallow Bowls and Plates
            153.1   Fish plates
            153.9   Miscellaneous shallow bowls and plates
    Type 158.   Megarian Bowls

201—299   Eastern Sigillata A

221—229   Jugs and Flasks
    Type 228.   Miscellaneous Jugs

251—259   Bowls, Cups, and Plates
    Type 251.   Small Deep Bowls
            251.2   Hemispherical (plain rim)
            251.2a   Hemispherical (everted rim)
            251.2b   Hemispherical (molded rim)
            251.6   Vertical rim
    Type 252.   Cups
            252.2   Everted sides
            252.3   Small craters
    Type 253.   Shallow Bowls and Plates
            253.1   Small with plain rim
            253.2   Small with molded rim
            253.3   Small with everted rim and flat base
            253.4   Large with simple rim
            253.5   Large with molded rim
            253.6   Large with everted rim
    Type 254.   Shallow Bowls with Vertical Sides
            254.2   Small

301—399   Miscellaneous Wares

Arretine Ware
    Type 354.2

Pompeian Red Ware
    Type 353.3

West Slope Technique
    Types 328, 345, 353.1, 353.2

11–19 JARS
TYPE 11. LARGE CYLINDRICAL TO BAG-SHAPED JARS WITH ROUNDED BASE

11.1 Simple rim (20 B.C.–A.D. 68)

Observations:

1. Least common rim treatment in jars of this type.
2. No certain evidence of this rim treatment until near the turn of the era.
3. Parallels: 'Ain Shems, Jerusalem, Qumrân Caves, 'Ain Feshkha, Samaria, Tulûl Abû el-'Alâyiq.

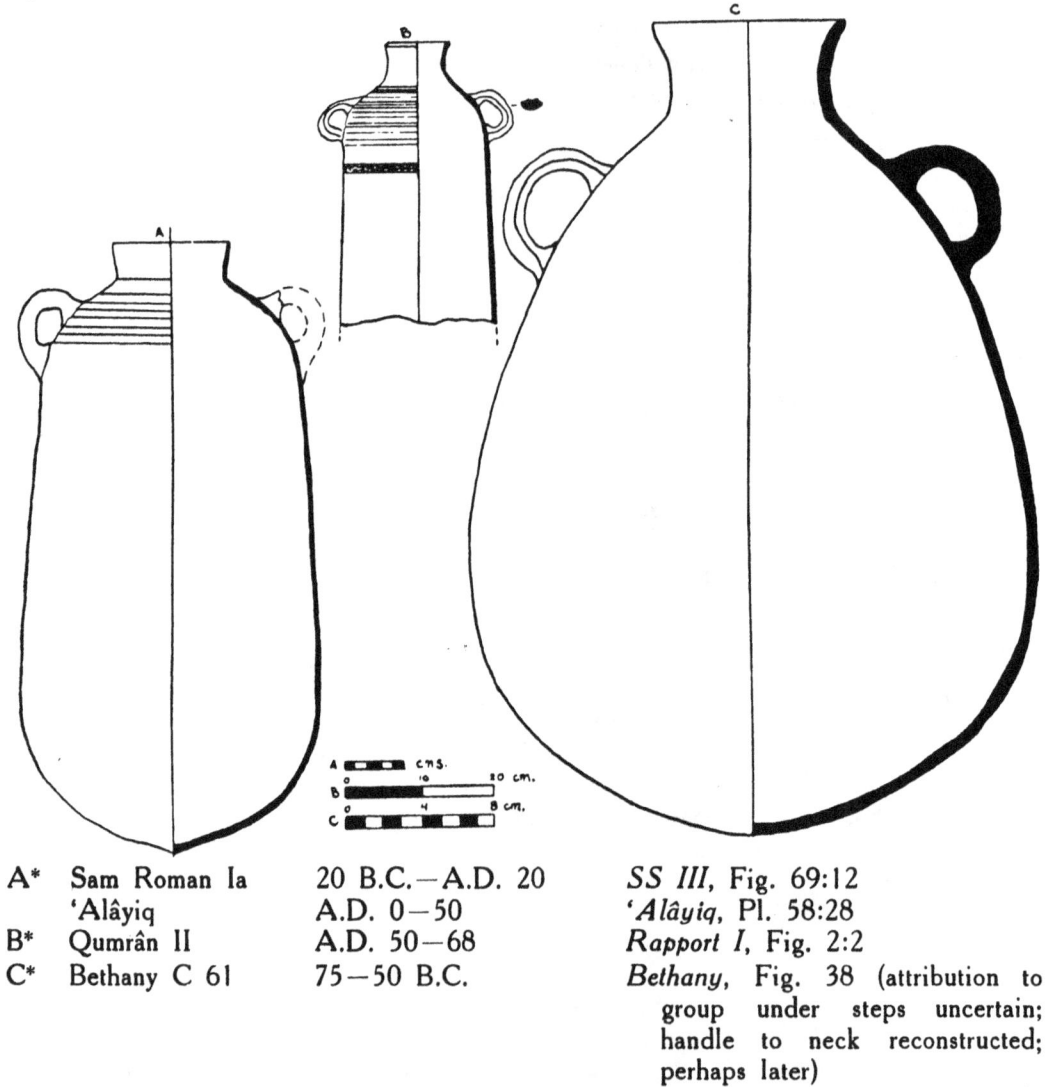

A*	Sam Roman Ia 'Alâyiq	20 B.C.–A.D. 20 A.D. 0–50	*SS III*, Fig. 69:12 *Alâyiq*, Pl. 58:28
B*	Qumrân II	A.D. 50–68	*Rapport I*, Fig. 2:2
C*	Bethany C 61	75–50 B.C.	*Bethany*, Fig. 38 (attribution to group under steps uncertain; handle to neck reconstructed; perhaps later)
	Qumrân II	A.D. 50–68	*Rapport II*, Fig. 5:6

continued page 145

11–19 JARS

TYPE 11. LARGE CYLINDRICAL TO BAG-SHAPED JARS WITH ROUNDED BASE

11.1 Simple rim (continued)

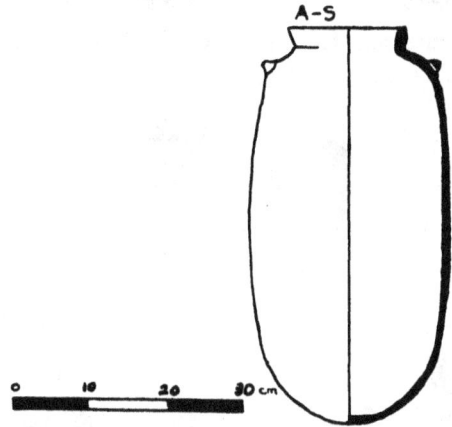

A–S* Qumrân Cave 26 A.D. 50–68   *Caves*, Fig. 2:5

11–19 JARS

TYPE 11. LARGE CYLINDRICAL TO BAG-SHAPED JARS WITH ROUNDED BASE

11.2 Squared rim (175 B.C.–A.D. 68)

Observations:

1. Gradual tendency to lengthen the collar throughout the period.
2. Parallels: Beth-zur, Jerusalem, Lachish, Pella, 'Ain Feshkha, Samaria, Tell el-Fûl, Tell en-Nasbeh, Tulûl Abû el-'Alâyiq.

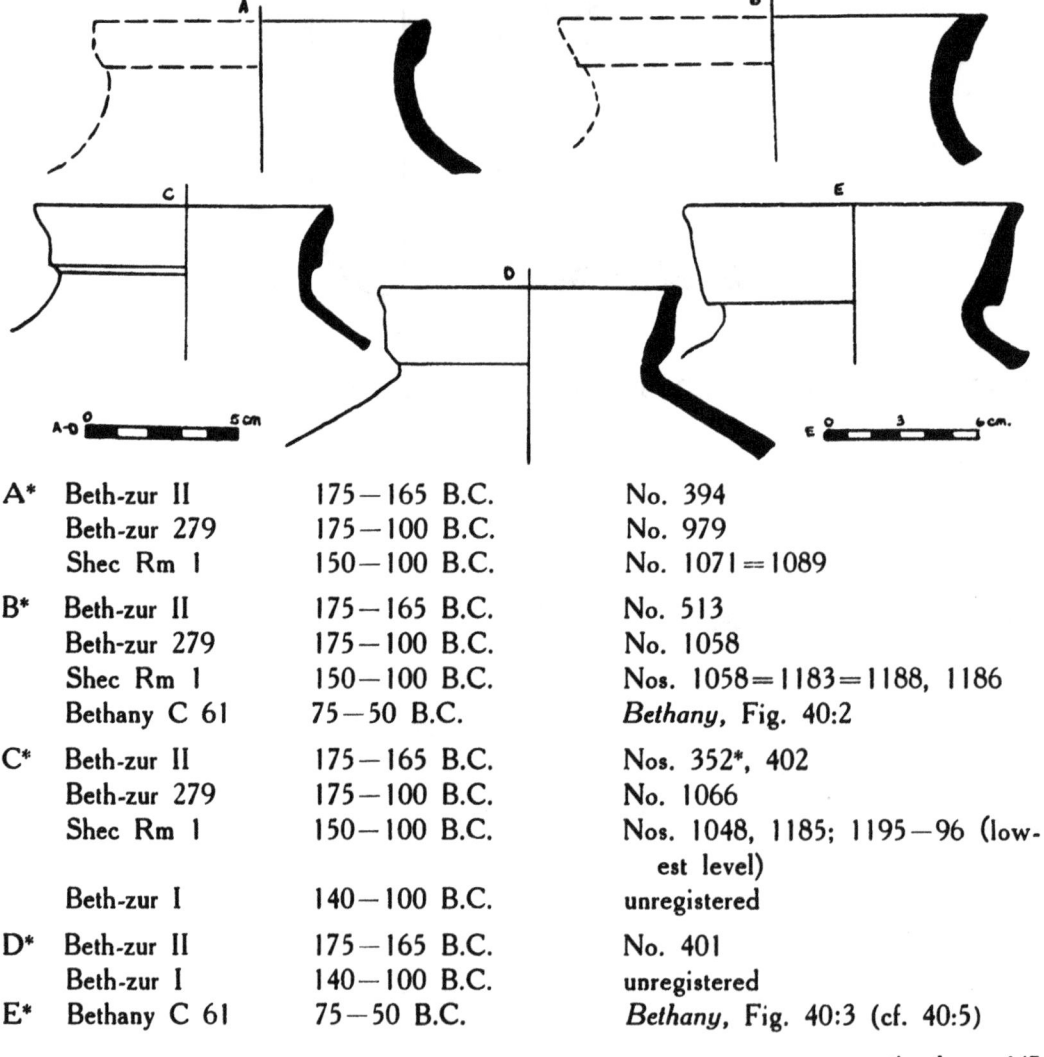

A*	Beth-zur II	175–165 B.C.	No. 394
	Beth-zur 279	175–100 B.C.	No. 979
	Shec Rm 1	150–100 B.C.	No. 1071=1089
B*	Beth-zur II	175–165 B.C.	No. 513
	Beth-zur 279	175–100 B.C.	No. 1058
	Shec Rm 1	150–100 B.C.	Nos. 1058=1183=1188, 1186
	Bethany C 61	75–50 B.C.	*Bethany*, Fig. 40:2
C*	Beth-zur II	175–165 B.C.	Nos. 352*, 402
	Beth-zur 279	175–100 B.C.	No. 1066
	Shec Rm 1	150–100 B.C.	Nos. 1048, 1185; 1195–96 (lowest level)
	Beth-zur I	140–100 B.C.	unregistered
D*	Beth-zur II	175–165 B.C.	No. 401
	Beth-zur I	140–100 B.C.	unregistered
E*	Bethany C 61	75–50 B.C.	*Bethany*, Fig. 40:3 (cf. 40:5)

continued page 147

11–19 JARS

TYPE 11. LARGE CYLINDRICAL TO BAG-SHAPED JARS WITH ROUNDED BASE

11.2 Squared rim (continued)

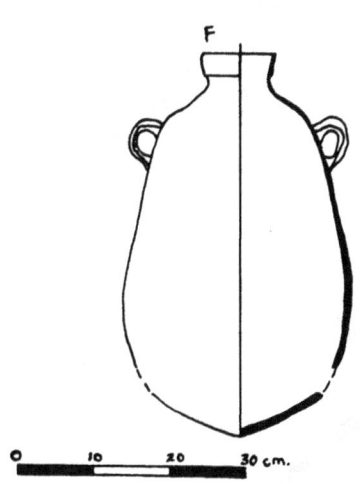 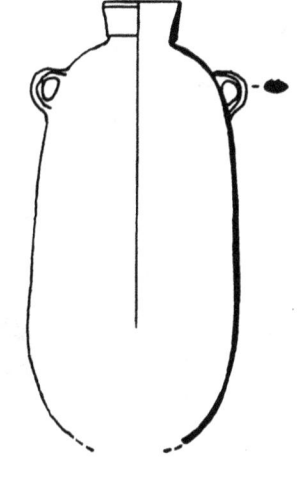

F*	Qumrân Tr A	50–31 B.C.	*Rapport II*, Fig. 1:4
	Jerus Ctdl C	37–29 B.C.	Johns, *QDAP*, XIV, Fig. 14:1 (first rim sherd)
G	Jerus Ctdl C	37–29 B.C.	Johns, *QDAP*, XIV, Fig. 14:1
	Sam Roman Ia	20 B.C.–A.D. 20	*SS III*, Fig. 69:11
*	Qumrân II	A.D. 50–68	*Rapport I*, Fig. 2:5

11–13 JARS

TYPE 11. LARGE CYLINDRICAL TO BAG-SHAPED JARS WITH ROUNDED BASE

11.3 Rounded rim (200–29 B.C.)

Observations:

1. Parallels: Lachish, Ramat Rahel, Tell el-Fûl, Tulûl Abû el-'Alâyiq.

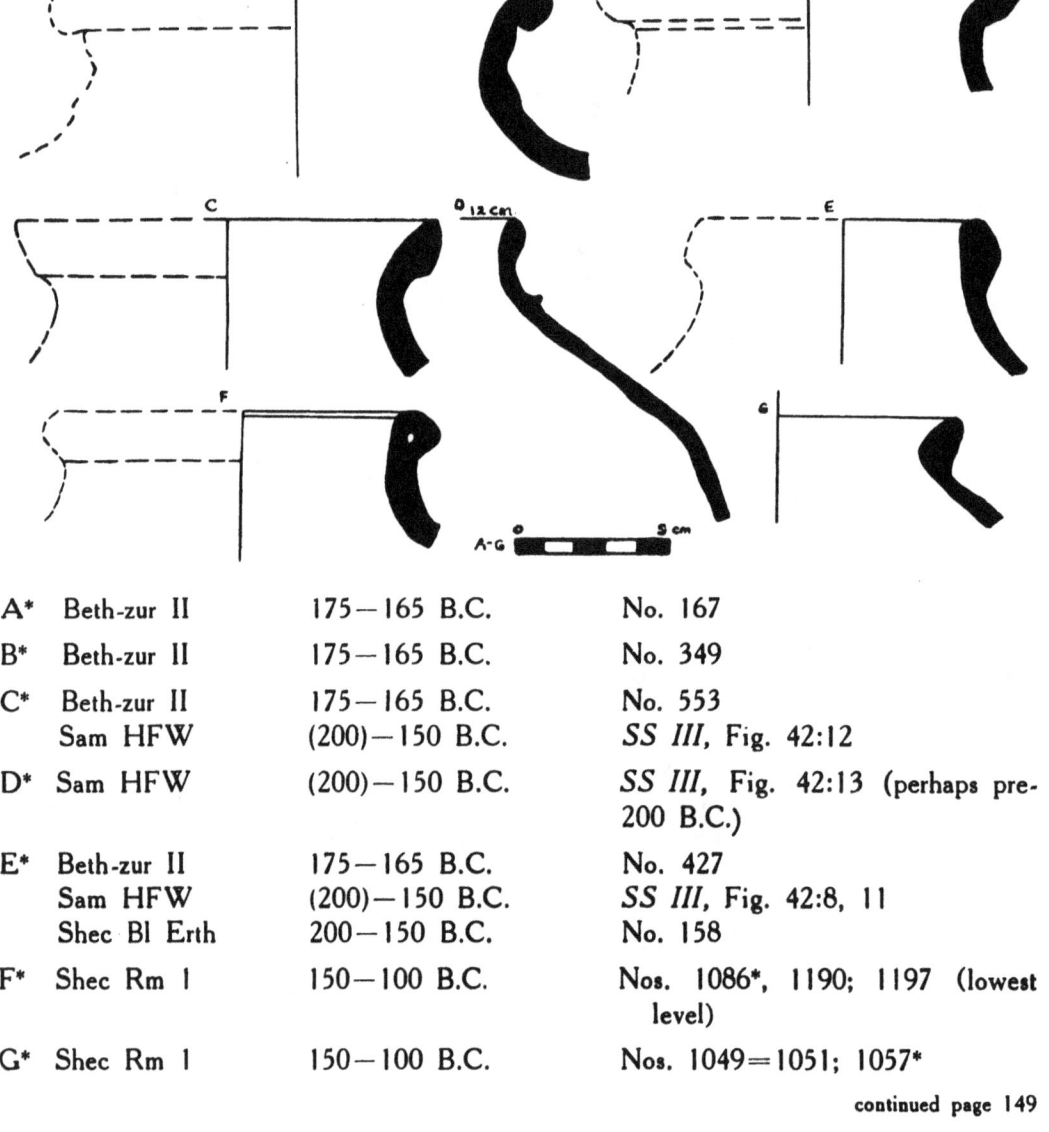

A*	Beth-zur II	175–165 B.C.	No. 167
B*	Beth-zur II	175–165 B.C.	No. 349
C*	Beth-zur II	175–165 B.C.	No. 553
	Sam HFW	(200)–150 B.C.	*SS III*, Fig. 42:12
D*	Sam HFW	(200)–150 B.C.	*SS III*, Fig. 42:13 (perhaps pre-200 B.C.)
E*	Beth-zur II	175–165 B.C.	No. 427
	Sam HFW	(200)–150 B.C.	*SS III*, Fig. 42:8, 11
	Shec Bl Erth	200–150 B.C.	No. 158
F*	Shec Rm 1	150–100 B.C.	Nos. 1086*, 1190; 1197 (lowest level)
G*	Shec Rm 1	150–100 B.C.	Nos. 1049=1051; 1057*

continued page 149

11–19 JARS

TYPE 11. LARGE CYLINDRICAL TO BAG-SHAPED JARS WITH ROUNDED BASE

11.3 Rounded rim (continued)

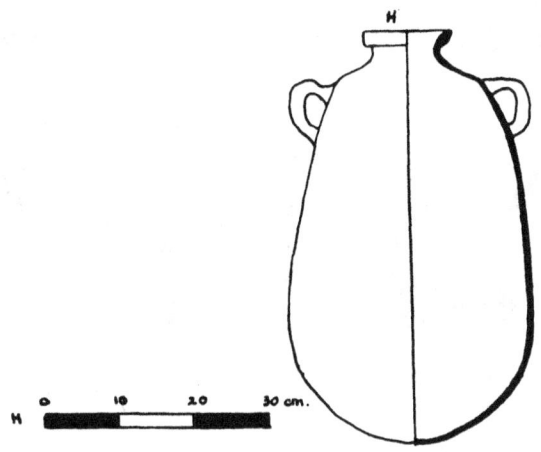

H* Qumrân Ib	50–31 B.C.	*Rapport II*, Fig. 1:2
Jerus Ctdl C	37–29 B.C.	Johns, *QDAP*, XIV, Fig. 14:1 (sixth fragment)

11–19 JARS

TYPE 11. LARGE CYLINDRICAL TO BAG-SHAPED JARS WITH ROUNDED BASE

11.9 Miscellaneous parts of large jars (arbitrarily assigned to Type 11)

Observations:
1. The stances of the handles from 'Alâyiq are questionable.
2. The oval section (E) does not occur in pre–150 B.C. contexts.

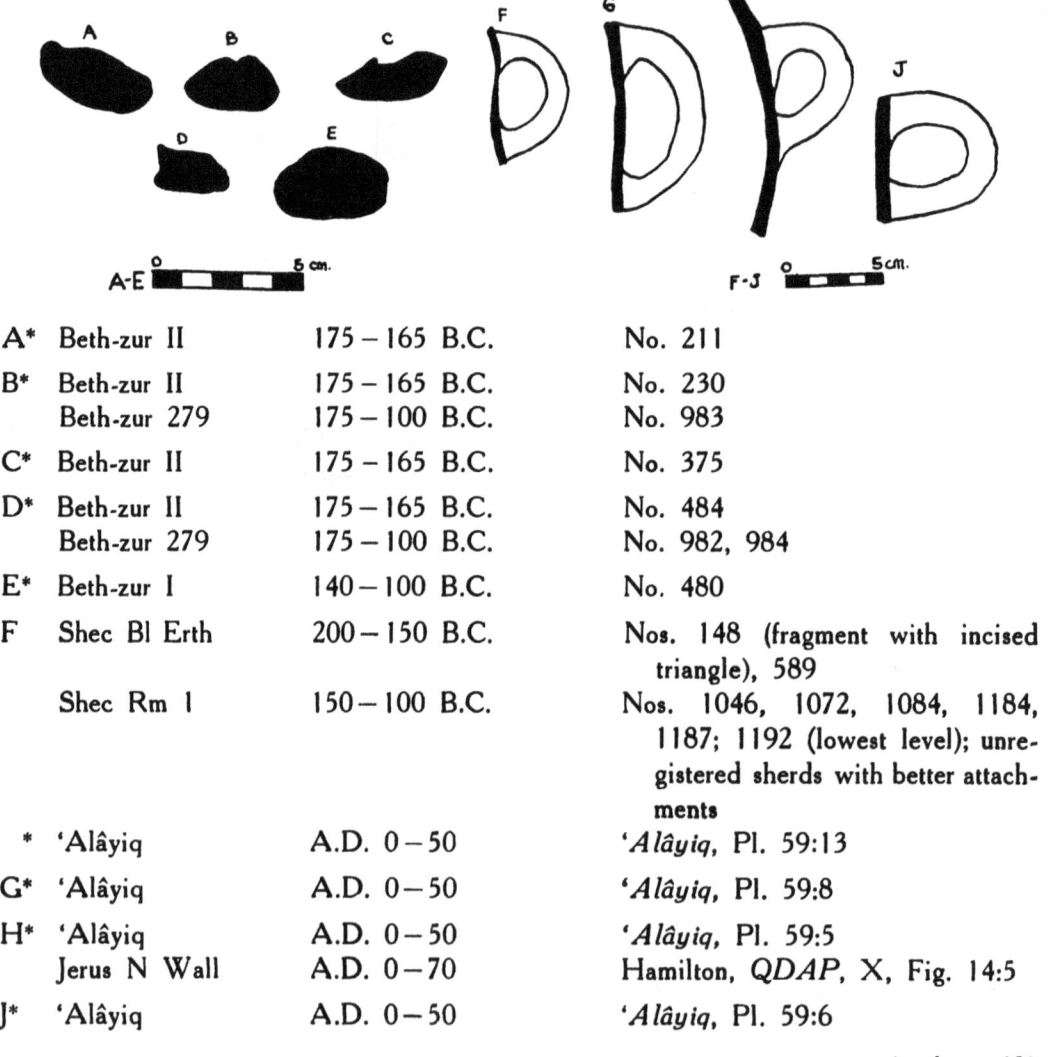

A*	Beth-zur II	175–165 B.C.	No. 211
B*	Beth-zur II	175–165 B.C.	No. 230
	Beth-zur 279	175–100 B.C.	No. 983
C*	Beth-zur II	175–165 B.C.	No. 375
D*	Beth-zur II	175–165 B.C.	No. 484
	Beth-zur 279	175–100 B.C.	No. 982, 984
E*	Beth-zur I	140–100 B.C.	No. 480
F	Shec Bl Erth	200–150 B.C.	Nos. 148 (fragment with incised triangle), 589
	Shec Rm 1	150–100 B.C.	Nos. 1046, 1072, 1084, 1184, 1187; 1192 (lowest level); unregistered sherds with better attachments
*	'Alâyiq	A.D. 0–50	*'Alâyiq,* Pl. 59:13
G*	'Alâyiq	A.D. 0–50	*'Alâyiq,* Pl. 59:8
H*	'Alâyiq	A.D. 0–50	*'Alâyiq,* Pl. 59:5
	Jerus N Wall	A.D. 0–70	Hamilton, *QDAP,* X, Fig. 14:5
J*	'Alâyiq	A.D. 0–50	*'Alâyiq,* Pl. 59:6

continued page 151

11-19

TYPE 11. LARGE CYLINDRICAL TO BAG-SHAPED JARS WITH ROUNDED BASE

11.9 Miscellaneous parts of large jars (continued)

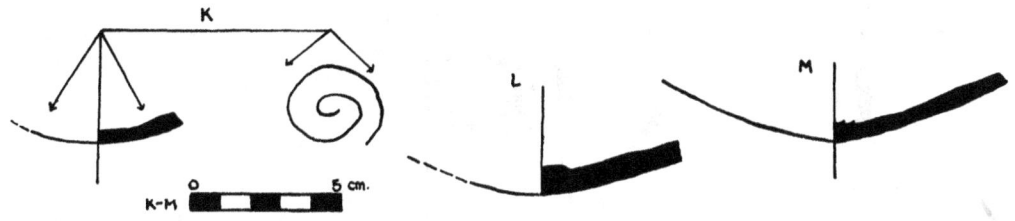

K*	Beth-zur II	175 – 165 B.C.	No. 210
L*	Beth-zur II	175 – 165 B.C.	No. 816
M*	Beth-zur II	175 – 165 B.C.	No. 822

11–19 JARS

TYPE 11. LARGE BELL-SHAPED JARS (75 B.C. – A.D. 70)

Observations:

1. Ridged rims of this type are at times difficult to distinguish from Type 11.2.
2. Parallels: ʻAin Shems, Beth-shan, En-gedi, Jerusalem, ʻAin Feshkha, Tell el-Fârʻah (South), Tell el-Fûl, Tell el-Qasîleh, Tell en-Nasbeh, Tulûl Abû el-ʻAlâyiq.

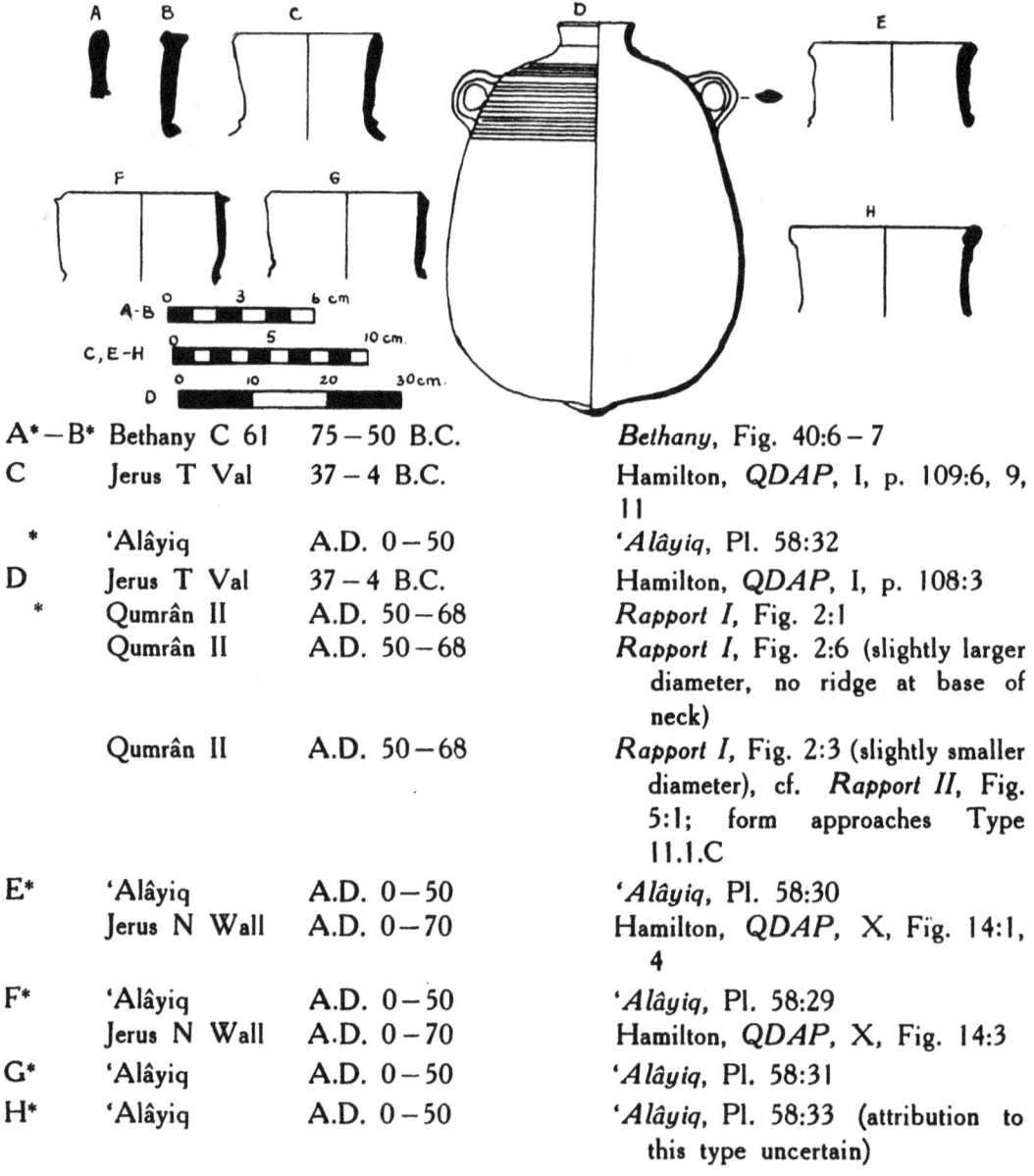

A*–B*	Bethany C 61	75–50 B.C.	*Bethany*, Fig. 40:6–7
C	Jerus T Val	37–4 B.C.	Hamilton, *QDAP*, I, p. 109:6, 9, 11
*	ʻAlâyiq	A.D. 0–50	*ʻAlâyiq*, Pl. 58:32
D	Jerus T Val	37–4 B.C.	Hamilton, *QDAP*, I, p. 108:3
*	Qumrân II	A.D. 50–68	*Rapport I*, Fig. 2:1
	Qumrân II	A.D. 50–68	*Rapport I*, Fig. 2:6 (slightly larger diameter, no ridge at base of neck)
	Qumrân II	A.D. 50–68	*Rapport I*, Fig. 2:3 (slightly smaller diameter), cf. *Rapport II*, Fig. 5:1; form approaches Type 11.1.C
E*	ʻAlâyiq	A.D. 0–50	*ʻAlâyiq*, Pl. 58:30
	Jerus N Wall	A.D. 0–70	Hamilton, *QDAP*, X, Fig. 14:1, 4
F*	ʻAlâyiq	A.D. 0–50	*ʻAlâyiq*, Pl. 58:29
	Jerus N Wall	A.D. 0–70	Hamilton, *QDAP*, X, Fig. 14:3
G*	ʻAlâyiq	A.D. 0–50	*ʻAlâyiq*, Pl. 58:31
H*	ʻAlâyiq	A.D. 0–50	*ʻAlâyiq*, Pl. 58:33 (attribution to this type uncertain)

11–19 JARS

TYPE 13. LARGE INVERTED OVOID JARS WITH RING BASE (50 B.C.– A.D. 68)

Observations:

1. Parallels: Tell el-Fûl, Tulûl Abû el-'Alâyiq.

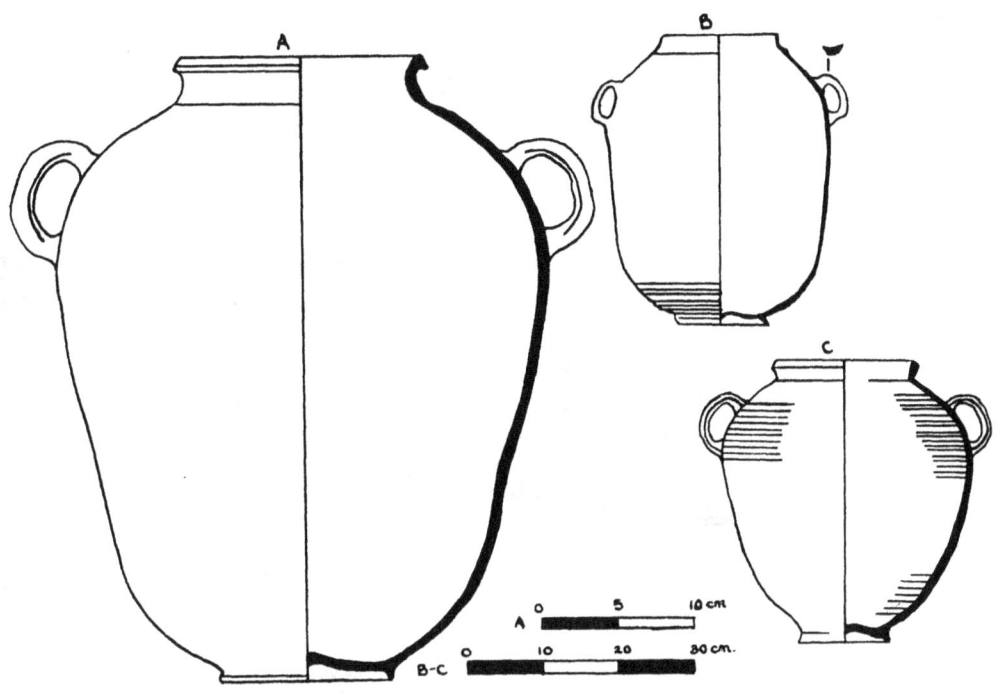

A*	Qumrân 89	50–31 B.C.	*Rapport III*, Fig. 2:10
	Qumrân Ib	50–31 B.C.	*Rapport II*, Fig. 1:3
B*	Qumrân II	A.D. 50–68	*Rapport I*, Fig. 2:7
	Qumrân II	A.D. 50–68	*Rapport II*, Fig. 5:2 (handle variant)
C*	Qumrân II	A.D. 50–68	*Rapport II*, Fig. 5:8

11–19 JARS

TYPE 14. LARGE CYLINDRICAL FOOTED JARS

14.1 Angular to rounded shoulder (A.D. 50–68)

Observations:

1. Parallels: Qumrân Caves, Tell el-Fûl, Tulûl Abû el-'Alâyiq.

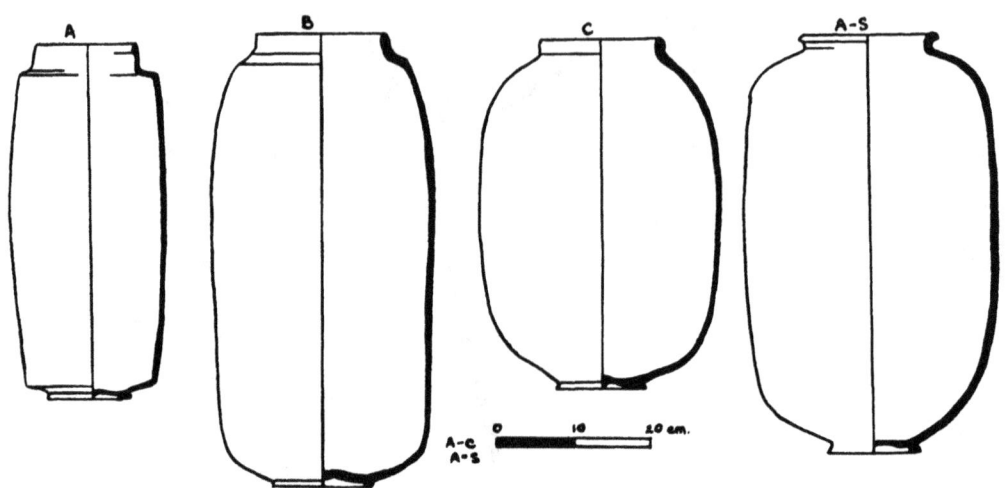

A*	Qumrân II	A.D. 50–68	*Rapport II*, Fig. 5:4
B*	Qumrân II	A.D. 50–68	*Rapport I*, Fig. 2:4
C*	Qumrân II	A.D. 50–68	*Rapport II*, Fig. 5:3
	Qumrân II	A.D. 50–68	*Rapport II*, Fig. 5:7 (with four pierced ear handles)
A–S*	Qumrân Cave 29	50–31 B.C.	*Caves*, Fig. 2:6 (probably Qumrân Ib horizon)

11–19 JARS

TYPE 14. LARGE CYLINDRICAL FOOTED JARS

14.2 With shoulder ledge (A.D. 50–68)

Observations:

1. Parallels: Qumrân Caves.

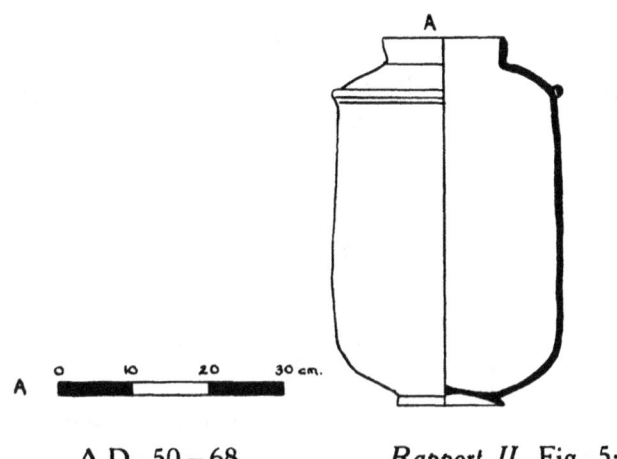

A*	Qumrân II	A.D. 50–68	*Rapport II*, Fig. 5:9

TYPE 15. SMALL CYLINDRICAL FOOTED JARS (A.D. 50–68)

Observations:

1. Parallels: 'Ain Feshkha, Tulûl Abû el-'Alâyiq.

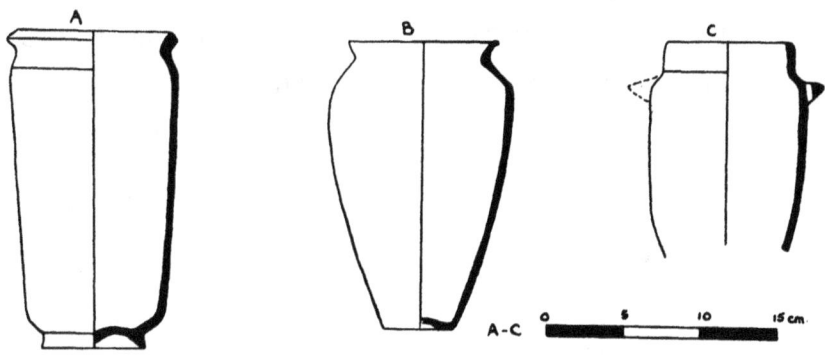

A*	Qumrân II	A.D. 50–68	*Rapport III*, Fig. 5:15 (perhaps from Qumrân Ib)
B*	Qumrân II	A.D. 50–68	*Rapport III*, Fig. 5:14
C*	Qumrân II	A.D. 50–68	*Rapport I*, Fig. 4:17

11–19 JARS

TYPE 19. MISCELLANEOUS JARS

Observations:
1. Parallels: Tulûl Abû el-'Alâyiq.

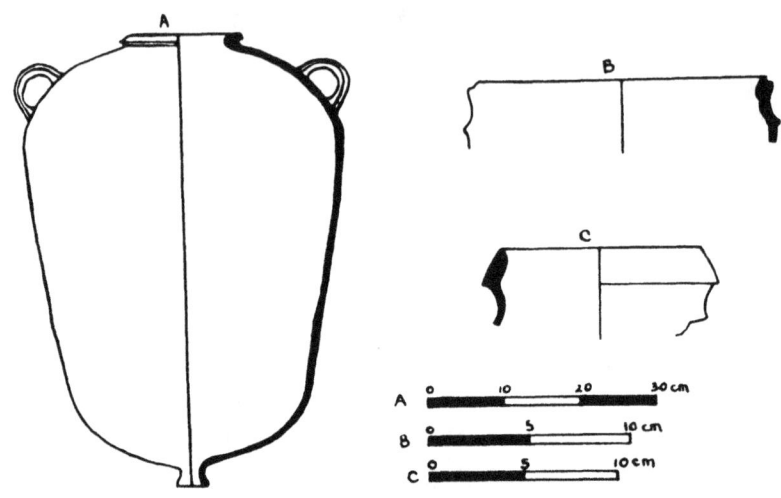

A*	Qumrân II	A.D. 50–68	*Rapport II*, Fig. 5:5 (note funnel base)
B*	'Alâyiq	A.D. 0–50	*'Alâyiq*, Pl. 58:7
C	Jerus T Val	37–4 B.C.	Hamilton, *QDAP*, I, p. 109:8
*	Jerus N Wall	A.D. 0–70	Hamilton, *QDAP*, X, Fig. 14:2

21–29 JUGS AND FLASKS

TYPE 21. LARGE JUGS

21.1 Wide neck (200 B.C.–A.D. 68)

Observations:

1. General trend toward angularity beginning at the end of the second century B.C. (cf. rims and bases).

2. Trend toward thinner ware during the second century B.C.

3. Parallels: Bethany, Beth-zur, Jerusalem, Lachish, Samaria, Tell el-Fûl, Tell en-Nasbeh, Tell Sandahannah, Tell Zakarîyeh, Tulûl Abû el-'Alâyiq.

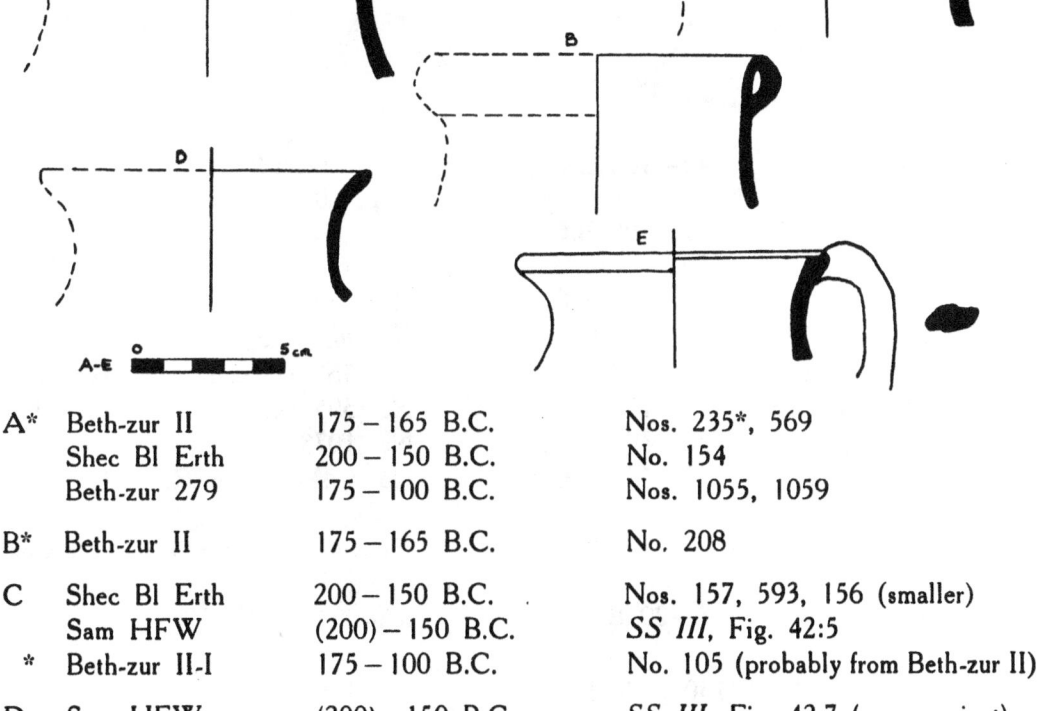

A*	Beth-zur II	175–165 B.C.	Nos. 235*, 569
	Shec Bl Erth	200–150 B.C.	No. 154
	Beth-zur 279	175–100 B.C.	Nos. 1055, 1059
B*	Beth-zur II	175–165 B.C.	No. 208
C	Shec Bl Erth	200–150 B.C.	Nos. 157, 593, 156 (smaller)
	Sam HFW	(200)–150 B.C.	*SS III*, Fig. 42:5
*	Beth-zur II-I	175–100 B.C.	No. 105 (probably from Beth-zur II)
D	Sam HFW	(200)–150 B.C.	*SS III*, Fig. 42:7 (ware variant)
*	Beth-zur 279	175–100 B.C.	No. 1014
E*	Shec Rm 1	150–100 B.C.	No. 1060 = 1061

continued page 158

21—29 JUGS AND FLASKS
TYPE 21. LARGE JUGS

21.1 Wide neck (continued)

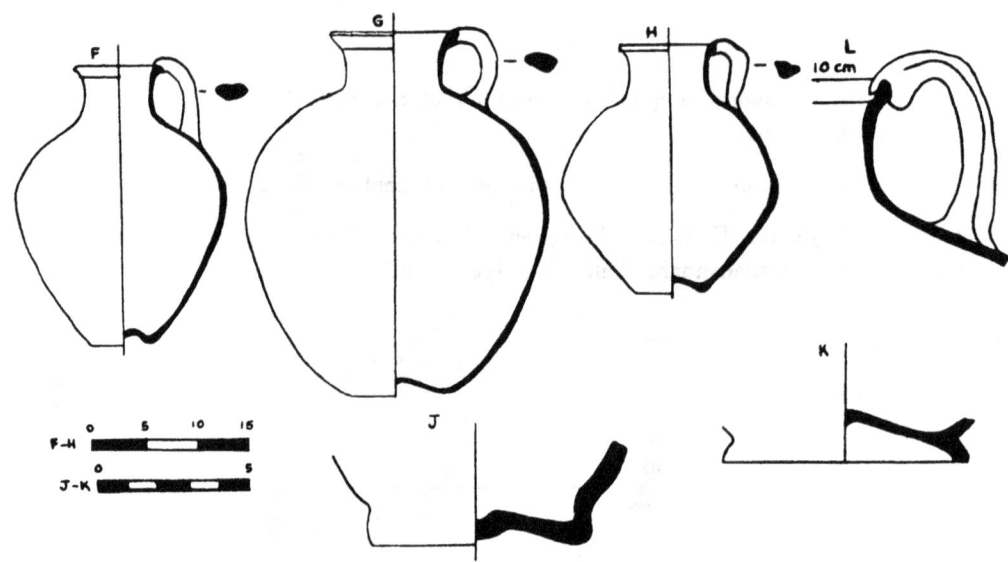

F*—G*	Beth-zur I	140—100 B.C.	Nos. 139, 136 (cf. *BASOR*, 151, p. 20, Fig. 2:5—8)
	Beth-zur 279	175—100 B.C.	Nos. 1025, 1046, 1056, 1060, 1065, 1073
	Shec Rm 1	150—100 B.C.	Nos. 1083 (base), 1050 (handle)
	Bethany C 61	75—50 B.C.	*Bethany*, Fig. 40:1 (not jar)
H	Beth-zur II	175—165 B.C.	No. 366 (thicker ware than H*)
	Shec Bl Erth	200—150 B.C.	No. 595 (thicker ware than H*)
	Shec Rm 1	150—100 B.C.	No. 1073
*	Beth-zur I	140—100 B.C.	No. 141 = *BASOR*, 151, p. 20, Fig. 2:4
	Qumrân 89	50—31 B.C.	*Rapport III*, Fig. 2:1 (more elongated)
	Jerus Ctdl C	37—29 B.C.	Johns, *QDAP*, XIV, Fig. 14:1, sherds 4, 8
J*	Shec Rm 1	150—100 B.C.	No. 1054
K*	Beth-zur II	175—165 B.C.	No. 406
	Beth-zur 279	175—100 B.C.	No. 980
L*	Sam PHFW	150—107 B.C.	*SS III*, Fig. 43:11

continued page 159

21–29 JUGS AND FLASKS

TYPE 21. LARGE JUGS

21.1 Wide neck (continued)

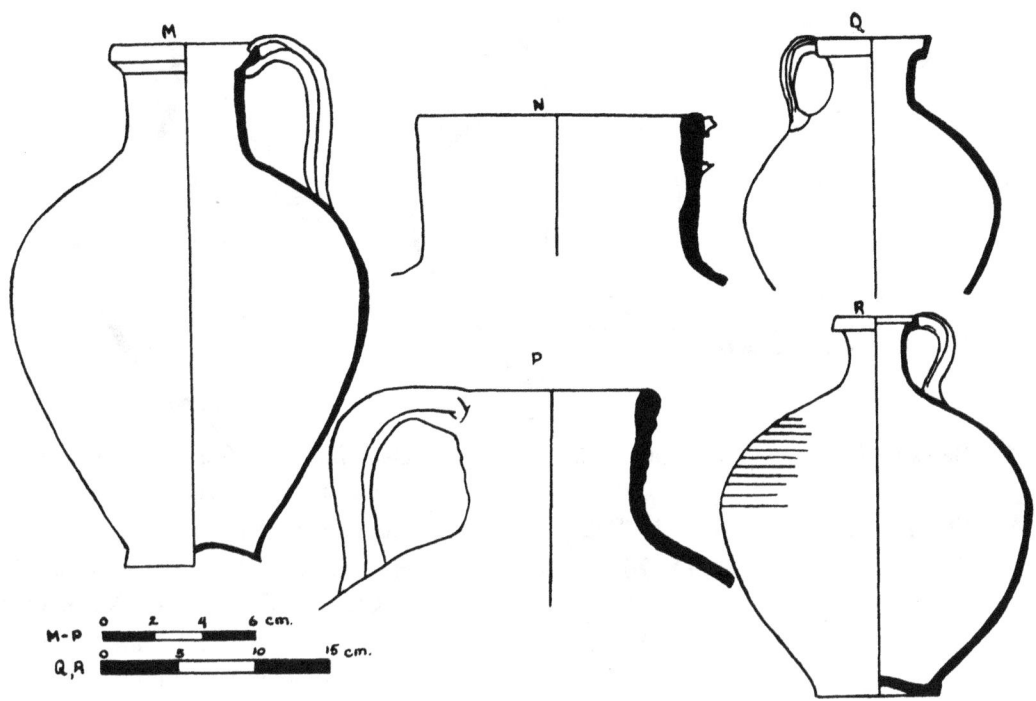

M*	Bethany C 61	75–50 B.C.	*Bethany*, Fig. 61:1*, 2
N*–P*	Bethany C 61	75–50 B.C.	*Bethany*, Fig. 60:1828, 1846
Q*	Qumrân Ib	50–31 B.C.	*Rapport III*, Fig. 1:5
R	'Alâyiq	A.D. 0–50	*'Alâyiq*, Pl. 58:23, 25; Pl. 59:9
*	Qumrân II	A.D. 50–68	*Rapport II*, Fig. 4:12
	Qumrân II	A.D. 50–68	*Rapport III*, Fig. 4:3

21–29 JUGS AND FLASKS
TYPE 21. LARGE JUGS

21.2 Narrow neck (75 or 50 B.C. – A.D. 70)

Observations:
1. Parallels: Beth-shan, Qumrân Caves, Tell en-Nasbeh.

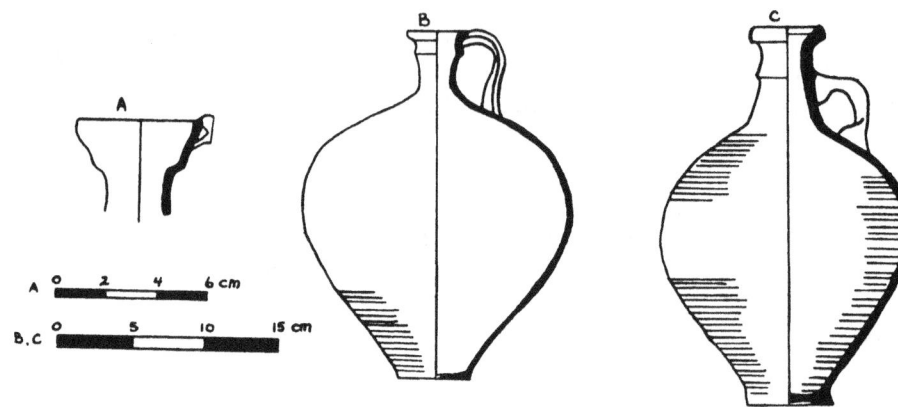

A*	Bethany C 61	75 – 50 B.C.	*Bethany*, Fig. 61:10 (attribution to this type uncertain)
B*	Qumrân Ib	50 – 31 B.C.	*Rapport II*, Fig. 3:19
C*	Qumrân III	A.D. 70+	*Rapport II*, Fig. 6:7 (occurs in Qumrân II; cf. Chap. V, n. 153)
	Bethany C 61	75 – 50 B.C.	*Bethany*, Fig. 40:4 (attribution to this type uncertain)

TYPE 28. MISCELLANEOUS JUGS AND FRAGMENTS

Observations:
1. Attribution to the jug class uncertain.

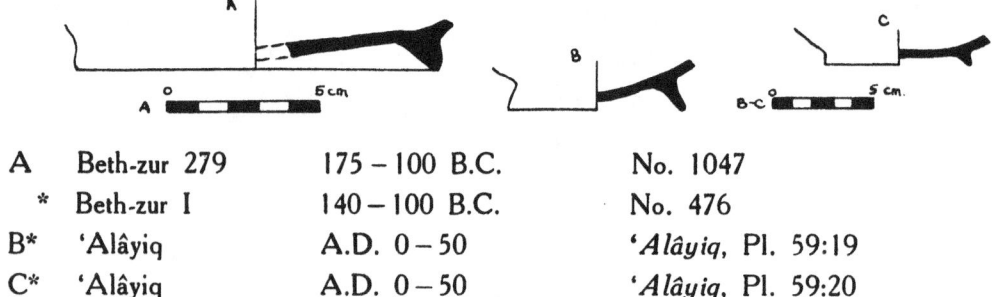

A	Beth-zur 279	175 – 100 B.C.	No. 1047
*	Beth-zur I	140 – 100 B.C.	No. 476
B*	'Alâyiq	A.D. 0 – 50	*'Alâyiq*, Pl. 59:19
C*	'Alâyiq	A.D. 0 – 50	*'Alâyiq*, Pl. 59:20

21–29 JUGS AND FLASKS
TYPE 29. FLASKS (200 B.C.–A.D. 70)

Observations:
1. Possible development of a longer neck during the second century B.C.
2. Parallels: Beth-shan, Beth-zur, Jerusalem, Lachish, 'Ain Feshkha, Samaria, Tell el-Fûl, Tell Sandahannah, Tulûl Abû el-'Alâyiq.

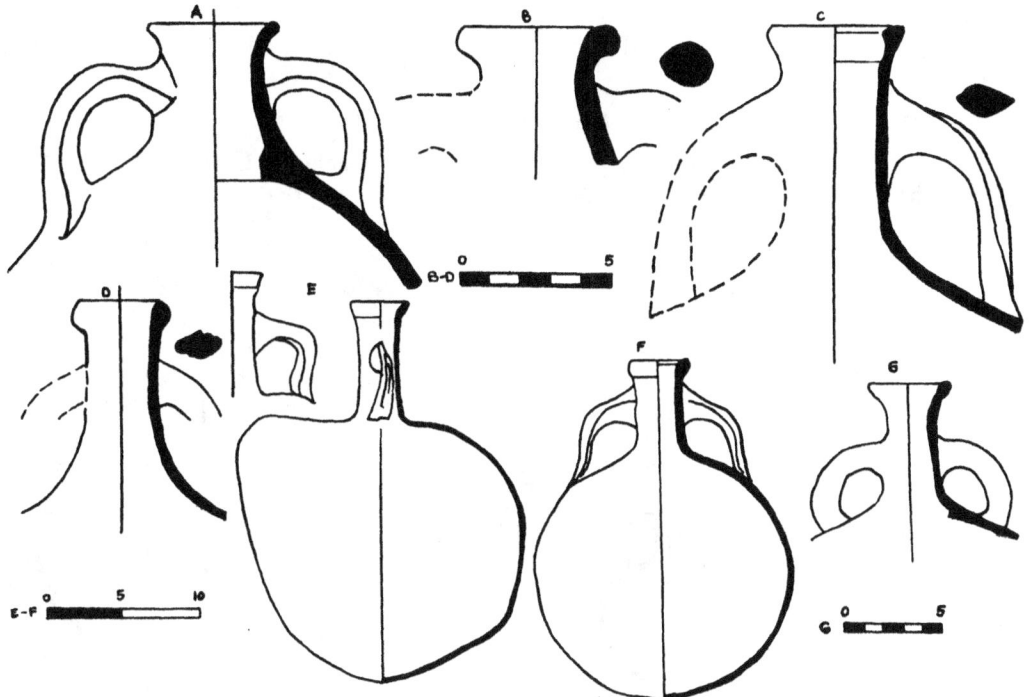

A*	Sam HFW	(200)–150 B.C.	*SS III*, Fig. 42:3 (possibly pre-200 B.C.)
B*	Beth-zur II	175–165 B.C.	No. 584
C*	Beth-zur II	175–165 B.C.	No. 372
	Beth-zur I	140–100 B.C.	No. 332
D*	Beth-zur 279	175–100 B.C.	No. 1013
E*	Qumrân Ib	50–31 B.C.	*Rapport II*, Fig. 3:18
	Jerus Ctdl C	37–29 B.C.	Johns, *QDAP*, XIV, Fig. 14:4a
	Jerus T Val	37–4 B.C.	Hamilton, *QDAP*, I, p. 109:4
F*	Qumrân Tr A	50–31 B.C.	*Rapport II*, Fig. 2:21
G*	'Alâyiq	A.D. 0–50	*'Alâyiq*, Pl. 59:21
	'Alâyiq	A.D. 0–50	*'Alâyiq*, Pl. 59:35 (neck interior variant)
	Jerus N Wall	A.D. 0–70	Hamilton, *QDAP*, X, Fig. 14:9

31 – 39 JUGLETS, BOTTLES, AND VASES
TYPE 31. GLOBULAR JUGLETS

31.1 Round base (200 B.C. – A.D. 70)

Observations:

1. Second century B.C. examples tend to be larger than those from the first century B.C.
2. Sharper lines of the rim and neck (better differentiated neck) in the first century B.C.
3. Tendency toward elongation in the first century A.D.
4. Parallels: Bethlehem, Beth-zur, Gezer, Jerusalem, Lachish, Qumrân Caves, 'Ain Feshkha, Tell en-Nasbeh, Tulûl Abû el-'Alâyiq.

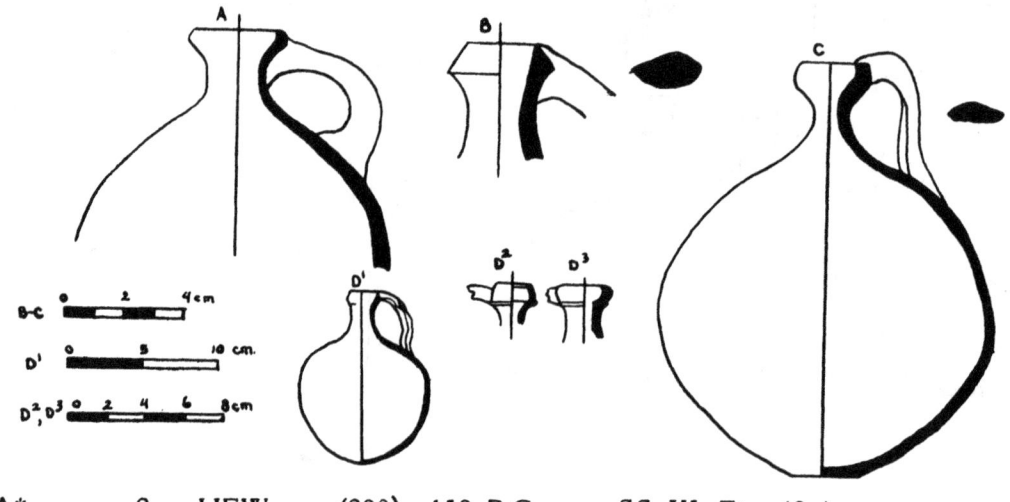

A*	Sam HFW	(200) – 150 B.C.	*SS III*, Fig. 42:4
	Beth-zur II-I	175 – 100 B.C.	No. 93
B*	Beth-zur 279	175 – 100 B.C.	No. 1030 (attribution to this type uncertain)
C	Beth-zur II	175 – 165 B.C.	No. 370
*	Beth-zur I	140 – 100 B.C.	No. 155 = *BASOR*, 151, p. 20, Fig. 2:3
D₁	Bethany C 61	75 – 50 B.C.	*Bethany*, Fig. 61:11
	Bethany C 61	75 – 50 B.C.	*Bethany*, Fig. 61:5
*	Qumrân Ib	50 – 31 B.C.	*Rapport II*, Fig 3:20
	Sam VIt C 2	75 – 25 B.C.	*HE I*, Fig. 183:25a
	Qumrân II	A.D. 50 – 68	*Rapport I*, Fig. 3:1 (cf. Fig. 3:3)
D₂* – D₃*	Sam VIt C 2	75 – 25 B.C.	*HE I*, Fig. 183:25b (both examples)

continued page 163

31–39 JUGLETS, BOTTLES, AND VASES
TYPE 31. GLOBULAR JUGLETS
31.1 Round base (continued)

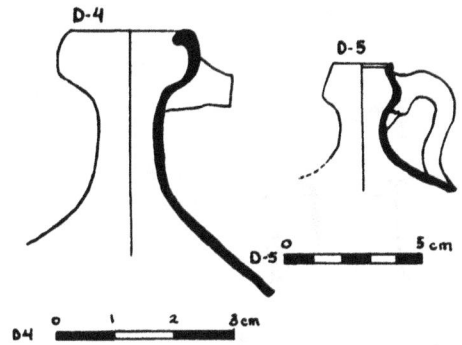
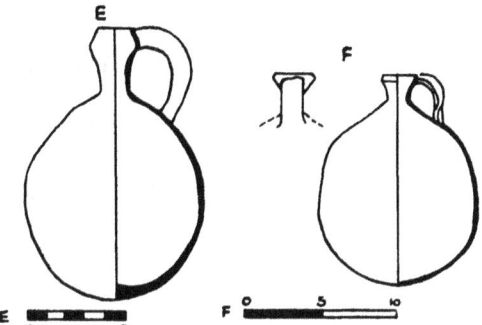

D₄*	Jerus T Val	37–4 B.C.	Hamilton, *QDAP*, I, p. 109:7
D₅*	Jerus T Val	37–4 B.C.	*PEFA*, 1927, Pl. XII:25
	Qumrân II	A.D. 50–68	*Rapport II*, Fig. 4:9
E	Qumrân Tr A	50–31 B.C.	*Rapport II*, Fig. 2:20 (possibly first century A.D.)
*	'Alâyiq	A.D. 0–50	*'Alâyiq*, Pl. 59:30 (cf. Pl. 59:38, 39; 42:5, 9)
	Jerus N Wall	A.D. 0–70	Hamilton, *QDAP*, X, Fig. 14:10
	Qumrân II	A.D. 50–68	*Rapport I*, Fig. 3:1 (cf. Fig. 3:3)
F*	Qumrân II	A.D. 50–68	*Rapport III*, Fig. 4:8

31.2 Flat base (75–25 B.C.)

Observations:
1. Parallels: Jerusalem, 'Ain Feshkha, Ramat Rahel, Samaria, Tulûl Abû el-'Alâyiq.

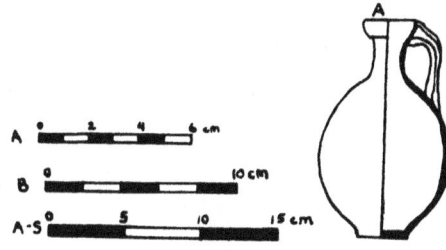
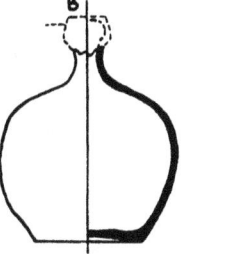

A*	Bethany C 61	75–50 B.C.	*Bethany*, Fig. 61:6
B*	Sam Vlt C 2	75–25 B.C.	*HE I*, Fig. 183:26a (possibly earlier)
A–S*	'Ain Feshkha II	A.D. 50–68	*Feshkha*, Fig. 2:1

31–39 JUGLETS, BOTTLES, AND VASES
TYPE 32. SPHERICAL, STRAIGHT-NECKED JUGLETS

32.1 Round base (75–29 B.C.)

Observations:

1. Parallels: Bethany, Tulûl Abû el-'Alâyiq.

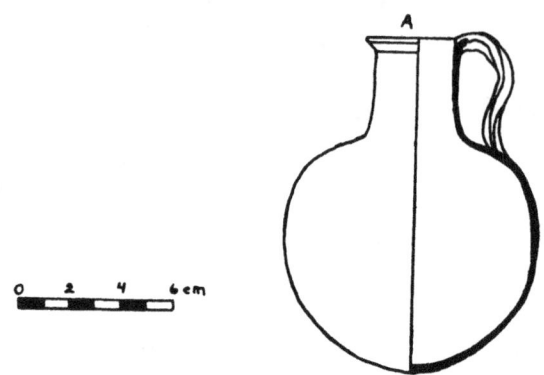

A*	Bethany C 61	75–50 B.C.	*Bethany*, Fig. 61:3 (cf. Fig. 61:4, 9)
	Jerus Ctdl C	37–29 B.C.	Johns, *QDAP*, XIV, Fig. 14:4c

32.2 Flat base (A.D. 50–68)

Observations:

1. Parallels: Qumrân Caves, Tulûl Abû el-'Alâyiq.

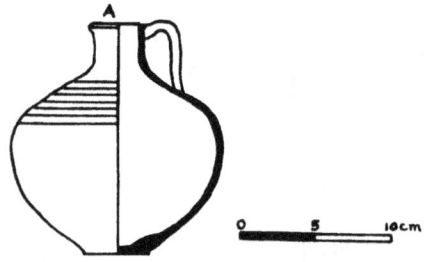

A*	Qumrân II	A.D. 50–68	*Rapport III*, Fig. 5:18

31–39 JUGLETS, BOTTLES, AND VASES

TYPE 33. ELONGATED PIRIFORM JUGLETS (37 B.C.–A.D. 68)

Observations:

1. Parallels: Ramat Rahel, Tell el-Fâr'ah (South).

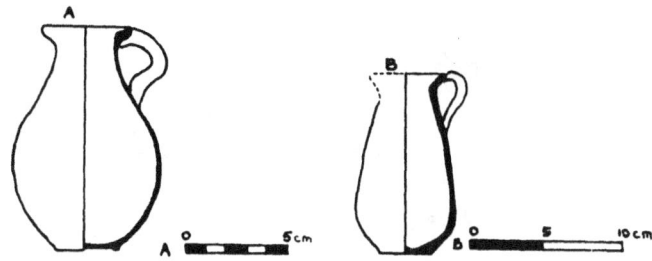

A	Jerus T Val	37–4 B.C.	Hamilton, *QDAP*, I, p. 109:1
*	'Alâyiq	A.D. 0–50	*'Alâyiq*, Pl. 58:26
B*	Qumrân II	A.D. 50–68	*Rapport II*, Fig. 4:10

TYPE 34. WIDE-MOUTHED, SQUAT JUGLETS (A.D. 0–68)

Observations:

1. Parallels: Ramat Rahel, Tulûl Abû el-'Alâyiq.

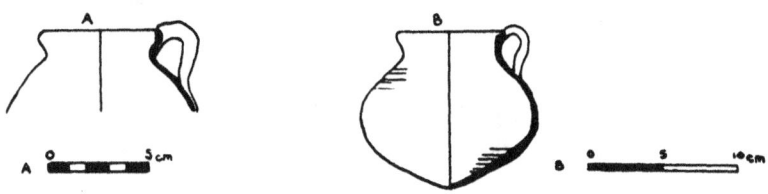

| A* | 'Alâyiq | A.D. 0–50 | *'Alâyiq*, Pl. 59:2 |
| B* | Qumrân II | A.D. 50–68 | *Rapport II*, Fig. 4:16 |

31–39 JUGLETS, BOTTLES, AND VASES

TYPE 38. MISCELLANEOUS BOTTLES AND VASES

Observations:

1. Parallels: Jerusalem (to 38.A—S*, 38.B—S*), Ramat Rahel (to 38.B—S*), Tulûl Abû el-'Alâyiq (to 38.A—S*).

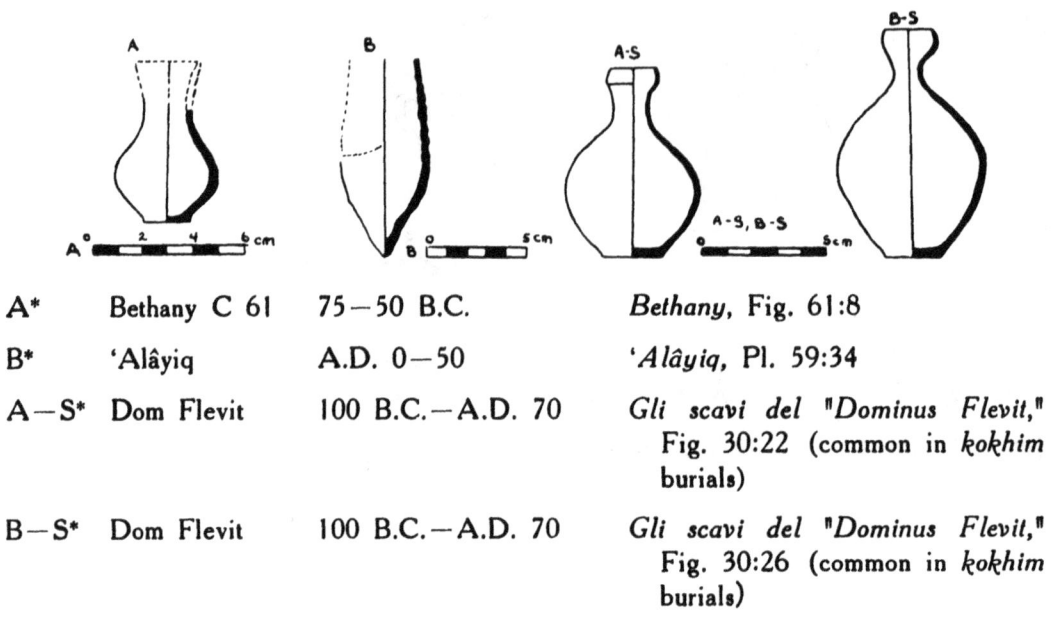

A*	Bethany C 61	75–50 B.C.	*Bethany*, Fig. 61:8
B*	'Alâyiq	A.D. 0–50	*'Alâyiq*, Pl. 59:34
A—S*	Dom Flevit	100 B.C.–A.D. 70	*Gli scavi del "Dominus Flevit,"* Fig. 30:22 (common in *kokhim* burials)
B—S*	Dom Flevit	100 B.C.–A.D. 70	*Gli scavi del "Dominus Flevit,"* Fig. 30:26 (common in *kokhim* burials)

TYPE 39. MISCELLANEOUS FRAGMENTS

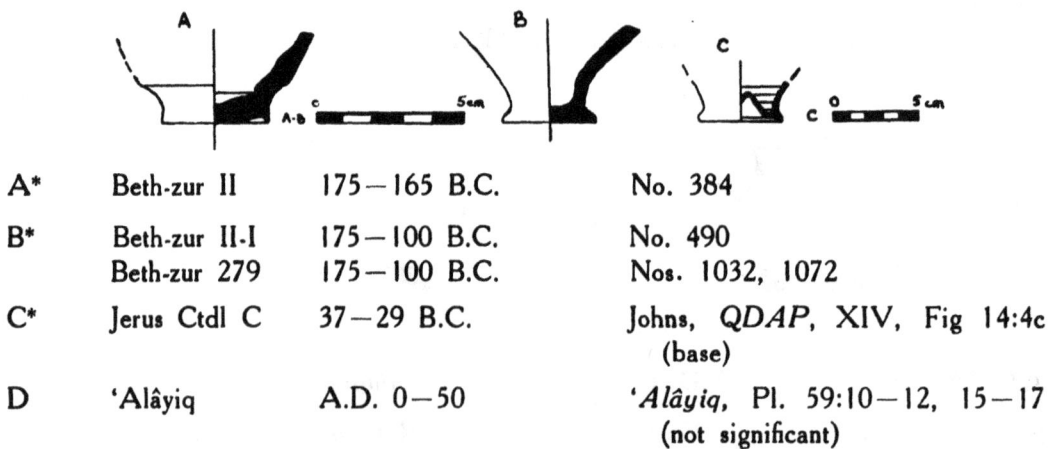

A*	Beth-zur II	175–165 B.C.	No. 384
B*	Beth-zur II-I	175–100 B.C.	No. 490
	Beth-zur 279	175–100 B.C.	Nos. 1032, 1072
C*	Jerus Ctdl C	37–29 B.C.	Johns, *QDAP*, XIV, Fig 14:4c (base)
D	'Alâyiq	A.D. 0–50	*'Alâyiq*, Pl. 59:10–12, 15–17 (not significant)

41–49 MORTARIA AND CRATERS

TYPE 41. MORTARIA (200–100 B.C.)

Observations:

1. Parallels: Beth-zur, Qubeibeh, Ramat Rahel.

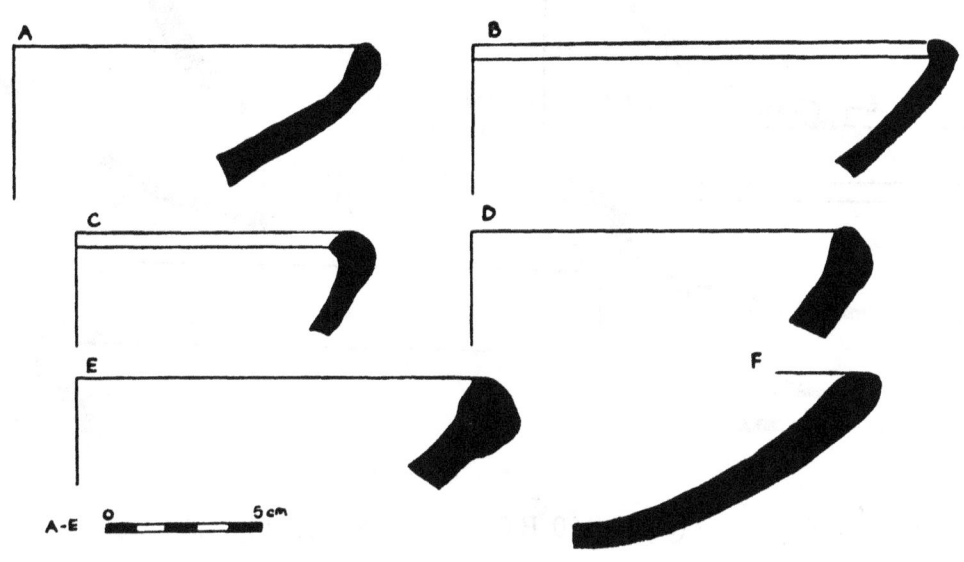

A*	Beth-zur II	175–165 B.C.	No. 198
B*	Beth-zur II	175–165 B.C.	No. 392
	Sam PHFW	150–107 B.C.	*SS III*, Fig. 43:8
C*	Beth-zur II	175–165 B.C.	No. 824
D	Shec Bl Erth	200–150 B.C.	No. 778
	Shec Rm 1	150–100 B.C.	No. 1063 (thinner ware)
*	Beth-zur I	140–100 B.C.	No. 479
E*	Beth-zur II	175–165 B.C.	No. 374
F*	Sam HFW	(200)–150 B.C.	*SS III*, Fig. 40:2

continued page 168

41–49 MORTARIA AND CRATERS

TYPE 41. MORTARIA (continued)

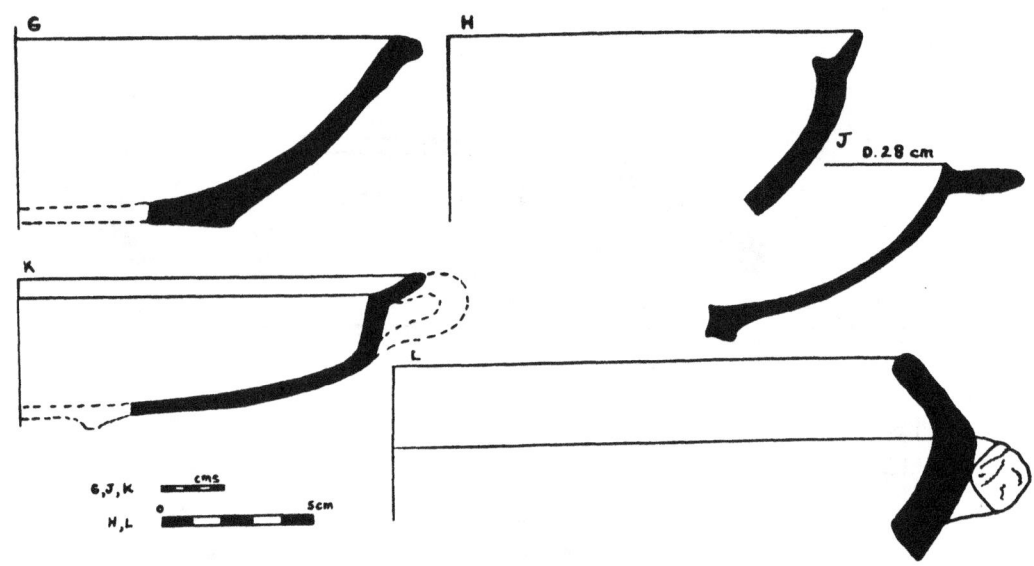

G*	Sam HFW	(200)–150 B.C.	*SS III*, Fig. 40:3
H*	Shec Bl Erth	200–150 B.C.	No. 150
J*	Sam HFW	(200)–150 B.C.	*SS III*, Fig. 40:4
K*	Sam HFW	(200)–150 B.C.	*SS III*, Fig. 40:5
	Beth-zur II	175–165 B.C.	Nos. 171, 403 (bases)
L*	Beth-zur II-I	175–100 B.C.	No. 181
	Beth-zur 279	175–100 B.C.	No. 1080

41 - 49 MORTARIA AND CRATERS

TYPE 45. CRATERS

45.1 Large, without handles (50 B.C. – A.D. 68)

Observations:
1. Parallels: Tulûl Abû el-'Alâyiq.

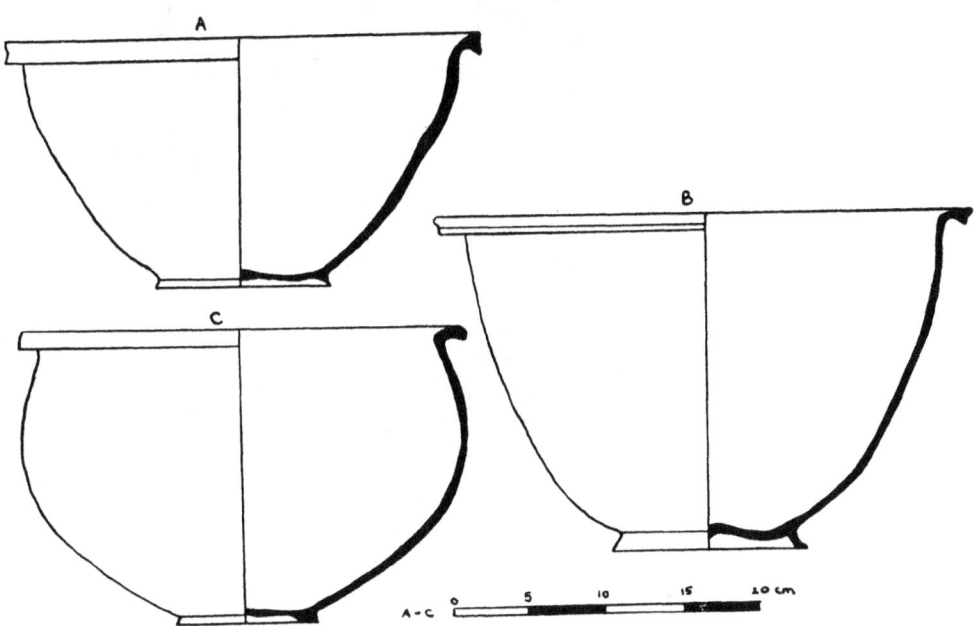

A*	Qumrân 89	50 – 31 B.C.	*Rapport III*, Fig. 2:2
	'Alâyiq	A.D. 0 – 50	*'Alâyiq*, Pl. 58:14, 18
B*	Qumrân II	A.D. 50 – 68	*Rapport I*, Fig. 3:8
C	'Alâyiq	A.D. 0 – 50	*'Alâyiq*, Pl. 58:12
*	Qumrân II	A.D. 50 – 68	*Rapport III*, Fig. 4:15

41–49 MORTARIA AND CRATERS

TYPE 45. CRATERS

45.2 Small, without handles (50 B.C.–A.D. 68)

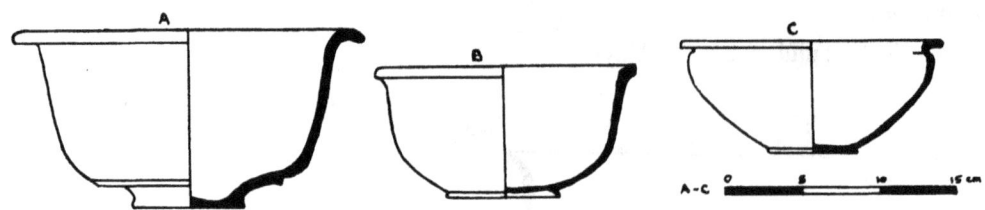

A*	Qumrân Ib	50–31 B.C.	*Rapport II*, Fig. 3:21
B*	Qumrân II	A.D. 50–68	*Rapport III*, Fig. 5:16
C*	Qumrân II	A.D. 50–68	*Rapport III*, Fig. 4:11

45.3 Large, with two handles (A.D. 0–68)

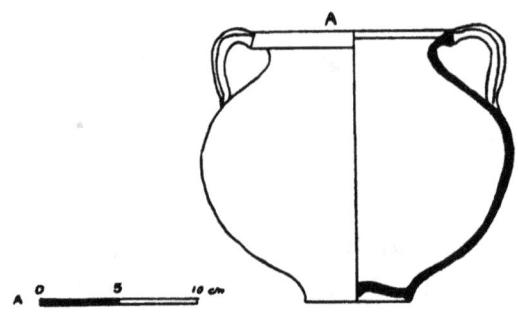

A	'Alâyiq	A.D. 0–50	*'Alâyiq*, Pl. 58:8, 9, 15 (possibly also 58:10 if stance is inaccurate); Pl. 59:14
	Qumrân II	A.D. 50–68	*Rapport I*, Fig. 3:2
	Qumrân II	A.D. 50–68	*Rapport II*, Fig. 4:17
*	Qumrân II	A.D. 50–68	*Rapport III*, Fig. 5:17

41–49 MORTARIA AND CRATERS

TYPE 49. MISCELLANEOUS CRATERS

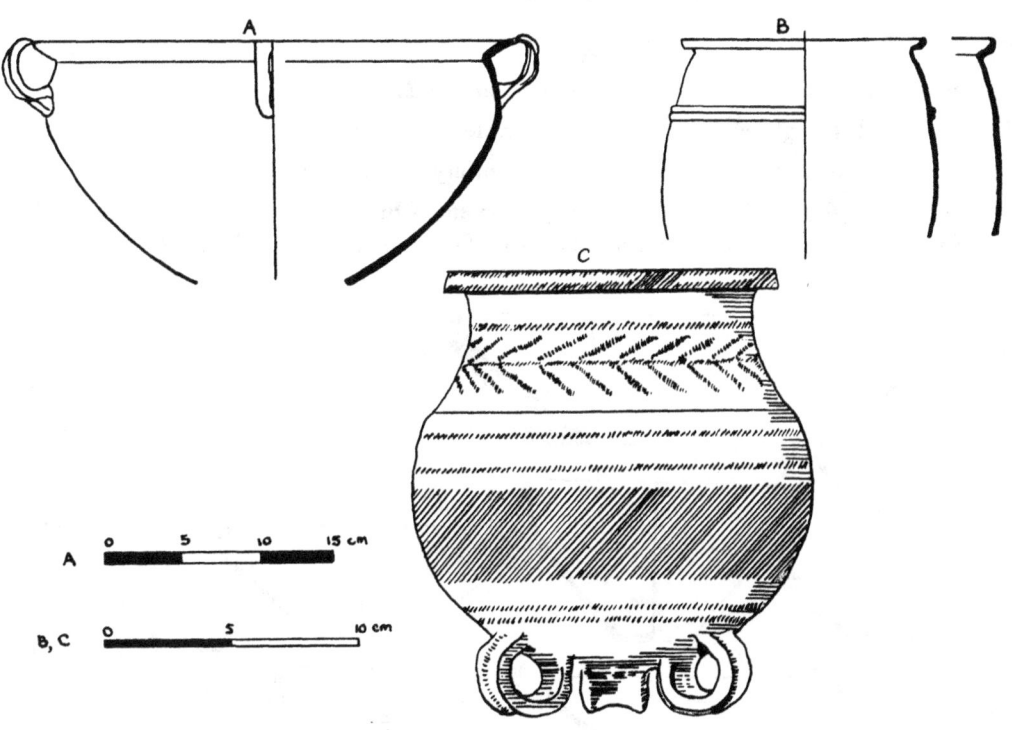

A*	Qumrân Ib	50–31 B.C.	*Rapport III*, Fig. 3:14
B*	Sam Roman Ia	20 B.C.–A.D. 20	*SS III*, Fig. 69:3
C*	Sam Roman Ia	20 B.C.–A.D. 20	*SS III*, Fig. 69:1 (dating questionable; a sherd probably from a similar vessel in a third century B.C. context at Shechem, No. 2129)

51–59 BOWLS, CUPS, AND PLATES

TYPE 51. SMALL DEEP BOWLS

51.1 Incurved rim (200 B.C. – A.D. 68)

Observations:
1. Some examples arbitrarily segregated from 51.2.
2. Cf. 151.1 for glazed and painted examples.
3. Note the heavier ware in the second century B.C. examples.
4. Parallels: 'Athlît, Beth-zur, Gezer, Jerusalem, Qumrân Caves, 'Ain Feshkha, Ramat Rahel, Samaria, Tell el-Fâr'ah (North), Tell Sandahannah, Tulûl Abû el-'Alâyiq.

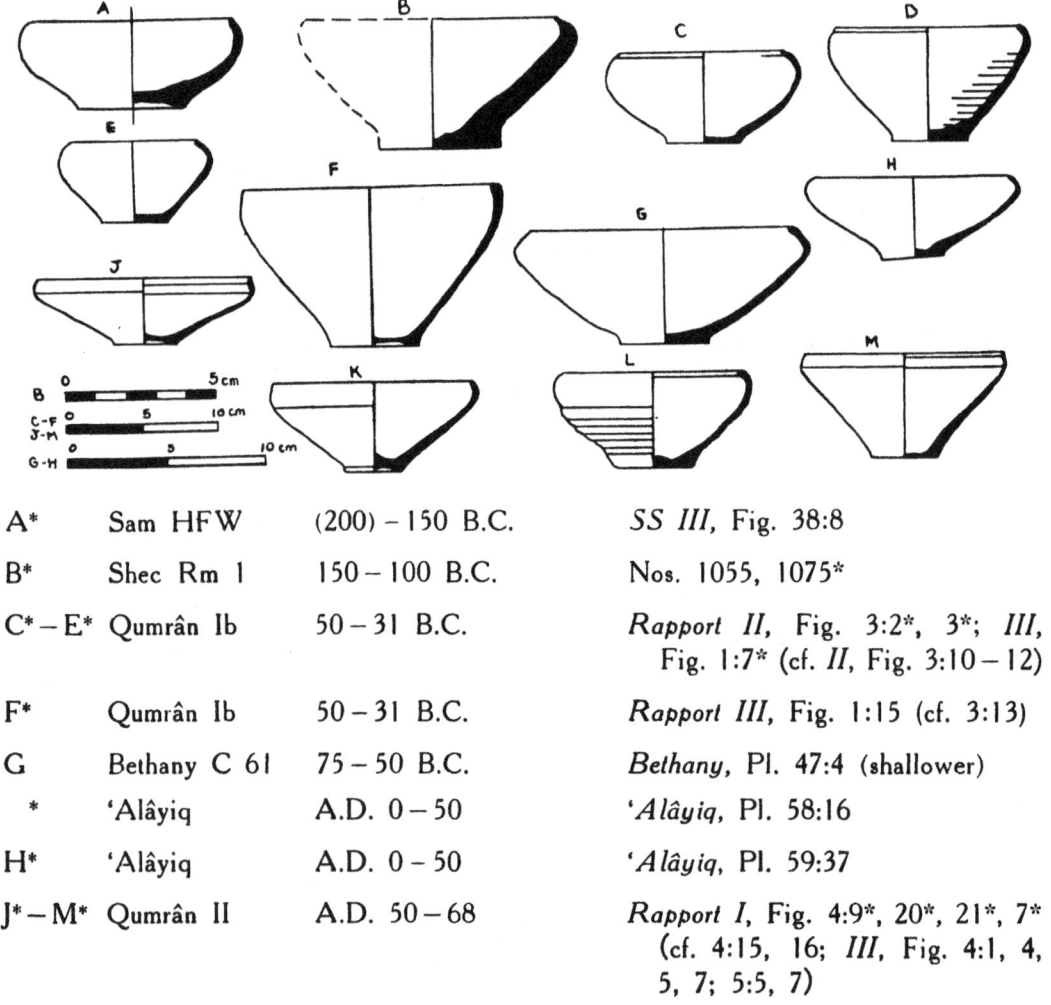

A*	Sam HFW	(200) – 150 B.C.	*SS III*, Fig. 38:8
B*	Shec Rm 1	150 – 100 B.C.	Nos. 1055, 1075*
C*–E*	Qumrân Ib	50 – 31 B.C.	*Rapport II*, Fig. 3:2*, 3*; *III*, Fig. 1:7* (cf. *II*, Fig. 3:10–12)
F*	Qumrân Ib	50 – 31 B.C.	*Rapport III*, Fig. 1:15 (cf. 3:13)
G	Bethany C 61	75 – 50 B.C.	*Bethany*, Pl. 47:4 (shallower)
*	'Alâyiq	A.D. 0 – 50	*'Alâyiq*, Pl. 58:16
H*	'Alâyiq	A.D. 0 – 50	*'Alâyiq*, Pl. 59:37
J*–M*	Qumrân II	A.D. 50 – 68	*Rapport I*, Fig. 4:9*, 20*, 21*, 7* (cf. 4:15, 16; *III*, Fig. 4:1, 4, 5, 7; 5:5, 7)

51–59 BOWLS, CUPS, AND PLATES
TYPE 51. SMALL DEEP BOWLS
51.2 Hemispherical (200 B.C. – A.D. 68)

Observations:
1. Some examples arbitrarily segregated from 51.1.
2. Note the heavier ware of the second century B.C. examples.
3. Parallels: Jerusalem, Qumrân Caves, 'Ain Feshkha, Tell Sandahannah.

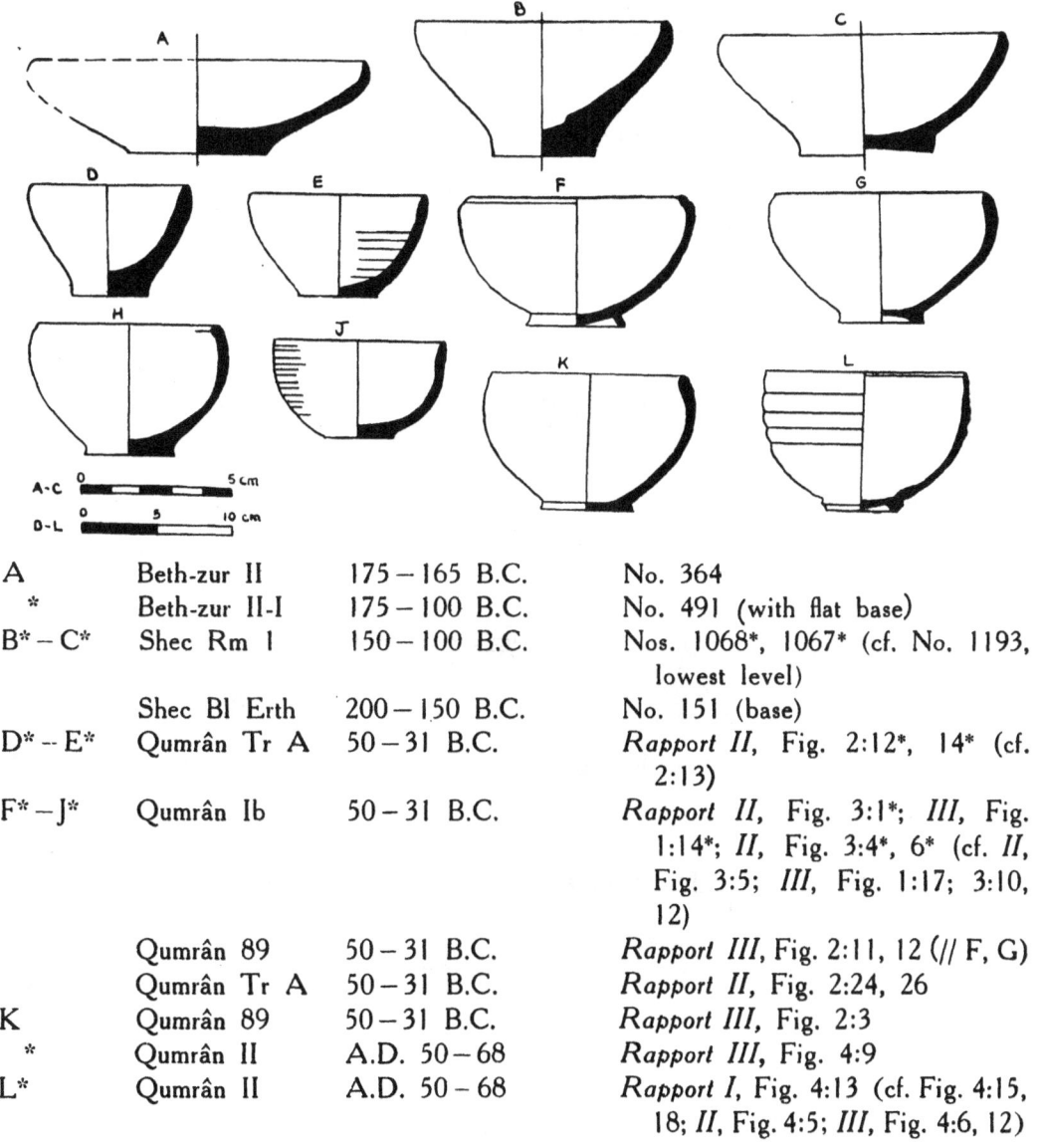

A	Beth-zur II	175–165 B.C.	No. 364
*	Beth-zur II-I	175–100 B.C.	No. 491 (with flat base)
B*–C*	Shec Rm 1	150–100 B.C.	Nos. 1068*, 1067* (cf. No. 1193, lowest level)
	Shec Bl Erth	200–150 B.C.	No. 151 (base)
D*–E*	Qumrân Tr A	50–31 B.C.	*Rapport II*, Fig. 2:12*, 14* (cf. 2:13)
F*–J*	Qumrân Ib	50–31 B.C.	*Rapport II*, Fig. 3:1*; *III*, Fig. 1:14*; *II*, Fig. 3:4*, 6* (cf. *II*, Fig. 3:5; *III*, Fig. 1:17; 3:10, 12)
	Qumrân 89	50–31 B.C.	*Rapport III*, Fig. 2:11, 12 (// F, G)
	Qumrân Tr A	50–31 B.C.	*Rapport II*, Fig. 2:24, 26
K	Qumrân 89	50–31 B.C.	*Rapport III*, Fig. 2:3
*	Qumrân II	A.D. 50–68	*Rapport III*, Fig. 4:9
L*	Qumrân II	A.D. 50–68	*Rapport I*, Fig. 4:13 (cf. Fig. 4:15, 18; *II*, Fig. 4:5; *III*, Fig. 4:6, 12)

51–59 BOWLS, CUPS, AND PLATES

TYPE 51. SMALL DEEP BOWLS

51.6 Vertical rim (A.D. 50–68)

A*   Qumrân II   A.D. 50–68   *Rapport I*, Fig. 3:6

51.7 Incurved sides with everted rim (A.D. 50–68)

Observations:
1. Parallels: Qumrân Caves, Tulûl Abû el-'Alâyiq.

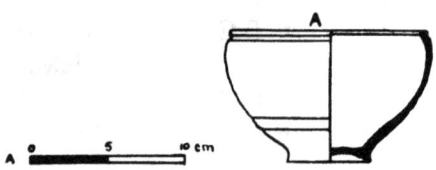

A*   Qumrân II   A.D. 50–68   *Rapport I*, Fig. 4:19

51–59 BOWLS, CUPS, AND PLATES
TYPE 51. SMALL DEEP BOWLS
51.8 Everted rim or sides (50 B.C.–A.D. 68)

Observations:
1. Note the slight cyma profile and carefully formed foot of the first century B.C. examples.
2. Parallels: Qumrân Caves, 'Ain Feshkha.

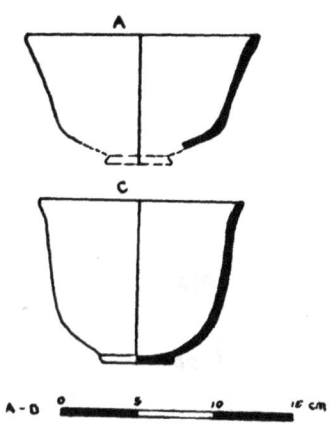

A*	Qumrân Ib	50–31 B.C.	*Rapport III*, Fig. 3:11
B*	Qumrân Ib	50–31 B.C.	*Rapport III*, Fig. 1:12 (cf. 3:7, 8)
	Qumrân 89	50–31 B.C.	*Rapport III*, Fig. 2:8; 9 (smaller)
	Qumrân Tr A	50–31 B.C.	*Rapport I*, Fig. 2:25
C*–D*	Qumrân II	A.D. 50–68	*Rapport III*, Fig. 4:13, 10

TYPE 52. CUPS
52.1 Inverted to vertical sides (50 B.C.–A.D. 68)

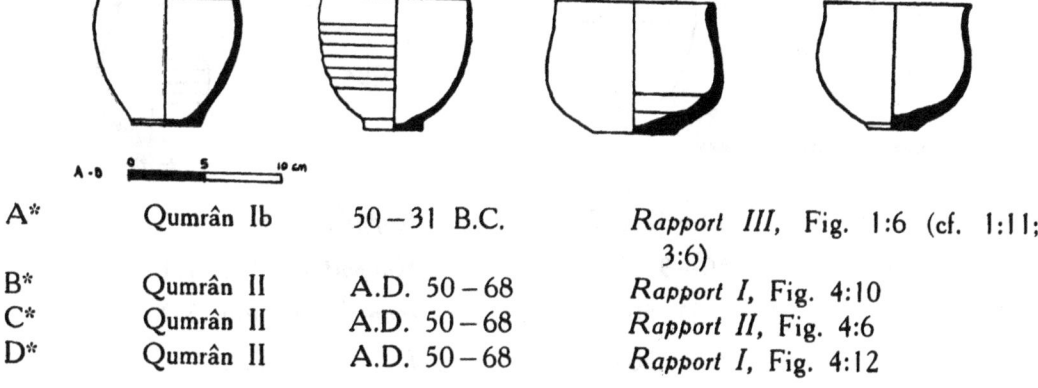

A*	Qumrân Ib	50–31 B.C.	*Rapport III*, Fig. 1:6 (cf. 1:11; 3:6)
B*	Qumrân II	A.D. 50–68	*Rapport I*, Fig. 4:10
C*	Qumrân II	A.D. 50–68	*Rapport II*, Fig. 4:6
D*	Qumrân II	A.D. 50–68	*Rapport I*, Fig. 4:12

51–59 BOWLS, CUPS, AND PLATES
TYPE 52. CUPS

52.2 Everted sides (50 B.C.–A.D. 68)

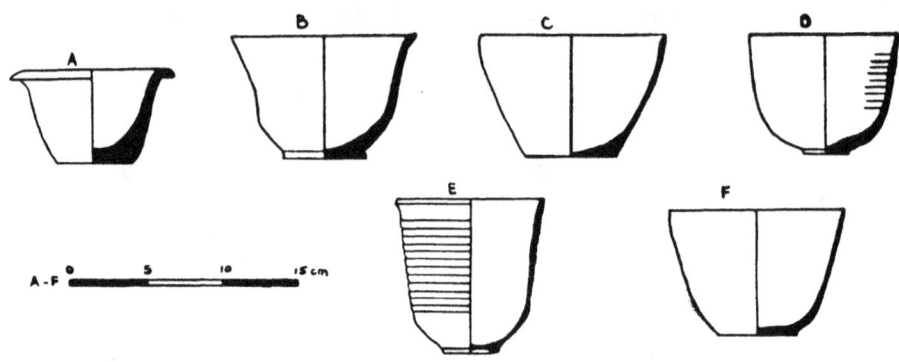

A*	Qumrân Tr A	50 – 31 B.C.	*Rapport II*, Fig. 2:19*, 18 (shallower)
B*	Qumrân Ib	50 – 31 B.C.	*Rapport II*, Fig. 3:8
C*	Qumrân Ib	50 – 31 B.C.	*Rapport III*, Fig. 1:13
D*	Qumrân Ib	50 – 31 B.C.	*Rapport II*, Fig. 3:7
E*	Qumrân II	A.D. 50 – 68	*Rapport I*, Fig. 3:9 (cf. II, Fig. 4:7)
F*	Qumrân II	A.D. 50 – 68	*Rapport III*, Fig. 4:16

52.9 Miscellaneous cups

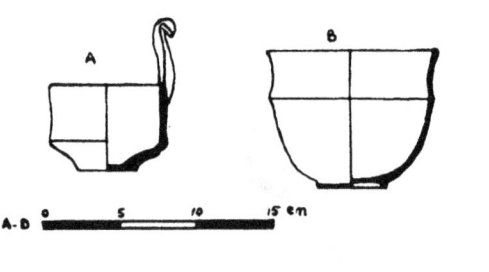
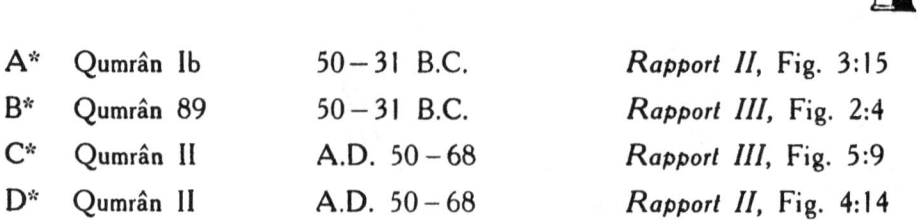

A*	Qumrân Ib	50 – 31 B.C.	*Rapport II*, Fig. 3:15
B*	Qumrân 89	50 – 31 B.C.	*Rapport III*, Fig. 2:4
C*	Qumrân II	A.D. 50 – 68	*Rapport III*, Fig. 5:9
D*	Qumrân II	A.D. 50 – 68	*Rapport II*, Fig. 4:14

51–59 BOWLS, CUPS, AND PLATES

TYPE 53. SHALLOW BOWLS AND PLATES (175–0 B.C.)

Observations:
1. The single example of this type from 'Alâyiq does not justify general extension of the type into the first century A.D.
2. All examples have flat bases.
3. Parallels: Beth-shan, Beth-zur, Lachish, Qubeibeh, Qumrân Caves, 'Ain Feshkha, Ramat Rahel, Samaria, Tell el-Fûl, Tell Sandahannah, Tulûl Abû el-'Alâyiq.

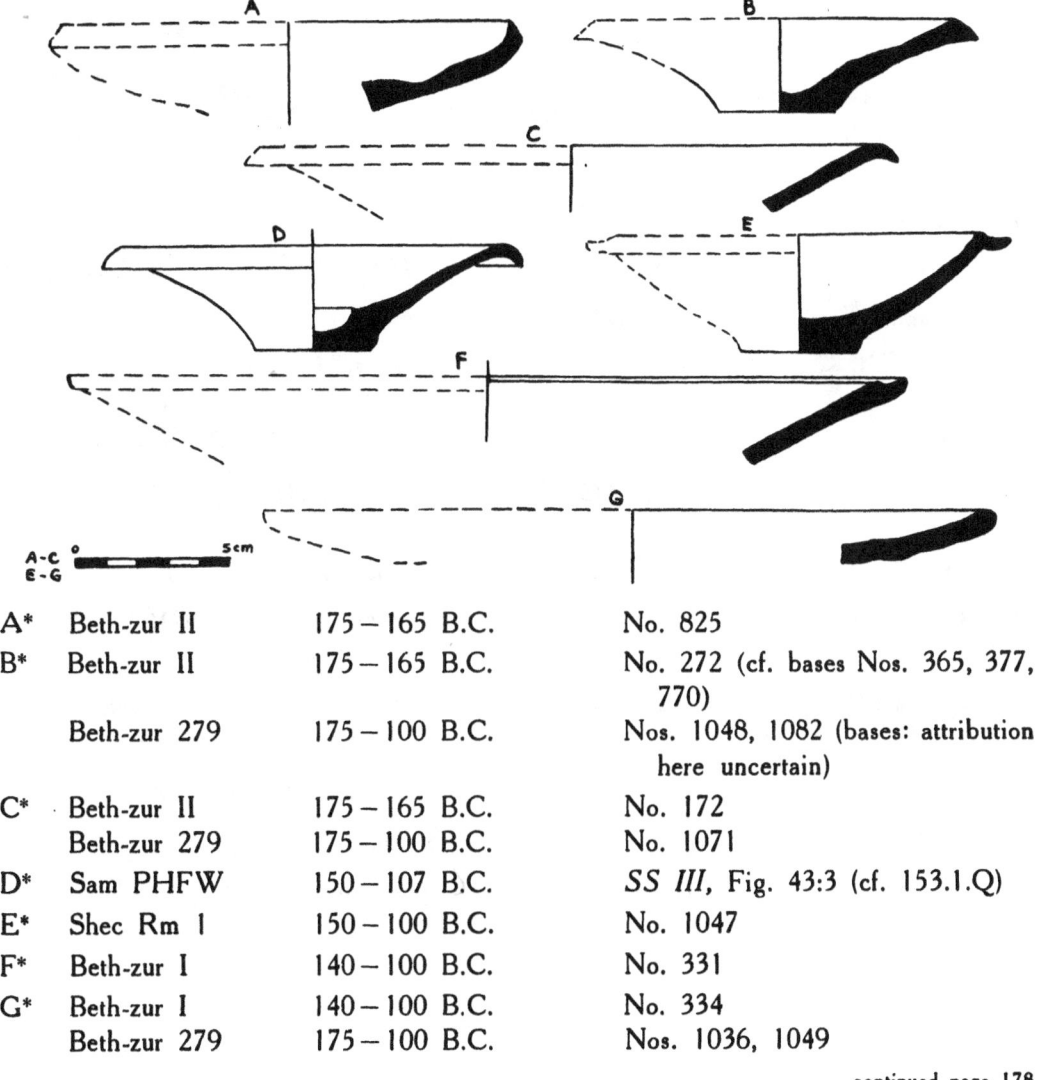

A*	Beth-zur II	175–165 B.C.	No. 825
B*	Beth-zur II	175–165 B.C.	No. 272 (cf. bases Nos. 365, 377, 770)
	Beth-zur 279	175–100 B.C.	Nos. 1048, 1082 (bases: attribution here uncertain)
C*	Beth-zur II	175–165 B.C.	No. 172
	Beth-zur 279	175–100 B.C.	No. 1071
D*	Sam PHFW	150–107 B.C.	*SS III*, Fig. 43:3 (cf. 153.1.Q)
E*	Shec Rm 1	150–100 B.C.	No. 1047
F*	Beth-zur I	140–100 B.C.	No. 331
G*	Beth-zur I	140–100 B.C.	No. 334
	Beth-zur 279	175–100 B.C.	Nos. 1036, 1049

continued page 178

51–59 BOWLS, CUPS, AND PLATES

TYPE 53. SHALLOW BOWLS AND PLATES (continued)

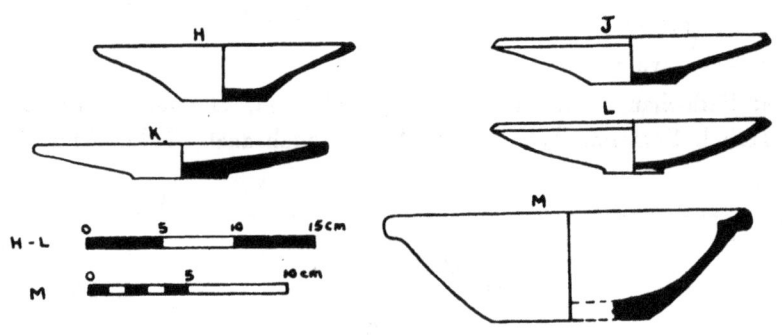

H	Bethany C 61	75–50 B.C.	*Bethany*, Fig. 47:5, 6
*	Qumrân Ib	50–31 B.C.	*Rapport III*, Fig. 3:1 (cf. 1:10; 3:4)
	Qumrân Tr A	50–31 B.C.	*Rapport I*, Fig. 2:8, 9
	Jerus Ctdl C	37–29 B.C.	Johns, *QDAP*, XIV, Fig. 14:3 (top)
	Jerus T Val	37–4 B.C.	*PEFA*, 1927, Pl. XII:1–4
J*	Qumrân Ib	50–31 B.C.	*Rapport III*, Fig. 1:9 (cf. *II*, Fig. 3:9)
	Qumrân Tr A	50–31 B.C.	*Rapport II*, Fig. 2:3
	Jerus Ctdl C	37–29 B.C.	Johns, *QDAP*, XIV, Fig. 14:3 (bottom)
K*	Qumrân Ib	50–31 B.C.	*Rapport III*, Fig. 3:3 (cf. *II*, Fig. 3:13)
L*	Qumrân Ib	50–31 B.C.	*Rapport III*, Fig. 3:2
	Qumrân Tr A	50–31 B.C.	*Rapport II*, Fig. 2:5
M*	'Alâyiq	A.D. 0–50	*'Alâyiq*, Pl. 59:40 (cf. E)

51–59 BOWLS, CUPS, AND PLATES

TYPE 54. SHALLOW BOWLS WITH VERTICAL SIDES

54.1 Large (35 B.C.–A.D. 68)

Observations:
1. The single Qumrân 89 example seems to indicate the introduction of this form shortly before 31 B.C.
2. Type 54.1 and 54.2 apparently replaced Type 53 in the first century A.D.

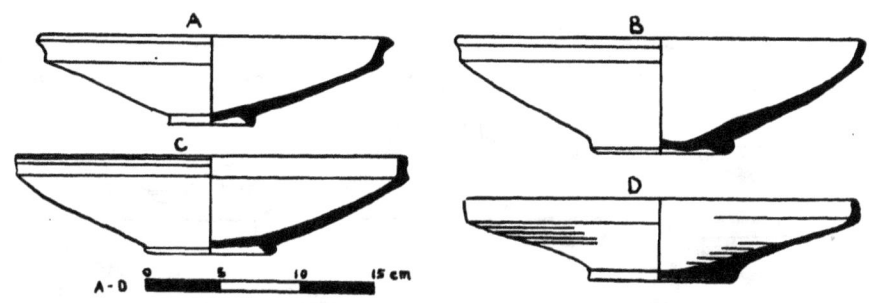

A*	Qumrân 89	50–31 B.C.	*Rapport III*, Fig. 2:5
	Qumrân II	A.D. 50–68	*Rapport I*, Fig. 4:8
B*	Qumrân II	A.D. 50–68	*Rapport I*, Fig. 4:11
C*	Qumrân II	A.D. 50–68	*Rapport I*, Fig. 4:14
D*	Qumrân II	A.D. 50–68	*Rapport II*, Fig. 4:11

51–59 BOWLS, CUPS, AND PLATES

TYPE 54. SHALLOW BOWLS WITH VERTICAL SIDES

54.2 Small (50 B.C.–A.D. 68)

Observations:
1. Cf. Type 254.2.
2. Examples with sharply vertical sides probably do not occur before the first century A.D.
3. Parallels: Jerusalem, 'Ain Feshkha, Tulûl Abû el-'Alâyiq.

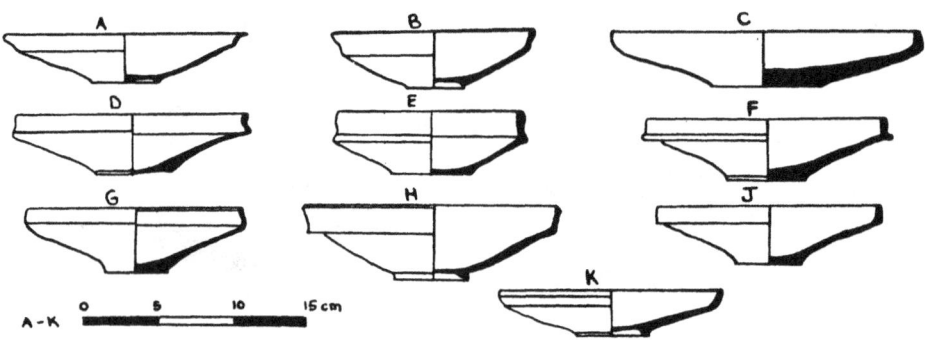

A*	Qumrân 89	50–31 B.C.	*Rapport III*, Fig. 2:6
B*	Qumrân 89	50–31 B.C.	*Rapport III*, Fig. 2:7
C*	Qumrân Tr A	50–31 B.C.	*Rapport II*, Fig. 2:1 (cf. 2:2)
D	Qumrân Tr A	50–31 B.C.	*Rapport II*, Fig. 2:4 (probably early first century A.D.)
*	Qumrân II	A.D. 50–68	*Rapport I*, Fig. 4:4 (cf. 4:3, 5; II, Fig. 4:3)
E*	Qumrân II	A.D. 50–68	*Rapport II*, Fig. 4:2
F*	Qumrân II	A.D. 50–68	*Rapport III*, Fig. 5:4
G*	Qumrân II	A.D. 50–68	*Rapport I*, Fig. 4:2
H*	Qumrân II	A.D. 50–68	*Rapport III*, Fig. 5:6
J*	Qumrân II	A.D. 50–68	*Rapport I*, Fig. 4:1
K*	Qumrân II	A.D. 50–68	*Rapport I*, Fig. 4:6 (cf. Type 53)

61–69 LIDS, STANDS, AND FUNNELS

TYPE 61. SHALLOW LIDS (200–31 B.C.)

Observations:
1. Cf. Type 51.2.

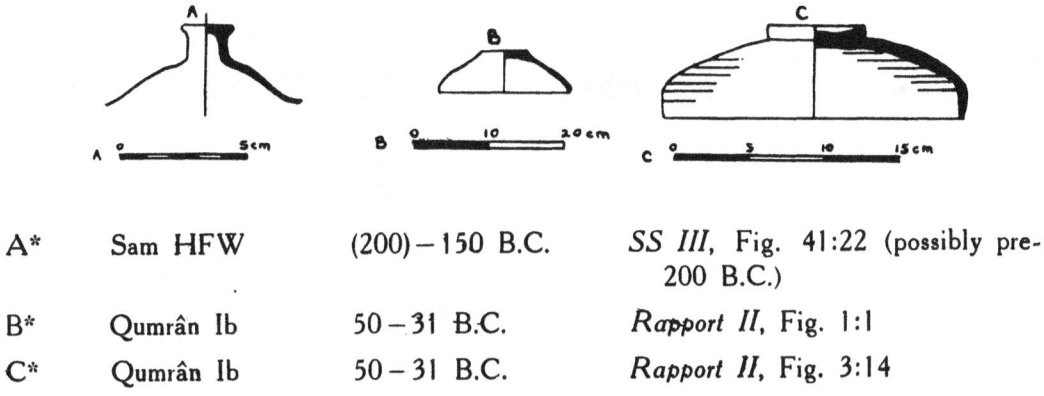

A*	Sam HFW	(200)–150 B.C.	*SS III*, Fig. 41:22 (possibly pre-200 B.C.)
B*	Qumrân Ib	50–31 B.C.	*Rapport II*, Fig. 1:1
C*	Qumrân Ib	50–31 B.C.	*Rapport II*, Fig. 3:14

TYPE 62. LIDS WITH VERTICAL SIDES (50 B.C.–A.D. 68)

Observations:
1. Cf. A* with 51.1 or 54.2.
2. A Beth-zur example indicates that this type occurs in the latter part of the second century B.C. Cf. p. 108 *supra*.
3. Parallels: Beth-zur, Qumrân Caves, 'Ain Feshkha.

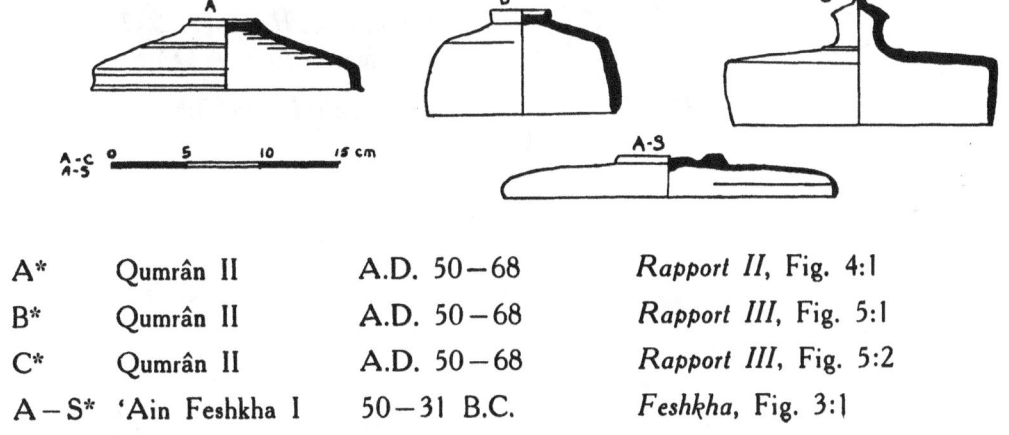

A*	Qumrân II	A.D. 50–68	*Rapport II*, Fig. 4:1
B*	Qumrân II	A.D. 50–68	*Rapport III*, Fig. 5:1
C*	Qumrân II	A.D. 50–68	*Rapport III*, Fig. 5:2
A–S*	'Ain Feshkha I	50–31 B.C.	*Feshkha*, Fig. 3:1

61-69 LIDS, STANDS, AND FUNNELS

TYPE 63. MISCELLANEOUS LIDS

| A* | Qumrân Ib | 50 – 31 B.C. | *Rapport III*, Fig. 1:8 |

TYPE 65. STANDS (50 B.C.–A.D. 70)

Observations:
1. Parallels: Beth-shan, Lachish.

| A | Qumrân Tr A | 50 – 31 B.C. | *Rapport II*, Fig. 2:17 (possibly first century A.D.) |
| * | Qumrân II | A.D. 50 – 68 | *Rapport I*, Fig. 3:5 |

61–69 LIDS, STANDS, AND FUNNELS

TYPE 68. FUNNELS

Observations:

1. Parallels: Tulûl Abû el-'Alâyiq.

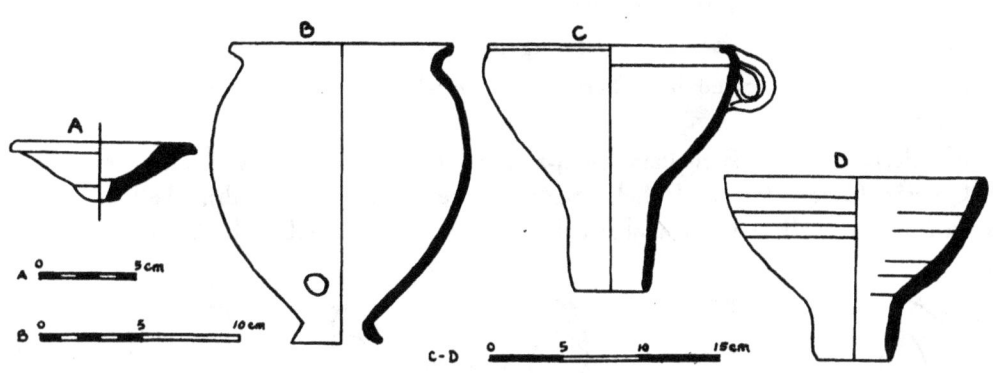

A*	Sam Vlt C 2	75–25 B.C.	*HE I*, Fig. 184:32a (possibly earlier)
B*	'Alâyiq	A.D. 0–50	*'Alâyiq*, Pl. 59:28 ("flower pot")
C*	Qumrân II	A.D. 50–68	*Rapport III*, Fig. 5:11
D*	Qumrân II	A.D. 50–68	*Rapport III*, Fig. 5:12

71–79 COOKING POTS, PANS, AND BRAZIERS

TYPE 71. GLOBULAR COOKING POTS

71.1 Without lid device (200 B.C.–A.D. 70)

Observations:
1. Second century B.C. material (A–J) has been separated from later material (K–Q) even though some of the later examples have parallels earlier.
2. Ware tends to become thinner during the second century B.C.
3. Necks tend to become less sharply differentiated and body more squat in the first century A.D.
4. Parallels: Bethany, Beth-shan, Beth-zur, En-gedi, Gezer, Jericho, Jerusalem, Lachish, Qumrân Caves, Ramat Rahel, Samaria, Tell el-Far'ah (South), Tell el-Fûl, Tell en-Nasbeh, Tell Sandahannah, Tell Zakarîyeh, Tulûl Abû el-'Alâyiq.

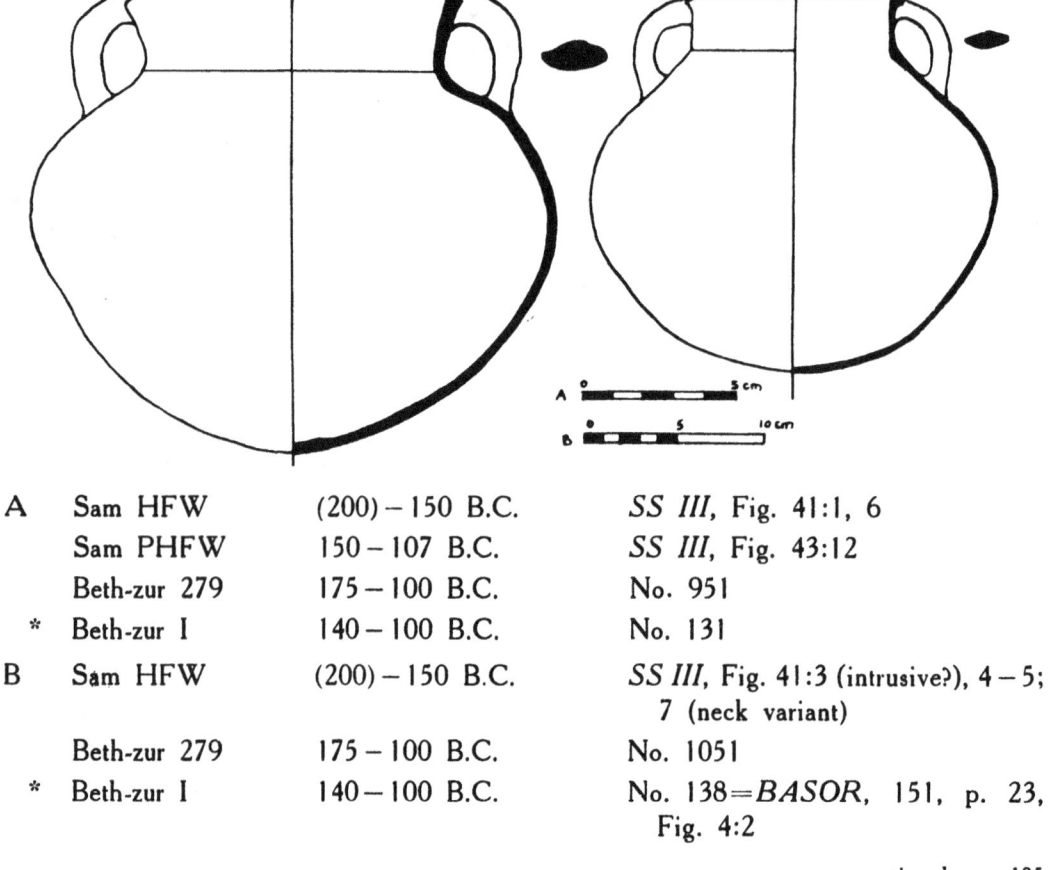

A	Sam HFW	(200)–150 B.C.	*SS III*, Fig. 41:1, 6
	Sam PHFW	150–107 B.C.	*SS III*, Fig. 43:12
	Beth-zur 279	175–100 B.C.	No. 951
*	Beth-zur I	140–100 B.C.	No. 131
B	Sam HFW	(200)–150 B.C.	*SS III*, Fig. 41:3 (intrusive?), 4–5; 7 (neck variant)
	Beth-zur 279	175–100 B.C.	No. 1051
*	Beth-zur I	140–100 B.C.	No. 138=*BASOR*, 151, p. 23, Fig. 4:2

continued page 185

71-79 COOKING POTS, PANS, AND BRAZIERS
TYPE 71. GLOBULAR COOKING POTS
71.1 Without lid device (continued)

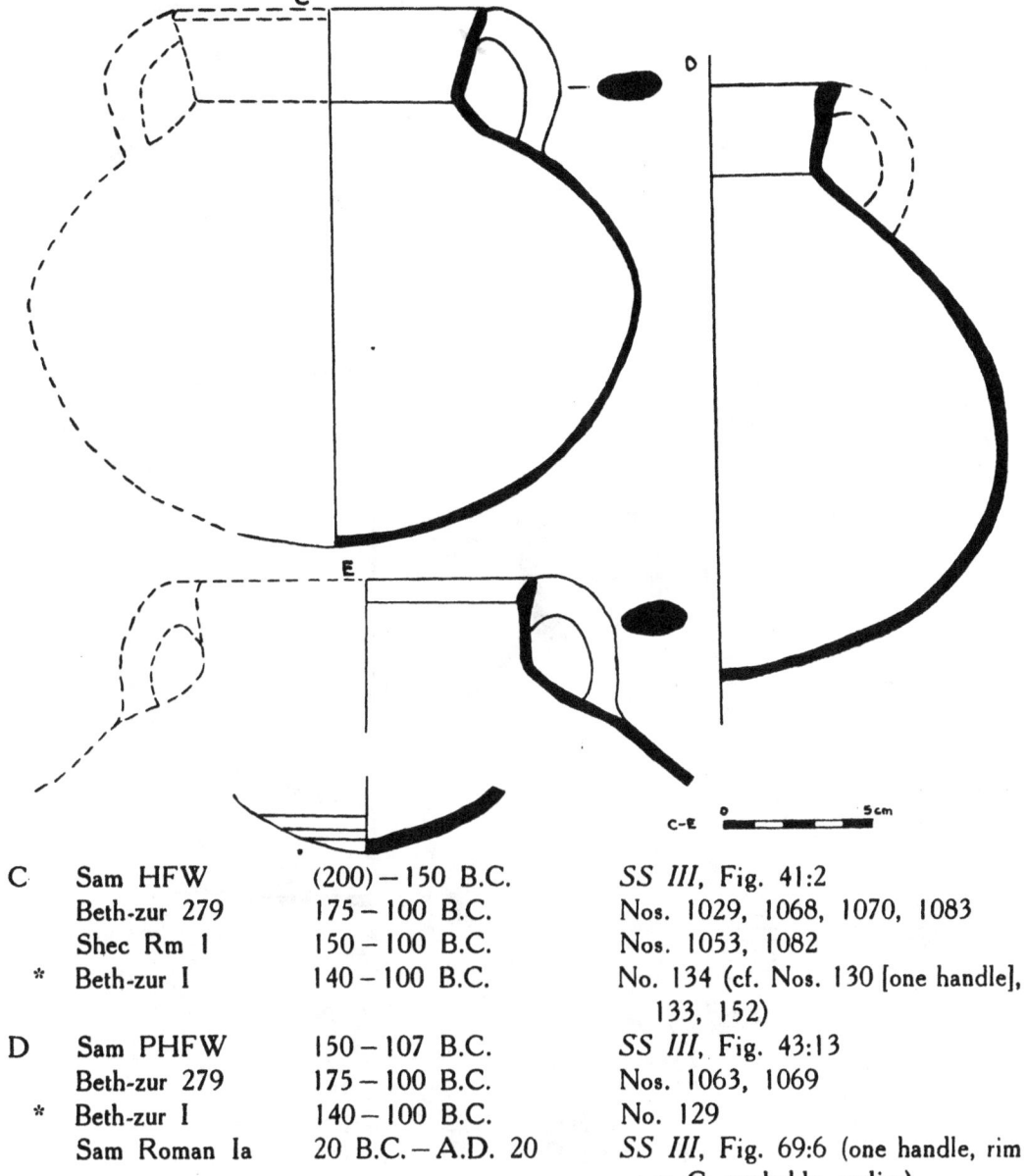

C	Sam HFW	(200)–150 B.C.	*SS III*, Fig. 41:2
	Beth-zur 279	175–100 B.C.	Nos. 1029, 1068, 1070, 1083
	Shec Rm 1	150–100 B.C.	Nos. 1053, 1082
*	Beth-zur I	140–100 B.C.	No. 134 (cf. Nos. 130 [one handle], 133, 152)
D	Sam PHFW	150–107 B.C.	*SS III*, Fig. 43:13
	Beth-zur 279	175–100 B.C.	Nos. 1063, 1069
*	Beth-zur I	140–100 B.C.	No. 129
	Sam Roman Ia	20 B.C.–A.D. 20	*SS III*, Fig. 69:6 (one handle, rim as C; probably earlier)
E	Beth-zur 279	175–100 B.C.	Nos. 1023, 1028
*	Beth-zur I	140–100 B.C.	No. 153

continued page 186

71–79 COOKING POTS, PANS, AND BRAZIERS
TYPE 71. GLOBULAR COOKING POTS
71.1 Without lid device (continued)

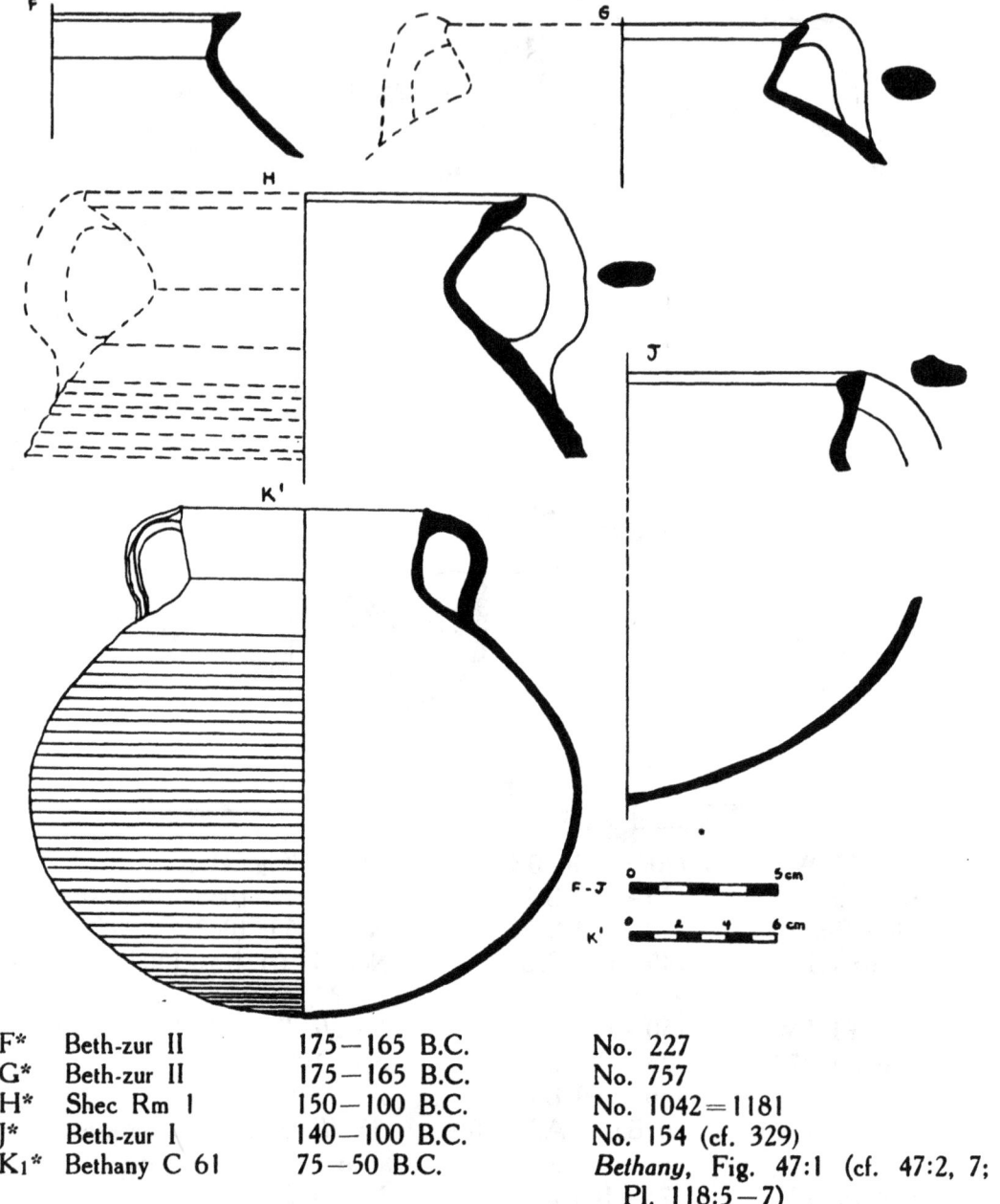

F*	Beth-zur II	175–165 B.C.	No. 227
G*	Beth-zur II	175–165 B.C.	No. 757
H*	Shec Rm 1	150–100 B.C.	No. 1042=1181
J*	Beth-zur I	140–100 B.C.	No. 154 (cf. 329)
K₁*	Bethany C 61	75–50 B.C.	*Bethany*, Fig. 47:1 (cf. 47:2, 7; Pl. 118:5–7)
	Sam Pre-Gab	75–55 B.C.	*SS III*, p. 289

continued page 187

71–79 COOKING POTS, PANS, AND BRAZIERS

TYPE 71. GLOBULAR COOKING POTS

71.1 Without lid device (continued)

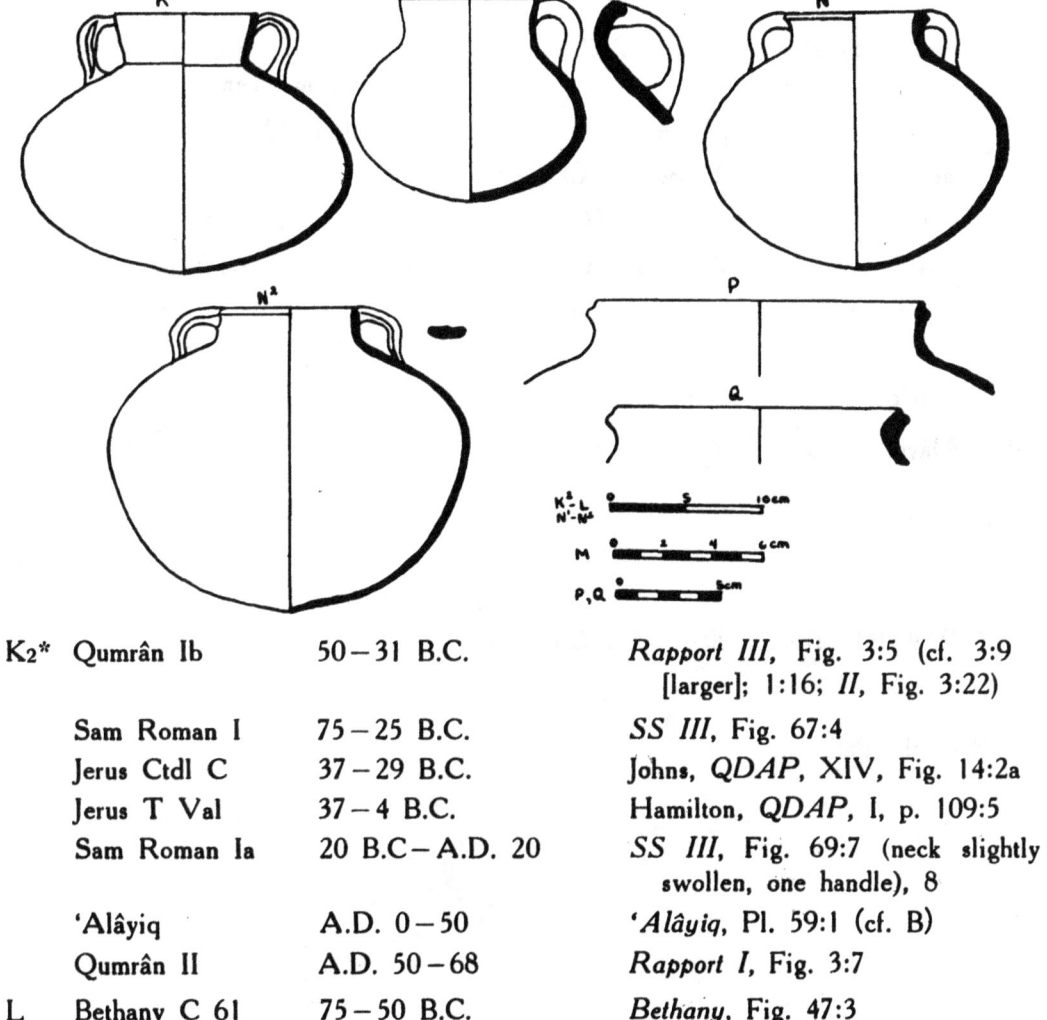

K₂*	Qumrân Ib	50–31 B.C.	*Rapport III*, Fig. 3:5 (cf. 3:9 [larger]; 1:16; *II*, Fig. 3:22)
	Sam Roman I	75–25 B.C.	*SS III*, Fig. 67:4
	Jerus Ctdl C	37–29 B.C.	Johns, *QDAP*, XIV, Fig. 14:2a
	Jerus T Val	37–4 B.C.	Hamilton, *QDAP*, I, p. 109:5
	Sam Roman Ia	20 B.C.–A.D. 20	*SS III*, Fig. 69:7 (neck slightly swollen, one handle), 8
	'Alâyiq	A.D. 0–50	*'Alâyiq*, Pl. 59:1 (cf. B)
	Qumrân II	A.D. 50–68	*Rapport I*, Fig. 3:7
L	Bethany C 61	75–50 B.C.	*Bethany*, Fig. 47:3
*	Qumrân Tr A	50–31 B.C.	*Rapport II*, Fig. 2:22
	Sam Roman Ia	20 B.C.–A.D. 20	*SS III*, Fig. 69:4
	'Alâyiq	A.D. 0–50	*'Alâyiq*, Pl. 59:4
M*	Bethany C 61	75–50 B.C.	*Bethany*, Fig. 47:13

continued page 188

71–79 COOKING POTS, PANS, AND BRAZIERS

TYPE 71. GLOBULAR COOKING POTS

71.1 Without lid device (continued)

N₁*	Qumrân Tr A	50–31 B.C.	*Rapport II*, Fig. 2:23 (probably early first century A.D.)
	Jerus T Val	37–4 B.C.	Hamilton, *QDAP*, I, p. 109:2
	Sam Roman Ia	20 B.C.–A.D. 20	*SS III*, Fig 69:9
	'Alâyiq	A.D. 0–50	*'Alâyiq*, Pl. 58:36
	Jerus N Wall	A.D. 0–70	Hamilton, *QDAP*, X, Fig. 14:7
N₂*	Qumrân II	A.D. 50–68	*Rapport I*, Fig. 3:11 (cf. *II*, Fig. 4:15)
P*	'Alâyiq	A.D. 0–50	*'Alâyiq*, Pl. 58:3
Q*	'Alâyiq	A.D. 0–50	*'Alâyiq*, Pl. 58:6 (cf. 58:4)

71.2 With lid device (200–150 B.C.)

Observations:
1. Parallels: Beth-zur.

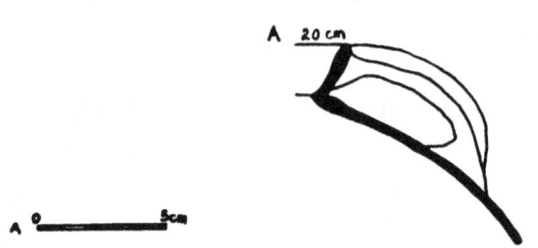

A*	Sam HFW	(200)–150 B.C.	*SS III*, Fig. 41:12 (cf. 41:16–17; 18 with horizontal loop handle; possibly also 41:21)

71–79 COOKING POTS, PANS, AND BRAZIERS
TYPE 72. SHALLOW COOKING POTS (CASSEROLES)

72.1 With lid device (200–100 B.C. and rarely thereafter).

Observations:
1. Only two examples from post–100 B.C. contexts (D, K*).
2. Parallels: Beth-zur, Tell en-Nasbeh.

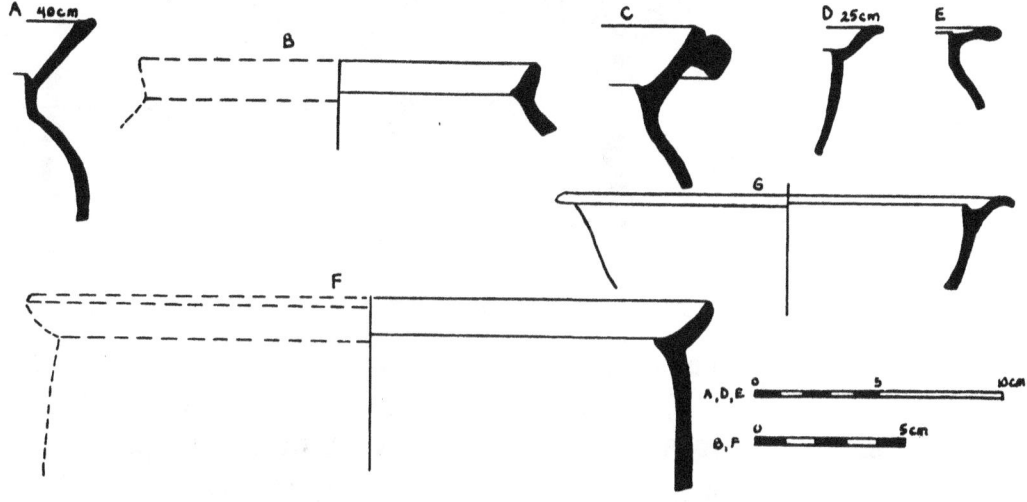

A*	Sam HFW	(200)–150 B.C.	*SS III*, Fig. 41:8 (cf. 41:9; 10 with loop handles; 41:11, 13, 15)
B*	Shec Bl Erth	200–150 B.C.	No. 781
	Beth-zur II	175–165 B.C.	No. 169 (possibly deep type)
C	Shec Bl Erth	200–150 B.C.	No. 583
*	Sam PHFW	150–107 B.C.	*SS III*, Fig. 43:14
D*	Sam HFW	(200)–150 B.C.	*SS III*, Fig. 41:14 (cf. 19)
	Jerus Ctdl C	37–29 B.C.	Johns, *QDAP*, XIV, Fig. 14:2b
E*	Sam HFW	(200)–150 B.C.	*SS III*, Fig. 41:20
F*	Beth-zur II	175–165 B.C.	No. 390
	Shec Bl Erth	200–150 B.C.	No. 588
	Beth-zur I	140–100 B.C.	unregistered sherds
G*	Sam PHFW	150–107 B.C.	*SS III*, Fig. 43:15

continued page 190

71–79 COOKING POTS, PANS, AND BRAZIERS

TYPE 72. SHALLOW COOKING POTS (CASSEROLES)

72.1 With lid device (continued)

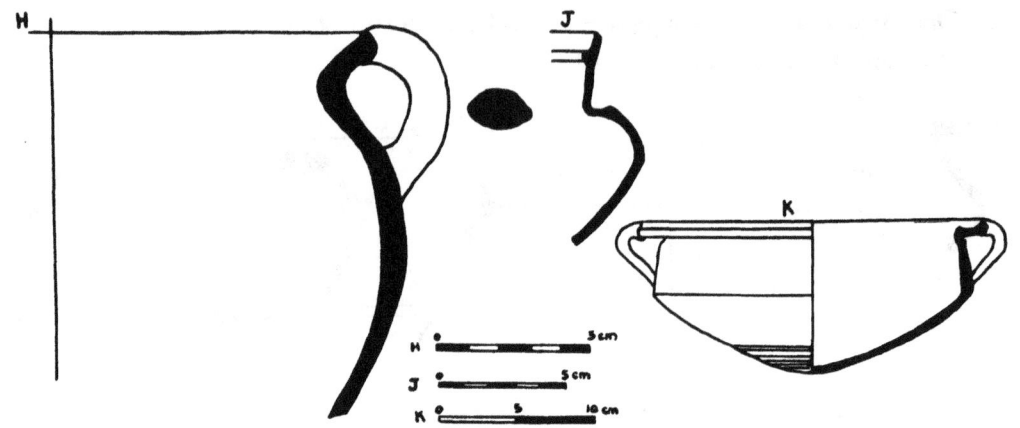

H*	Shec Rm 1	150–100 B.C.	No. 1043 (cf. No. 1064=1066 with thinner ware)
J*	Sam Roman Ia	20 B.C.–A.D. 20	*SS III*, Fig. 69:10 (possibly earlier)
K*	Qumrân II	A.D. 50–68	*Rapport III*, Fig. 5:8

72.2 With shoulder (A.D. 0–70)

Observations:
1. Parallels: Bethany, Jerusalem, 'Ain Feshkha, Tulûl Abû el-'Alâyiq.

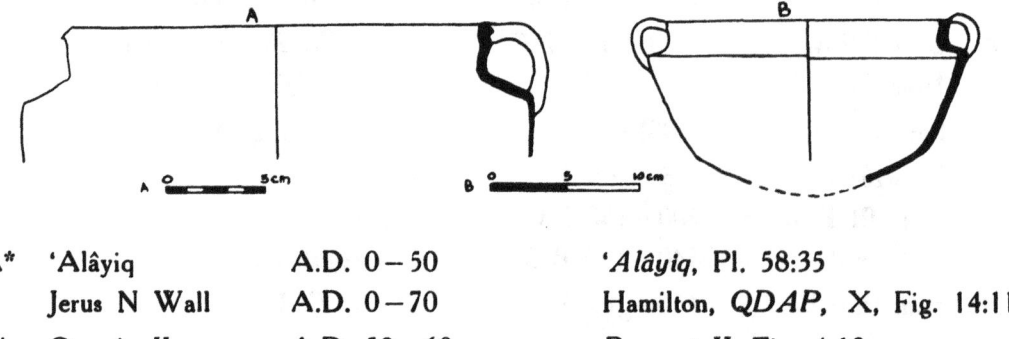

A*	'Alâyiq	A.D. 0–50	*'Alâyiq*, Pl. 58:35
	Jerus N Wall	A.D. 0–70	Hamilton, *QDAP*, X, Fig. 14:11
B*	Qumrân II	A.D. 50–68	*Rapport II*, Fig. 4:13

71–79 COOKING POTS, PANS, AND BRAZIERS

TYPE 72. SHALLOW COOKING POTS (CASSEROLES)

72.3 Simple rim (A.D. 50 – 68)

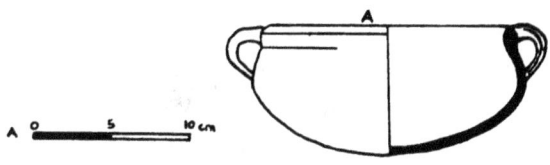

A*	Qumrân II	A.D. 50 – 68	*Rapport III*, Fig. 5:3

TYPE 78. FRYING PANS (200 – 150 B.C.)

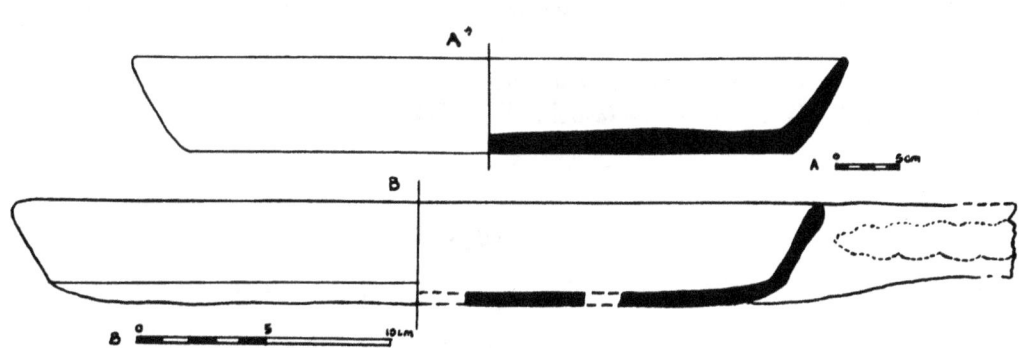

A*	Sam HFW	(200) – 150 B.C.	*SS III*, Fig. 40:1 (possibly pre-200 B.C.)
B*	Sam HFW	(200) – 150 B.C.	*SS III*, Fig. 41:23 (possibly pre-200 B.C.)

81–89 LAMPS

TYPE 81. SMALL FOLDED LAMPS

81.1 Open

Observations:
1. Parallels: 'Ain Shems, Bethany, Jerusalem, Ramat Rahel, Tell el-Fûl, Tell Sandahannah.

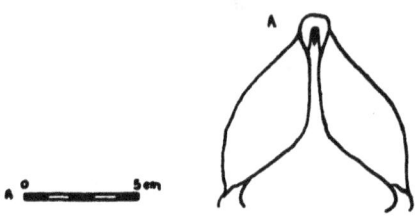

A	Bethany C 61	75–50 B.C.	*Bethany*, p. 161, No. 18
*	Jerus T Val	37–4 B.C.	*PEFA*, 1927, Pl. XVII:1

81.2 Closed

Observations:
1. Beth-zur evidence indicates that this type also occurs in the second century B.C. Cf. p. 108 and p. 107, n. 67, *supra* and *CBZ*, Fig. 41.
2. Parallels: 'Ain Shems, Bethany, Beth-zur, Gezer, Jericho, Jerusalem, Ramat Rahel, Samaria, Tell el-Fûl, Tell en-Nasbeh, Tell Zakarîyeh.

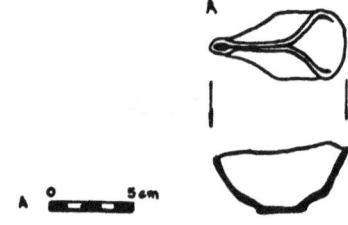

A	Bethany C 61	75–50 B.C.	*Bethany*, p. 165, Nos. 5–6
*	Jerus Ctdl C	37–29 B.C.	Johns, *QDAP*, XIV, Fig. 14:5
	Jerus T Val	37–4 B.C.	*PEFA*, 1927, Pl. XVII:2

81–89 LAMPS

TYPE 82. BOW-SPOUTED ("HERODIAN") LAMPS

82.1 Undecorated (75 B.C.–A.D. 70)

Observations:

1. Parallels: Bethany, Beth-shan, Gezer, Jerusalem, Qubeibeh, Qumrân Caves, 'Ain Feshkha, Ramat Rahel (?), Silet edh-Dhahr, Tell el-Fâr'ah (South), Tell en-Nasbeh, Tulûl Abû el-'Alâyiq, Zâharîyeh.

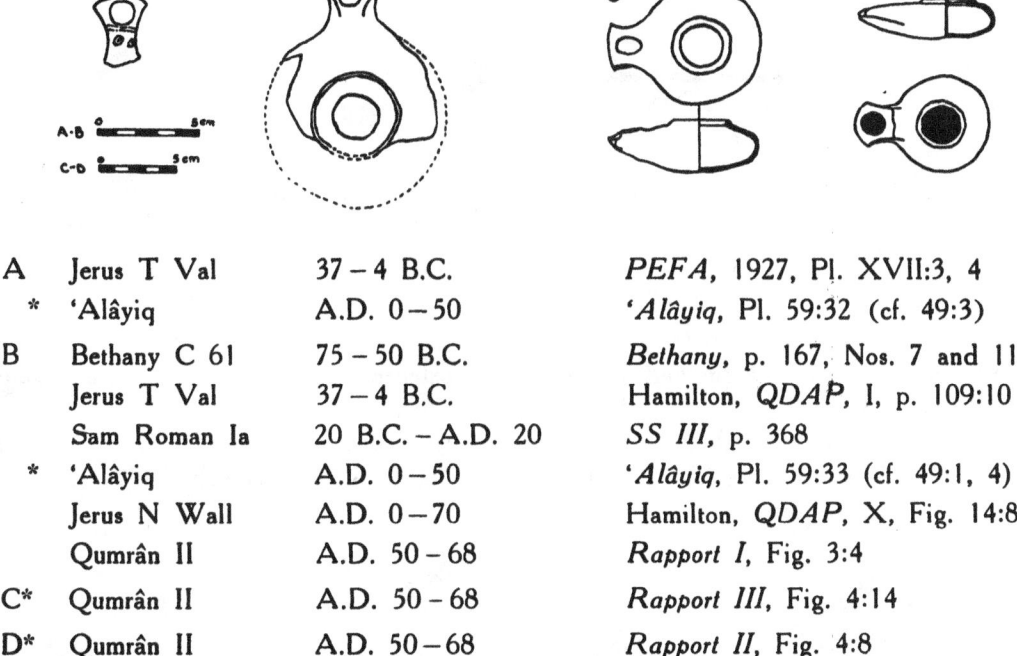

A	Jerus T Val	37 – 4 B.C.	*PEFA*, 1927, Pl. XVII:3, 4
*	'Alâyiq	A.D. 0 – 50	*'Alâyiq*, Pl. 59:32 (cf. 49:3)
B	Bethany C 61	75 – 50 B.C.	*Bethany*, p. 167, Nos. 7 and 11
	Jerus T Val	37 – 4 B.C.	Hamilton, *QDAP*, I, p. 109:10
	Sam Roman Ia	20 B.C. – A.D. 20	*SS III*, p. 368
*	'Alâyiq	A.D. 0 – 50	*'Alâyiq*, Pl. 59:33 (cf. 49:1, 4)
	Jerus N Wall	A.D. 0 – 70	Hamilton, *QDAP*, X, Fig. 14:8
	Qumrân II	A.D. 50 – 68	*Rapport I*, Fig. 3:4
C*	Qumrân II	A.D. 50 – 68	*Rapport III*, Fig. 4:14
D*	Qumrân II	A.D. 50 – 68	*Rapport II*, Fig. 4:8

82.2 Decorated (50 – 31 B.C.)

A*	Qumrân Ib	50 – 31 B.C.	*Rapport II*, Fig. 3:17

81–89 LAMPS
TYPE 83. DELPHINIFORM LAMPS

83.1 Plain

Observations:

1. Parallels: 'Athlît, Beth-zur, Gezer, Jerusalem, Lachish, Megiddo, Ramat Rahel Tell el-Fâr'ah (South), Tell el-Fûl.

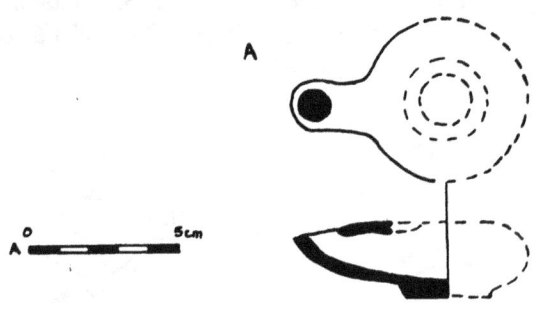

A*	Beth-zur II	175–165 B.C.	No. 449

83.2 Ray motif

Observations:

1. Examples from Beth-zur and Gezer suggest extension of provenience to the second century B.C.
2. Parallels: 'Athlît, Beth-zur, Gezer, Jericho, Jerusalem, Lachish, Qubeibeh, Ramat Rahel, Tell el-Fâr'ah (South), Tell el-Qasîleh, Tell Sandahannah, Tulûl Abû el-'Alâyiq, Zâharîyeh.

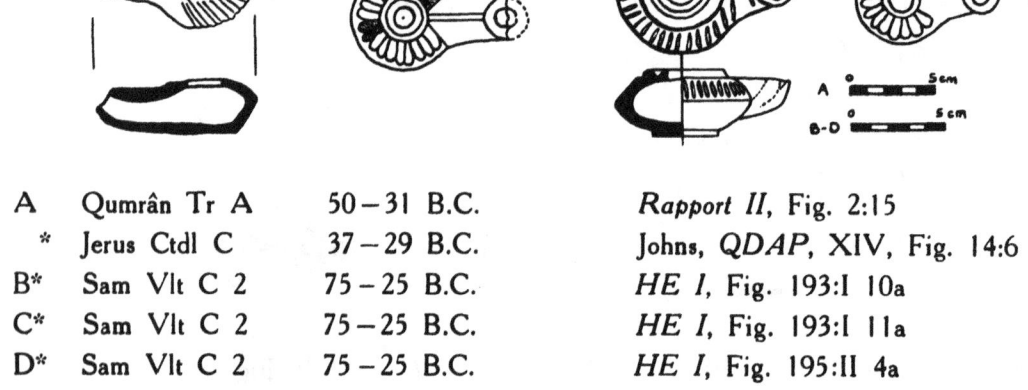

A	Qumrân Tr A	50–31 B.C.	*Rapport II*, Fig. 2:15
*	Jerus Ctdl C	37–29 B.C.	Johns, *QDAP*, XIV, Fig. 14:6
B*	Sam Vlt C 2	75–25 B.C.	*HE I*, Fig. 193:I 10a
C*	Sam Vlt C 2	75–25 B.C.	*HE I*, Fig. 193:I 11a
D*	Sam Vlt C 2	75–25 B.C.	*HE I*, Fig. 195:II 4a

81–89 LAMPS

TYPE 83. DELPHINIFORM LAMPS

83.3 Volute motif

Observations:
1. No stratified evidence.
2. Parallels: 'Athlît, Beth-shan.

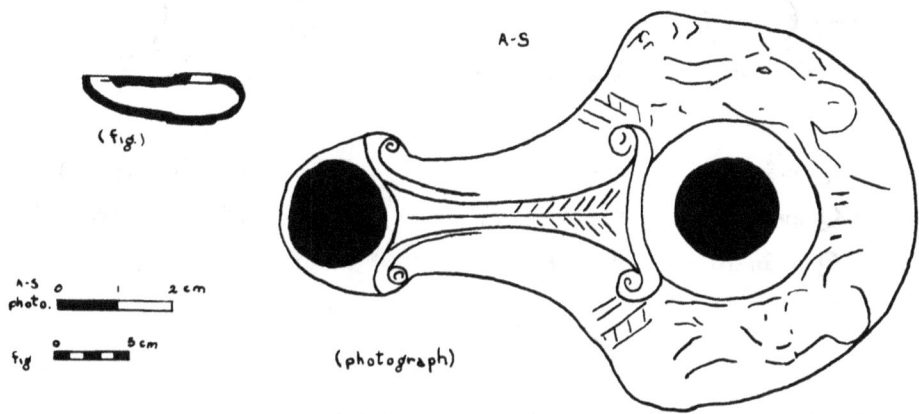

A–S* 'Athlît Tomb L 24   ± 200 B.C.   Johns, *QDAP*, II, Pl. XXXIV: 907, Fig. 83.

81–89 LAMPS

TYPE 84. LOOP-HANDLED LAMPS

Observations:
1. Parallels: Lachish, Qumrân Caves, Tell el-Fâr'ah (South).

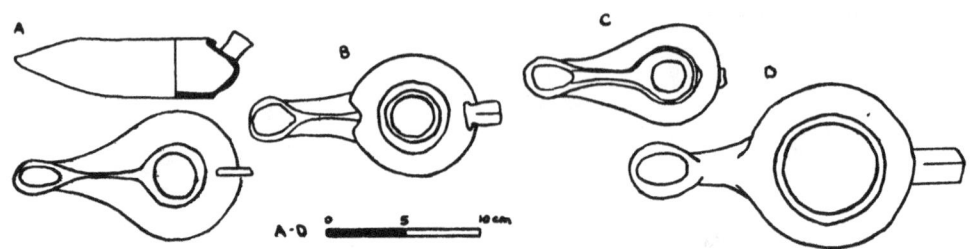

A*–D*	Qumrân Ib	50–31 B.C.	*Rapport III*, Fig. 1:1–4
B	Qumrân Tr A	50–31 B.C.	*Rapport II*, Fig. 2:16
D	Qumrân Ib	50–31 B.C.	*Rapport II*, Fig. 3:16

TYPE 85. MOLDED LAMPS WITH SLIGHT NOZZLE

Observations:
1. Apparently rare before A.D. 70.
2. Parallels: Tell el-Fâr'ah (South).

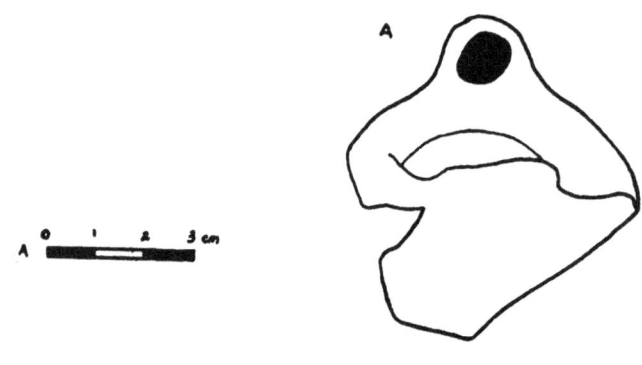

A*	'Alâyiq	A.D. 0–50	*'Alâyiq*, Pl. 49:6 (photograph)

91–92 UNGUENTARIA

TYPE 91. FUSIFORM UNGUENTARIA

91.1 Heavy ware (200–150 B.C.)

Observations:
1. Apparently characteristic of the second century B.C.
2. Parallels: Beth-shan, Beth-zur, Gezer, Jericho, Jerusalem, Lachish, Megiddo, Samaria, Tell Abû Hawâm, Tell el-Fâr'ah (North), Tell el-Qasîleh, Tell en-Nasbeh, Tell Jemmeh, Tell Sandahannah, Zâharîyeh.

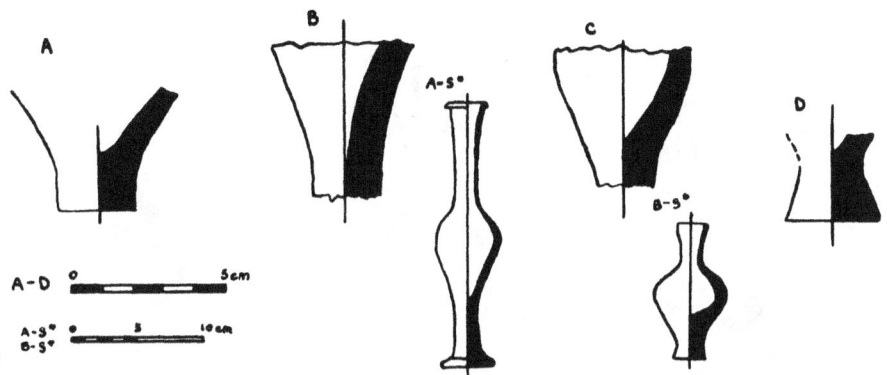

A*	Shec Bl Erth	200–150 B.C.	No. 590 (for shape cf. *HE I*, Fig. 178:9)
B*–D*	Beth-zur II	175–165 B.C.	Nos. 373, 843, 438
A–S*	Beth-zur		*CBZ*, Pl. X:14 (illustrates second century B.C. form)
B–S*	Beth-zur		*CBZ*, Pl. X:13 (cf. 91.1.D; illustrates second century B.C. form)

91–92 UNGUENTARIA

TYPE 91. FUSIFORM UNGUENTARIA

91.2 Thin ware (75 B.C. – early first century A.D.)

Observations:

1. Apparently characteristic of the first century B.C., disappearing in early first century A.D.
2. All examples rather bulbous.
3. Parallels: Beth-shan, Beth-zur, Jerusalem, Ramat Rahel, Samaria, Tell el-Qasîleh, Tell Sandahannah.

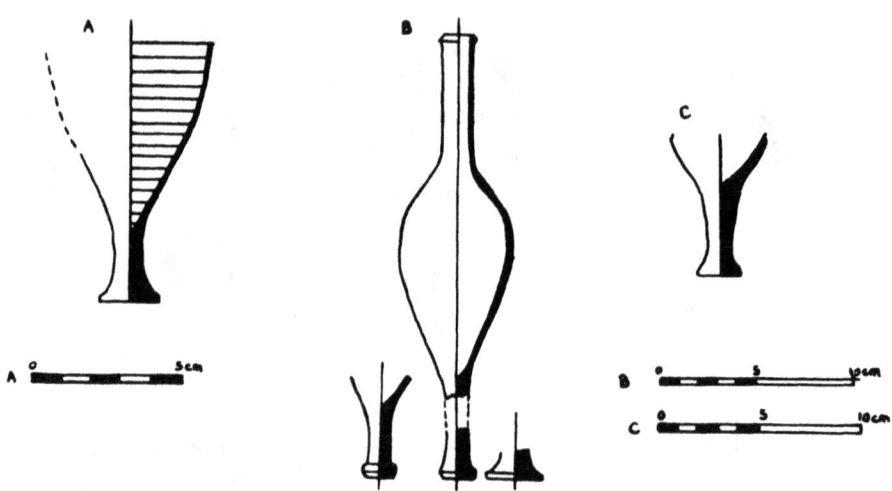

A*	Beth-zur 279	175 – 100 B.C.	No. 1050 (intrusive?)
	Sam Vlt C 2	75 – 25 B.C.	*HE I*, Fig. 178:2, 3 (?)
B	Jerus Ctdl C	37 – 29 B.C.	Johns, *QDAP*, XIV, Fig. 14:7 (four fragments)
*	Sam Vlt C 2	75 – 25 B.C.	*HE I*, Fig. 178:1
	Jerus T Val	37 – 4 B.C.	*PEFA*, 1927, Pl. XI:34, 39
C*	'Alâyiq	A.D. 0 – 50	*'Alâyiq*, Pl. 59:31

91–92 UNGUENTARIA

TYPE 92. PIRIFORM UNGUENTARIA (20 B.C. – A.D. 68)

Observations:

1. Parallels: 'Athlît, Bethany, Bethlehem, Jerusalem, 'Ain Feshkha, Ramat Rahel, Samaria, Silet edh-Dhahr, Tell en-Nasbeh, Tulûl Abû el-'Alâyiq.

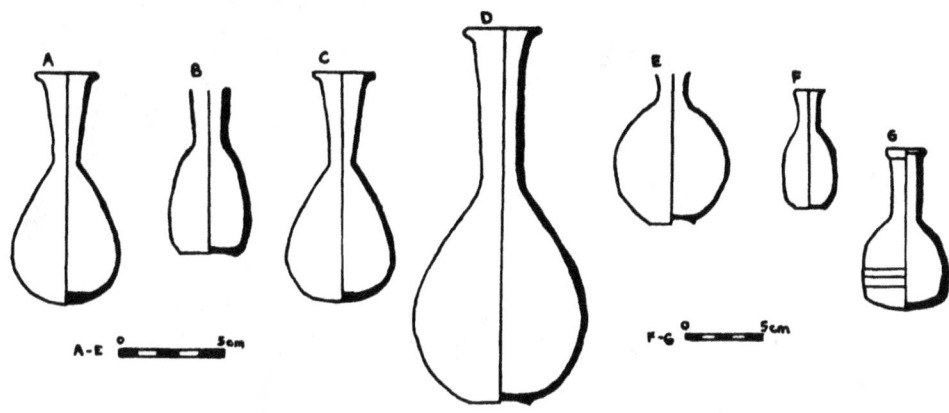

A	Sam Roman Ia	20 B.C. – A.D. 20	*SS III*, Fig. 69:2
*	'Alâyiq	A.D. 0 – 50	*'Alâyiq*, Pl. 59:27
B*	'Alâyiq	A.D. 0 – 50	*'Alâyiq*, Pl. 59:23
C*	'Alâyiq	A.D. 0 – 50	*'Alâyiq*, Pl. 59:26
D*	'Alâyiq	A.D. 0 – 50	*'Alâyiq*, Pl. 59:29
	Qumrân II	A.D. 50 – 68	*Rapport I*, Fig. 3:10
E*	'Alâyiq	A.D. 0 – 50	*'Alâyiq*, Pl. 59:24 (cf. 59:25)
F*	Qumrân II	A.D. 50 – 68	*Rapport II*, Fig. 4:4
G*	Qumrân II	A.D. 50 – 68	*Rapport III*, Fig. 5:10

101–199 HELLENISTIC DECORATED WARE
121–129 JUGS AND FLASKS
TYPE 128. MISCELLANEOUS JUGS

Observations:
1. Parallels: Samaria (B and C).

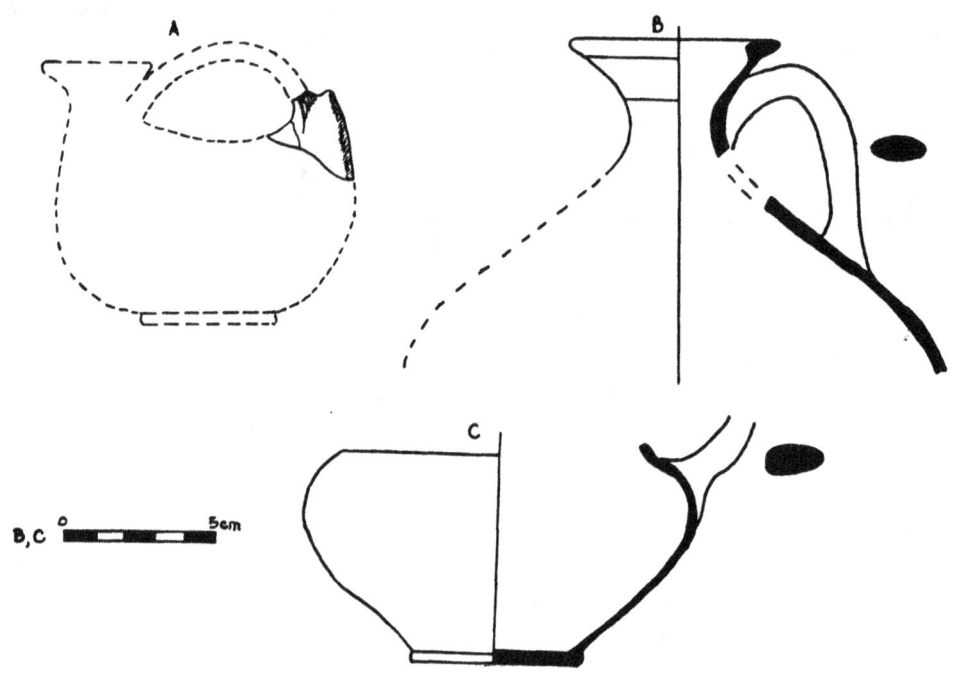

A*	Sam HFW	(200)–150 B.C.	*SS III*, Fig. 39:6 (askos; probably pre-200 B.C.)
B*	Shec Bl Erth	200–150 B.C.	No. 779 (possibly pre-200 B.C.)
C*	Shec Rm 1	150–100 B.C.	No. 1189 (possibly earlier)

131–139 JUGLETS, BOTTLES, AND VASES
TYPE 139. MISCELLANEOUS FRAGMENTS

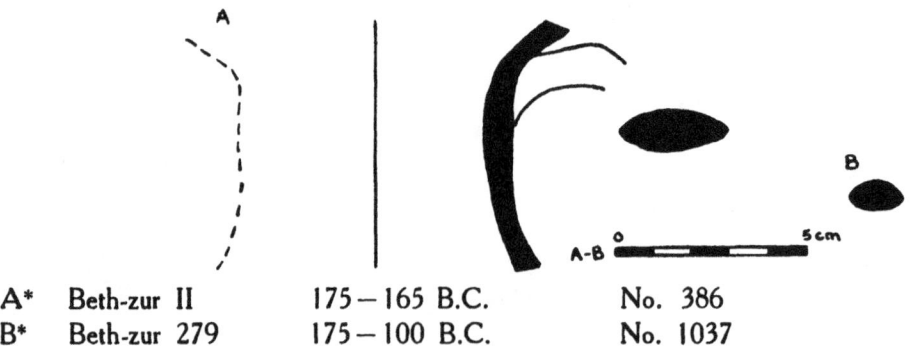

A*	Beth-zur II	175–165 B.C.	No. 386
B*	Beth-zur 279	175–100 B.C.	No. 1037

151–159 BOWLS, CUPS, AND PLATES

TYPE 151. SMALL DEEP BOWLS

151.1 Incurved rim (200–100 B.C.)

Observations:
1. Decoration consists of glaze, paint, slip, or wash in black to red.
2. Cf. 51.1.
3. Parallels: Beth-shan, Jerusalem, Lachish, Samaria, Tell Sandahannah, Zâharîyeh.

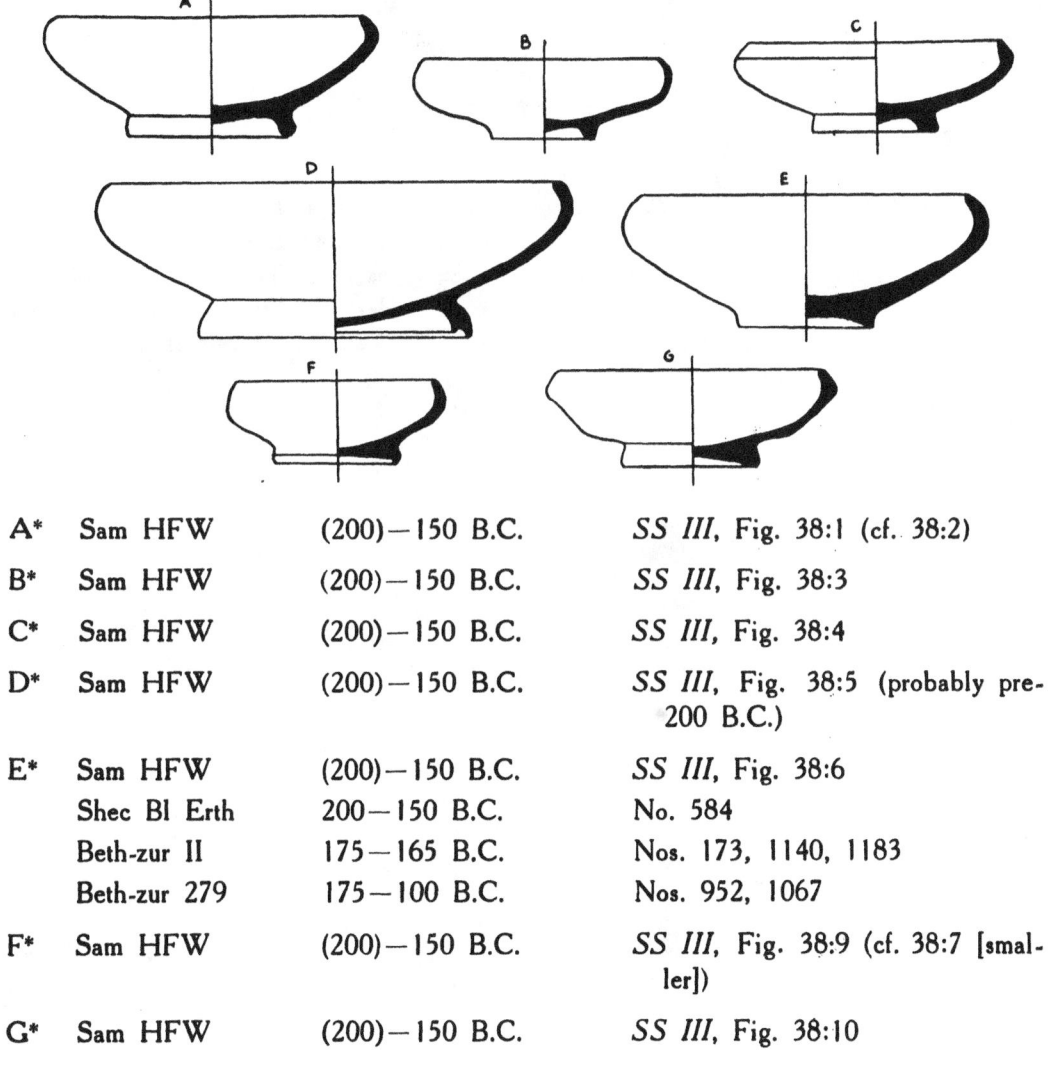

A*	Sam HFW	(200)–150 B.C.	*SS III*, Fig. 38:1 (cf. 38:2)
B*	Sam HFW	(200)–150 B.C.	*SS III*, Fig. 38:3
C*	Sam HFW	(200)–150 B.C.	*SS III*, Fig. 38:4
D*	Sam HFW	(200)–150 B.C.	*SS III*, Fig. 38:5 (probably pre-200 B.C.)
E*	Sam HFW	(200)–150 B.C.	*SS III*, Fig. 38:6
	Shec Bl Erth	200–150 B.C.	No. 584
	Beth-zur II	175–165 B.C.	Nos. 173, 1140, 1183
	Beth-zur 279	175–100 B.C.	Nos. 952, 1067
F*	Sam HFW	(200)–150 B.C.	*SS III*, Fig. 38:9 (cf. 38:7 [smaller])
G*	Sam HFW	(200)–150 B.C.	*SS III*, Fig. 38:10

151–159 BOWLS, CUPS, AND PLATES

TYPE 151. SMALL DEEP BOWLS

151.2 Hemispherical (75–25 B.C.)

Observations:
1. Parallels: Samaria.

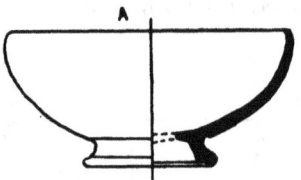

A*   Sam Roman I   75–25 B.C.   *SS III*, Fig. 67:1 (best considered in connection with 251.2 as glaze is much better than that of Hellenistic Decorated Ware in the Late Hellenistic period)

151–159 BOWLS, CUPS, AND PLATES

TYPE 151. SMALL DEEP BOWLS

151.3 Outcurved rim (200–25 B.C.)

Observations:
1. Decoration consists of glaze, paint, slip, or wash in black to red.
2. Parallels: 'Athlît, Beth-shan, Beth-shearim, Lachish, Samaria, Tell Sandahannah.

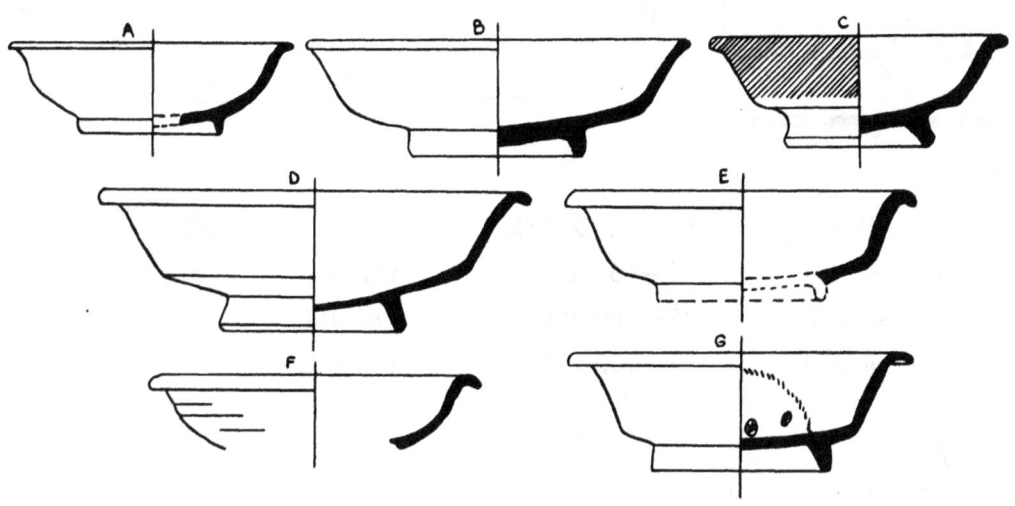

A*	Sam HFW	(200)–150 B.C.	*SS III*, Fig. 37:14
	Beth-zur II–I	175–100 B.C.	No. 189
B*	Sam HFW	(200)–150 B.C.	*SS III*, Fig. 37:15
C*	Sam HFW	(200)–150 B.C.	*SS III*, Fig. 37:16
D*	Sam PHFW	150–107 B.C.	*SS III*, Fig. 43:4
E*	Sam PHFW	150–107 B.C.	*SS III*, Fig. 43:5
F*	Sam PHFW	150–107 B.C.	*SS III*, Fig. 43:6
G*	Sam Roman I	75–25 B.C.	*SS III*, Fig. 67:2 (perhaps earlier)

151–159 BOWLS, CUPS, AND PLATES

TYPE 151. SMALL DEEP BOWLS

151.4 Pinched handle (200–100 B.C.)

Observations:

1. Parallels: Beth-shan, Beth-zur, Jerusalem, Lachish, Samaria, Tell Sandahannah.

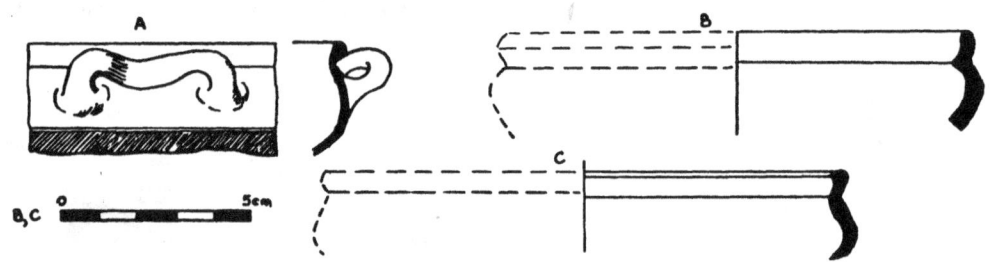

A*	Sam HFW	(200)–150 B.C.	*SS III*, Fig. 39:5
	Beth-zur II	175–165 B.C.	No. 378
B*	Beth-zur II-I	175–100 B.C.	No. 108
C*	Beth-zur 279	175–100 B.C.	No. 992

151.5 Skyphos (200–150 B.C.)

Observations:

1. Parallels: Beth-shan, Samaria.

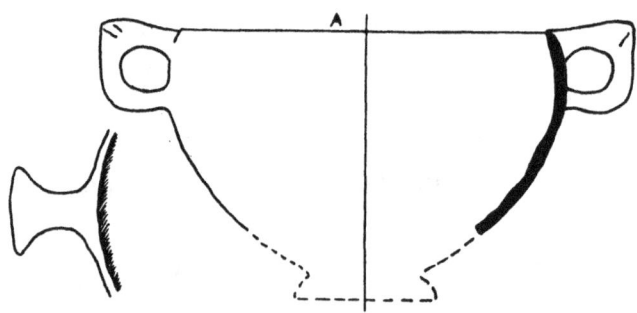

A*	Sam HFW	(200)–150 B.C.	*SS III*, Fig. 39:4

151–159 BOWLS, CUPS, AND PLATES

TYPE 151. SMALL DEEP BOWLS

151.9 Miscellaneous fragments

Observations:
1. Decoration consists of glaze, paint, slip, or wash in black to red.
2. Some parts may belong with Type 153.
3. Parallels: Jericho.

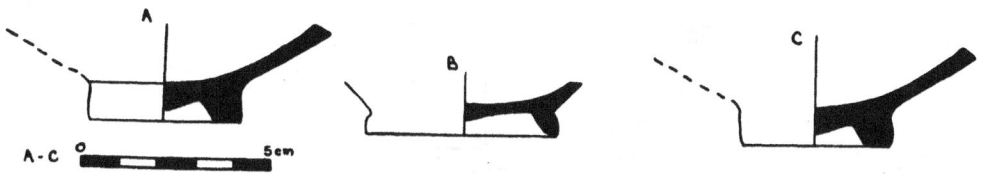

A	Beth-zur II	175–165 B.C.	Nos. 356, 362, 930
	Beth-zur 279	175–100 B.C.	No. 1040
*	Beth-zur I	140–100 B.C.	No. 455 (cf. No. 337)
B*	Beth-zur II	175–165 B.C.	Nos. 355, 540 (// No. 1338*)
	Beth-zur 279	175–100 B.C.	No. 1053
C	Beth-zur II	175–165 B.C.	No. 363
*	Beth-zur 279	175–100 B.C.	No. 1024

151–159 BOWLS, CUPS, AND PLATES

TYPE 153. SHALLOW BOWLS AND PLATES

153.1 Fish plates (200–100 B.C.)

Observations:

1. Elongated drooping rims (N) and buff ware are characteristic of the last half of the second century B.C.
2. Parallels: Beth-shan, Beth-zur, Lachish, Samaria, Tell Sandahannah.

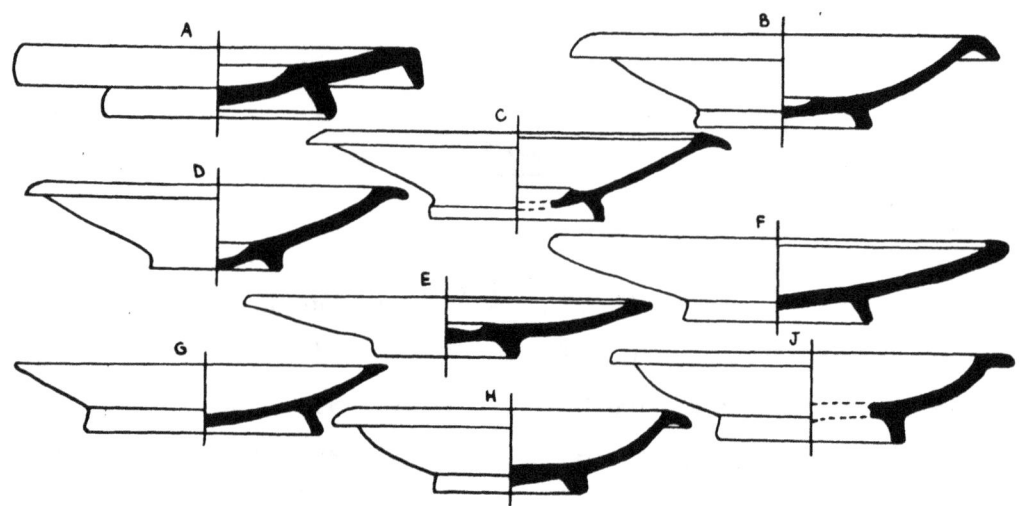

A*	Sam HFW	(200)–150 B.C.	*SS III*, Fig. 37:1 (probably pre-200 B.C.)
B*	Sam HFW	(200)–150 B.C.	*SS III*, Fig. 37:3 (cf. 37:2, 4, 5)
C*	Sam HFW	(200)–150 B.C.	*SS III*, Fig. 37:6
D*	Sam HFW	(200)–150 B.C.	*SS III*, Fig. 37:7
E*	Sam HFW	(200)–150 B.C.	*SS III*, Fig. 37:8
F*	Sam HFW	(200)–150 B.C.	*SS III*, Fig. 37:9 (pre-200 B.C. ?)
	Shec Bl Erth	200–150 B.C.	Nos. 531, 587
G*	Sam HFW	(200)–150 B.C.	*SS III*, Fig. 37:10
H*	Sam HFW	(200)–150 B.C.	*SS III*, Fig. 37:11 (cf. 37:13)
J*	Sam HFW	(200)–150 B.C.	*SS III*, Fig. 37:12

continued page 207

151–159 BOWLS, CUPS, AND PLATES
TYPE 153. SHALLOW BOWLS AND PLATES
153.1 Fish plates (continued)

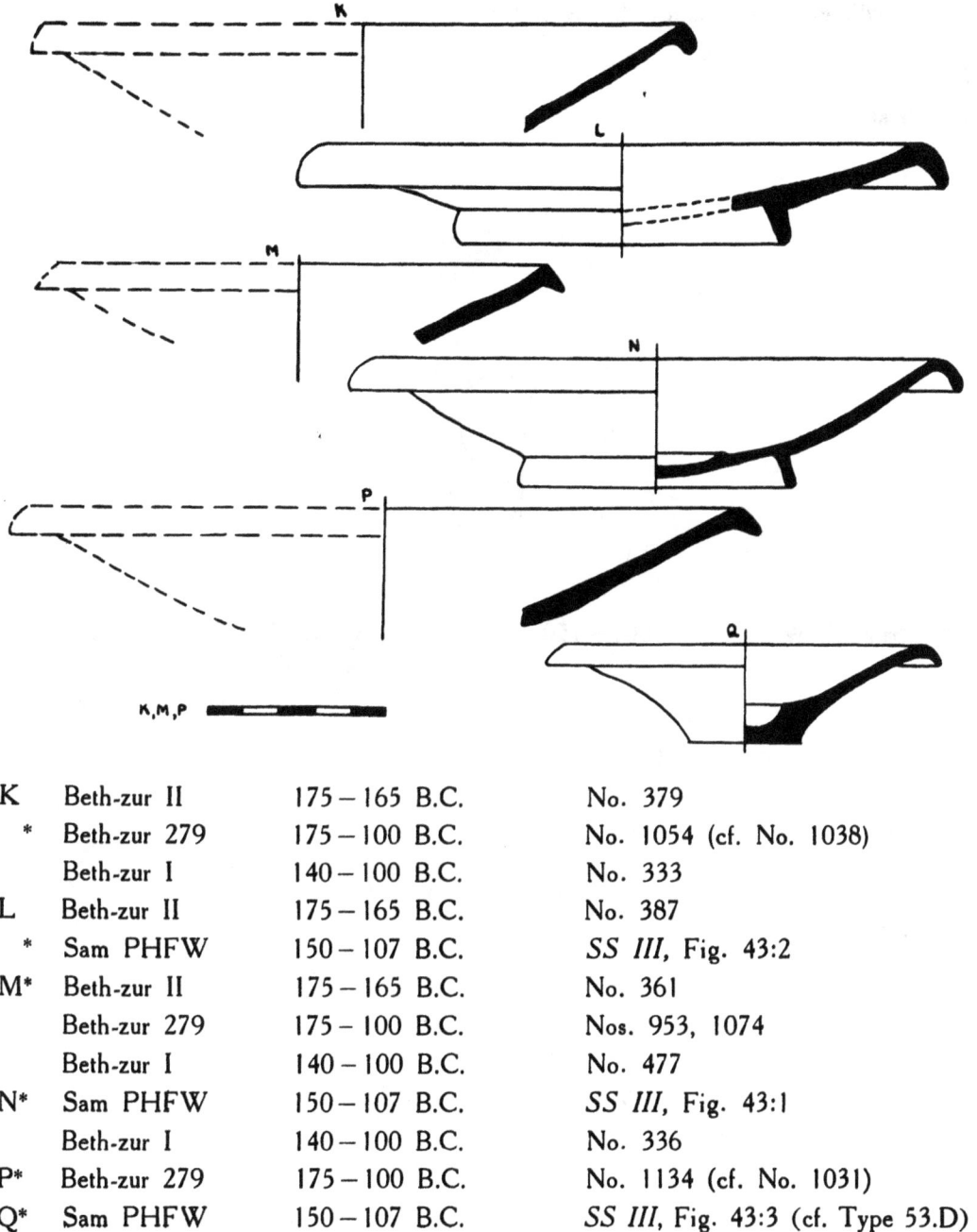

K	Beth-zur II	175 – 165 B.C.	No. 379
*	Beth-zur 279	175 – 100 B.C.	No. 1054 (cf. No. 1038)
	Beth-zur I	140 – 100 B.C.	No. 333
L	Beth-zur II	175 – 165 B.C.	No. 387
*	Sam PHFW	150 – 107 B.C.	*SS III*, Fig. 43:2
M*	Beth-zur II	175 – 165 B.C.	No. 361
	Beth-zur 279	175 – 100 B.C.	Nos. 953, 1074
	Beth-zur I	140 – 100 B.C.	No. 477
N*	Sam PHFW	150 – 107 B.C.	*SS III*, Fig. 43:1
	Beth-zur I	140 – 100 B.C.	No. 336
P*	Beth-zur 279	175 – 100 B.C.	No. 1134 (cf. No. 1031)
Q*	Sam PHFW	150 – 107 B.C.	*SS III*, Fig. 43:3 (cf. Type 53.D)

151–159 BOWLS, CUPS, AND PLATES

TYPE 153. SHALLOW BOWLS AND PLATES

153.9 Miscellaneous shallow bowls and plates

Observations:
1. Parallels: Samaria.

A*   Sam HFW   (200)–150 B.C.   SS III, Fig. 39:7 (could be considered a stand; cf. SS III, pp. 269–70; perhaps pre-200 B.C.)

151–159 BOWLS, CUPS, AND PLATES

TYPE 158. MEGARIAN BOWLS (150 B.C.–A.D. 20)

Observations:
1. Parallels: Beth-shan, Beth-shearim, Beth-zur, Gezer, Jericho, Samaria, Tell Sandahannah.

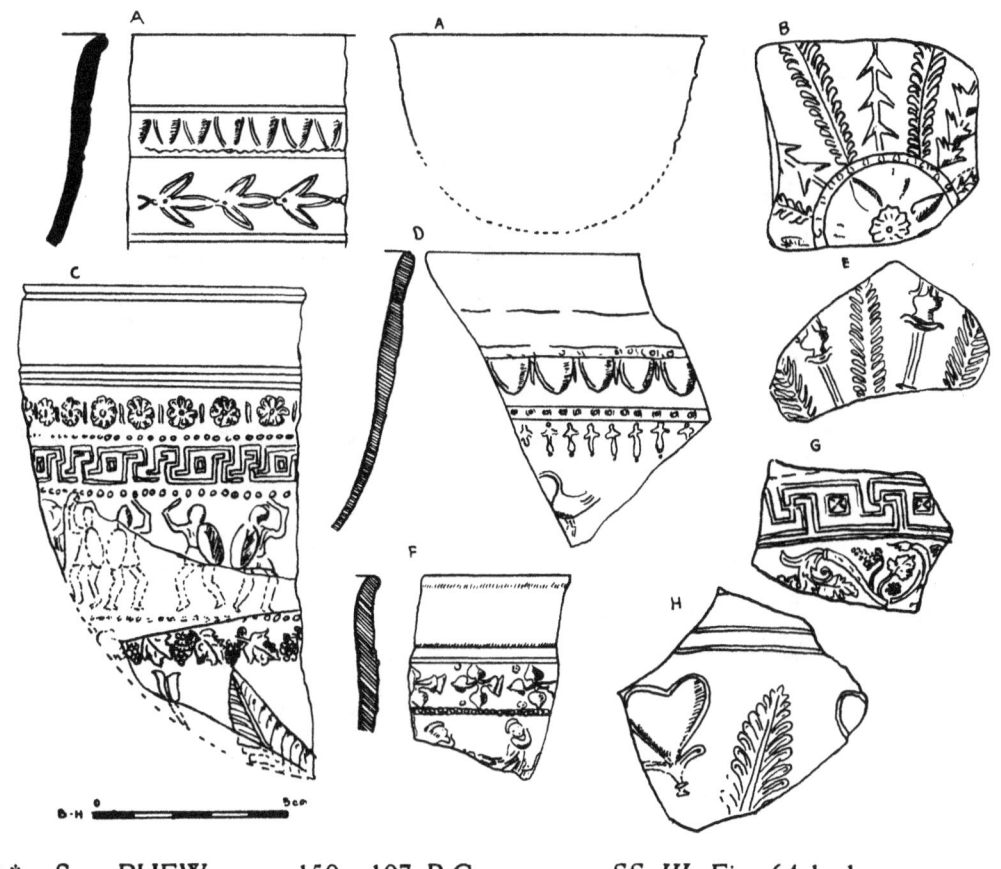

A*	Sam PHFW	150–107 B.C.	*SS III*, Fig. 64:1, 1a
B*	Sam PHFW	150–107 B.C.	*SS III*, Fig. 64:2
C*	Sam Pre-Gab	75–55 B.C.	*SS III*, Fig. 61
D*	Sam Pre-Gab	75–55 B.C.	*SS III*, Fig. 62:12
E*	Sam Pre-Gab	75–55 B.C.	*SS III*, Fig. 63:20
F*	Sam Roman I	75–25 B.C.	*SS III*, Fig. 62:13
G*	Sam Roman I	75–25 B.C.	*SS III*, Fig. 63:1
H*	Sam Roman Ia	20 B.C.–A.D. 20	*SS III*, Fig. 63:22 (sigillata)

201–299 EASTERN SIGILLATA A

221–229 JUGS AND FLASKS

TYPE 228. MISCELLANEOUS JUGS

Observations:
1. Parallels: Samaria (A and B).

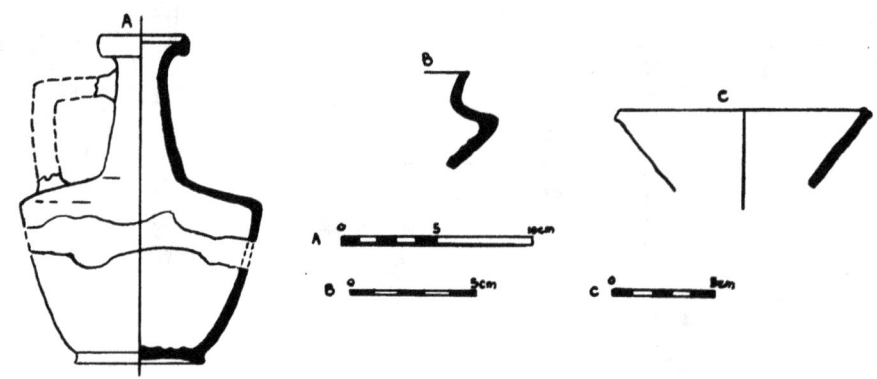

A*	Sam VIt C 2	75 – 25 B.C.	*HE I*, Fig. 185:14a
B*	Sam Roman Ia	20 B.C. – A.D. 20	*SS III*, Fig. 68:7
C*	'Alâyiq	A.D. 0 – 50	*'Alâyiq*, Pl. 58:20

251–259 BOWLS, CUPS, AND PLATES
TYPE 251. SMALL DEEP BOWLS

251.2 Hemispherical (plain rim) (75 B.C.–A.D. 20)

Observations:

1. Parallels: Beth-shan, Samaria, Tell Sandahannah, Tulûl Abû el-'Alâyiq.

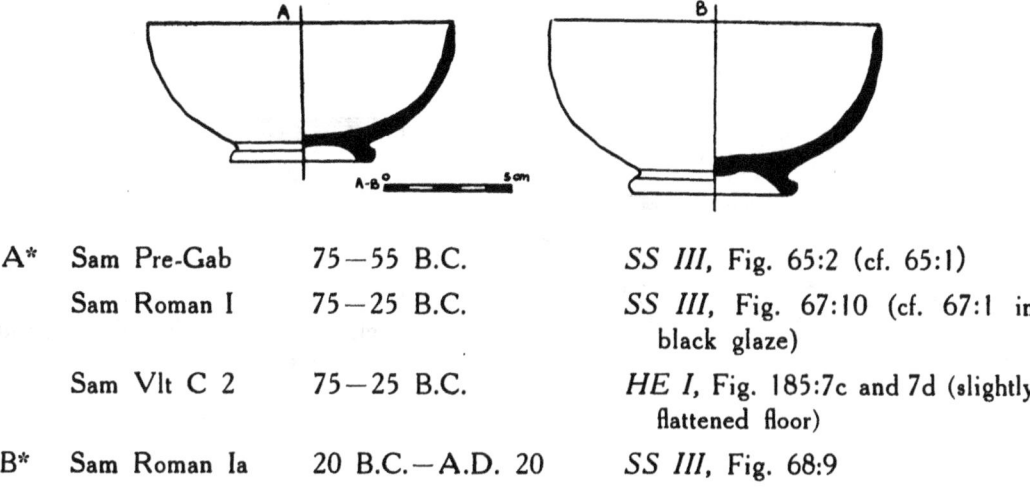

A*	Sam Pre-Gab	75–55 B.C.	*SS III*, Fig. 65:2 (cf. 65:1)
	Sam Roman I	75–25 B.C.	*SS III*, Fig. 67:10 (cf. 67:1 in black glaze)
	Sam Vlt C 2	75–25 B.C.	*HE I*, Fig. 185:7c and 7d (slightly flattened floor)
B*	Sam Roman Ia	20 B.C.–A.D. 20	*SS III*, Fig. 68:9

251.2a Hemispherical (everted rim) (75–25 B.C.)

Observations:

1. Parallels: Beth-shan, Samaria, Tell Sandahannah.

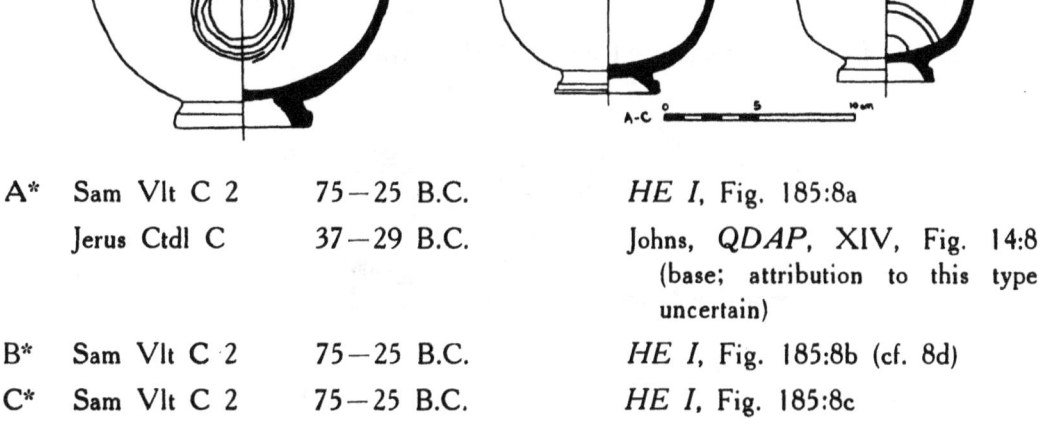

A*	Sam Vlt C 2	75–25 B.C.	*HE I*, Fig. 185:8a
	Jerus Ctdl C	37–29 B.C.	Johns, *QDAP*, XIV, Fig. 14:8 (base; attribution to this type uncertain)
B*	Sam Vlt C 2	75–25 B.C.	*HE I*, Fig. 185:8b (cf. 8d)
C*	Sam Vlt C 2	75–25 B.C.	*HE I*, Fig. 185:8c

251–259 BOWLS, CUPS, AND PLATES

TYPE 251. SMALL DEEP BOWLS

251.2b Hemispherical (molded rim) (75 – 25 B.C.)

Observations:
1. Parallels: Samaria.

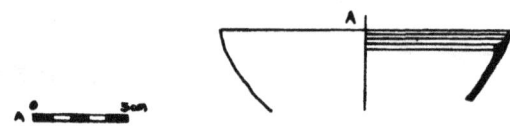

A* Sam Vlt C 2   75 – 25 B.C.   *HE I*, Fig. 185:9a (occurs in black glaze also, *SS III*, p. 259 and Fig. 53:5)

251.6 Vertical rim (20 B.C. – A.D. 20)

Observations:
1. Parallels: Beth-shan, Samaria, Tulûl Abû el-'Alâyiq.

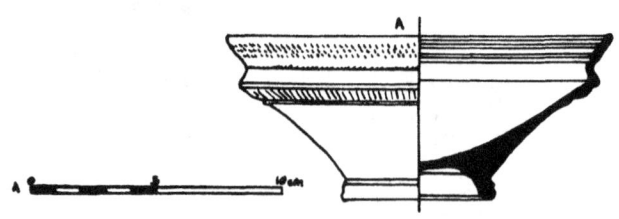

A* Sam Roman Ia   20 B.C. – A.D. 20   *SS III*, Fig. 68:8

251–259 BOWLS, CUPS, AND PLATES

TYPE 252. CUPS

252.2 Everted sides (75–25 B.C.)

Observations:
1. Parallels: Beth-shan, Samaria.

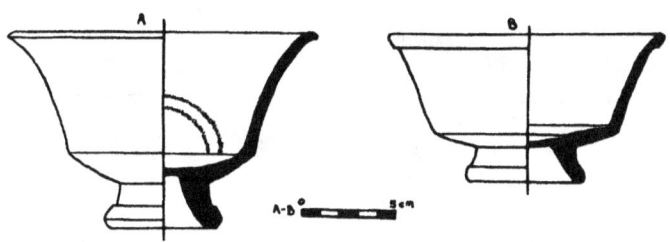

A*	Sam VIt C 2	75–25 B.C.	*HE I*, Fig. 185:10a
B*	Sam VIt C 2	75–25 B.C.	*HE I*, Fig. 185:10b

252.3 Small craters (75–25 B.C.)

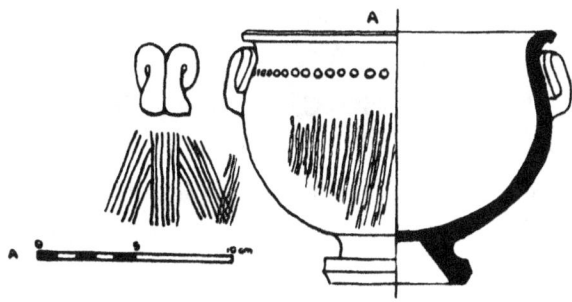

A*	Sam VIt C 2	75–25 B.C.	*HE I*, Fig. 185:11a (cf. 11b)

251–259 BOWLS, CUPS, AND PLATES

TYPE 253. SHALLOW BOWLS AND PLATES

253.1 Small with plain rim (75 B.C. – early first century A.D.)

Observations:
1. Parallels: Beth-shan, Samaria, Tell Sandahannah, Tulûl Abû el-'Alâyiq.

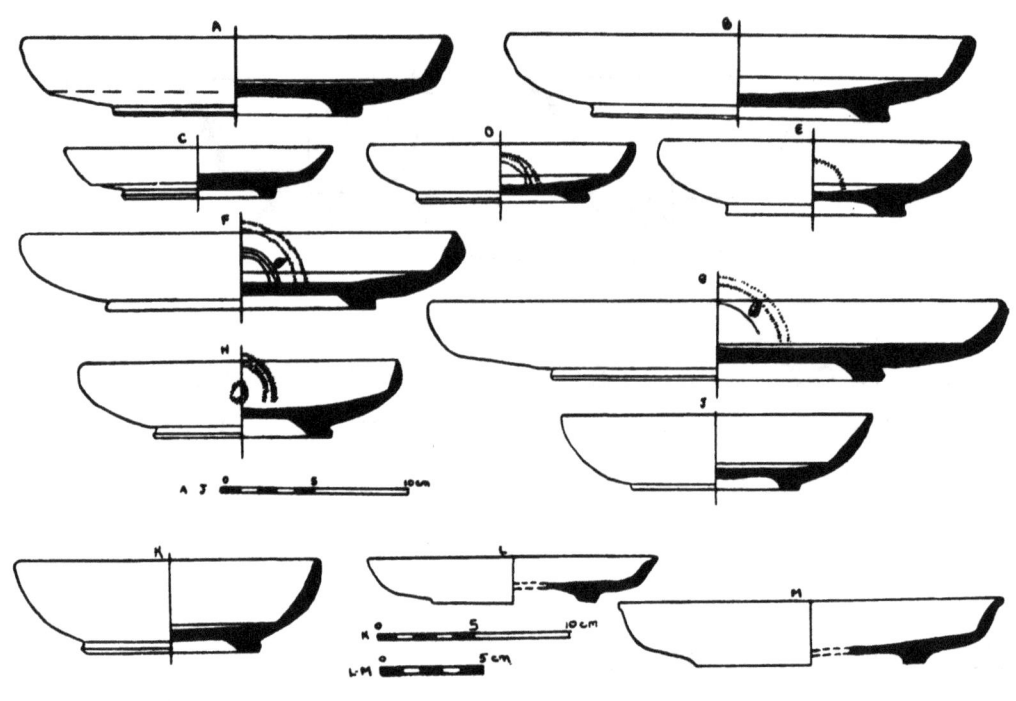

A*–E*	Sam VIt C 2	75–25 B.C.	*HE I*, Fig. 185:2a–2e
F*	Sam VIt C 2	75–25 B.C.	*HE I*, Fig. 185:2f (cf. 2h)
G*	Sam VIt C 2	75–25 B.C.	*HE I*, Fig. 185:2g (cf. 2j with step in base)
H*–K*	Sam VIt C 2	75–25 B.C.	*HE I*, Fig. 185:2i, 7a, 7b
L*	'Alâyiq	A.D. 0–50	*'Alâyiq*, Pl. 58:19 (probably early first century A.D.)
M*	'Alâyiq	A.D. 0–50	*'Alâyiq*, Pl. 58:17 (cf. 21, 27; 59:36; probably early first century A.D.)

251–259 BOWLS, CUPS, AND PLATES

TYPE 253. SHALLOW BOWLS AND PLATES

253.2 Small with molded rim (75–25 B.C.)

Observations:
1. Parallels: Samaria, Tell Sandahannah.

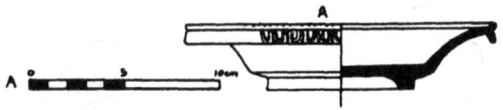

A*	Sam Vlt C 2	75–25 B.C.	*HE I*, Fig. 185:6a

253.3 Small with everted rim and flat base (75–25 B.C.)

Observations:
1. Parallels: Samaria, Tell Sandahannah.

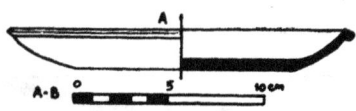 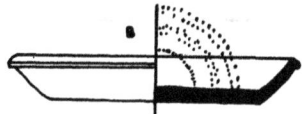

A*	Sam Vlt C 2	75–25 B.C.	*HE I*, Fig. 185:1b
B*	Sam Vlt C 2	75–25 B.C.	*HE I*, Fig. 185:1c (cf. 1a – without design)

251–259 BOWLS, CUPS, AND PLATES
TYPE 253. SHALLOW BOWLS AND PLATES
253.4 Large with simple rim (75 B.C.–A.D. 20)

Observations:
1. Parallels: Beth-shan, Samaria.

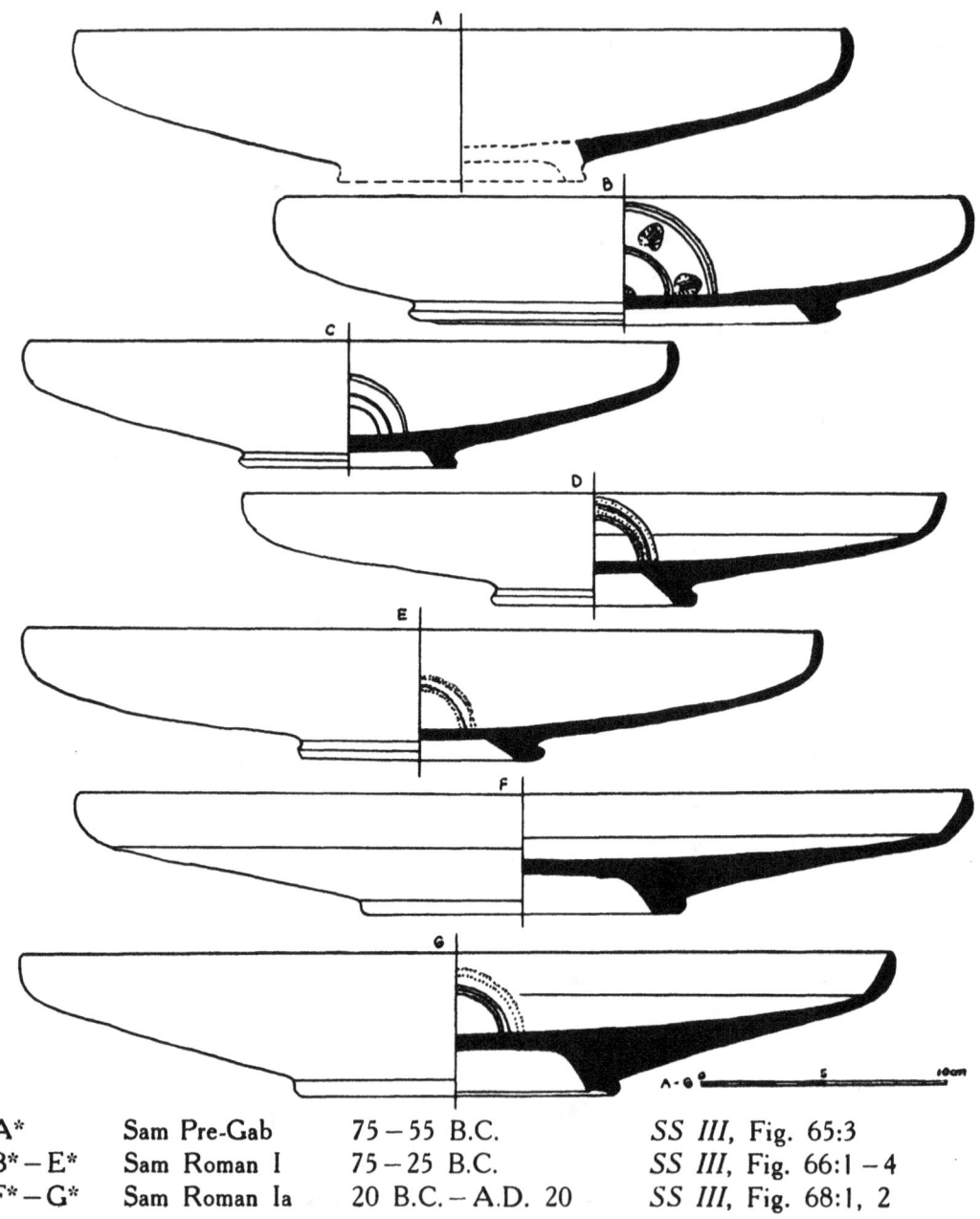

A*	Sam Pre-Gab	75–55 B.C.	*SS III*, Fig. 65:3
B*–E*	Sam Roman I	75–25 B.C.	*SS III*, Fig. 66:1–4
F*–G*	Sam Roman Ia	20 B.C.–A.D. 20	*SS III*, Fig. 68:1, 2

251–259 BOWLS, CUPS, AND PLATES

TYPE 253. SHALLOW BOWLS AND PLATES

253.5 Large with molded rim (75–25 B.C.)

Observations:
1. Parallels: Samaria.

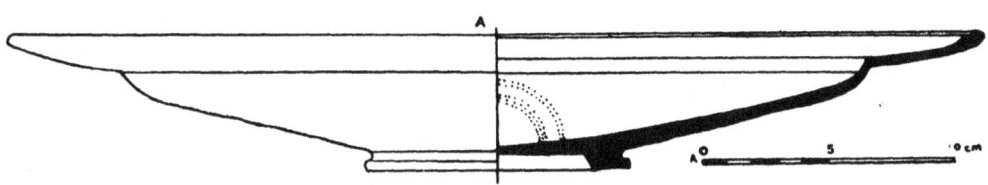

A*	Sam Roman I	75–25 B.C.	*SS III*, Fig. 66:5

253.6 Large with everted rim (75 B.C.–A.D. 20)

Observations:
1. Parallels: Samaria.

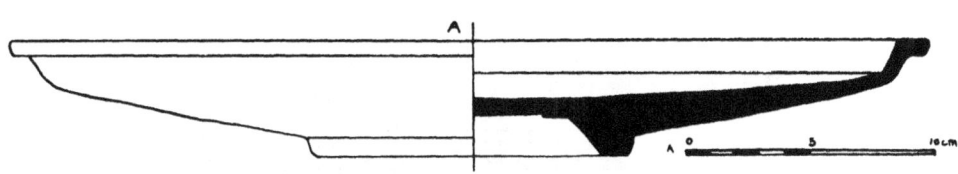

A	Sam Roman I	75–25 B.C.	*SS III*, p. 287
*	Sam Roman Ia	20 B.C.–A.D. 20	*SS III*, Fig. 68:3

251–259 BOWLS, CUPS, AND PLATES

TYPE 254. SHALLOW BOWLS WITH VERTICAL SIDES

254.2 Small (75 B.C.–A.D. 20)

Observations:

2. Parallels: Beth-shan, Samaria, Tell en-Nasbeh, Tulûl Abû el-'Alâyiq.

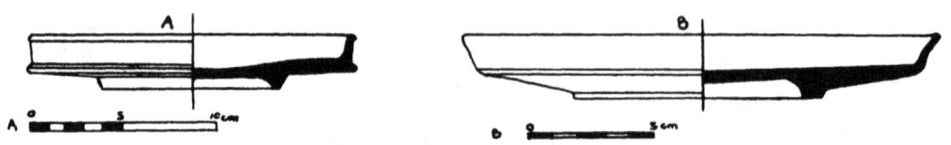

A*	Sam Vlt C 2	75–25 B.C.	*HE I*, Fig. 185:4b
	Sam Roman Ia	20 B.C.–A.D. 20	*SS III*, Fig. 68:6
B*	Sam Roman Ia	20 B.C.–A.D. 20	*SS III*, Fig. 68:4

301–399 MISCELLANEOUS WARES

ARRETINE WARE

Observations:

1. Parallels: Beth-shan (354.2).

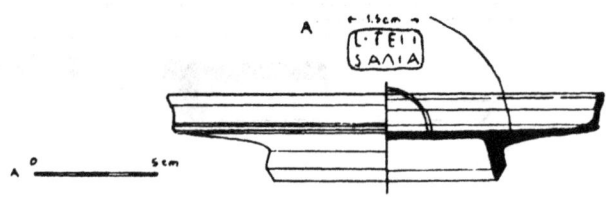

354.2.A*	Sam Roman Ia	20 B.C.–A.D. 20	*SS III*, Fig. 68:5

POMPEIAN RED WARE

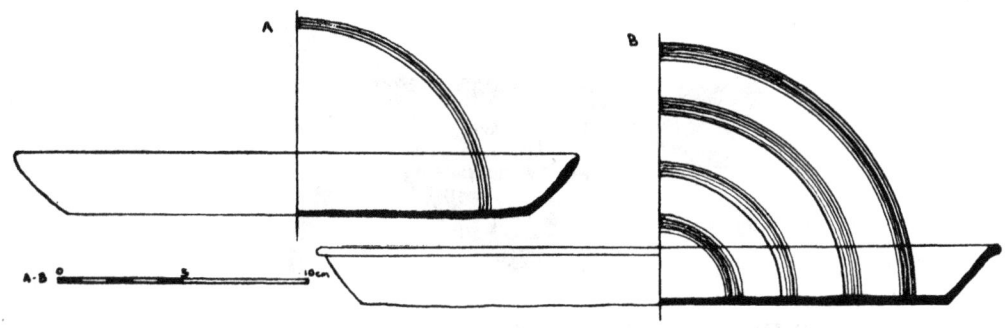

353.3.A*	Sam Roman Ia	20 B.C. – A.D. 20	*SS III*, Fig. 68:10
353.3.B*	Sam Roman Ia	20 B.C. – A.D. 20	*SS III*, Fig. 68:11

WEST SLOPE TECHNIQUE

Observations:

1. Parallels: Beth-shan (353.2.A), (Gezer 353.1.A), Samaria (345.1.A, 353.1.A, 353.2.A).

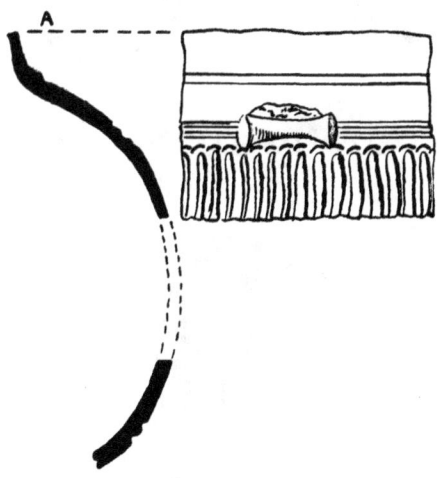

328.A*	Sam HFW	(200) – 150 B.C.	*SS III*, Fig. 39:8 (probably earlier)

continued page 220

WEST SLOPE TECHNIQUE
(continued)

345.1.A*   Sam HFW   (200) – 150 B.C.   *SS III*, Fig. 39:1 (cf. 2; probably earlier)

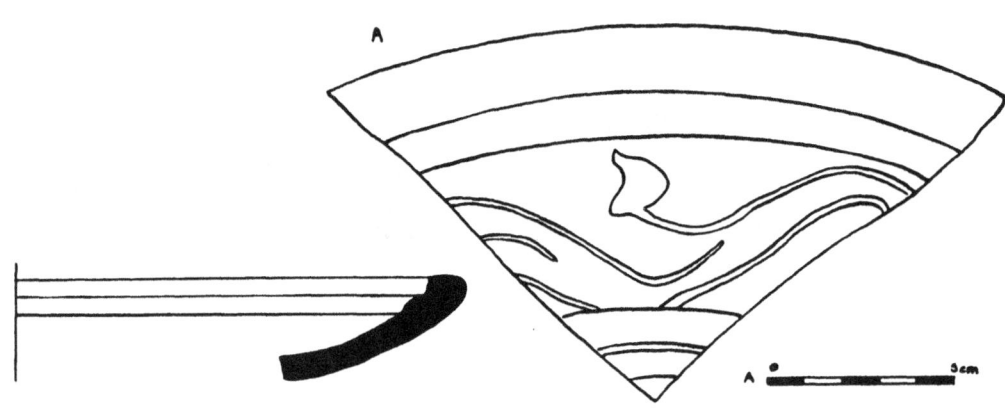

353.1.A*   Beth-zur II   175 – 165 B.C.   No. 515

353.2.A   Sam PHFW   150 – 107 B.C.   *SS III*, Fig. 43:7

APPENDIX A

ECONOMIC AND CULTURAL IMPLICATIONS

An attempt to draw from this ceramic study significant implications for the economic and cultural life of the times is beset with difficulties.[1] There is the danger of imposing a modern economic or cultural frame of reference upon the evidence.[2] There is the temptation to draw conclusions from too little evidence, and, in this instance, from only one facet of the evidence. It is easy to find formal relationships and assume that these involve material relations.[3] A further handicap in the Hellenistic period is the lack of a body of correlative Hellenistic literature.[4] Yet, it is hoped that this brief treatment will prove useful and suggest the trends which a detailed study of these implications might take.

Implications may be drawn at two levels. There are the more technical and local types of implications regarding such specifics as establishment of routes of trade or tracing the origin and spread of a particular ceramic ware. Then, there are broad, inclusive generalizations about such phenomena as directions of cultural influence, periods of rapid cultural transition, and general trends toward decentralized manufacture. It would seem sound to assume that the latter implications should be built upon the foundation of the former. As one looks at the related literature, however, one is impressed by an imposing group of broad generalizations and, frequently, a corresponding lack of technical substructure. Either the material for the substructure is lacking or the task of analyzing the technical evidence has not been seriously undertaken. There seems to be an urgent need for more technical data and their systematic treatment. The Corpus has been developed as a chronological tool which will aid primarily in gathering local technical data; in its development certain technical data have come to light, and their implications for the economy or culture of the times have been alluded to occasionally. The implications of the study are, in the nature of the case, oriented primarily to the technical local level. Accordingly, there follows below

---

1. For an excellent treatment of the methodology to be used in deriving cultural and economic implications from ceramic evidence cf. Anna O. Shepard, *Ceramics for the Archaeologist* (Washington, 1956), pp. 348–63.

2. A Marxian interpretation of the economic background of the New Testament, for example, was widely held early in this century. Cf. F. C. Grant, "The economic background of the New Testament," in *The Background of the New Testament and its Eschatology*, ed. W. D. Davies and D. Daube (Cambridge, 1956), pp. 98, 101.

3. Cf., e.g., the position of W. W. Tarn, *The Greeks in Bactria and India* (Cambridge, 1938), p. 67: "Considered broadly, what the Asiatic took from the Greek was usually external only, matters of form; he rarely took substance..."

4. Cf. Norman H. Baynes, *The Hellenistic Civilization and East Rome* (London, 1946), pp. 7–8.

a consideration of some of the major economic and cultural generalizations in the light of some of this technical evidence; then attention is directed to one of the chief local problems for which the study has implications.

There are widely diverging views of the economic structure of the Graeco-Roman world. Special attention should be given to the views of M. Rostovtzeff because of his broad comprehension of the technical substructure. He flatly rejects the common *Oikenwirtschaft* view because it is not supported by technical evidence.[5] This view, that industry could not develop because the Graeco-Roman world never got beyond the primitive forms of "house-economy," is even partially espoused by F. C. Grant in the latest survey of literature on the economic backgrounds of this period.[6] The evidence reviewed in this study would certainly tend to support Rostovtzeff's speaking of a "world-market" for Arretine pottery despite the fact that some theorists reserve even "city-economy" and "state-economy" for modern times.[7] More allusions to such evidence as the contemporary transition from fusiform to piriform unguentaria in Palestine and on the Rhine and sigillata from Arezzo found in contemporary deposits from England to Arabia and the east coast of India are sufficient to reject the case of *Oikenwirtschaft*.[8]

Related to industrialization are questions concerning standardization of product and centralization of manufacture. Regarding the former Rostovtzeff notes that although

> there was a certain tendency among the Hellenistic potters to make the work more mechanical and more speedy by standardizing the ware produced, the method of manufacture was not that of a factory, was not a mass production of the same types of vases from the same forms by purely mechanical devices. The craft was still to a very large extent individualistic, especially in the field of painted pottery.[9]

He points to the lack of duplication among the lagynoi and Megarian bowls, the latter having been noted also in this study.[10] A similar lack of standardized product can be noted in the local ware of the Hellenistic era in Palestine; the mortaria and cooking pots are typical.[11] The same variety characterizes the plates and bowls of Hellenistic Decorated Ware wherever they occur. In Eastern Sigillata A, and perhaps in contemporary local wares, a stronger tendency toward a standardized product appears. Although there is a wider variety of forms than was extant in later Hellenistic Decorated Ware,[12]

---

5. M. Rostovtzeff, *The Social and Economic History of the Roman Empire* (second ed. rev. by P. M. Fraser; Oxford, 1957), I, p. 349, and II, p. 693, n. 107.

6. Grant frequently relies on Rostovtzeff's views, but his view that "factories were few and far between" (Grant, p. 112) contrasts strikingly with Rostovtzeff's reference to "the large industrial centres of the ancient world." Rostovtzeff, *The Social and Economic History of the Roman Empire*, I, p. 36. Cf. by the same author, *The Social and Economic History of the Hellenistic World*, II, p. 1211.

7. Rostovtzeff, *The Social and Economic History of the Roman Empire*, I, pp. 70, 349; II, p. 603, n. 107.

8. Cf. *supra*, p. 56, n. 1; p. 62, n. 41.

9. Rostovtzeff, *The Social and Economic History of the Hellenistic World*, II, p. 1210.

10. Cf. *supra*, p. 67, n. 95.

11. Corpus 41, 71.1. A–J, 72.1.

12. Cf., e.g., *SS III*, pp. 235, 309–312.

there are frequently a number of nearly identical vessels.[13] The standardization of at least a number of local ceramic forms at the same time that sigillata was beginning to be used in Palestine is indicated by evidence from Qumrân Locus 89 where 204 plates, 75 cups, and 708 small bowls of very similar form occur.[14]

Attention to the process of decentralized manufacture sheds some light on the sharp increase in product standardization in the first century B.C. Rostovtzeff uses Megarian bowls as a typical example of decentralized manufacture that was characteristic of most of the Hellenistic period.[15] He points to the effort of the East to become self-sufficient, to increase production and export as much as possible. In Greece this meant that "economic production became more and more dispersed, each city trying to supply its own requirements."[16] In this connection Rostovtzeff predicted that "further archaeological exploration will probably show that there was hardly any place in the Hellenistic world which had not its own Megarian bowls." Megarian molds from Antioch and Samaria fulfil this prediction, at least in part.[17] This tendency toward decentralized manufacture provides a very satisfactory explanation of the second century B.C. groups at Shechem, Samaria, and Beth-zur in which practically no obviously imported ware occurs, and the same inferior local attempt to manufacture Hellenistic Decorated Ware characterizes each site.[18]

While the Roman government had no official economic policy and a system of *laissez-faire* prevailed,[19] the inter-provincial trade was the chief source of wealth to the Empire.[20] There certainly seems to be a relation between the sudden shift in the character of Palestinian deposits in the latter part of the first century B.C. and the advent of Roman control.[21] The sudden appearance of Eastern Sigillata A in quantity and shortly thereafter of Arretine, Pompeian Red, and other wares seems obviously

---

13. A perusal of the General List of sigillata at Samaria described beginning on *SS III*, p. 312, will indicate how frequently a number of fragments seem to represent identical vessels. Cf. p. 332, Fig. 80:1, where twenty-six hemispherical bowls of identical ware and glaze are mentioned. Cf. pp. 91 and 93 *supra* for the observation that the same situation obtains at other sites.

14. *Rapport III*, Fig. 2:6—7, 8—9, and 11—12 respectively. Note that these vessels do display the variations to be expected from the fact that each was individually made. Yet, the variety is not nearly as great as is displayed by the group of small bowls from the Room 1 deposit in the Hellenistic House at Shechem. Cf. pp. 46—47 *supra*.

15. Rostovtzeff, *The Social and Economic History of the Hellenistic World*, II, pp. 615—16.

16. *Ibid.*, p. 615.   17. Cf. *supra*, p. 67, n. 94.

18. "Local" should not necessarily be limited to each individual site. The characteristic buff ware of fish plates of Hellenistic Decorated Ware at both Samaria and Beth-zur in the second half of the second century B.C., for example, suggests a common place of manufacture. Cf. p. 32 *supra*.

19. Rostovtzeff, *The Social and Economic History of the Roman Empire*, I, pp. 89—90, 99. Cf. Grant, pp. 112—13.

20. Rostovtzeff, *The Social and Economic History of the Roman Empire*, I, p. 158.

21. More precisely, it is tempting to relate the beginning of sigillata importation (which has been roughly set in this study at 75 B.C. because of the limited archaeological evidence and for which Miss Kenyon suggests the date 60 B.C.) to the time of Roman annexation in 63 B.C.

related to the trade practices fostered in the Empire especially in the Augustan period.[22] Interesting in this connection are similar crater rims in kitchen ware from Athens and Qumrân in this period.[23]

Turning to cultural generalizations, the ground is much less certain. There are diverse and complex types of evidence that must be considered, and ceramic evidence is not one of the most significant. Yet, perhaps a discussion of two problems in this area will at least indicate the difficulty of drawing cultural implications from ceramic evidence. First, there is the problem of the extent to which Hellenistic culture has been orientalized. (The extent of Hellenization in Palestine is discussed below.) The question is sometimes phrased in terms of the extent to which the major cultural trend was westward or eastward. In the second and early first centuries the notable import of Palestine was wine in the commonly found jars of Rhodes and other Aegean islands. Other imported vessels were uncommon throughout Palestine at this time, but these came from the same direction. There seems to be no evidence that these imports influenced the local typological development. Yet, the local development is not isolated or unusual but part of the *koine* development in Syria-Palestine and, indeed, throughout the Mediterranean world.[23a] It would seem that this entire region had a similar material culture, at least in its ceramic aspect, and that the ceramic products of the period were, to say the least, quite unimaginative. There seems to have been no creative development susceptible of being traced eastward or westward.

The introduction of Eastern Sigillata A is a creative advance which can definitely be traced from east to west even though the ceramic picture in Italy at this time is not adequately published.[24] It seems clear that Eastern Sigillata A originated in Syria and was the obvious inspiration for the similar wares which developed in the Greek cities, Arezzo, and from there in Gaul and Germany.[25] But only a half-century after Eastern Sigillata A appeared in Palestine the eastern markets were penetrated by western wares, and the complicated profiles characteristic of western wares were imitated in Eastern Sigillata A.[26] So the direction was rapidly reversed. This evidence suggests that the latest technical and stylistic advances moved rapidly eastward and

---

22. In the Tiberian period, already, the reassertion of decentralized manufacture is noted throughout the Empire. Potteries in Gaul and Germany began producing ware to replace Italian Arretine, Tarsus was manufacturing sigillata, and a typical Arretine form occurs in Eastern Sigillata A at Samaria and in other wares elsewhere. Rostovtzeff, *The Social and Economic History of the Roman Empire*, I, pp. 172–73, 223; II, p. 617, n. 39. *Tarsus I*, pp. 176, 181. Corpus 251.6. A and cf. *supra*, p. 38, n. 144.

23. Cf. *TCHP*, F 60–61 with Corpus 45.1. A–B.

23a. *E.g.*, note the similarities in kitchen ware between Tarsus and Palestinian sites, pp. 60–61 *supra*; the similar repertory of forms and wares in Italy is mentioned *supra*, p. 56, n. 1.

24. Cf. the criticism of Waagé's attempt to describe a development in Italian ceramic *supra*, p. 90, n. 298. *V.* also J. H. Young, Review of *Cyprus IV*, *AJA*, LXIII (1959), p. 96; Einar Gjerstad, *Early Rome I* (Lund, 1953), p. 80, n. 2. A work comparable to Gjerstad's *Early Rome III* (Lund, 1960) for the periods here studied would be most helpful.

25. Cf. *supra*, p. 91, n. 310. For the earliest evidence for Samian and Arretine ware, cf. *supra*, pp. 80–82 and pertinent notes.

26. Cf. Corpus 251.6. A and *Tarsus I*, Nos. 412–419.

westward across Mediterranean lands, but no one would suggest that developing cultural trends copied the directions indicated by ceramics.

Perhaps a more fruitful approach might be to concentrate on shapes of vessels to determine popularity of distinct shapes or decorative motifs originating in the east which became popular in the west and vice versa. Movements in both directions are apparent. The earliest Eastern Sigillata A forms are reproduced in the west, and the new western forms are reproduced in Eastern Sigillata A and local Palestinian ware. To attempt a modern parallel to the late first century B.C. Palestinian, a contemporary German housewife buying a set of dishes can choose several patterns manufactured in Sweden and several from Czechoslovakia. Some "Swedish" patterns originated in Czechoslovakia and vice versa. To determine the origin of the pattern she selects would not determine her "iron curtain" or "free world" sympathies or tastes. Likewise, the Palestinian would reflect purely personal tastes in choosing crockery, and the sum of the tastes of Palestinians in their purchases would reflect what might be called an homogenized *koine* material culture that would be found throughout the Mediterranean world.

The other question concerns the ceramic reflection of cultural breaks. Here a balanced judgment, weighing all available evidence, is essential, for attempts to postulate a sharp cultural break on the basis of a few obvious changes or new forms are too common.[26a] The local pottery of Palestine in the last two centuries B.C. and the first century A.D. does not reflect any specific point when there is a sharp break in ceramic forms or repertory, but obvious changes do occur during this period. The small incurved-rim and hemispherical bowls, Corpus 51.1–2, and flasks, Corpus 29, continue through the period with no apparent developments. Collars of cylindrical to bag-shaped jars, Corpus 11.2, display a lengthening tendency throughout the period. The large, wide-necked jug, Corpus 21.1, the globular juglet, Corpus 31.1, and the globular cooking pot, Corpus 71.1, are other examples of types that continued through this period with certain specified developments. On the other hand, mortaria, Corpus 41, and the poor local Hellenistic Decorated Ware, Corpus 101–199, seem to disappear during the first half of the first century B.C., and large craters, Corpus 45.1 and 3, and "Herodian" lamps, Corpus 82.1, begin to appear at this same time. Small shallow bowls and plates, Corpus 53, seem to disappear about the turn of the era. In general, the changes in the forms during the period seem to be in the direction of more sharply angular profiles and, beginning at the end of the second century B.C., of better artisanship. The similarity of the angular crater rims at Qumrân and the Agora might suggest outside influences on this local development.[27]

In imported wares there does seem to be the distinct break about the time of Roman annexation alluded to above. Only in pottery groups dated after the accession

---

26a. *E.g.*, cf. *supra*, p. 83, n. 250.

27. Cf. n. 23 *supra*. In this connection it is interesting to note Rostovtzeff's observation that the local eastern pottery displays "a combination of eastern and Greek forms." Rostovtzeff, *The Social and Economic History of the Hellenistic World*, II, p. 1208. The globular cooking pot (Corpus 71.1) certainly reflects a continuing eastern tradition while many bowls in kitchen ware are copies of Hellenistic developments of Greek forms (Corpus 51.1–2).

of Rome is there a significant quantity of imported ware.[28] The Samaria evidence also indicates that there may be another rather abrupt change in the early first century A.D. after which Eastern Sigillata A may not have any longer been imported into Palestine in quantity.[29] But the evidence for this is not yet conclusive.

These ceramic data fit well with what is known of the history of this period in the Levant. The continuous local tradition is related to the fact that there is no evidence of major shifts in population or cultural orientation in Palestine in this period. The chauvinistic tendencies of the Maccabean period and the extensive inter-provincial trade in the Roman Empire that reaches its climax in the Augustan era is reflected in the sudden appearance of substantial quantities of imported wares toward the middle of the first century B.C. The restiveness and resistance that grew up against Rome in the first century A.D. may be related to the decline in importations at this time. The trends and breaks in Palestine, however, do not seem to be as related to broad, general cultural trends as they are to local conditions in Palestine with the exception of the influx of imports during the period of Roman control in the first century B.C.

Another attempt to draw broad generalizations from archaeological evidence is the symbolic approach of E. R. Goodenough. His concern is primarily with decorative motifs, which are uncommon on pottery of this period. A study of these motifs has led him to conclude that "the spiritual history of the development of Western man... must be seen to be a continuous adaptation of certain basic symbols."[30] This is not the proper place to attempt a refutation of the major conclusion, but his misuse of some of the ceramic evidence from the period under study should be noted. An examination of his use of a tomb group published by Sukenik[31] is "symbolic" of his method. He suggests that two of the Herodian lamps "show traces of an ornament which has largely disappeared." He sees hints of vine or scroll designs around the central oil hole. He "feels that Sukenik might have told us more of the ornament" but suggests that "probably the original [lamp] is equally inscrutible."[32] He notes clear evidence of "round objects" in one example. These remarks of Goodenough do not take cognizance of the

---

28. The relation of the early sigillata forms to the forms in Hellenistic Decorated Ware and to the first century A.D. sigillata forms should be mentioned in this connection. Some of the early sigillata forms have definite prototypes in Hellenistic Decorated Ware. Corpus 152.A and *TCHP*, E 46–48, are related to Corpus 251.2. *Tarsus I*, No. 290, in sigillata is related to the bowl with outcurved rim, Corpus 151.3. The broad-floored plate with offset rim, Corpus 253.5, has Hellenistic parallels at Athens, *TCHP*, D 1, E 22–26. The sigillata example, Corpus 228.A, carries on the lagynos tradition. Cf. *TCHP*, pp. 450–51. The sharp break between Hellenistic and Roman sigillata has been rejected *supra*, p. 66 and n. 80.

29. Mrs. Crowfoot notes that "during the Roman period sigillata flourished at Tarsus while it dwindled away at Samaria." *SS III*, p. 348. No Corpus forms certainly postdate A.D. 20, and the survey of material in Chap. V did not reveal any sites with substantial quantities of the sigillata characteristic of the first century A.D. at Tarsus. Cf. pp. 67–70 *supra*.

30. Erwin R. Goodenough, *Jewish Symbols in the Greco-Roman Period*, Vol. I: *The Archaeological Evidence from Palestine* (New York, 1953), p. viii.

31. Sukenik, *AJA*, LI, pp. 351–65. Cf. Goodenough, p. 145.

32. Goodenough, p. 145 and n. 32. The lamps are found in Sukenik, *AJA*, LI, Pl. LXXXV A (lower left and lower right).

fact that, except for lines and circles at the spout, such ornament on this omnipresent lamp type is unknown.[33] Further, there seems to be no reason to consider the double circles as anything beyond an identifying or decorative motif. Certainly the erotic implications of "round objects" are totally unnecessary.[34] Later Goodenough states that this tomb was not disturbed since it was last used for burial, and he concludes that "it may be supposed that the pots and vases had been put into the tomb originally in this fragmentary form."[35] In marked contrast, however, Sukenik states:

> The ceiling of the burial chamber was damaged by blasting during recent building operations. There was clear evidence that the tomb was entered once and left open; masses of earth penetrated through the opening into the burial chamber and filled it up to about two-thirds of its height.[36]

If such symbolic interpretations are to be given serious attention, they must certainly deal more realistically with the evidence!

The problem of the extent of the Hellenization of Judaism in Palestine in the period under study has received considerable attention. P. Kahane has undertaken the investigation of the ceramic evidence relevant to the study of the Hellenization of Judaism in the Herodian Period, and his chronological conclusions have been discussed above.[37]

Kahane concludes that the globular cooking pot (his Type A) "shows no elements of form which are specifically Hellenistic."[38] This conclusion seems beyond dispute, but his statement that there is no certain evidence for the occurrence of this type pot outside Palestine needs correction.[39] His view that the only innovation in this form is the "ribbing" of the body should also be revised.[40] Regarding the shallow type cooking pot (his Type B), on the other hand, Kahane suggests that "this is a Late Hellenistic type, independent to a great extent of local ceramic tradition."[41] He bases his conclusion on "aesthetic" grounds and on the fact that the type only occurs in ossuary tombs, but the first is extremely dubious and the last is wrong.[42] Yet, this

---

33. A single decorated example from Qumrân Ib, Corpus 82.2, might be considered exceptional, but its loop handle also sets it apart from ordinary Herodian lamps.

34. Cf., e.g., Goodenough, pp. 151–52.

35. Goodenough, p. 164.

36. Sukenik, *AJA*, LI, p. 354.

37. *Kahane I-III*. Cf. pp. 111–12 *supra*.

38. *Kahane I*, p. 129.

39. *Kahane I*, p. 129, but cf. *Tarsus I*, Fig. 201:727, H. This publication apparently was studied by Kahane after he had written his first article. Cf. *Kahane II*, p. 177. Cf. also *TCHP*, C 69 and D 71.

40. The term preferred in this study for the phenomenon occurring at this time is rippling. Cf. *supra*, p. 19, n. 111. That this should be considered an "innovation" and not merely the result of making vessels of very thin ware is dubious. The fact that rippling occurs sporadically on various parts of the body indicates that it is not a decorative technique.

41. *Kahane I*, p. 131.

42. The sharp lines of the type suggest to Kahane a Hellenistic metallic prototype without any evidence for such metal vessels. This is certainly dubious especially in view of the fact that there was a definite trend toward angularity in local Palestinian pottery forms as noted above. There is no intrinsic necessity of associating angularity with metallic prototypes. Note, e.g., Corpus 253.5 .A, which has ceramic

type may have Hellenistic origins. Its provenience in a deposit at the Jerusalem Citadel may provide a link between the first century A.D. examples from Tarsus and the Corpus and the second century B.C. shallow lid-type pot in Palestine which was also common at Athens.[43]

Kahane gives a rather comprehensive treatment of the broad provenience of the fusiform unguentarium and concludes that it is a "purely Hellenistic type."[44] This conclusion is assured, and his case for Egyptian origin is strong, but there hardly seems to be enough evidence from Palestine for postulating unguentarium manufacture in Palestine in the Herodian Period.[45] The chronological significance attached by Kahane to his piriform unguentarium variants has been rejected in Chapter V,[46] but his conclusion that the form is "a Hellenistic heritage, most probably of eastern (Alexandrian?) provenience" is clearly indicated by the evidence he cites.[47]

The lekythos with its variant, the globular juglet of Corpus Type 31.1, Kahane considers "a local creation of the Hellenistic period."[48] The aryballos, on the other hand, he relates to a "(Syrian?) metal aryballos"[49] because of its cup-shaped mouth. This seems inconsistent in view of the fact that the cup-shaped mouth is also characteristic of the globular juglet. In view of what has been said about the use of "metallic prototypes,"[50] the writer would prefer to consider both local Palestinian creations.

The evidence cited by Kahane suggests the conclusion that some pottery forms display a continuing development of the Palestinian tradition while others are received from the surrounding Hellenistic world. But it would be imprudent to suggest any significant Hellenistic influence on the basis of the use of certain Hellenistic ceramic forms. The fact that the form of the containers in which the Jews obtained the unguents required for their burials was not Palestinian in origin certainly should not be understood as any kind of compromise with Hellenism. These containers were used throughout the Maccabean period, and there is no indication that they were introduced by Hellenizing Jews.[51]

---

prototypes in *TCHP*, Fig. 116:D 1 and cf. p. 435 and E 22–26. Whether or not the black-glazed Agora vessels were derived from metallic types, it seems clear that the Eastern Sigillata form was copied from the Hellenistic ceramic tradition with its sharply offset rim. Note also that common pottery forms such as the unguentaria are copied in metal. Ref. cited in *Kahane I*, p. 135. Cf. *Kahane III*, p. 51. Especially objectionable is Kahane's conjecture that the bulge in the center of the shoulder is an attempt to copy a metallic joint. The metallic joint would not be expected in the center of the shoulder, but at a sharp joint. Further, if the craftsman who formed the vessel did have a sense of "primitive aesthetics," one would not expect the reproduction of an "unaesthetic" joint. That this is merely an imperfection in the vessel is indicated by the lack of such a bulge in other examples of this type. Cf. Corpus 72.2; note also proveniences outside ossuary tombs.

43. Cf. *Tarsus I*, Fig. 201:726. *SS III*, p. 230. Corpus 72.1–2 and pp. 54, 78 *supra*.
44. *Kahane I*, p. 137.
45. *Kahane I*, pp. 138–39.
46. Cf. p. 112 *supra*.
47. *Kahane II*, p. 182.
48. *Kahane III*, p. 51.
49. *Kahane III*, p. 54.
50. Cf. n. 42 *supra*.
51. Kahane's suggestion that fusiform unguentaria were introduced into Palestine by Gentiles or Hellenized Jews is a pure conjecture. *Kahane I*, p. 139.

In this connection it may prove instructive to raise the question of Hellenization in connection with the Qumrân evidence where the conservatism of the community might perhaps be reflected in its ceramic predilections.[52] The conspicuous absence of imported ware, particularly in Qumrân Ib, seems to be a clear indication of the rejection of foreign influence by these Essenes. It is also possible that certain bowl and jar types were creations of the Qumrân community.[53] The tall collar may have been slower in developing at Qumrân.[54] Yet, it is also true that sigillata forms turned up very soon in the local ware at Qumrân,[55] and none of the forms common at Qumrân and other Corpus sites provide any clear evidence of cultural lag or conservatism.[56] Accordingly, there is no uniform indication of Qumrân religious conservatism in the ceramic evidence.

---

52. Cf. *supra*, p. 12 and n. 28.

53. Cf., *e.g.*, Corpus 14.1—2; 51.8. The finding of a jar of Corpus Type 14.1 near Abila with an inkpot identical with one discovered at Qumrân may suggest that this jar is distinctive of the group and indicate the place of their habitation after A.D. 68. (Oral communication from Dr. Awni Dajani).

54. Cf. Corpus 11.2. G.

55. Cf. *supra*, p. 18 with n. 101 and p. 51.

56. It may be noted that these parallels to Qumrân vessels occur both in the north and in the south. The same is true in the second century B.C. where similar forms and repertory occur at Beth-zur, Shechem, and Samaria. There do not seem to be any major differences between the pottery of northern and southern Palestine in the Late Hellenistic and Early Roman periods. This situation contrasts strikingly with that of Iron II times. Cf. pp. 33—34 *supra*. A difference between northern and southern cooking pots in the second century B.C. should be noted as an exception. Cf. p. 44 *supra*.

APPENDIX B

HISTORICAL IMPLICATIONS

The Hellenistic era was characterized by almost constant warfare and the accompanying conditions of insecurity, devastation, and decline in wealth and population.[1] Conditions were especially bad in the East and grew worse as the era wore on. That Palestine was no exception is indicated also in the ceramic evidence. The poor pottery from the first half of the second century B.C. becomes poorer in the last half of the century and the first part of the next. The unsettled conditions and decline in prosperity are reflected in the archaeological evidence; a number of major sites were abandoned or substantially declined in the last half of the second century B.C. or shortly thereafter. These include Gezer, Samaria, Beth-shan, Shechem, Beth-zur, Lachish, and possibly also Bethel, Dothan, Shiloh, and Tell Zakarîyeh.[2]

The relation between the urban decline and the battles of Hyrcanus and Jannaeus, the latter almost an addict of war, is obvious. The abandonment of a number of cities after their capture by a Maccabean suggests the possibility that they may have been razed in a venture of holy war. While the attempt of the Maccabees to reëstablish the Davidic monarchy through tactics similar to those used in that earlier period cannot be denied, the urban decline can be explained by the unsettled political conditions of the times, and resort to the holy war interpretation seems unnecessary. This view is upheld by the fact that the abandonment of a number of the sites cannot be related to the holy war pattern. Beth-zur was captured, apparently without destruction, and became a comparatively prosperous Maccabean community. Its decline and abandonment is attributable to the extension of the borders of the Jewish state into Idumea.[3] Shechem was not abandoned until some time after the capture by Hyrcanus in 128 B.C.[4] Evidence does not clearly demonstrate that Beth-shan and Samaria were completely abandoned after Hyrcanus' capture in 107 B.C.[5] Josephus specifically mentions a resettlement of Gezer by Simon after 143 B.C.[6]

The short-lived stability brought by the Romans is reflected in the building operations of Gabinius at Samaria and Beth-shan and the later building operations of Herod

---

1. For a recent description v. F. C. Grant, pp. 102–104 and the literature there cited.
2. Cf. Chap. V where these sites are discussed in alphabetical order. V. also p. 10 for Beth-zur, pp. 26–27 for Samaria, and p. 48 for Shechem. Beth-shan was captured by Hyrcanus at the same time as Samaria, 107 B.C.
3. Cf. *CBZ*, p. 13.
4. Cf. Wright, *BASOR*, 148, p. 27; Toombs and Wright, *BASOR*, 161, p. 47.
5. Cf. *supra*, p. 27 with n. 36.
6. Cf. *supra*, p. 110, n. 82.

at Samaria, 'Alâyiq, and elsewhere. That conditions were still far from stable is reflected in the destruction of Tell Sandahannah by the Parthians in 40 B.C., the general lack of any quantity of good imported ware of the first century A.D., and finally in the Roman campaign which destroyed Qumrân and culminated in the destruction of Jerusalem.

www.ingramcontent.com/pod-product-compliance
Lightning Source LLC
Chambersburg PA
CBHW080243170426
43192CB00014BA/2543